Information Management
Voluntary Sector

Information Management in the Voluntary Sector

Diana Grimwood-Jones and Sylvia Simmons
Editors

Published by
Aslib, The Association for Information Management.
Staple Hall, Stone House Court, London EC3A 7PB

Tel: +44 (0) 171 903 0000
Fax: +44 (0) 171 903 0011
Email: *pubs@aslib.co.uk*
WWW: *http://www.aslib.co.uk/*

© Aslib, 1998

ISBN 0 85142 394 9

Except as otherwise permitted under the Copyright, Designs and Patents Act 1988, this publication may only be reproduced, stored or transmitted in any form or by any means, with the prior permission in writing of the publisher.

The editors and authors of the individual chapters assert their moral rights to be identified as such in accordance with the terms of the Copyright, Designs and Patents Act 1988.

Aslib, The Association for Information Management, founded in 1924, is a world class corporate membership organisation with about 2000 members in some 70 countries. Aslib actively promotes best practice in the management of information resources. It lobbies on all aspects of the management of, and legislation concerning, information at local, national and international levels.

Aslib provides consultancy and information services, professional development training, conferences, specialist recruitment, Internet products, and publishes primary and secondary journals, conference proceedings, directories and monographs.

 THE ASSOCIATION FOR INFORMATION MANAGEMENT

Contents

Preface viii
    Sylvia Simmons and Diana Grimwood-Jones

Introduction 1
    Professor Nicholas Deakin

Part A – The Voluntary Sector: The Context

1. Introducing the Voluntary Sector 9
    Colin Rochester

2. Charity Financial Reporting, Fiscal Matters and Governance 23
    Pesh Framjee

3. Managing Change in the Voluntary Sector 45
    Christine Forrester

4. Information and Communication in the Voluntary Sector 59
    Kevin Harris

5. The Role of Information in Developing Policy 73
    Sylvia Simmons

6. International Perspectives 103
    Carys Hodges

Part B – Technical and Professional Issues

7. Managing the Library and Information Service in a Voluntary Organisation 125
    Graham Bennett

8. The National Children's Bureau Library and Information Services: User Services 149
    Nicola Hilliard

9. Developing New Products and Services, including Electronic Publishing 163
    Mark Watson

10. Acquiring and Organising Material 187
    Frances Tait

11. Library Automation for Voluntary Organisations 207
    Jacqueline Cropley

12. Knowledge Management: Why Get Involved with the Internet? . 231
    Emma Hallam and Mark Walker

13. Copyright and Information: Issues in Protection and Liability ... 251
    Jeremy Phillips

14. Records Management and Archives in the Voluntary Sector 263
    Rodney Breen

15. Staffing Issues in the Voluntary Sector Library 283
    Lynette Cawthra

16. Marketing the Information Service in Voluntary Sector
    Organisations 305
    Diana Grimwood-Jones

Part C: Case Studies

I   Archives and Records Management at Leonard Cheshire 325
    Jill Roberts

II Christian Aid: Evaluation of Library Services 339
    Sarah Heery

III Library Automation at the NSPCC Library 349
    Gerry Power

IV Launching a Web Page: Alcohol Concern 361
    Caroline Bradley

V   Information Audit at Charities Aid Foundation 379
    Susan K. E. Saxon-Harrold

VI Information Collection and Dissemination in an International
    Context: the Case of CRIN 389
    Becky Purbrick

Appendix

Electronic Information Resources for the Voluntary and
   Community Sector 413
   Compiled by Communities Online Forum and Partnerships Online

Notes on Contributors 421

Index 429

Preface

The voluntary sector – diverse, dynamic and driven by a desire for change – is an evolving and growing force in society. Libraries and information centres in all sectors are changing, diversifying to adapt to the opportunities and challenges posed by information and communication technologies (ICTs). Good information and knowledge management is recognised as essential for organisations in all sectors if they are to remain relevant, viable and competitive in the new millennium.

Information professionals are examining how they will meet the growing expectations of their community of readers, users and customers in an information-rich society. How will users demand, acquire and share information? How can library and information centres contribute to the corporate knowledge base? What role will information workers have in offering guidance, adding value, facilitating and enabling these demanding users?

This volume brings together these themes and suggests how librarians and information workers can contribute to the strategic and operational development of voluntary sector organisations. We offer twenty-two contributions by senior practitioners from the voluntary sector and the information management field who deal with different aspects of these issues. The book is divided into three parts, whose style and focus range deliberately from theoretical overview for senior managers to practical guidance and case studies for information workers.

Part A sets out the context for information management in the voluntary sector; Part B deals with technical and professional issues in information management; six practical case studies are offered in Part C. A guide to electronic information resources for the voluntary and community sector is provided in the Appendix.

The book has been designed with three groups of readers in mind (for whom different chapters or sections may be of more immediate relevance or interest):

1. Chief executives, directors and senior managers in voluntary organisations – general managers who may have little or no experience of information management issues – for whom the book seeks to offer an understanding of the information function, the potential of the Library and Information Service (LIS) to support a diverse range of internal and external customers and the difficulties faced by information staff.

2. Information staff in the voluntary sector, who may be qualified and experienced Library and Information Science (LIS) professionals but new to the voluntary sector, or unqualified staff seeking practical guidance – for whom the book is designed to help gain an understanding of how the services they are offering, managing or marketing must operate – i.e. within the context of their own organisation and the voluntary sector as a whole. Services must be client-led, in line with the organisation's objectives and responsive to the changes it undergoes. For both groups the book offers an opportunity to 'benchmark' their library and information service against others in the sector.
3. Trainers, tutors and course developers in the voluntary and not-for-profit sector – including MBA, DMS and related training, in-service management development and training – for whom we offer a snapshot of recent developments in information management, trends in ICTs and implications for the sector.

A number of recurring themes are dealt with by more than one contributor, for which we make no apology. We hope readers will find it stimulating to see the issues addressed from more than one perspective. The voluntary sector has undergone significant changes in recent years: growth of the contract culture; increased emphasis on staff development and professionalism; quality, standards, monitoring and evaluation; an awareness of governance issues and changes in the way Boards operate. Understanding this framework must underpin the function of information management.

In Part A, Colin Rochester traces the growth of the nonprofit sector: its history, definitions, diversity, functions, common features, challenges and implications for future development. Pesh Framjee examines financial reporting, taxation and governance and offers best practice recommendations for charity financial reporting.

Strategies for coping with the impact of change are central to voluntary sector management. Christine Forrester sets out a strategic framework for change at the micro level and the macro level, demonstrating how change, if managed well, can have a positive impact on the life and work of an organisation.

Information in communities is diverse, multi-faceted and dynamic; the challenge for information management at a local level is to help establish and sustain healthy conditions for community initiatives to flourish. A print-based knowledge culture works against the interests of disadvantaged people and ICTs offer a potentially significant transformation of information flow into and within communities (issues taken up by Watson,

Hallam and Walker). Kevin Harris's focus is on the community sector as a distinct feature of the third sector; he examines the contribution of information to social inclusion and implications for information management.

The role of information and the information manager in the formulation of policy is explored by Sylvia Simmons who sets out their contribution in supporting the organisation's policy objectives both on the internal and wider social policy agenda and offers a suggested model for good practice: The Information Cycle in Policy Development.

International organisations working globally on disaster relief, development, health and welfare issues may have centralised or de-centralised management structures; both present challenges for information management. Carys Hodges considers needs assessment, internal documentation, linguistic, cultural and technological differences and the contribution of information management to a global learning network. The international context for information collection and dissemination is the focus of Becky Purbrick's case study of the Child Rights Information Network (CRIN).

In Part B, Graham Bennett sets out the key management issues for the voluntary sector. A successful voluntary sector LIS manager must understand the organisational context and range of perceptions of his or her organisation. The stages in an organisation's development and accompanying changes in management style are traced: from collective to a high degree of bureaucracy and specialisation. Identifying organisational culture, where the LIS sits in the management structure, and aspirations of staff and volunteers, all influence ways of working. Voluntary organisations are complex hierarchical entities which informal styles of working may disguise. Designing the LIS demands an understanding of strategic, operational and financial planning; management of staff, technology, materials and collections; marketing and promotion.

These issues are explored in greater detail in ensuing chapters. The dilemma in managing User Services is summarised by Nicola Hilliard: the provider has to know what the user wants and provide it and only users know what they want to access – dual and potentially conflicting demands to be met within the constraints of budget, the limitless number and variety of user and the impossibility of stocking 'everything'. Acknowledging that there is neither typical library nor user within the voluntary sector, Hilliard emphasises it is no longer viable to offer a reactive service; dissemination is vital and information has to be actively marketed.

Marketing – a major area of concern for librarians in all sectors – is taken up by Diana Grimwood-Jones. Marketing the voluntary sector library involves understanding the environment in which we operate; customers (actual or potential); which services are used and what for; intensive users and non-users; the nature of the competition; identifying Strengths, Weaknesses, Opportunities and Threats; what customers say they need and how they want it delivered. Case studies are offered by Sarah Heery (evaluation and promotion of LIS at Christian Aid) and Susan Saxon-Harrold (information audit at CAF).

Are traditional libraries to be replaced with a global information superhighway and a Virtual Library? Mark Watson sets out the case for investment in LIS services, staff and the development of new services. ICTs have revolutionised the potential for developing new services with emerging opportunities for income generation, managing information overload and exploiting corporate wisdom. The voluntary sector must look to the model of the commercial sector to achieve a market lead. The emphasis must be on information needs, not the technology; Watson analyses options for electronic publishing, marketing CD-ROMs and in-house databases, and using the World Wide Web to provide information services. A case study on launching a Web site at Alcohol Concern by Caroline Bradley and the potential for Internet technology discussed in Saxon-Harrold's case study develop these issues. ICTs offer the prospect of raising the profile of the voluntary sector in society and fostering closer links with public and private sector agencies. Organisations need clear objectives and coherent strategies for communications management but the rewards – collaboration, more cost effective and open communication and greater visibility – are many. Emma Hallam and Mark Walker discuss voluntary sector information and communication and the opportunities offered by electronic networking, using Internet tools for knowledge management, offering examples of new ways of working for staff and service users.

Much of the literature in voluntary sector libraries does not appear in regular bibliographies. Frances Tait – stressing the need to be pragmatic, flexible, consistent and relevant to users' needs – offers a down-to-earth set of guidelines for selecting and organising print and non-print material; the 'just-in time' versus 'just in case' approach to collection management; cataloguing, classification and thesaurus building are discussed.

The constraints imposed by scant human and financial resources are taken up by Jacqueline Cropley in dealing with library automation (and Gerry Power's case study of library automation at NSPCC). Cropley addresses the rationale for new IT solutions, planning, the potential for change offered by new systems, and outlines requirements, finance, applications and systems issues. Automation is not an end in itself and the principle of creating real benefits to the user must be retained.

Jeremy Phillips sets out the legal framework of copyright, information provision and liability: the legal status of information, copyright in author's works, protection of databases, information on the Internet and intranets and liability for false or damaging information.

Archivists and records managers have much in common but the two roles – although closely related – are different from other information functions as they deal with information generally produced within the organisation which cannot be replicated elsewhere. Rodney Breen discusses specialist problems arising in the voluntary sector, (a budget-conscious culture and a casual attitude to systems and procedures) and records management and archives as part of an information strategy. His outline of procedures (security, electronic records, access to and use of archives) are explored in depth by Jill Roberts in her case study of the Leonard Cheshire archive.

Lynette Cawthra examines staffing issues: skills and experience required; selection, recruitment and staff induction; team management, alternative working patterns, solo librarianship; continuing professional development; working for a manager from another discipline and securing organisational recognition of the library's work. Voluntary sector librarians need to 'understand the purpose and culture of their organisation, so they can define the value which the information service can add ... and [must] have a determination to make their voice heard outlining methods by which the library can contribute to the wider organisation's strategic vision'. As Bennett confidently asserts: if you embrace the culture and learn to understand it, the rewards will be great!

Whilst we have sought to draw readers' attention to common and overlapping themes, the style of each contribution remains different. Although we have made comments and suggestions, we have encouraged authors to adopt their own style best suited to the subject. We are immensely grateful to all who have contributed their experience and expertise to this publication, which we believe to be a first – synthesizing the management needs of the voluntary sector with the discipline of information management.

Understanding these issues is fundamental to information management in the voluntary sector. The Quality Standards Task Group – which grew out of recommendations made by the Deakin Commission – set out its proposed quality principles in its "White Paper" on quality in the voluntary sector (published February 1998). A quality voluntary organisation it states, inter alia ' ... uses recognised standards or models as a means to continuous improvement and not as an end' and '… adds value to its end users and beneficiaries'. We hope this publication will contribute to the development of quality standards in the key function of information management in the voluntary sector.

We wish to thank Professor Nicholas Deakin for his recognition of the pivotal role played by information in voluntary sector development and for writing the introductory essay to this volume; his initial enthusiasm and continuing support is deeply appreciated. Sarah Blair, and latterly Nigel Wood, at Aslib, our publishers, have provided valued professional and personal encouragement at every stage of this project, from embryonic idea to final publication. We acknowledge this support and the comments of colleagues in the voluntary sector, past and present, whose commitment and dedication to information provision in the sector have inspired this publication.

Sylvia Simmons and Diana Grimwood-Jones
London, August 1998

Introduction
Professor Nicholas Deakin

The world of voluntary organisations and charities – the terms overlap, sometimes confusingly – has changed in all sorts of fundamental ways over the past decade. Voluntary and community-based bodies, call them what you will, have taken on many more tasks and developed a wide variety of different ways of doing them. They face a steadily increasing number of demands and as a direct consequence have more responsibilities, and are accountable to a wider group of potential or actual stakeholders. This process has accelerated as a result of the election of a Labour government on 1st May 1997, which has led to the closer involvement of voluntary bodies and their leading figures in a whole range of new policy initiatives.

If the circumstances of voluntary organisations (as I'll call them for shorthand) have been changing, so have public perceptions of these bodies. In some respects, their higher profile has increased the public's awareness of the importance of the role that they perform and hence the potential, at least, for higher levels of public approval. But in other ways, more intense scrutiny has produced a more demanding environment. The public wants to know not just that voluntary bodies are performing important tasks but that they are performing them well, with the minimum amount of bureaucracy and maximum impact on the problems that they have been funded to address. Partly, this is a result of the success of the National Lottery, which was sold to Parliament and the public partly on the back of the contribution that proceeds from the Lottery would make to 'good causes'. Wider public interest in the activities of charities, which has been one of the results of the Lottery's success has also created a market for stories that aim to cut the pretensions of charities down to size. The media, whose appetite for exposés of what they choose to define as hypocrisy sometimes seems insatiable, have found additional scope for this approach in the charity world.

The external environment in which voluntary action takes place in this, the last decade of the twentieth century, sometimes seems eerily familiar to that of the first decade. The scope and form of the role that the state should perform is a matter of constant controversy, as are the changes in attitudes and behaviour patterns in the public at large: questions like the role of women and the future of the family are continually rehearsed, now as then. Although the material context is now entirely different, the content of these debates still has a familiar ring. Another repeated concern centres on the limits which can (or should) properly be set on the extent to which private or philanthropic activity can substitute for state action, given that the distinctiveness of voluntary action lies in large measure in its independence of the state. This has sometimes been portrayed, at both ends of the century, as a contest for 'the soul of the voluntary sector'.

The influence of the market is another key factor in shaping the environment in which the contemporary voluntary sector operates. This is as much a matter of style as it is of content. In seeking to shake off the stigmata of insensitivity and uniformity in service delivery which critics see as typical of large bureaucracies, welfare organisations of all kinds have turned to the market to learn new skills. Advertising, fund raising, marketing, campaigning and, in particular, managing are all skills that voluntary organisations have had to learn as their functions have expanded. And in the field of information and communications technologies which provides the context for the present collection of essays, new developments have opened up a whole range of new opportunities with which the voluntary and community sector are only just beginning to come to terms.

In one sense, all these changes and adaptations to a new working environment can be seen as an increase in professionalism – another term that often sets the alarm bells ringing. Yet while this new sophistication in styles of operation is developing, the basic structure of governance of voluntary bodies still remains largely unchanged. The definition of charity has scarcely been modified; the role and responsibilities of trustees and management committees is much as it always was. There is an amateurism at the heart of the sector, which makes for an increasingly uncomfortable fit with its expanded functions. Yet amateurism has its virtues as well as its drawbacks: if we discard its better features in the name of greater professionalism, we do so at our peril.

The twin pressures of modernisation and expansion give particular prominence to the role of regulation. The Charity Commission looks after the charitable sector in England and Wales, so its coverage of the whole field of voluntary action in the UK is necessarily incomplete, but it is nonetheless a player of increasing significance. One of the most striking changes in a decade of change has been the way in which the Commission has changed its manner of operating and its general approach. In (almost) one bound, it has gone from a Victorian world of ledgers and card indices to the radically updated universe of a register of charities posted on the World Wide Web. The role of the regulator has also been rethought – in some respects controversially so. This has been most clearly exposed in the advisory functions of the Commission: the input to the training of trustees to help them discharge their ever more demanding role and advice to those managing charities operating in a changing and complex environment. The pressure on resources that has become one of most frequently debated questions in the voluntary sector world has added an edge to these issues. Competition is now a standard feature of that world – and it is one in which the main competitors are often from within the sector and the contest is sometimes far from amicable.

In this changing environment the introduction and development of information and communications technologies has a greatly enhanced potential. To take only one important example, the increased stress on the role of users of services provided by voluntary bodies places a premium on efficient means of communication and facilitating rapid and effective responses to users' needs. The use of new techniques to inform and empower has already begun to take hold within the voluntary sector and its significance is certain to increase over the next few years. As the essays in this collection demonstrate, a whole range of new opportunities that have opened up on which imaginative 'social entrepreneurs' can draw.

However, these new opportunities are not without their attendant risks. Leaping too rapidly on to passing bandwagons has its dangers – who now remembers the revolution in personal communications that citizen band radio was supposed to usher in? New technologies can also be as excluding as the traditional systems they are now threatening to replace. Complexity in operation, expense and the use of off-putting jargon are all dangers of which we need to be aware. The early success of the French post office in introducing their easily operated Minitel system linked to a low-cost and widely available public service has lessons for innovators on this side of the Channel.

New technology and changing management styles are now being employed to help voluntary organisations to address problems that were only too familiar to their Edwardian predecessors – in particular, the problem of poverty, or in late twentieth century terminology the issue of 'social exclusion'. This has also been an arena in which the importance of developing partnerships between voluntary and community bodies, the state (both local and central) and the market has begun to emerge as a key theme. However, the concept of partnership imperfectly conceals problems of asymmetry of power, especially as between small community-based bodies and government departments. In that situation, ready access to relevant information can make the difference between a supine falling into line with an agenda set from above and the capacity to argue successfully for different priorities.

In sum, then, the new operating environment poses important challenges for voluntary bodies of all kinds, although the range of tasks that they are now being asked to perform defies easy generalisation. Changing circumstances make increasing demands on their capacity to respond effectively while not sacrificing their independence or their equally important role in advocacy and campaigning. These new demands can distort the agenda of voluntary action and limit the ability of organisations to plough their own furrow. On the other hand, taking up new challenges can help to empower them, by providing a role and resources to match from which the users of services can benefit directly. The balancing act remains a delicate and often difficult one.

Those of us who came together two years ago as the Independent Commission on the Future of the Voluntary Sector in England (1995/6) to advise the sector on the directions that it might follow in future were clear that the independence of the sector should not be compromised. Our recommendations for reformulating relationships between the voluntary sector, the state and the market were based on that fundamental principle. The proposed compact between government and voluntary organisations that emerged from our deliberations is now being actively considered by the potential partners. If it works out in practice as we hoped it would, this compact should give the voluntary sector the security of not again being conscripted to implement programmes which it has had no say in designing. Similarly, we wanted to see a more constructive relationship between voluntary and corporate sectors based on better mutual understanding about the extent (and limits) of potential collaboration between them. At the same time, we felt that it was essential to provide for the efficient governance of voluntary bodies delivering services, often to the most vulnerable members of society. We were therefore particularly glad that the Joseph Rowntree Foundation was willing to fund some follow-up work, which has led to the publication of suggested Codes of Governance for organisations. Other initiatives that are being actively pursued include a review of relations between the voluntary sector and business and a task force on quality assurance and standards. In parallel, the issue of resources is being pursued by a group convened by the Council for Charitable Support.

We were not so successful with some of our other recommendations – for example, those on the modernisation of charity law. But the general picture that has emerged from debates (in Parliament and outside) on our report and that of our Scottish opposite numbers and the Labour party's own inquiry, conducted at the end of their period in opposition, is remarkably consistent. All parties concerned are anxious for the voluntary and community sector to continue to exercise an effective but at the same time independent role. The key debate is about how this role can be safeguarded. The sector has to modernise its practice and deliver services of at least equivalent quality to those previously provided by the state or currently available through the market, while not compromising its capacity to act as advocate. Implementation of the principles of public life enunciated by Lord Nolan's committee on standards in the public sector, requiring those concerned with delivering services, at all levels, to observe the fundamental imperatives of integrity, accountability and efficiency also poses a challenge for voluntary and community organisations – indeed one part of the sector, housing associations, has already been subjected to the Nolan committee's scrutiny. In particular, we can expect the importance of accountability, both to those funding the activities of the sector and to those on whose behalf it acts, to increase steadily as the role of the sector continues to expand.

The collection of essays brought together in this book should help the voluntary sector and its allies in the demanding task of charting a course for the future. The particular emphasis on the significance of information and communications technologies, itself a rapidly evolving feature of a speedily changing scene, should prove to be of particular value to organisations of all kinds in every part of the field. I hope that it will be widely read.

Part A

The Voluntary Sector: The Context

1

Introducing the Voluntary Sector
Colin Rochester

Setting the Scene

One of the most striking features of public and social policy in the late twentieth century has been the remarkable growth in importance and size of what is variously termed the 'voluntary', 'nonprofit', 'nongovernmental' or 'third' sector. This is both a national and an international phenomenon. In Britain, as in most of the western world, the change has been driven by widespread disillusion with the cost and quality of social welfare provided by government bureaucracies. In developing countries it is underpinned by the distrust felt by donors and local people alike of governments which are widely seen as incompetent or corrupt – or both. In the former Soviet Union and Central and Eastern Europe the sector has been given a key role in rebuilding 'civil society' – 'that set of diverse non-governmental institutions which is strong enough to counterbalance the state and, whilst not preventing the state from fulfilling its role as keeper of the peace and arbitrator between major interests, can nevertheless prevent the state from dominating and atomising the rest of society' (Gellner, 1995: 32).

The apparently irresistible rise of the voluntary sector has been accompanied by the development of a research community that can support three international academic journals. Nonetheless the subject of their research and theory-building remains largely unknown and is bedevilled by problems of definition and confusing differences of terminology. The aim of this chapter is to provide a guide through these complexities and a 'roadmap' of the sector's major features. In the process it will examine some of the current challenges facing voluntary agencies and introduce some key pieces of literature that will enable the reader to pursue some of the issues in greater depth. Its focus will be on the voluntary sector in Britain but it will also draw on experience and the literature of other countries where this is appropriate.

Historical Background

While the growing scale and significance of the third sector is common to many countries, there is a distinctive form and flavour to its manifestation in any single society which is shaped by its unique history. Britain in particular has a long and important 'voluntary tradition'. It has recognised the important role that can be played by voluntary organisations in meeting social need since the sixteenth century at least when the dissolution of the monasteries destroyed the institutions that had borne the brunt of providing health care and relieving poverty in the middle ages. The social turmoil of the reign of the first Elizabeth provided the conditions under which charities became a feature of the social landscape. It also led to their recognition and regulation through the Charitable Uses Acts of 1597 and 1601 which still provide the framework of charity law at the end of the twentieth century (Davis Smith, 1995).

A later period of social upheaval – nineteenth century industrialisation – has been described as 'the golden age of voluntary organisations' (*ibid*: 14). The creation almost overnight of modern London and the other major urban centres made poverty more visible and led to a plethora of philanthropic responses. Middle class women, prevented by a patriarchal society from engaging in paid employment, found an outlet for their skills and energy in voluntary work: one commentator of the time (quoted by Prochaska, 1980) estimated that half a million women were working on a regular basis for the new charitable organisations. By the 1880s *The Times* reported that the aggregate income of charities in London alone exceeded that of the Swedish, Danish and Portuguese governments and was double that of the Swiss Confederation (Owen, 1964: 469). The importance of the role of these new organisations was underlined by the establishment in 1860 of the Charity Commission which remains the body which monitors, regulates and investigates the conduct of charities in England and Wales.

But charities and the philanthropic impulse they embody represent only one of the roots of the contemporary voluntary sector. The other significant tradition is that of mutual aid and self-help. While less well documented than philanthropy 'the working man's voluntary action' (Davis Smith, 1995: 17) of mutual aid and self-help was arguably of equal importance both to the social fabric of Victorian England and to the development of the voluntary sector. Friendly Societies, building societies and working men's clubs, moreover, attracted more members than the other two working class institutions of the nineteenth century, the trades unions and the co-operative movement.[1]

Another important and sometimes neglected feature of the 'golden age of charitable organisations' was the role of the state. The accepted view of the history of the sector is that charities and government operated in self-contained and separate spheres for most of the nineteenth century until the inadequacy of the charities' provision led the state to take over their functions – reluctantly but ineluctably. This is misleading on two counts.

In the first place, government inspection and funding of charitable activity such as schools and reformatories for poor children was established practice as early as the 1850s. And, secondly, the increasing role of the state did not lead to the destruction of the voluntary sector – merely to a change in its character (G.D.H. Cole, quoted in Davis Smith, *op cit*).

Thus the general expectation that the post Second World War welfare settlement would mean the relegation of charities and voluntary organisations to the margins of the welfare state was not realised. While voluntary activity was displaced by the state in some fields – noticeably the hospitals – other long established organisations continued to play an important role. They were joined by newer bodies – like the Citizen's Advice Bureaux – which had demonstrated their value in wartime and a new generation of agencies including household names like SHELTER and the Child Poverty Action Group as well as organisations known only in their locality which were born during the 60s and 70s.

Today the voluntary sector is a substantial part of British society and a not insignificant segment of the economy. Measuring its size is a hazardous operation – as we shall discuss below – but one recent estimate suggests that the total income of the 200,000 to 240,000 organisations in the sector was about £15 billions in 1995, that the sector may employ as many as 620,000 people, and that 750,000 people act as the unpaid trustees of charities (Commission on the Future of the Voluntary Sector, 1996).

Defining the Sector

In 1978 a committee set up by two major grant-making foundations and chaired by Lord Wolfenden published its report on the Future for Voluntary Organisations. This brought currency to the idea that there was such a thing as a voluntary sector – one of four arenas of activity to meet social need. It was thus distinguished from the statutory or governmental sector; the private for profit sector; and the informal sector. Wolfenden's major concern was the future relationships between the sectors (Deakin, 1995). Interestingly, at much the same time the Filer Commission in the USA had arrived at the concept of a nonprofit sector (Hall, 1992). Since then the idea of a sector has been widely accepted and has underpinned the development of a number of institutions such as the National Council for Voluntary Organisations, the Charities Aid Foundation and what is now called the Voluntary and Community Unit at the Home Office.

On the other hand the search for an adequate and robust definition of the sector has proved difficult. The different terminology in use is symptomatic of this. In Britain the terms 'voluntary sector' and 'voluntary organisation' reflect and reveal an historic assumption that what is important about voluntary sector organisations is that they exist because a group of people have chosen freely to bring them into being and to sustain them without expectation of material reward. In North America the term 'nonprofit' makes the important distinction between these organisations and private for-profit enterprises which needs to be established if they are to be granted the tax exemptions which nonprofit organisations enjoy. In developing countries (and in British agencies which work in them) as well as in the former communist countries the term nongovernmental organisation (usually abbreviated to NGO) is used to distance them from the state. The term 'third sector' is being increasingly used to avoid the specific emphases of these different labels and has been adopted by the international society formed by scholars interested in the field.

A valiant attempt to develop a definition which will cross national boundaries has been made by the researchers involved in a thirteen country cross-national study conducted by Johns Hopkins University (Salamon and Anheier, 1996). Their 'structural-operational definition' is based on five core criteria. Third sector organisations are:

1. *Formally organised*: that is 'formal, structured entities, with a charter, constitution or set of rules' (Kendall and Knapp, 1995: 86);
2. Constitutionally or legally *independent of government*;
3. *Self-governing*: with its own internal decision-making structures and not controlled by a private (for-profit) firm or by government;
4. *Not profit-distributing and primarily non-business*: profits may be earned but must be ploughed back into the organisation and not distributed to members, officers or trustees; and
5. *Voluntary*: the organisation 'benefits to a meaningful degree from philanthropy or voluntary citizen involvement' (*ibid*). At a minimum this means that it must have an unpaid management committee, board of trustees or governing body.

This is probably the most adequate definition we have but it has not solved all of the difficulties of delineating this 'loose and baggy monster'. As it stands it would include both political parties and churches which do not fall within most subjective 'common sense' ideas of what we mean by the voluntary sector.[2] And the boundaries of what remains are unclear.

The boundary with government: as Kendall and Knapp (*op cit*) have remarked organisations which are legally separate from the state and whose assets are independently owned may yet be subject to a great deal of government influence. Many are wholly or very largely dependent on the state for their income. Others have government appointees as members of their boards. A few have been constituted or reformed by Act of Parliament. At what point does their ability to act independently become a matter of doubt?

The boundary with the private sector: many voluntary organisations engage in vendorism (selling services like training and information services in order to produce income) and venturism (unrelated trading like Christmas cards and mail order catalogues). While they may continue to meet the criterion of being non-profit distributing, their activities are seen by some commentators to be otherwise indistinguishable from similar commercial operations.

The boundary with the informal sector: the great majority of the organisations that make up the voluntary sector are small (90% of charities have an income of less than £10,000 a year) and relatively informal. How valid is it to make a distinction between them and self-help groups and other less organised forms of voluntary action? Exactly where can the boundary line be drawn?

A further problem is raised by the heterogeneity of what is unambiguously contained within these permeable boundaries. The full extent of the sector's diversity will be examined below but at this point it is worth noting some of the difficulties encountered at the definitional level by treating the voluntary sector as a single entity. One important aspect of this is the increasingly common distinction between the minority of comparatively well funded, professionally staffed and formally organised voluntary agencies on the one hand and the huge majority of small, informal organisations wholly or largely dependent on the voluntary efforts of their members. In the US this has been described as the difference between 'paid staff nonprofits' and 'grassroots associations' (Smith, 1997). In Britain the idea that there is a 'community sector' which either forms a distinctive sub-sector within the voluntary sector or is a separate sector in its own right is gaining ground (Rochester, 1997). A group of national federations and networks of these associations together with organisations that provide them with support and training has formed the Community Sector Coalition to promote their interests.

The Coalition argues that the lion's share of the attention given to the voluntary sector by policy-makers and researchers alike has been focused on professionally-led, service providing agencies. As a result the contribution of the community sector to the improvement of collective life and living conditions and its claims for recognition and support have been neglected. This is explained in part by the emphasis placed by public policy on transferring the provision of social welfare from the state to the voluntary sector. The focus is on organisations which can deliver services and operate in a similar fashion to the statutory bodies they are supplanting. The tide may be beginning to run in favour of community sector organisations as the result of a second powerful trend in social policy – the rediscovery of 'civil society' and the importance of maintaining stocks of 'social capital'. Instead of being judged by their ability to deliver social welfare and other services responsively, flexibly and at low cost, voluntary organisations are beginning to be valued for their ability to integrate people into society, to provide opportunities for personal and social learning and for collective voluntary action.

The Diversity of the Sector

The distinction between voluntary agencies and community sector organisations goes to the heart of the voluntary sector's diversity. Among the more significant variations between the organisations of which it is composed are: differences of function; diversities of scale and area of operation; the variety of legal and constitutional forms; the nature and mixtures of funding sources; differences in relationships with government; variations in levels of formalisation; and the extent of the voluntary contribution to their work.

Functions

Maria Brenton (1985) has identified four principal functions carried out by voluntary agencies. The first of these is the provision of services; voluntary agencies provide a range of care, information and advice services for a variety of client groups and also undertake various activities aimed at improving the environment. Others promote mutual aid between people who share a health problem, disability or common interest. A third strand is the pressure group function where the principal aim is to bring about changes in policy and practice by campaigning and lobbying decision-makers. Brenton's fourth area of work involves the resource and co-ordinating functions typically undertaken by Wolfenden's 'intermediary bodies' which bring together, represent the interests of and provide services to other voluntary agencies. General intermediaries operate on a national basis (these include the National Council for Voluntary Organisations and the National Centre for Volunteering) locally – notably Councils for Voluntary Service, Volunteer Bureaux or Rural Community Councils. There is also a wide range of specialist intermediaries working in particular fields. This basic list of functions can be extended. Kendall and Knapp (1995) suggest the addition of individual advocacy to help people to secure services which meet their specific needs. Other functions include fund-raising, research and grant-making.

Scale and area of operation

Voluntary organisations range in size from the 'household names' like Oxfam and the NSPCC which dispose of substantial incomes and employ large numbers of staff to local neighbourhood groups entirely dependent on volunteers and raising small sums from jumble sales and similar activities. They may operate on a local, regional, national or even international level.

Legal and constitutional forms

Many but not all voluntary agencies are registered charities. This brings a number of benefits including a limited amount of tax exemptions and a right to a rebate on business rates as well as the less tangible advantages of what appears to be official recognition as a 'good cause'. But charitable status also brings responsibilities including making annual returns and submitting properly audited accounts to the Charity Commission. And it is not open to all; in order to register as a charity an organisation must demonstrate that its purposes are charitable in law. The legal definition of charity is based on the Charitable Uses Act of 1601 and has been developed by a series of decisions taken in the courts and by the Charity Commission. The most important of the barriers to registration is that campaigning and pressure group activities, by and large, are not regarded as charitable. As well as the distinction between the charitable and the non-charitable we can distinguish between organisations which are incorporated as companies limited by guarantee or as friendly societies and unincorporated associations or trusts.

Funding

A few fortunate voluntary sector organisations are endowed with capital assets that bring them a guaranteed annual income. A number receive all or most of their funds from national or local government sources either in the form of grants or purchase of service contracts. Other sources of income include individual donations and subscriptions, charitable trusts and foundations, commercial sponsorship, vendorism (selling training, consultancy and other services), venturism (unrelated commercial activities like mail order catalogues) and fund-raising events from charity balls to sponsored walks. Funding may be closely tied to particular projects, activities or expenditure or it may be free of such constraints and available to be spent as the organisation wishes. It may take the form of a 'one-off' payment, a short term arrangement or guaranteed support for a number of years.[3]

Relationship with government

We have noted earlier that some agencies may have been set up or re-formed by Act of Parliament, many have representatives of central or local government on their governing bodies and may be heavily dependent on the state for their income. More generally and especially with the development of the 'contract culture' there is a widespread concern that many agencies have become so involved with the delivery of services on behalf of the state that they have put their ability to act autonomously at risk. At the other end of the spectrum are the pressure groups and campaigning bodies for whom freedom from government penetration is vital. And, in between, many organisations have a set of relationships with the state which may change according to particular circumstances.

Formalisation

A popular view of voluntary agencies is that they are characterised by flexibility and unbureaucratic forms of organisation. Undoubtedly informal organisations with little if any form of hierarchical structure exist within the sector. On the other hand, so do agencies whose organisation is as formal as any statutory agency or large corporation. Again, a whole range of intermediate arrangements can also be found.

Voluntarism

Similarly the degree of voluntary contribution made to the agency varies considerably – from the organisation where the existence of an unpaid governing body is the sole manifestation of voluntarism to the group whose entire work is carried out by volunteers. Some depend heavily on volunteer effort supported by paid staff, others on paid staff who are assisted by volunteers.

Common Features

Given the difficulty of delineating its boundaries and the bewildering diversity of the organisations found within them is there any sense in talking about a voluntary sector? One answer developed through the work of the London School of Economics' pioneering Centre for Voluntary Organisation and summed up by Margaret Harris is that coherence can be given to the idea of the sector if we concentrate on the distinctive organisational features that voluntary agencies have in common (Harris, 1990). The argument is not that any one such feature exists only in the voluntary sector but that the combination of most, if not all, of them is unique to voluntary organisations. These key features are:

The importance of values
The absence of a 'bottom line' or clear expectations defined in a statute means that voluntary agencies are driven or guided by a mission or a set of values. This can have a number of consequences. It may mean that the organisation will judge its performance as much on the degree to which it expresses its values as on the successful execution of tasks (Jeavons,199). And it can also mean that 'a particular form of organisational conflict – the values issue' is more likely to arise (Paton, 1996: 43). Such differences cannot be resolved as easily as other forms of conflict – like disagreements over budgets – where compromise is possible (*ibid*).

Voluntary governing bodies
While the terminology varies –'management committee', 'board of trustees', 'council of management' or 'executive committee' are just some examples – every voluntary organisation is governed by a group of people who receive no reward for the often onerous responsibilities they undertake as the final point of accountability for the agency's work. The effective functioning of the governing body and, in particular, the establishment of a constructive relationship between it and the paid or unpaid staff is a central challenge for every voluntary agency.

Multiple accountabilities
Accountability in the public and for-profit sectors is straightforward; in the former, officers are responsible to the electorate through elected representatives while, in the latter, the board is responsible to the shareholders. Voluntary organisations, by contrast, may have a range of accountabilities – to those who provide the funds, to those who benefit from their activities, to their own paid staff and volunteers, to a local community or community of interest, and to the wider public.

Human resources
Volunteering is not restricted to the voluntary sector; it is common in the public services and far from unknown in the for-profit sector. Many voluntary agencies, moreover, rely entirely on paid staff to undertake their operational activities. But others face the unique challenge of a situation in which paid staff and volunteers work side-by-side, often carrying out the same tasks.

Funding
Another characteristic challenge to voluntary agencies is the short-term and insecure nature of much of their funding and the resulting need to constantly seek income in a variety of ways from a range of sources.

Charismatic leaders
Many organisations exist only because of the activities of a charismatic and energetic individual who has identified a need and created a means of addressing it. At a later stage, however, the qualities that were required for the successful launch of the enterprise become less relevant to the needs of a growing organisation and painful decisions may have to be taken about the founder's continuing role.

Explaining the sector

David Billis, the founder of the Centre for Voluntary Organisation and the pioneer of voluntary sector studies in the UK, has developed a theory which helps to explain the distinctive nature of this constellation of organisational features (Billis, 1993). In the first place, he suggests, voluntary agencies do not conform to the traditional 'ABC' organisational model.

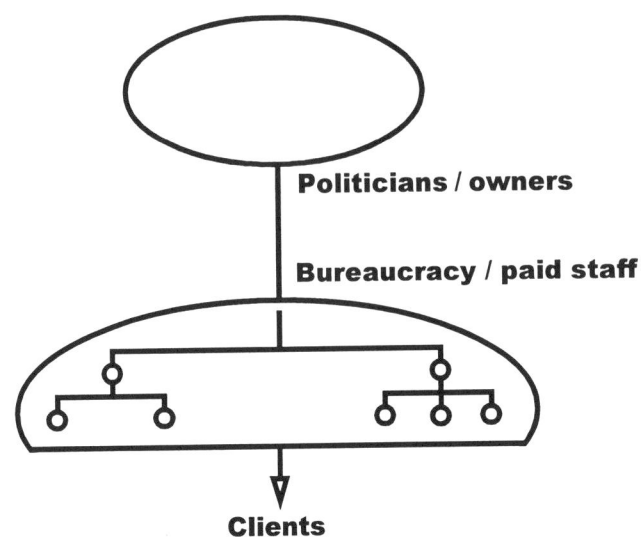

Figure 1 – The Traditional Model

The clear-cut division in a commercial venture between the owners (A), the work-force (B) and customers (C) has been mirrored in the public sector's distinction between members, officers and the beneficiaries of services. The workforce who produce the goods or provide the services are organised in a hierarchy with clear boundaries to their activities and authority and equally clear lines of managerial accountability.

In voluntary agencies, by contrast, the roles are far less clearly distinguished. Users or beneficiaries may also be members of the governing body or may play their part in the operational activities of the organisation. Paid staff may have been recruited from those who use the agency's services and they, or past employees, may be involved in the work of the governing body. And there are tensions within the organisation between the idea that commitment to the work was unbounded (the expectation staff should work 24 hours a day) and the need for job descriptions and conditions of employment, and between collaborative and collegiate ways of working and organisation as a bureaucratic hierarchy.

In seeking to explain these – and other – characteristic challenges to voluntary agencies Billis has described voluntary agencies as hybrid or 'blurred' organisations sharing the characteristics of two different 'worlds'. He suggests that there are three such unambiguous worlds or 'scenes of human existence':

The *personal world* where 'social problems are resolved by relatives, friends, neighbours, on a private basis' (Billis, 1993:160);

The *world of voluntary associations* comprised of 'groups of people who draw a boundary between themselves and others in order together to meet some problem, to do something'(*ibid*). An association will have a name, make a distinction between members and non-members and agree some rules for the election of officers and the conduct of its business;

The *bureaucratic world* characterised as 'a system of paid staff who are organised into hierarchical roles ... bound together by concepts such as accountability and authority' (*op cit*:161).

The worlds can be depicted as three overlapping circles:

Bureaucratic   Associational   Personal

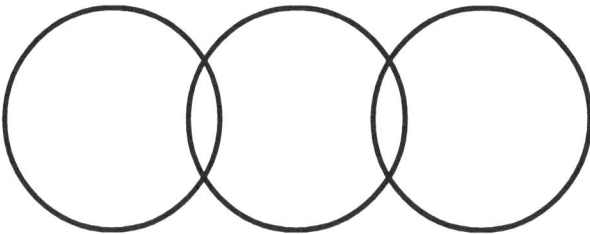

Figure 2 – Three Worlds Model

The key to the theory lies in the ambiguous zones created where the circles overlap. Between the personal and the associational world we find unorganised groups which 'represent the first step from the personal to the associational world' (Billis, 1993: 162) but lack a constitution or legal identity. This analysis throws light on the issue discussed above of the boundary between the voluntary and the informal sectors. The characterisation of the inhabitants of the other overlapping zone as 'ambiguous voluntary agencies' sheds more light on the distinctive nature of these organisations.

The key feature which distinguishes these agencies from associations is their employment of paid staff to carry out operational tasks. As a consequence they find themselves balancing and managing two very different sets of rules and expectations – those of the membership association where authority is derived from election to office and those associated with the managerial hierarchies of the bureaucratic form of organisation.

Current Challenges and Their Implications

The increased expectations on voluntary sector organisations that have developed over the past twenty years have brought with them a number of issues and challenges. For a start the expanded role in the provision of social welfare has had a number of organisational impacts which go beyond a significant change in the scale of their operations. As Billis and Harris (1992) have reported, these include changes in:

The nature of the users of services: voluntary agencies have increasingly been required to focus their activities on the more severe cases of social need – such as the most vulnerable of older people and children 'at risk';

The kind of services delivered: this has been accompanied by a shift from less to more intensive kinds of care – such as from luncheon clubs to day care; from domiciliary to residential care;

Professionalisation: in order to meet these demands agencies are tending to employ specialist professionals rather than generalist staff; replacing volunteers with paid staff to secure a more 'reliable' service; and applying a 'workplace' approach to the organisation of the work of those volunteers who remain;

Formalisation: these changes have been accompanied by the adoption of more formal structures and practices which tend to resolve the tensions between associational and bureaucratic approaches in favour of the latter; and

Isomorphism: in the process voluntary agencies have tended to lose their distinctive characteristics. Isomorphism is the term used by DiMaggio and Powell (1983) to describe a process in which organisations in the same field take on a similar 'shape'. This may be the result of coercion – taking on particular structures in order to gain access to funding or other advantages – or of copying existing models in order to be accepted into the field. It is suggested that voluntary contractors are increasingly coming to resemble the statutory agencies they are replacing as service providers.

The dilution of the distinctive nature of much of the voluntary sector undermines the principle on which voluntary agencies have been preferred to government bureaucracies. It also has direct implications for the sector. As the state comes to play a greater role in the funding and activities of the voluntary sector and voluntary agencies lose their special identity there will be little incentive for people to give time and money to them. And the outlook is gloomy; research commissioned by the Commission on the Future of the Voluntary Sector (Halfpenny and Scott, 1996) suggested that donations are static or falling and that the minority of larger agencies are gaining ground at the expense of smaller organisations.

The higher profile of the sector, fears about the loss of its distinctive identity and a handful of well publicised 'scandals' have created a situation in which the voluntary sector is coming under scrutiny. The Commission on the Future of the Voluntary Sector recognised the need to address these concerns and laid the primary responsibility on the agencies themselves to maintain and improve their effectiveness:

> The operational definition of efficiency adopted must be appropriate to the mission, values and objectives of the organisation itself and not imposed from outside. It needs to be clearly defined and expressed and may include criteria less common in other sectors, such as acting on the views of service users, empowering communities and building working alliances with other groups (*op cit*: 11).

The advent of a new Labour Government in May 1997 has brought with it an undertaking to enter into a 'compact' with the voluntary sector. This has been given a cautiously optimistic reception by those who hope that it will bring a clearer recognition by government of the distinctive nature and role of the sector. This in itself, however, will not be enough; for their part, voluntary sector organisations need to ask themselves some searching questions if the 'golden goose of voluntarism and altruism on which the future of the voluntary sector depends' (Harris 1997: 5) is to avoid slaughter.

References

Billis, D. *Organising public and voluntary agencies*, London, Routledge, 1993

Billis, D. and Harris, M. 'Taking the strain of change; UK voluntary agencies enter the post-Thatcher period', *Nonprofit and Voluntary Sector Quarterly* 21(3) (1996) pp.211-25

Brenton, M. *The voluntary sector in British social services*, London, Longman, 1985

Commission on the Future of the Voluntary Sector. *Meeting the challenge of change: voluntary action into the 21st century*, London, NCVO, 1996

Davis Smith, J. 'The voluntary tradition: philanthropy and self-help in Britain 1500-1945' in Davis Smith, J., Rochester, C. and Hedley, R. (eds.) *An introduction to the voluntary sector*, London, Routledge, 1995

Deakin, N. 'The perils of partnership: the voluntary sector and the state 1945-1992' in Davis Smith, J., Rochester, C. and Hedley, R. (eds.) *An introduction to the voluntary sector*, London, Routledge, 1995

DiMaggio, P. and Powell, W.W. 'The iron cage revisited; institutional isomorphism and collective rationality', *American Sociological Review* 48 (1983)

Gellner, E. 'The importance of being modular' in Hall, John A. *Civil society: theory, history, comparison*, Cambridge, Polity Press, (1995)

Halfpenny, P. and Scott, D. 'Future Developments in Funding for the Voluntary Sector' in *Meeting the challenge of change: voluntary action into the 21st century; summary of evidence and selected papers*, London, NCVO, 1996

Hall, P.D. *Inventing the nonprofit sector and other essays on philanthropy, voluntarism and nonprofit organisations*, Baltimore, Johns Hopkins University Press, 1992

Harris, M. *The Jewish voluntary sector in the United Kingdom: its role and future*, London, Institute for Jewish Policy Research, 1997

Harris, M. 'Working in the Voluntary Sector', *Work, Employment and Society* 4 (1) (1990) pp.125-140

Jeavons, T. *When the bottom line is faithfulness: the management of Christian service organisations*, Bloomington, Ind., Indiana University Press, 1994

Kendall, J. and Knapp, M. 'A loose and baggy monster; boundaries, definitions and typologies' in Davis Smith, J., Rochester, C. and Hedley, R. (eds.) *An introduction to the voluntary sector*, London, Routledge, 1995

Owen, D. *English philanthropy 1660-1960*, Oxford, Oxford University Press, 1964

Paton, R. 'How Are Values Handled in Voluntary Agencies' in Billis, D. and Harris, M. (eds.) *Voluntary agencies: challenges of organisation and management*, London/Basingstoke, Macmillan, 1996

Prochaska F. *Women and philanthropy in nineteenth century England*, Oxford, Clarendon Press, 1980

Rochester, C. 'The Impact of Funding Changes on the Voluntary Sector' in *Meeting the challenge of change: voluntary action into the 21st century; selected evidence and papers*, London, NCVO, 1996

Rochester, C. *Social benefits; measuring the value of community sector organisations*, London, Charities Aid Foundation, 1997

Salamon, L. and Anheier, H. *The emerging voluntary sector: an overview*, Manchester, Manchester University Press, 1996

Smith, D.H. 'The rest of the nonprofit sector: grassroots associations as the dark matter ignored in prevailing 'flat earth' maps of the sector', *Nonprofit and Voluntary Sector Quarterly* 26 (2) (1997)

Wolfenden Committee. *The future for voluntary organisations*, London, Croom Helm, 1978

Notes

1 For a fuller treatment of the importance of the mutual aid 'roots' of the voluntary sector see Davis Smith, 1995.

2 A distinction is generally made between the sacramental activities of religious organisations which are not seen as part of the voluntary sector and their involvement in social welfare provision which is.

3 For a fuller discussion of the sector's funding see Rochester, C. (1996).

2

Charity Financial Reporting, Fiscal Matters and Governance

Pesh Framjee

This chapter examines issues relating to financial reporting, taxation and governance. It is, of course, possible to have books dedicated to each of these interesting and diverse issues. The intention here is to highlight significant issues and signpost how to obtain more detailed information. The chapter also discusses best practice recommendations for charity financial reporting, explains the principles and focuses on areas where interpretation may be contentious so that those involved with charity financial reporting can understand the rationales and ensure compliance. There is also a section on reserves. The various topics will be looked at in the following order:

- Home Office Regulations and SORP compliance
- The purpose of a set of accounts
- The statement of financial activities – the rationale
- Fund accounting
- Classification of expenditure
- A tax overview
- Rates/council tax
- Tax effective giving
- Charity governance: measuring up to Cadbury

Home Office Regulations and SORP compliance

With over 170,000 charities accounting for over £17 billion of income it is somewhat surprising that there was until relatively recently no mandatory audit and accounting regime for charities. This changed when in October 1995 the Home Office published regulations on the new accounting, auditing and reporting regime under the Charities Act 1993, to come into force for accounting periods beginning on or after 1 March 1996.

To facilitate a better understanding of the regulations they have been published along with the revised Statement of Recommended Practice (SORP) on accounting by charities.

The Regulations set up the detailed statutory framework for the maintenance of accounting records and introduce the Statement of Financial Activities (SOFA) as the basis of a charity's accounts. There is also a requirement to prepare a trustees report and charities which breach certain financial thresholds will have to be independently examined or audited.

The Regulations stipulate the minimum accounting requirement for charities which are not also companies, in effect the statutory framework. The revised SORP will, as best practice for all charities, provide the flesh on the bones. The accounting regulations and the SORP have been drafted to ensure that compliance with the SORP will ensure full compliance with the accounting regulations. Although the SORP being recommended practice is not mandatory the Charity Commissioners have explained that they would expect charities to comply with the requirements unless another SORP which is more specific to them is published. Charity accounts should specifically note compliance with the SORP as part of the accounting policies.

Charities with income under £100,000 if preparing accounts on a receipts and payment basis can adopt a simplified basis. It is important to recognise that the SORP only applies to material items.

Furthermore, in certain cases a departure from the principles of the SORP may be necessary to give a true and fair view and in such cases the departure should be explained stating the reasons for such departure.

When considering the principles expressed in the SORP readers should understand the underlying reasons for the recommendations and adopt a common sense approach to their application. Narrow and rigid interpretations are often made on certain aspects when clearly this is not the rationale behind those aspects. Above all, a charity's accounts should be transparent and the accounting policies and the notes should explain what has been done.

In addition to the Charity SORP there are other SORPs which are applicable to specific classes of charities. There are SORPs for Universities, Housing Associations and Unit Trusts (the last should be followed by Common Investment Funds). This material does not cover these specific SORPs and concentrates on accounting for charities that do not have to follow alternative regimes.

Relationship with accounting standards

Statements of Standard Accounting Practice (SSAPs) and more recently issued Financial Reporting Standards (FRSs) are together seen as being authoritative statements on accounting practice. They aim to narrow the areas of difference and variety in the accounting treatments of the matters with which they deal to ensure that accounts are prepared on a broadly similar basis. They are applicable to all financial statements which are intended to give a true and fair view of the organisation's state of affairs at the balance sheet date and of income and expenditure for the financial period ending on that date. Compliance with accounting standards will normally be required if financial statements are to give a true and fair view.

It is important to recognise that many charities are already following the principles of the revised SORP as indication of best practice since nothing in the new SORP conflicts with existing accounting principles. In fact the SORP has received the 'negative franking' from the Accounting Standards Board.

The SORP specifically does not reiterate all the principles of generally accepted accounting practice. Therefore charities preparing accounts to give a true and fair view must also consider Accounting Standards.

Relationship with other legislation

The SORP has been written to ensure that it is in line with the accounting requirements of the Charities Act 1993. In fact, charities preparing accounts under the SORP will automatically meet the Charities Act accounting requirements.

In addition, there is nothing in the SORP that would be unacceptable for charitable companies. In certain cases a summary income and expenditure account may be required (see Section on Charity Law).

The Purpose of a Set of Accounts

Many charity accountants have long complained that the traditional income and expenditure account did not reflect or explain fully all the financial activities of the charity. They consider that the very nature of raising and using of charity resources requires a different approach from that of commercial profit oriented companies.

Charities do not usually have shareholders with an equity interest, so matters such as distributable profit and dividends do not feature. A charity's resource providers do not usually expect a direct return on their donations. The users of charity financial statements need to assess the services that the charity is providing and its ability to continue providing them. The accounts should also show how the trustees have discharged their stewardship responsibilities during the year and, whilst it may be that the bottom line surplus or deficit provides some of this information, any presentation that focuses on such a bottom line tends to ignore some fundamental differences between accounting for charities and commercial organisations.

In summary, charities exceeding £100,000 of gross income will have to prepare full accounts in accordance with the SORP. If their gross income is under £100,000 they can prepare a simple receipts and payments account. Those charities exceeding £250,000 of gross income or total expenditure in the current or the preceding two years will have to have a full audit. If they fall under this band but exceed £10,000 of gross income they will require an independent examination. The regulations do not apply to charities that are incorporated under the Companies Act and these charities have further hurdles before they are entitled to the audit exemption. In addition to income having to be under £250,000 they are not entitled to the audit exemption if they are a parent or subsidiary company or if their net asset exceeds £1.4 million. There is no requirement for independent examination and Companies Act charities with income above £90,000 but under £250,000 will require an accountant's report.

Although the objectives of charity accounting have remained unchanged, experience has shown that the original guidelines needed to be strengthened and clarified in certain areas. The thrust of the changes stems from the desire for greater accountability of all the resources entrusted to a charity.

Many of these concepts mirror important aspects of trust law and to comply with that law charities are expected to maintain records that should allow much of the information required by the SORP to be easily obtained. In many areas the requirements are virtually identical to the original SORP 2 but additional clarification and refinements have been made so that the accounting treatment and public presentation reflects the legal requirement and the needs of users of charity accounts.

The Statement of Financial Activities – the Rationale

In recognition that charities do not generally have any one single indicator of performance comparable to a business enterprise bottom line, it is perhaps more important to consider changes in the *nature* as well as the *amounts* of the net resources of a charity. This, coupled with other information about the charity's efforts and accomplishments, will assist in assessing performance. Accordingly, the SORP and the Regulations recommend a primary statement that records all the resources entrusted to the charity and reflects all the financial activities in the period under review. The proposals are that this statement will be called the Statement of Financial Activities (SOFA) (SORP para 69 et seq).

In producing the SORP this departure from an 'operating' statement format had to be carefully considered and certain options were considered. For example, that the reporting statement should be divided into two parts, a statement of 'operations' and a statement of other changes in net assets. The suggestion was that the first statement would report operating income and expenses and would be followed by another statement that would report all other income, expenses, gains and losses. There is, however, no consensus on how to define an operating measure and on which income and expenses should be included or excluded from 'operations'.

For example, some would include in 'operations' only donations and resources available for current period use, whether restricted or not. Others suggested the exclusion of restricted income if the restrictions were not met in the current period. Some would exclude from 'operations', revenues, gains or losses from non-recurring, unexpected or unusual events such as a very large legacy.

Fund Accounting

The distinction between income and capital permeates through trust law. Income includes all resources which become available to the charity and which the trustees are legally required to apply in furtherance of the charitable purposes within a reasonable time. Capital, on the other hand, must be invested or retained.

In addition, due to the constraints of trust law and the important matter of donor imposed restrictions it is vital that users of the accounts can see what the increase or decrease in net resources represents. A charity may, for example, have maintained the level of its net assets only because it received restricted income earmarked for a particular purpose that compensated for a significant decrease in general income. This would not be obvious in the traditional single column format that usually does not distinguish between the types of funds. It is important that to ensure compliance with the terms of the special trusts and funds, that the accounts assist this understanding.

Many charities receive significant amounts of restricted resources and these restrictions often affect types and levels of services. Consequently, information about the change in the nature of net assets is vitally useful in assessing a charity's ability to respond to short term needs or higher levels of service. Therefore, the recommendations are that the resources of a charity should be grouped according to the restrictions on their use as follows:

1. Unrestricted funds

These are funds available for general use and include those that have been designated for particular purposes by the trustees of a charity.

2. Restricted income funds

These are funds that are restricted for particular purposes, either by the wishes of the donor or by the nature of the appeal. Therefore those preparing and auditing charity accounts will have to consider carefully appeal literature, direct mail and other forms of solicitation to ascertain whether income received as a result of the solicitation should be restricted.

3. Capital funds

These funds are funds that are not for direct application. Where the trustees have no power to apply capital as income it will be permanent endowment. Where the trustees have a power to expend it if necessary, this will be expendable endowment. Expendable endowment should be treated as capital until the right to expend it is exercised in which case it should be transferred to income prior to application.

Appendix 3 to the SORP provides a useful explanation on the principles of Fund Accounting and the definition of income and capital are covered in the glossary.

An analysis and visible segregation on the face of the SOFA and in the Balance Sheet is vital to be able to identify what services and activities a charity could continue to carry out. For example, if an international aid charity has received income specifically for Kurdish Refugees, this will be shown as a restricted fund and will highlight that the money is unavailable for other purposes. This information would be far more important than a composite surplus or deficit on revenue income and revenue expenditure.

Use of designated funds

When a charity's trustees propose to use general funds for a particular purpose they can set aside amounts for future expenditure. In these circumstances such amounts should be treated as designated funds. These transfers to and from designated funds are an allocation of the general fund balance carried forward and not a reduction of unrestricted funds, there will therefore be no change to total net assets. However, it will highlight that some of these are designated for a particular purpose. Designated funds should not be confused with restricted funds. The former are usually a result of an internal decision (which can be altered) whilst the latter arise from donor imposed restrictions or the terms of a specific appeal.

It is also possible to use designated funds to create a distinction between funds. For example, a charity with significant amounts of mission initial fixed assets such as care homes or hospices may decide to set up a property or fixed asset fund which will equate to the net book value of the assets. This fund will then segregate from the general fund the amount that has already been 'utilised' and is represented by fixed assets.

Classification of Expenditure

The size of charities is often measured by their income. Perhaps this is due to the fact that with commercial companies size is often measured through turnover. However, there is a fundamental difference: the sales of a commercial company is its raison d'être; with a charity it is its expenditure and not its income which fulfils its objectives. For this reason it is vital that the analysis and presentation of expenditure in the accounts is given particular importance. The aim should be to reflect fairly the activities of a charity so that readers of the accounts can understand how the charity's expenditure fulfils its objectives.

Functional classification

The new SORP expands on the recommendations that although expressed in the SORP2 were not clearly explained and hence not always followed. SORP2 required that expenditure was split between charitable and non-charitable expenditure. It suggested further that non-charitable expenditure should be divided between fund-raising, publicity and administration.

A number of charities have ignored this and many income and expenditure accounts merely list expenditure by their natural expense classification, such as rent, salaries and wages, printing and stationery etc. This information does not convey very much about the activities of the charity to the reader. In fact, when looking at these accounts it is often not clear how the charity is spending money on its objectives. Expenditure information by natural classification has its uses but it is more important to identify the costs incurred on each of the different activities of the charity. Charities should continue to disclose certain expenses such as salaries by natural classification, but this could be done in the notes to the accounts.

The SORP therefore recommends that expenditure should be listed by functional classification (para 136). This is the aggregation of costs incurred in pursuit of a defined purpose – for example, provision of services to the elderly or counselling. It is achieved by adding together all the costs (salaries, rent, depreciation etc.) relating to that specific activity. It is likely therefore to include an allocation exercise as well as aggregation since it summarises expenditure according to the purpose for which costs are incurred. The SORP recommends a two-fold functional classification that reports expenditure on major projects or services and the costs of supporting those charitable activities (charitable expenditure) distinguishing them from expenditure on fund-raising, publicity and administration (other expenditure) (paras 92 and 93).

The Regulations under the Charities Act 1993 endorse this classification and require resources expended to be divided into:

- expenditure directly relating to the objects of the charity;
- expenditure on fund-raising and publicity; and
- expenditure on the management and administration of the charity.

Tabulating information in this way would move towards the user being able to see information that may assist in linking a charity's expenses with its accomplishments. Charities should attempt to select appropriate headings for functional costs that best explain the areas of their work. A good start is to review the annual report to see what it says about how the charity has expended its resources. The headings on the SOFA should then tie in with the narrative comment.

Contrary to popular misconception, charities are not automatically exempt from taxation. Charities are in fact affected by income/corporation tax, VAT, employee taxes and capital-gains tax. There are of course fiscal benefits associated with charitable status and charities should ensure that they are aware of the opportunities and pitfalls.

A Tax Overview

It is not only registration with the Charity Commission that allows a charity to get these benefits. The concept of Charity Commission registration only started in 1960 and is limited geographically to England and Wales. As far as tax benefits go, the entitlement to the special tax status is determined in Scotland exclusively by the Inland Revenue, and in England and Wales the Inland Revenue normally do not question registration with the Charity Commissioners. This chapter takes an overview of the taxation of charities. It does not intend to be fully comprehensive but simply highlights some of the more important tax aspects.

Primarily, it is important for a charity to consider carefully where its income has come from, whether it is doing anything in exchange for the income and how it is spending its money. When considering the tax and legal position of charities, the concept of being established 'for charitable purposes only' is used time and time again in tax legislation but this phrase is not defined in any legislation. Consequently one has to turn to case law.

Taxes on Income and Profits

Whether a charity is liable to pay income tax or corporation tax depends entirely on the constitution of the charity. If it is incorporated under the Companies Acts, Industrial and Provident Act, Royal Charter or is incorporated in another way its income or profits may be subject to corporation tax. Otherwise income tax may be charged.

The main statutory exemptions from taxation for charities is found in Sections 505 and 506 of the Income and Corporation Taxes Act 1988 (ICTA 88) and Section 256 of the Taxation of Capital Gains Act 1992 (TCGA 92).

For income and corporation tax purposes the key sections of ICTA 88 directly relevant to charities are:

Section
- 235   Distributions to exempt funds
- 339   Charges on income, donations to charity
- 347a General rules on financial payments and interest
- 505   Charity exemption general
- 506   Qualifying and non qualifying expenditure
- 507   Extension of S505 to certain other bodies
- 508   Scientific research organisations
- 510   Agricultural societies
- 660   Covenanted payments
- 671   Recoverable settlements allowing release of obligations
- 776   Transactions in land: taxation of capital gains
- 832   Interpretation section
- 839   Connected persons

VAT

In theory VAT is simple – recover VAT on inputs (business purchases) and charge VAT on outputs (supplies). However, VAT is particularly complex in its application to charities since it is likely to involve standard rated, zero rated and exempt supplies in any organisation. A commercial business may have one business line, e.g. publishing; a charity may have many types of supply and activity; this is the basis for complexity. In addition, there is the important distinction between non-business and business activities. These terms have no special meaning in the charity context and, although they have not been explained in detail, some explanation is merited where there are charity specific issues.

There are three basic questions that must be addressed in considering the correct VAT treatment of a particular transaction:

- Is the income derived from a business activity?
- If so, is that activity exempt from VAT or taxable?
- If it is taxable, is it subject to VAT at 17.5% or 0% (or 8%)?

Simple questions that, more often than not, are not so simple to answer. Before we go into further detail, it is also important to set down four fundamental points:

(a) VAT is a tax based on transactions;
(b) For the purposes of VAT, transactions can be defined as supplies made for consideration;
(c) Consideration can be monetary or non-monetary; *and*
(d) If a supply is made in the course or furtherance of business, it will be subject to VAT at the standard rate unless the legislation specifically provides for it to be treated as zero rated or exempt.

Business or non-business

The underlying issue, therefore, before we look at whether an activity is standard rated, zero rated or exempt, is whether the income is received by way of business. If it is, there will be VAT implications; if it is not, the income will be outside the scope of VAT.

It is an unpromising start in attempting to define business for VAT purposes to have to say that there is no comprehensive definition of business in the VAT legislation. VAT legislation mentions only two specific activities that are always considered to be business activities:

(a) the provision by a club, association or organisation (for a subscription or other consideration) of the facilities or advantages available to its members; *and*
(b) the admission of persons to any premises for a consideration.

(a) above does not apply where a body has objects which are in the public domain and are of a political, religious, philanthropic, philosophical or patriotic nature, provided the subscription contains no facility or advantage for the subscriber (other than the right to participate in its management or receive reports on its accounts).

Registration

VAT registration is compulsory when the VAT registration threshold is exceeded. This can happen in two circumstances:

a) Where at the end of any month the value of **taxable supplies** in the period of one year then ending exceeds the threshold; *or*

b) At any time when there are reasonable grounds for believing that the value of **taxable supplies** in the next 30 days will exceed the threshold.

Taxable supplies are standard rated and zero rated supplies, they do not include exempt and non-business supplies.

For VAT registration purposes the disposal of 'capital assets' of the taxpayer are disregarded when considering whether the threshold has been exceeded. Capital assets include office furniture, office machinery (including computers), and used company vehicles. (The procedure for VAT registration can be found in VAT Notice 700/1 'Should I be registered for VAT?'.)

However, VAT law is never as simple as that and the waters are clouded further since, for example, a concert held once a year when an admission fee is charged is a business activity. However, if it fulfils the conditions to be treated as a one off fundraising event (Group 12 Sch 9 VAT Act 1994), it would be exempt.

Exempt supplies

Exempt supplies are within the scope of VAT law but no VAT is charged when making supplies. Similarly, subject to certain limits, generally no VAT can be recovered on expenditure incurred in making those supplies. This is to be contrasted with zero rated supplies.

Zero rated supplies

These are taxable supplies, albeit at the zero rate. No VAT is chargeable on the making of these supplies but, since they are treated as taxable supplies, the VAT incurred in making these supplies can usually be recovered.

Non Business Supplies

Non business activities such as the receipt of donations, bequests, grants and provision of voluntary services free of charge are outside the scope of VAT. Charities whose activities are wholly outside the scope of VAT are not allowed to register for VAT.

Registering for VAT is often seen as an unnecessary complication but it may be beneficial for the charity to be registered to enable it to reclaim input VAT. For example, many charities sell goods that have been donated for resale. This is a business activity that is zero rated. This means that VAT is not charged on the goods sold but the charity can recover all of the associated input VAT – e.g. on the VAT-able costs of running charity shops.

Input VAT directly related to taxable supplies can be recovered in full and the proportion of input VAT on general overheads that can be attributed to taxable activities can also be recovered. VAT incurred on expenditure relating to non-business activities cannot be reclaimed in any circumstances. This means that all expenditure with VAT on it must be attributed to each source of income to ensure that VAT recovery is maximised.

VAT – the key issues

VAT for charities is a very complex area and charities must recognise that even if they are not registered for VAT, they are almost always involved in VAT that is charged on goods and services provided to them.

The aim for charities is to:

- Ensure that full advantage is taken of any VAT reliefs so that the minimum amount of VAT is incurred on expenditure;
- Maximise the recovery of any VAT incurred; *and*
- Where possible, charge VAT if customers are able to recover it and use reliefs to zero rate or exempt supplies where the VAT would be an additional cost and would, therefore, reduce income.

For VAT purposes it is useful to know the schedules that provide zero rating and exemptions. These schedules of the VAT Act 1994 that are relevant for charities are:

Schedule 8 – zero rating
   Group
3   Books etc.
4   Talking books for the blind and handicapped and wireless sets for the blind
5   Construction of dwellings
6   Protected buildings
12   Drugs, medicines, aids for the handicapped
15   Charities etc.

Schedule 9 – exemptions
   Group
6   Education
7   Health and Welfare

| 9 | Trade unions and professional bodies |
| 12 | Fundraising events by charities and other qualifying bodies |

Rates/Council Tax

The Local Government Finance Act 1988 (LGFA 88) introduced a distinction between domestic property and non-domestic property for rating purposes.

Domestic

The LGFA 88 introduced the community charge which was from 1st April 1993 replaced by the council tax introduced by the Local Government Finance Act 1992 (LGFA 92). Council tax is primarily a domestic property tax based on the assessed freehold value of the property. 'Domestic property' is property that is used wholly for the purpose of living accommodation. It would include gardens, outhouses and garages (S66 LGFA 88). Certain unoccupied properties are exempt from the tax under the council tax (Exempt Dwellings) Order 1992. Charities may be able to obtain relief of up to 50% of council tax. For example, if there is only one chargeable person occupying the property, a 25% discount can be obtained and if as a result of persons qualifying for exemptions, such as the severely mentally impaired, there are no chargeable persons in occupation, a 50% discount applies.

Non-Domestic

Ss43 and 44 of LGFA 88 introduced the system of non-domestic rating. Non-domestic properties are subject to the unified business rate. Non-domestic properties will include offices occupied by the charity. However a large residential 'home' including offices will not be subject to the unified business rate but rather to domestic council tax.

Mandatory relief for non-domestic or unified business rates is provided to charities and certain other organisations at 80% where the ratepayer is: *'a charity or trustees for the charity and the hereditament is wholly or mainly used for charitable purposes (whether of that charity or of that charity and other charities)'.*

S47 LGFA 88 conveys power on local authorities to allow discretionary relief that would be additional to the mandatory relief. This is given when the property is used wholly or mainly for charitable purposes by a charity or other non profit body whose main objects are charitable or benevolent or concerned with education, social welfare, science, literature or the arts. Discretionary relief is also available where the property is wholly or mainly used for recreation by a non-profit club or society.

The Government has issued guidance to charging authorities on certain criteria that should be considered when making a decision as to allow discretionary relief. These include: whether membership of an organisation is open to all sections of the public, whether it provides facilities such as training and education, what its affiliates are, whether the membership is drawn from the area of that authority and what the charity has done for the area.

It is important to appreciate the impact of the wording 'wholly or mainly used for charitable purpose' and a distinction must be made between activities that are directed to the achievement of the objects of the charity and activities that, although they help the charity, cannot be described as carrying out or part of the carrying out of its charitable purposes.

In this respect activities such as management of assets and fund raising fall into the second category and such activities are not eligible for relief.

Tax Effective Giving

It is important to consider ways in which charities can benefit in a tax efficient manner, the donor possibly benefiting as well as the charity: see also Inland Revenue Leaflets *Giving to Charity*, IR64 (businesses) and IR65 (individuals).

Tax effective methods

Deeds of covenant – A payment under a deed of covenant is an annual payment. Where income tax has been deducted from such a payment it is treated as tax at the basic rate paid by the person to whom the payment is being made. Consequently charities, which are exempt from income tax under the ICTA 1988 s 505, are entitled to recover the basic rate income tax deducted from the annual payments made to them. In some cases there are also benefits to donors.

To be valid the covenants must fulfil at least the following legal requirements:

i) There must be a binding legal obligation such as a deed. This is necessary in order to transfer the legal title of income from the covenantor to the charity.
ii) It must be recurring and be capable of exceeding three years (therefore they are usually made for four years) and it should not be capable of termination without the consent of the charity concerned. It could be variable or contingent on external facts.
iii) It must be made otherwise than for consideration. It must be paid out of income and be pure income profit in the hands of the charity, that is, there must be no cost incurred in receiving the income.

Consequently, it must be clear that there are no conditions or benefits in return for the covenant. If the covenant is in fact in return for a benefit then it would be invalid. Essentially, the gross annual payment should be regarded as an addition to the total income of the charity and cannot be a payment for any goods or services.

The Inland Revenue clarified in a press release issued in March 1989 that in the case of ordinary small subscriptions the benefits available to subscribers are in practice ignored if they are worth less than 25% of the covenanted subscription. It is the availability of the benefit that matters and even if it is not availed by the covenantor it will be taken into account. In addition, S59, FA 1989 brought in a further concession – where the charity's sole and main purpose is to preserve the national heritage or wildlife for the benefit of the public the benefit of a member's rights of entry to view the charity's property is left out of account altogether.

Gift aid – This scheme enables tax paid on gifts (in the case of individuals and close companies of [now] £250 or more) to be recovered.

Gift Aid was launched on 1 October 1990 and was seen to be an important boost to charitable giving. For the first time both individuals and closed companies can make tax effective single donations to charities. The relevant legislation for companies is found in Section 339 ICTA 1988 as amended by S26, FA 1990 and for individuals in Section 25 Finance Act 1990.

The main advantage over the deed of covenant route is simplicity and that the payments do not have to extend more than three years. Discussed below are some of the important Gift Aid principles.

There is a minimum limit for individuals and close companies. Each gift must be for at least £250 (£400 between 7 May 1992 and 16 March 1993 and £600 prior to 7 May 1992) net of basic rate tax. There is no such minimum limit for non close companies.

Only outright gifts can qualify and payments by individuals and close companies in return for goods and services cannot be made under Gift Aid. However, very small benefits will be acceptable. These should not exceed 2.5% of the net gift and the total benefit from a charity must not exceed £250 in a tax year.

Payroll giving – Employees can now participate in approved 'give as you earn' schemes (maximum [now] £1,200 in any year) and obtain tax relief on those payments.

The legislation for the payroll deduction scheme is found in 202 ICTA 1988. It was introduced in 1986 and was enacted to encourage modest giving without the formalities of deeds of covenants or minimum threshold required for Gift Aid.

In practice the scheme has not been as popular as was initially hoped because it involves a certain amount of paper work and there are many restrictive conditions. The scheme operates as follows:

(i) The individual's employer must operate the scheme for an employee to participate;

(ii) The employee can decide whether to join the scheme and how much to donate. The maximum annual limit was increased to £1,200 with effect from 6 April. In practice many employers have imposed a minimum limit to counter the administrative burden. The employee can also decide to which charity the money is to be paid.

(iii) The employer must deduct the appropriate sum from the employee's salary and pay it to an agent who must be a charity. In all cases the Inland Revenue generally must approve the agent and terms of the scheme.

(iv) The tax relief is available to the employee for the sum donated and PAYE is calculated after the donation. However, the sum is not deductible for the purpose of National Insurance Contributions.

Capital gains – Section 257 of the Taxation of Chargeable Gains Act 2992 (TCGA 1992) confers exemption on donors who make outright gifts to charity. A gain will not be chargeable where the disposal is to a body mentioned in the Inheritance Tax Act 1984, Sched 3 (TCGA 1992, s 258). These gifts for national purposes can be made to universities, museums, art galleries and other national institutions. The provision caters for the situation where an individual has made a gift or a sale at under-value.

Transfers on death – Section 23 of the Inheritance Act 1984 (IHTA 1984) exempts transfers of value to the extent that the values transferred by them are attributable to property which is given to charities, i.e. becomes the property of charities of is held on trust for charitable purposes only: see e.g. *Guild v IRC* (1992) 2 A11 ER 10.

It is important that the gift be immediate and unconditional: transfers will not constitute exempt transfers where the donor has stipulated restrictions. Section 23 provides that where a gift is conditional on something happening and the condition is not met within a period of 12 months of transfer, the gift will not be exempt. If a charity is offered a gift subject to a prior condition and there is a likelihood that the condition will not be satisfied within 12 months then it should try to arrange for the transfer to be treated as a loan and not as a transfer of value until such a time as the condition has been satisfied. At that stage the loan could be written off and this would be treated as an exempt transfer of value under s 23.

Secondment of employees – In certain circumstances employers may treat as tax deductible expenditure attributable to an employee seconded to a charity.

Charity Governance: Measuring up to Cadbury

Issues of Governance are moving centre stage. Charities have particular issues in this area due to their two-tier structure of voluntary trustees and paid management. This is a difficult area and whilst trustees can delegate they must not abdicate. This section considers how trustees and management should adapt the Cadbury guidelines on Corporate Governance to the voluntary sector environment.

The Cadbury code requires that directors should report on the effectiveness of the company's system of internal control. In December 1994 a joint working party made up of representatives of the 100 group of finance directors, the ICAEW and the ICAS published 'Internal control and financial reporting: Guidance for directors of listed companies registered in the UK.' Since then some charities have thought it right to make a Cadbury type statement in their trustees' report.

To meet best practice guidelines this report should contain as a minimum:

a) acknowledgement by the trustees that they are responsible for the charity's system of internal financial control;

b) explanation that such a system can provide only reasonable and not absolute assurance against material misstatement or loss;

c) description of the key procedures that the trustees have established and which are designed to provide effective internal financial control;

d) confirmation that the trustees or a committee, such as the finance or audit committee have reviewed the effectiveness of the systems of internal financial control; *and*

e) description of corrective action taken or intended to be taken, if any, to correct weaknesses in internal financial control which have resulted in material losses, contingencies or uncertainties which require disclosure in the financial statements or in the auditors' report. Where no changes are considered necessary an explanation should be given.

Prima facie it may appear that such a statement is easy to make. In reality it does require careful consideration of a number of criteria. Unfortunately, there is little published information on how charities can establish whether or not they meet these criteria. Consequently, before making the statements trustees must, in effect, carry out a 'health check' over their internal control systems to ascertain that it does fulfil the criteria. This requires identification of the control procedures currently in place. Inevitably, these procedures will not be perfect and the trustees must consider how they might be improved or strengthened to support a statement in the Trustees' Report. The Charities Act, Accounting, Auditing & Reporting Regulations do not have a requirement for a statement on internal financial controls. However, the Housing Corporation requires a Cadbury style report for all registered housing associations owning 50 homes or more.

Internal financial controls need to be considered at two levels: higher level controls that are of the overall organisational type and lower level controls which deal with the nitty-gritty. The Charity Commissioners have published a useful leaflet dealing with internal financial control. This leaflet deals with the minimum financial and supervisory controls that are expected in a charity. The Cadbury code focuses on the higher level organisational controls and the criteria for effectiveness from the guidance for directors identifies the following key areas.

(The bullet points in each section cover the issues that would need to be considered/evaluated and perhaps included in a statement of internal controls).

Criteria for assessing effectiveness

Control environment

- A commitment by directors/trustees, management and employees to competence and integrity (e.g. leadership by example, employment criteria);
- Communication of ethical values and control consciousness to managers and employees (e.g. through written codes of conduct, formal standards of discipline, performance appraisal);
- An appropriate organisational structure within which operations can be planned, executed, controlled and monitored to achieve the charity's objectives;
- Appropriate delegation of authority with accountability which has regard to acceptable levels of risk; and
- A professional approach to financial reporting which complies with generally accepted accounting practice (SORP, Charities Act Regulations, Financial Reporting Standards etc.).

Trustees and management must ensure that there is an appropriate control environment. This includes the establishment of clear management responsibilities in relation to internal financial control and unambiguous responses to control failures. This requires a documented organisational structure clearly defining lines of responsibility and delegation of authority between the trustees, management and operating units. My experience is that policies, practices and procedures are usually better understood and disseminated when they are articulated in a code of conduct which becomes part of the organisation's culture rather than something to gather dust on the shelves.

There are a number of matters to address. Starting at the top there must be commitment to quality and integrity and the mission statement should reflect the ethical values of the charity. The prominence of the ethical climate should not be inward facing and external literature and external relationships should also reflect these values.

Identification and evaluation of risks and control objectives
- Identification of key business risks in a timely manner;
- Consideration of the likelihood of risks crystallising and the significance of the consequential financial impact on the charity; and
- Establishment of priorities for the allocation of resources available for control and the setting and communicating of clear control objectives.

This is where the charity considers the process used to identify major risks (including optionally a brief explanation of the major financial risks identified).

Senior management and trustees should be aware of the risks facing their charity and the implications of these. This means that they must assess risks arising from both external and internal sources. It also means that they must consider the political, economic and sociological trends that may affect the charity.

There are many examples of external risk. Changes in the market place affecting services provided by the charity or the introduction and development of new methods of providing services need to be regularly assessed. Charities are often operating in an environment which is no less competitive than in the for profit sector. Competition can be from various sources and the risk assessment should carefully consider competitors and the impact that new entrants, changes in practice etc., have on the operation of the charity.

Many charities are over-dependant on particular funders. This dependence is a risk factor if the funders are likely to cut direct funding or make onerous requirements on the charities.

Charities operating overseas or charities which are dependent on supplies and/or services from overseas have their own particular risk factors which are inherent in their operating environment. For example, they are exposed to adverse fluctuations in foreign exchange and to the local political climate.

Internal risk would include the risk of information loss and will require an overview of the adequacy of back-up systems in the event of failure of systems that could significantly affect operations. There is always a risk associated with people and with the human resources of a charity the danger of changes in key management affecting the ability of the charity to function effectively.

Information and communication
- Performance indicators which allow management to monitor the key operational and financial activities and risks, and the progress towards financial objectives, and to identify developments which require intervention (e.g. forecasts and budgets).
- Information systems which provide ongoing identification and capture of relevant, reliable and up-to-date financial and other information from internal and external sources (e.g. monthly management accounts, including earnings, cashflow and balance sheet reporting); and
- Systems that communicate relevant information to the right people at the right frequency and time in a format that exposes variances from the budgets and forecasts and allows prompt response.

This area considers the major information systems that are in place and the performance indicators which are used to monitor and evaluate the progress to achieving objectivity. The trustees should lay out the long term objectives in terms of service provision, market share, stakeholder satisfaction etc. in line with the long term goals and objectives and the vision of the charity.

There should be a three to five year plan broken down into annual plans. The annual plan should be supported by integrated operating budgets, capital budgets and cash flow forecasts which are prepared by management and approved by the board of trustees who ensure that it is consistent with strategic goals.

Key performance indicators (KPIs) and factors that are critical for success must be identified and measured. Importantly, staff should be aware of these KPIs and how they impact on the charity's success and indeed their own appraisal.

Control procedures
- Procedures to ensure complete and accurate accounting for financial transactions;
- Appropriate authorisation limits for transactions that reasonably limit the charity's exposures;
- Procedures to ensure the reliability of data processing and information reports generated;
- Controls that limit exposure to loss of assets/records or to fraud (e.g. physical controls, segregation of duties);
- Routine and surprise checks which provide effective supervision of the control activities; and
- Procedures to ensure compliance with laws and regulations that have significant financial implications.

Financial transactions
An area that often requires attention is the interfacing and reconciliation of different sources of information. For example, fund-raising information from a fund-raising department should be matched and reconciled with information in the financial accounting systems. Where possible standard reconciliation formats should be used and the reconciliations should be carried out independently, with procedures being properly documented. My experience is that, although reconciliations may be seen as important, they are rarely seen as urgent, so in times of pressure they are postponed. The control procedure should lay down the deadlines for reconciliations.

Another area which is not given importance is amendments and interventions to standard procedure. For example, all non-recurring journals must be supported by adequate documentation and should only be put through after they are authorised at the appropriate level. The senior management team or the trustees must agree on the situations and frequency with which intervention may be needed to flex budgets or to plan transfer cost allocations, etc. Where management has intervened these interventions should be documented and explained appropriately. As a general rule management override outside the agreed cycle should be prohibited.

Monitoring and corrective action
- A monitoring process which provides reasonable assurance to the trustees that there are appropriate control procedures in place for all of the charity's significant operations and that these procedures are being followed (e.g. consideration by the board or board committee of reports from management, from an internal audit function or from independent accountants).
- Identification of change in the operations and its environment which may require changes to the system of internal financial control;
- Formal procedures for reporting weakness and for ensuring appropriate corrective action; *and*
- The provision of adequate support for public statements on internal control or internal financial control.

Senior management should ensure that there is an independent evaluation of the internal control system on a rolling basis. This may be carried out by internal audit, external audit or by independent members of the charity staff. An appropriate element of internal control systems should be evaluated and the scope, depth, coverage and frequency of this evaluation should be enough to give a reasonable level of assurance over the systems being reviewed. The aim should be to create an understanding of how the system is supposed to work and how it actually does work. It is useful to use checklists, questionnaires, or other evaluation methodology tools to simplify this process.

In conclusion

A chapter of this length can merely scratch the surface of non-profit financial reporting, fiscal issues and governance. The aim of this chapter has been to highlight emerging and current issues on which charity trustees and management must focus.

3

Managing Change in the Voluntary Sector

Christine Forrester

Change – The Context

A changing environment – a changing sector

It has become almost a truism to say that managing change has become a key area for the voluntary sector over the past decade. A new and rapidly changing environment, more competitive and more pressurised, has had a significant impact on many of the traditional ways in which voluntary sector organisations have operated. As the sector has developed, and new patterns of working and new demands have affected all organisations, from small local organisations to the large national level charities, strategies for coping with the impact of these changes have become central to voluntary sector management.

Introducing new information technologies

In this context, the introduction and use of new information management systems has in many cases enabled organisations to manage change more effectively; in others, the introduction of new technology applications has caused transition problems as organisations have needed to adjust to a changed internal environment as well as respond to changes in the external environment. The introduction of new technologies can be both a part of the change and a response to change. It can assist in making the impact of change more measurable and can also create uncertainties.

Change – A Strategic Framework

The Change Process

The change process in all organisations involves altering behaviours and practices that relate to:

- priorities and targets;
- methods and procedures;
- tasks within the organisation and how these are organised;
- the information and skills required to action the work.

Developing responses to the change process means examining decision-making processes, reviewing organisational cultures and enabling effective communication to ensure that there is full ownership of the change process throughout an organisation.

Internal responses to external change

As the external environment requires organisations to change and adapt, so the internal environment of organisations needs to respond to these changes. The change process is fundamental for organisations that are willing to respond to the changing external environment in a positive way, and should involve reviewing and evaluating the strategy, the culture, the work to be undertaken and the information and skills required to do the work. Organisations which do not respond to change may for a while continue as they have always done, but will often face either a crisis, without the mechanisms to be able to respond, or they gradually fade. Organisations which see change as a positive process can redirect their resources to adapt, to grow, and to continue to be responsive to the needs that they were established to meet.

Strategy and review in the change process

Fundamental to the change process are the linked areas of strategy and review. Strategy development and strategic planning were until comparatively recently seen as areas of activity that were only relevant to larger organisations – increasingly, even very small voluntary sector organisations are starting to see the advantages of strategic planning, to enable the organisation to make a positive response to a changing external environment. Without an effective planning and review framework, it is very difficult for organisations to develop services in the most appropriate direction to meet needs, respond to changes in the external environment and use resources in the most efficient and effective way. Good planning underlies good organisational performance and is the foundation on which effective service provision is built. Effective planning also requires access to information and data which ensures that existing and new services are responsive to real needs and demands for the organisation's services.

Planning for positive change

Planning can also help people involved in organisations cope with the change process. All too often, change becomes a frightening process, with individuals, staff, volunteers and Committee or Board members not knowing how to cope with even the small adjustments that are needed in their methods of operating. When major life experiences are effectively planned, when people feel in control of and informed about the process (despite the fact that the experience may be difficult to handle), it is possible to find mechanisms for enabling the change to become a positive factor. When the change is unexpected, or brought about through unforeseen circumstances, it can be difficult to make the adjustment, and the process will be uncomfortable and, in some cases, can lead to major problems. As an individual faced with unforeseen and uncomfortable change can become depressed and unable to cope, so organisations that deal inadequately with change become demotivated, confused and often dysfunctional.

Whilst planning or creating a well-thought out response to change, will not necessarily ensure that there are no problems to be encountered in the process, it will help the change process to be handled with sensitivity and with a responsiveness that takes account of the broadest impact of that change.

Effective planning sets a framework – a guide which enables the organisation to see where they are going and why and to know, through monitoring and evaluation when they have achieved certain goals and what has been achieved in the process. From the strategic plan, annual work plans can be set, as well as business plans and monitoring mechanisms can enable performance to be measured against the plans. Where change has at its root the improvement of services, monitoring how services are developing is crucial. Linking planning to the process of managing change is of critical importance for all voluntary sector organisations, whatever their size or area of activity.

Change – What Kind of Change?

At the micro level – the organisation

Acknowledging the need to accept change as an important part of creating effective responses to identified needs and demands is essential in the voluntary sector. For many smaller organisations, however, change is not necessarily welcomed, but is seen as threatening.

A small community-based, volunteering organisation[1] was faced with the impact of the local social services department deciding to move from grants to contracts. The organisation was concerned as to how it could continue its current work – primarily providing volunteers to support a wide range of organisations in its locality. With limited staff resources, it did not know how it could meet the requirements of the new contracts. It would have to shift the focus of its activities under the contract from being a generalist volunteer provider, to meeting the volunteer needs of specified organisations. It needed to increase the skills within its staff team to manage more complex volunteer placements. It would be able to continue its more general work, but only with money raised separately from the proposed contract. Existing staff were very concerned that their traditional user organisations would receive an inferior service, but accepting the contract from Social Services was essential for the well-being of the organisation. The Management Committee was divided as to whether the contract would bring real benefits for the organisation. In undertaking a brief organisational review, it needed to identify how it could deploy its staff more effectively, and how it could raise additional funds. The review also highlighted the lack of planning mechanisms within the organisation and gaps in the committee's understanding of their governance role. The organisation needed to change in order to be able to respond to these issues.

There are no easy answers to this kind of problem – for a large number of small, community based voluntary organisations, facing this kind of externally determined change can feel very threatening. The impact of this change would affect staff, committee members, organisations currently using the volunteer placement service and the volunteers themselves. What the organisation needed to find was a strategy for coping with the change. Inevitably, this strategy would involve some difficult decisions being made. The eventual outcome from this process could result in a stronger, more adaptive organisation, or could lead to internal tensions which would fundamentally weaken the organisation's ability to deliver any kind of volunteer service at all.

The case study noted above highlights a number of the changes which have impacted on the sector in recent years:

- the growth of the contract culture;
- an increased emphasis on staff development, and on increasing the professionalism of staff;
- an increased emphasis on quality, standards, monitoring and evaluation;
- an awareness of a range of governance issues and changes in the way Boards and committees operate in managing organisations.

Each of these issues were examined in the organisational review that took place in this organisation. This comprehensive review highlighted a number of key areas where the organisation was weak and was therefore not in a position to cope with the change. These included:

- a lack of strategic and corporate planning processes, including no annual work plans;
- a lack of staff supervision and appraisal mechanisms, which could highlight staff training needs and skills gaps, as well as support staff;
- a lack of understanding of governance issues and a lack of information reaching the management committee which would enable the committee to take effective decisions;
- a lack of adequate performance indicators and processes for monitoring and evaluating the work of the organisation ;
- a lack of financial control mechanisms, beyond the annual budget setting process;
- a lack of communication between committee, staff, volunteers, and stakeholders, such as funders and receiving organisations;
- lack of data collection systems that would enable more effective monitoring to be undertaken and enable more timely information to be passed to staff and to the committee.

The identified management gaps in the organisation were a major barrier to the organisation being able to cope with the key decision that needed to be made – should the contract be accepted or not? Because the organisation had no clear strategic plan and no way of knowing how well it was currently performing, it could not judge what the real impact of the contract would be within the organisation. It was at risk of going on doing what it had traditionally done, not as a result of a positive and proactive choice, but more from inertia.

What are the ways in which an organisation in this position can cope with the change needed? In this case, what was needed was:

- The setting up of a planning process, which could refocus the organisation on its mission and vision, determine a strategic plan, write a business plan that would identify the strengths of its current services and the services that would be provided under contract, develop annual plans or work plans that could be used for members of staff, and which could be linked into a new supervision and appraisal process.
- The development of a staff supervision and appraisal process, to enable training needs to be identified and skills gaps identified, which could be used to monitor how staff were coping with the potentially conflicting demands of the new contracted service and existing demands of traditional service-using organisations. It also

needed to extend supervision and support to its core team of volunteers, to help them cope with the demands of more complex cases.

- The introduction of effective control mechanisms, that would enable:
  - on the financial side, the tracking of more complex financial information to enable the contract income and expenditure to be identified and separately accounted for the local authority;
  - on the service provision side, better monitoring of volunteer placements and requests for volunteers that could be separated into those linked to the contract and those resulting from work outside the contract.

The use of the new control mechanisms to enable better information flows to the management committee, both to enable them to monitor performance more effectively and also to enable review of the strategy and the business plan on a regular basis.

Teams also needed to be built – particularly the management committee. They needed to spend time thinking about their governance role, and 'away days' and training were recommended.

Identifying clear line management was also needed – some staff were not clear who managed them and who they reported to, and this was part and parcel of the lack of supervision and management within the organisation.

Without these kinds of changes, the organisation was experiencing uncertainty, internal tension and the risk of conflict. It was unable to respond to a challenge that could enable it to develop significant work with new client groups. Without understanding the need for change, organisations become ossified and less able to meet new needs and demands. Without identifying mechanisms and strategies for coping with the impact of changes, organisations can become inert, and lose opportunities for continuing innovation and response to changing needs and demands.

Developing the strategies needed to respond to the challenge of change meant examining decision-making processes, reviewing organisational culture and enabling effective communication to ensure that there was full ownership of the change process throughout the organisation.

The impact of change at the organisational level

Change impacts at a number of different levels in organisations. Organisations which have been through a process of management review and organisational restructuring will often need to change their management structures and means of delivering services, creating new teams, new reporting mechanisms and introducing planning and performance measurement mechanisms which may change the relationships that individuals working in the organisation have with the users of service or beneficiaries, their colleagues and their managers. At the individual level, change is known to have a profound effect – the way in which a job or series of tasks has been undertaken traditionally will be altered, staff may find themselves working in new locations and with new groups of people and past patterns of working practice are altered.

At the macro level – the sector

The case study above highlighted how change impacted at the organisational level. The study also highlights one of the major changes to impact on the sector in recent years. Among these changes are:

- The growth of the contract culture, and with it, the need for many organisations to be more 'commercially minded'; a corollary of this growth has been a shift away from core funding to project funding where grants are still available within the sector.
- Key issues relating to governance and accountability in organisations, which relates closely to the development of new management responses and practices, with clearer definitions of the role of Boards and the partnership that needs to exist between Boards and managers to achieve efficiency and effectiveness within the organisation, as well as ensuring accountability – to a wide range of stakeholders.
- An increased emphasis on professionalism in the sector, with the need for training, staff supervision and appraisal systems becoming more acknowledged. Developing staff as the key resource within the sector is now taking a higher priority than previously, and increased demands are being made for resources for staff development in organisations.
- An increased emphasis on quality, standards, monitoring and evaluation, both within the sector itself and on the part of funders of voluntary sector activity. Performance measurement is now critical for voluntary sector organisations and requires more attention to planning processes, target setting and the development of indicators to measure progress.
- An increased awareness of the need to involve users and beneficiaries of services provided by voluntary sector organisations in the planning and review of services, as well as increasing accountability to other stakeholders, such as local communities, members and wider networks.

These changes will be examined below, in relation to how they impact on voluntary sector organisations.

The development of the contract culture

The development of the contract culture has meant that organisations which have traditionally played a key role in providing services which are complementary to and independent of public sector provision are increasingly becoming involved in contracts to run services either directly for a local authority or with the authority exercising more control over the services that are provided. This is one of the key areas where change management has been important.

Where statutory funding of the voluntary sector tended to be through a grants mechanism, monitoring and reporting procedures were often loose and relatively informal. In most areas, statutory funding has shifted to service level agreements and contracts, which can take a number of different forms. In the main, the shift to contracts has involved more stringent monitoring and performance review. Voluntary organisations have therefore have had to adjust to new levels of accountability. For some organisations, this change has also had a significant impact on their types of service provision, with greater emphasis being placed, inevitably, on those areas which are funded through specific contracts. New monitoring tools are required in organisations, to separate work undertaken under contract and work or services provided with other sources of funding. Contracts normally specify precisely who will be assisted and how referrals will be made, the length of time that services can be delivered for, and what standards will be adhered to in the delivery of services.

Whilst there are many questions that can be asked about the impact of the contract culture on a wide range of voluntary sector organisations, this chapter is not the place to deal with all of these. However, for organisations who have become involved, the impact, and the need for change within organisations to take account of the demands of contracts is significant. Contracts bring closer monitoring by the contracting agency and information gathering and reporting both externally and internally become more important.

Open Door Housing Trust, a specialist provider of supported services and accommodation for single people with special needs in London, is increasingly operating under contract to local authorities. A strategic review which highlighted Open Door's particular niche, and encouraged diversification into areas such as floating support services, meant that reorganisation into new teams and closer controls over the range of activities being carried out by the organisation was essential. The change has had a particular impact on staff, with a new senior management structure and in many cases either relocation of the workplace or changes to the particular client groups staff work with. For the Management Committee, the increasing complexity of the organisation has meant a review of the committee structure, with two audit committees replacing a number of committees. It has also identified the need for more detailed information on activities and performance, which has had to be presented in ways that the committee can readily grasp and use. External reporting has become more complex, with different information needed for different agencies who are contracting with Open Door for their services. This increased the need for more efficient information retrieval systems and for higher levels of staff training in recording information about clients and work undertaken with them. Accountability has increased at a number of different levels: from staff to senior management; from management to the committee and from the organisation to the funders.

The change process in Open Door has not been easy to manage. For a relatively small organisation working with clients with a range of complex needs, the day to day demands on staff, particularly front line staff, are considerable. On top of this, the Management Committee and senior managers were asking staff to cope with changes in working practices and in teams, including relocation in some cases, and with the introduction of a much tighter reporting structure, which made extra demands on staff time. The introduction of better communications systems within the organisation, including staff conferences, and work towards the Investors in People award have helped in ensuring that staff have felt more involved in both the decisions that have needed to be taken and the outcomes from those decisions.

Communication: a key to change

As noted above, one of the key ways in which change is being managed in Open Door has been through a review of communications within the organisation. In small organisations, where day to day contact between all staff and volunteers can be easily maintained, it is often assumed that everyone is involved and knows what is happening. As organisations grow, specific mechanisms need to be adopted which enable information to circulate within the organisation. However, even very small organisations can fail to communicate effectively at a number of different levels. If a change process is to be well managed, both formal and informal methods of communication need to be adopted, even in very small organisations. All too often, Management Committees fail to communicate effectively to volunteers and staff; in organisations with only one or two members of staff, the increased time needed to ensure that members of the organisation or volunteers know what is happening may prevent regular communication. Regular staff meetings, regular meetings for volunteers, newsletters, notice boards which are kept up to date – there are many small and medium sized organisations where these obvious communication tools are not employed.

Managing change – measuring performance

As a result of both the contract culture and an increased emphasis on standards and performance measurement, funders are placing increasing emphasis on the collection of a greater range of data. Funders and contractors will also demand that this information is provided in a standardised format to enable comparisons to be made between different organisations providing services and, in some cases, for instance in local authorities, to provide comparable data to those provided by the authority's own services.

A local authority[2] recently conducted a review of its advice and information services. These services were provided by a mix of voluntary sector and local authority providers, and the aims of the review included an examination of the cost effectiveness of different types of service provision, coupled with a review of service access, to examine how far the most socially excluded within the population had effective access to high quality services which met their needs. A range of indicators were used within the review. One of the difficulties for the authority was 'comparing like with like' as there was no standardised reporting system across the advice and information service providing agencies. A major outcome from the review has been the introduction of standard reporting procedures and key standards which all funded agencies are expected to meet. At a meeting with the voluntary sector agencies to discuss the outcomes from this review and the new standards that the authority wanted to introduce, many agencies complained that this would increase pressures on them and that they should be trusted to work effectively with their clients. The authority's response was that they needed to ensure accountability and effective monitoring and that they were willing to support agencies in moving towards a more efficient and standardised data collection system and the implementation of standards.

For some front line staff, increased levels of monitoring can appear very intimidating. There is often a feeling that they are not being trusted to do the job. However, on the part of the funder, the need for accountability, and the need for comprehensive and standardised information to assist with strategic planning of, for example, a local authority's services and resource allocation, or a charitable trust funder's strategic grant making priorities, is increasingly important. In addition, many funders are interested not only in measuring **outputs** relating to activities, but in measuring **outcomes** – the effect or impact that a particular service has, the difference a service has made. For many voluntary organisations, moves towards outcome measurement have been linked to funder's requirements for more information about service impact.

These changed approaches to performance measurement have had a significant impact in relation to change in organisations, and are closely related to a theme addressed earlier in this chapter – the need for voluntary organisations to see strategic planning as part of the process of managing change. Where an organisation has adopted a positive approach to strategic planning, it will have identified ways of measuring both outputs and outcomes.

Change, performance measurement and standards

Closer monitoring of performance also relates to the exercise of good governance and practice in voluntary sector organisations. Management Boards/Committees need to request regular information on a range of performance issues, not merely financial information to monitor budgets. This increased emphasis on internal monitoring has come in part from funders, in part from organisations which are involved in setting standards which relate to particular parts of the sector and to the whole of an organisation's activities.

Some coordinating and regulatory bodies (such as the National Housing Federation and the Housing Corporation for housing associations) have developed standards as well as giving clear guidance to organisations on the type of performance measurement that should be carried out. These include both internal and external audit. Whilst external audit has been a requirement for registered charities over a certain size since the introduction of the most recent Charities legislation, internal audit – the process of checking all control systems within the organisation on a regular basis – has been less commonly applied in smaller and medium sized organisations. The relationship between the control systems and the information produced by the systems is crucial. Every organisation needs to assess what information will provide them with the means to assess overall performance, not just in the service delivery area. Information on staff, Committee or Board members' attendance, external information enquiries to the organisation, response times to telephone calls, correspondence etc. are all increasingly important as measures of an organisation's efficiency. This information collection is not only important to ensure accountability to external agencies such as funders and standards setting bodies. It is also important to enable the success of change management to be assessed, both by senior management and by Management Boards or Committees.

Increasingly, in this context, standards and quality are important in the sector.

Scottish Homes HomePoint, a provider of support services and grants for housing advice and information providers in Scotland, undertook a standards setting exercise in 1995. National Standards for Housing and Advice Information providers were developed, and all organisations in receipt of grants from Scottish Homes HomePoint are being expected to work towards full implementation of these standards. The standards include planning mechanisms, issues related to service provision, including interpretation services, home visits and telephone advice provision, case management systems, communication and information resources management, staff and volunteer management issues and training. Working towards these standards has involved many agencies in change and in developing monitoring procedures that enable compliance with the standards.

Scottish Homes is not the only grant provider or standards monitoring agency whose work impacts on the voluntary sector. The Legal Aid Board, in developing franchising with non-solicitor based information and advice agencies has a rigorous set of standards that agencies applying for a franchise have to meet. Increasingly, local authorities in negotiating service level agreements and contracts with the voluntary sector are setting standards that have to be achieved. Whilst some quality systems, such as IS0 9000 and Bench Marking, are being used by larger voluntary organisations, they are often seen as less appropriate for smaller agencies. However, no organisation, large or small, can ignore the quality systems and standards that are being introduced within the sector. Standards enable a level of quality to be achieved, and for that achievement to be measured. Inevitably, the implication of the introduction of such systems leads to change.

Developing useful systems

Successful performance monitoring is not accomplished through immersion in a vast and unsifted mass of data. This will not help either to measure performance nor to identify the areas where change needs to take place, nor to measure and evaluate the impact of changes made within an organisation. As voluntary organisations identify the need to measure performance effectively, so the need for better data collection systems and technologies for data processing becomes more important. A number of networks in the information and advice field have been involved in developing software packages that can enable smaller organisations to collect complex statistical information in a simple and standardised way. This not only helps individual agencies, but also enables the networks to collect standard sets of statistics which can help them monitor responses to external changes such as the impact of new legislation on the users of these services.

Some Disability Advice and Information and Advice Lines (DIAL) have secured funding for new computer projects which not only enable more efficient data collection for the organisation, but also enable more effective information systems to be developed for public access to information. The introduction and management of new projects of this kind inevitably involves change within an organisation's culture and often in its overall management. Initiatives of this type not only enable individual organisations, but also parts of the diverse voluntary sector to respond more effectively to both external and internal change.

The complexities of change – some conclusions

Managing change is a complex and often fraught area for the voluntary sector. Whilst it is acknowledged very widely that change has to be accepted, at a wide range of levels, within many organisations there is a lack of basic processes which can ensure that change is managed well so that it can have a positive impact on the work and life of the organisation.

This chapter has set out some of the areas where change in the external operating environment and in expectations of the sector has had a major impact. It has also looked at some of the areas where change is initiated as a result of internal needs. There are a number of areas which have not been explored in detail – particularly areas connected with the day to day management of staff. However, it is suggested that where organisations have adopted a strategic approach to planning within the organisation, staff can be involved in the process and can be part of the change process. Where performance measurement processes and mechanisms enable effective monitoring to be carried out, this can also assist management in assessing individual staff performance, as well as enabling the organisation to respond to the needs for more accountability to funders and other stakeholders.

Where periodic review and evaluation are seen as an integral part of the planning process, then the impact of change can be measured and the process of change can be more effectively and efficiently managed, to the ultimate benefit of the beneficiaries of the wide range of types of organisations and areas of activity that make up the diversity of the voluntary sector.

References

The Standards and Good Practice Manual referred to in the text, which is produced by Scottish Homes HomePoint, is coupled with a series of distance learning packs on Strategic Planning and Managing Staff and

Volunteers. Further information is available from HomePoint, Scottish Homes, Thistle House, 91 Haymarket Terrace, Edinburgh EH12 5HE.

1   This organisation was the subject of an organisational review carried out by CAF Consultants in 1995. Its name is withheld to ensure confidentiality.
2   Review carried out by the author with Bob Widdowson. The name of the authority has been omitted to ensure confidentiality.

4

Information and Communication in the Community Sector

Kevin Harris

Introduction

The lives of people in communities are shaped and affected, often strongly, by forces beyond their community. Factors affecting the economy, or the environment, may present problems too complex for a given community easily to cope with. In areas with an accumulation of disadvantage, the expectation that 'the community' could change things solely by their own efforts is unrealistic and unfair. Such communities may face a future that strains their own natural level of organisation. Nonetheless, groups and agencies in a locality will organise themselves and network to confront or cope with disadvantage; and to develop and sustain leisure, celebratory, or educational initiatives. Information is fundamental to their requirements, and communication skills are fundamental to the success of their endeavours.

This chapter focuses on the community sector as a distinct feature of the so-called third sector. It will discuss the characteristics of information flow and communication at local level; the contribution of information to social inclusion; the importance of access to communication channels; and a number of issues to do with the management of information in community organisations.

The questions which this chapter seeks to address are: what are the characteristics of information flow in local communities; and what are the implications for information management within agencies working in this context?

The term 'people in communities' is used here to refer to the whole breadth of social life in local (spatial) communities. An individual may be, say, a small business owner, a member of a family, a user of public services; and may contribute in the community sector, for example through the organisation of school fundraising events. We need to recognise that most people are active in other communities as well as that in which they live – usually communities of interest such as a place of employment or sports club, or in communities of need, such as a campaign group. Some people contribute to more than one spatial community, as happens when young people leave the area in which they grew up but return frequently to spend time with their parents.

Often, communities which are strong and coherent, with a commonly-recognised identity, have developed these attributes through confronting adversity – the withdrawal of a dominant employer or the decline of a major local industry, for example. Nonetheless, many integrated communities which might be described as strong and healthy have not necessarily had a focus on some form of adversity, but may simply reflect a common (and relatively insulated) way of life (as with some coastal fishing villages, for example); a lively tradition of cultural expression or celebration; or some other aspect of their topography or cultural history (being located close to a large university or to a major tourist attraction, for example).

The 'community sector' comprises the whole range of formal and informal activity that lies beyond the family, where people give of their time and energy to achieve common aims or share interests.[1] Thus it will incorporate informal neighbourhood support and care, self-help groups, picking up a neighbour's children from school, school fundraising committees, local environmental campaigns, luncheon clubs for older people, allotment associations, darts clubs, and so on. In many respects it overlaps and seems to be part of the traditional voluntary sector. At the same time, it may be helpful to point out that traditional volunteering has fundamental values which are essentially philanthropic – the giving of time, energy or resources by those who have a surplus to those who have not. In contrast, voluntary activity in the community sector is essentially about people helping themselves and one another, and often community groups are the barely visible face of a crucial life-support culture. In historically disadvantaged communities, for example, such a culture may be extensive and well-established, providing knowledge to local networks about the availability of work, shelter, cheap food, second-hand clothes, and so on.

A coherent, healthy community will have *key conduits* for local information, and these will include individuals who are gatekeepers (for example, they will be active on local committees, on community initiatives, perhaps on the parish council, and so on); as well as *key occasions* such as at the school gates, at the pub, at the youth club or in the corner shop. Significant information exchanges take place in such contexts and it is critical for local information services that this is recognised. The point is that neighbourhood networks and gatekeepers are fundamental to information flow at local level, and any formal community information service needs to engage collaboratively with them.

From the information management perspective, what do we mean by 'strong' or 'healthy' communities? In a democratic society we should expect people in communities:

- to be fully informed about local issues which affect them, and about opportunities to participate in the decision-making processes which affect them;
- to have easy access to sources of such information and to channels of communication with relevant authorities;
- to have opportunities and access to appropriate media for publishing their own information and for communicating with others.

An integrated community will show these features.

In severely disadvantaged communities, however, people's energies and interests may be almost wholly consumed in keeping themselves going and in trying to escape. Isolation, inertia, and secrecy may constitute formidable barriers to the flow of information, and creative neighbourhood networks may function poorly if at all.[2] A disintegrated community – where there are relatively few community groups, where people are in conflict with authorities, with employers, or with one another; or where many people are isolated, uncommunicative, or live in fear – is unlikely to have the vital pulse of information flow through which residents share their experiences and act collectively to express their needs and improve their quality of life. The challenge for information management at local level is to help establish and sustain healthy conditions for community initiatives to flourish.

Information and communication in communities

Information in communities is diverse, multi-faceted and dynamic. People in communities tend to have relatively unstructured and unsystematic information environments, compared with, say, those working in academic or business organisations. At local level, much of an individual's information income may be coincidental, unauthenticated, informal, and highly variable according to time and context. In what follows, these points will be considered and we will note the contrast with formal information which is *imported* into their environment.

Information and communication at local level is diverse and multi-faceted. Many forms and formats are common currency (from chance encounters, through school bulletins and shop window notices, to local newspapers and local committee meetings); and the complexities reflect the various kinds of relationship between individuals, households, groups, umbrella agencies, intermediary agencies, local businesses, the local and central state, and so on.

Information and communication at local level is dynamic. Most information transfer at local level is very time- and context-sensitive; as people's needs and interests change, the information that they share and use is reshaped and communication may well be improvised. This is a function of the informality of much information and communication at local level. Thus a conversation between neighbours which begins with a moan about the mess left by the dustmen can easily become a discussion about the survival of the local corner shop or the virtues of traffic calming schemes or who's got a surplus of cooking apples and what can you do if the cats are fouling the garden right where your daughter plays. In passing, information may be shared about entitlement to benefit for a single mother working part-time. In such a context, we should note two conditions which are highly significant for social inclusion.

First, people make their own judgements, rightly or wrongly, about the authenticity, accuracy and currency of the information they receive on such occasions, and it is a critical role for our education system to ensure that people are as well equipped as possible to make such judgements. (Arguments about 'information quality' on the Internet are generally made from the perspective of formal information services and sometimes fail to take account of the fact that people receive, pass on, and make impromptu judgements about all kinds of unauthenticated information all the time).

Secondly, the availability and accessibility of a local, formal information service, to which the individual can turn as a first point of call to verify or to further explore information received in such a context, is of fundamental importance. Without such a facility being seen as a natural and uncomplicated place to turn, disempowerment through inadequate information will continue as a key feature of social exclusion. We will return to the importance of local information services as part of our discussion of the technological context, but it is worth stressing here that this point is neither radical nor new. For example, in a response to a government consultation document on the voluntary sector in 1978, the Joint Monitoring Steering Committee on resource centres commented: 'It is of paramount importance that those individuals and groups least able to influence policies and obtain resources should receive adequate information, services and support to enable them to put forward their own (informed) views.'[3]

Recent research into the role of public libraries in relation to black and ethnic minorities suggests that the interests of people in communities are best addressed by 'a mixed economy of cultural and information provisions at local level'. The researchers go on to note that: '... for many the network of community-based and religious bodies has become the principal provider – often taking precedence over the public library.'[4] This, of course, is not news to many information workers in the community and voluntary sectors.

It is also the case that much of what people know about their community is tacit, unacknowledged and unarticulated. A good example occurred in North Wales a few years ago, following a case of child abuse. Children in the offender's neighbourhood apparently were far more aware than adults of the behaviour of their local 'deviant' and knew how to avoid him.

Above all, perhaps, it is important to recognise that information shared by people in communities probably does not map neatly onto perceptions of 'need to know'. Certainly people will have their own perceived information needs – 'Who knows a reliable plumber? Who can look after my children on Wednesday afternoons?' – but a high proportion of their information income, as we have noted, will be *coincidental*, partial, unauthenticated, and partisan. In such contexts, the notion of information as some kind of 'product' delivered by a 'service' has only limited applicability. It may be that many attempts to run community information services have been relatively unsuccessful because of the difficulty of integrating a formal service with the dynamic informality of the neighbourhood communication networks. Furthermore, in community groups and local development agencies the formal provision of information tends to have low priority anyway:

> Often this is because, in under-resourced circumstances, information cannot be shown to be of direct relevance to their objectives. When you're dealing with the reality of poverty, ill-health, or unemployment, against other severe constraints, it is hard to justify the kind of investment, for uncertain return, which information demands.[5]

This raises questions about the relationship between information, power, and exclusion; and the justification for investing in information as a resource to improve people's quality of life, skills, opportunities, circumstances – the unproven potential for managed information and communication to contribute to social inclusion. In this respect, important research is underway, which should provide us with closer understanding of people's expressed or unexpressed needs for citizenship information.[6]

I have deliberately stressed the informal and coincidental nature of much information and communication at local level since this is seldom given appropriate recognition. At the same time, of course, most people's information income tends to include a high proportion of non-interactive, formal information provision. We buy newspapers and receive television broadcasts which contain pieces of national and international news and a lot of non-local entertainment snippets. This kind of information contrasts sharply with the highly interactive, local and informal knowledge culture which I have been discussing, and the contrast highlights certain political considerations which I address in the section on social inclusion below.

Between these two points on the spectrum there is information provided by, and communication with, public agencies and other intermediary institutions, particularly the local authority. Figure 1 illustrates this range of information and communication relationships. In the following section I explore the implications of the institutional context.

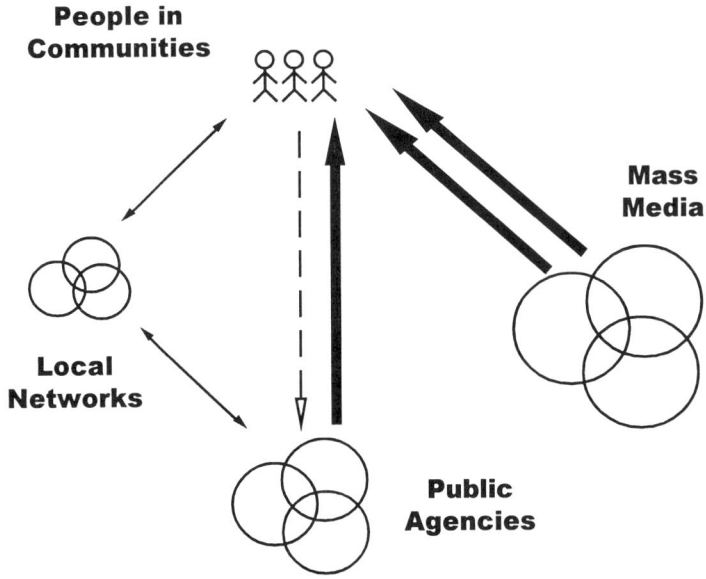

Figure 1 – The range of information and communication relationships

The changing institutional context

Institutions can generate huge amounts of information, can oblige others to provide it, and can affect its flow significantly. For institutions to function, a degree of bureaucracy is inevitable. One consequence is the formalisation of much information and communication. The purposes of this section are to outline how people in communities, particularly disadvantaged people, can be affected by the institutional context of information flow; to point out ways in which this is changing; and to identify possible implications for the information management function.

People who live much of their day-to-day lives within their own neighbourhood – for example those who work, go to school, or pursue their leisure interests locally – may well have relatively little experience (or none at all) of how bureaucracies operate. Historically, the institutions with which most people have had most contact are their school, local authority, and employer; they may have had quite a lot to do with others such as their bank or their church. Other agencies, such as the health service, the police, the Benefits Agency, tenants associations, and so on, occupy an increasingly important part in many people's lives.

On the whole, it is part of the role of institutions to collect information about people, and to tell them about what the organisation does and some of its procedures. Gradual increases in consumer influence over the past 20-30 years in the UK – particularly through the work of such agencies as the National Consumer Council, the Campaign for Freedom of Information, the Plain English Campaign, the regulators for former nationalised industries, the Citizens Charter Unit, and so on – have improved the extent to which information is provided, the ways in which it is presented, and, significantly, requirements to consult and to respond to enquiries and complaints.

In spite of these improvements, however, two significant facets of our information culture remain. First, a notorious attitude of paternalist secrecy among bureaucrats, who control what people in communities can find out about decisions and decision-making processes which affect them. And secondly, a conditioned attitude of compliance among many citizens, which reinforces the secretive information culture and by extension discourages participation, or discourages some bureaucrats who themselves are seeking to break down these barriers.

The upshot of this is a net cost for social policy. If people in communities are dissuaded from participating in the processes of social policy, then the policy measures are far more likely to fail. Thus, there are two major implications for information management. The first concerns openness and the accessibility of information; the second is about community involvement and engagement with those affected or potentially affected by any given decision. For many authorities, the way to address both these implications is seen to be through partnerships and issue forums, usually with the representation of appropriate voluntary and community agencies. There are many examples where the police for instance have shown how this can help in addressing crime and the fear of crime.

Increasingly, people are coming to expect intelligible statements from authorities, whether these require them to fulfil some obligation or legal duty, seek their views, or simply announce some developments in services. Nonetheless, for many people the institutional context for much of the important information in their life can be extremely off-putting. For those unused to office systems and the anonymity of officialdom, what happens in the name of efficiency may be extreme insensitivity; a referral to another office or voice is an abyss dropping them out of the system; a mouthful of jargon is threatening; above all, the separateness of different parts of the bureaucracy can be disheartening to the point of exhaustion. For those less articulate, less self-confident, who may not have access to their own telephone and no personal contacts with professional advisers who they trust – those who lack experience of bureaucracies except as its victims – for such people the availability of an approachable, local intermediary service, such as an advice bureau, remains of critical importance. Agencies such as some of those described elsewhere in this book, which can minimize the anti-participatory culture of bureaucracies, through information-sharing, advice, interpretation and guided referral, can go a long way towards reducing social exclusion.

I have referred generally to the changing consumer-orientation of institutions, and we should note here that the nature of information flow into, within, and from institutions is being changed fundamentally by new information technologies. In part this is because the range of options available, for example to a local authority in describing its services, has increased significantly with cable television, local radio, public access kiosks, automated information points of various kinds, the World Wide Web, and so on. But of course the potential is far greater, and this is still insufficiently recognised. A recent study of local authority Web sites in the UK concluded:'In the vast majority of cases local authorities regard the Internet simply as the latest device for the one way transmission of information to the public.'[7]

In addition, there are signs that the advent of electronic mail as a communications medium may be the most powerful device yet for opening up institutions, because of the way it allows users to communicate irrespective of hierarchies and other traditional controls.

Information and social inclusion

The increasing information-intensiveness of people's lives[8] at home and in the workplace has been reflected in the way the information requirements of community and voluntary agencies have risen and become more complex – in terms of funding information and proposals, the management of partnerships, monitoring and evaluation, reports, financial accounting, consumer research, policy contributions, public relations and advertising, and so on. This Information Society places increasing emphasis on the use of information for problem-solving and decision-making, and also generally as a resource for personal and social development. Partly as a consequence, the relationship between *information and power* has become a key focus for the unfolding debate about social inclusion.[9] In this section I will address briefly four key themes in this debate, concerning 'information culture', the social origin and location of information, access to the information highway, and information handling skills.

It is not uncommon to hear the slogan 'information is power': while this is a highly questionable over-simplification, it is useful shorthand to draw attention to the significance of this relationship. It is clear that there can be circumstances in which information (the wrong kind, or too much, or incomplete, or false information) can be disempowering; there are many people in positions of power who demonstrably are ill-informed; just as there may be circumstances in which a single 'nugget' of information, in the right place at the right time, can transform power relations.[10] There is much optimism among its advocates that the new information and communication technologies (ICTs) can help bring about changes in this respect, but there is little evidence that more information and better access to it, is genuinely empowering. And yet there is an assumption fundamental to democracy that freedom of access to information is desirable, and that the denial of access to information is disempowering.

I can suggest three related explanations for our uncertainty on this issue. First, there is widespread disillusion with the political process at all levels in the UK[11], which discourages information access and use because people may have little conviction that power relations will be affected. Secondly, investment in formal information services in the past has mostly focused on *access to stored records* – rather than on levels of information awareness and the skills people need to exploit information once they have it, or on the importance of communication channels for sharing information. And thirdly, the economics of conventional publishing and the broadcast media work against the interests of disadvantaged groups. The existing print-based knowledge culture 'is biassed in favour of those who already have power, wealth, and influence, and the levels of investment required of people who are outside this system are disproportionately high.'[12]

These characteristics of our inherited knowledge culture are seldom acknowledged but have critical implications for information management. This culture is based on the technology of print, and around it there have grown heavy institutions such as the education system, the publishing industry, libraries, professional organisations and so on. Institutions like this all depend to some extent on the economics of print publishing and its technology, which has to do with the production of multiple copies of documents, made available as physical objects and distributed.[13] The contrast with the logic of new ICTs – making a single copy universally available at very low cost – helps to explain the revolutionary potential of the changes we are experiencing.

A further consideration is the extent to which the print-based knowledge culture emphasises and gives status to *formal* information (published books, journals, broadcasts etc.) from reputable or authoritative sources, and devalues the experiential knowledge of ordinary people. The ICTs, by broadening access to formal and informal information at once (online databases, library catalogues, searchable archives of discussion lists, newsgroups, and email) appears to subvert this institutional domination to some extent.

This returns us to another key feature, referred to earlier: the extent to which people's information income is dominated by *imported information* from the mass media. Where the *social origin* of so much information is outside the community, with little or no interactive potential, it can lead to information and communication inertia or stagnation. Again, the new technology seems to offer significant opportunities, which information managers could be leading and stimulating, for community groups to generate and publish their own information. The value of a major shift in the availability of locally generated information is likely to be enormous. Communities can give validity to their experience by making it visible to others; and the *process* of preparing, say, a multimedia record of their initiatives, should be a capacity-building and confidence-building experience in itself.

Thirdly, we should note the segmented character of the prevailing knowledge culture. Information will always be available in a range of formats – indeed, the range is likely to go on increasing – but it is at best unhelpful that we have to go to one place for a leaflet, to a separate office for some other document, and phone elsewhere for something else while waiting for the arrival by post of a particular form, which we then have to take to the post office to photocopy before sending it off. Again, there is little appreciation of the degree to which social exclusion can be reenforced by this *segmented institutionalisation of access*, not least because the communication skills needed to understand and negotiate one's way through a bureaucratic 'Circumlocution Office' are often complex and culturally subtle. And again, the ICTs genuinely appear to offer real promise. Information management has an obvious role in helping to signpost related material on the information highway, and in helping people to gain access and to learn the skills to exploit the resources they find.

Indeed, this question of the need for information-handling skills should not be under-estimated. There is increasing stress on people's capacities to recognise and articulate their information needs; to identify sources and channels which might help address those needs; to access information and take decisions at the time about the appropriateness of what they receive; and to exploit the information which they deem to be of use and relevance. Undeveloped information capability, in any of these areas, can be a continuing and invisible factor in social exclusion. The role for information management is a complex mix of demonstrating the range of information resources in imaginative ways (public libraries have a strong tradition here), providing advice on particular resources, keeping information high in people's consciousness, and supporting (through training and by making suitable technology accessible) people's requirements for interpreting, repackaging and using what they find and what they already know.

The changing technological context

As I have already indicated, the new ICTs imply a potentially significant transformation in the information flow into and within communities. For this reason in particular, access to these technologies is a social policy issue. There is a growing movement worldwide (led in the UK by Communities Online[14]) among community agencies of various kinds, to seek to ensure that the benefits of the new technologies are made readily and fully accessible to people in communities. This section highlights some of the key features of the changing technological context, in order to explain why people think it matters.

There are signs already that the Internet is evolving from a dissemination conduit, to a more integrated 'social learning space', because of the integration of Web sites, linked mailing lists, newsgroups and email. Having said that, for people in most community organisations, email remains probably the most useful and powerful element in this technology. This is not to imply that online databases, multimedia, the World Wide Web and so on are not in themselves powerful tools and valuable resources. But email is significant because it multiplies the options for quickly disseminating and adding value to information, including information *about* other resources. I have already drawn attention to the importance of *informal* communication at local level, and to the rising requirements for *formal* information among community agencies, as many are obliged to become more organised in the pursuit of their objectives. Email gives us a refreshing facility for combining informal and formal communication – a section clipped from a report or Web site, say, forwarded with a note drawing attention to it and hoping the recipient can come to next week's meeting. The speed and convenience of sharing and exploiting information in this way is unprecedented.

This in turn draws attention to a possible re-balancing of communication and information. Fundamental to my argument has been the point that a print-based knowledge culture works against the interests of disadvantaged people, placing an emphasis on information provided from centres where power is concentrated, and diminishing the role of communication – particularly communication between the receivers and the disseminators of such information. It may be that wide, perhaps even universal, availability of email would narrow the difference here. People's willingness to respond to information provided *for* them is always likely to increase if (a) there are open and accessible channels for them to do so, and (b) they perceive a genuine receptiveness. Similarly, the *value* of the communication process – in terms of personal and community development – may well be a very positive feature of the unfolding information society: the pulse of information flow, through email, newsgroups, community calendars and so forth, could become a meaningful indicator of the health of a community. A key part of this, as I have suggested, will be the degree to which community self-publishing using the Web becomes a routine part of community activity.

For this to happen, access to the information highway needs to be far easier and more widely available than it is at present. This question of public access for people in communities was a fundamental issue for the 'INSINC' Working Party and is a focus for their report, *The Net Result*. Their recommendations include a call for 'community resource centres' to be established and developed, to provide access and to raise awareness of the potential of multimedia and online technologies.[15] A related study, the 'COMMIT' report on community-based IT initiatives[16], stressed issues to do with *organisational structures* and *partnership, community involvement* in the resource centres, and *sustainability* as the critical questions to be addressed if the communications infrastructure for social inclusion is to be adequate.

Community resource centres as envisaged by INSINC could be part of the library service, based on an independent advice centre, a new developing role for a community centre, a new initiative based in a primary school, or something else entirely. This returns us to the importance of local information and communication services. It seems to me that for the foreseeable future there will be a need for community buildings which people are comfortable going into, a common space where they find an appropriate range of resources and support, and where as a community they can have some genuine influence over what happens.[17] Such resource centres are becoming an essential part of the technological context for people in communities, and the information management issues have to do with: (i) making a major contribution to the organisational partnerships which enable such a facility to be funded and to be managed in a sustainable way; (ii) the extent to which such a centre is the hub of existing neighbourhood networks, and engaging with these networks as information sources and channels; (iii) the coordination of existing information resources and the development of local information resources; and (iv) support for learning and for exploiting the technology.

Concluding remarks

This chapter has introduced a number of issues which arise when we focus on information and communication in communities. I have deliberately not discussed the *range* of information services which exist at local level, since these tend to be a function of prevailing local conditions (of organisation, funding, support, and so on) irrespective of the general principles I have been exploring. Definitional distinctions between, for example, community (public) libraries and information services in local branches of voluntary organisations are unlikely to help us clarify the characteristics of information flow at local level or to identify key information management options: these characteristics and options are surely relevant to all types of local agency which have an information function. By way of conclusion I suggest three general areas in which information management issues arise.

First, any information facility intended to serve people in communities must be based on an understanding of the importance of communication as a process, and information as a resource. 'Process' means just that, an experience which people go through, which should have its own value irrespective of the end result. 'Resource' means something which people can draw on for their own and others' benefit. The contribution of information processes and resources to community development is a fundamental characteristic of community information services.

Secondly, information management calls for communication skills with a wide range of people and agencies – from the most marginalised and isolated in the neighbourhood, to the most politically influential figures. The ability to contribute the information management perspective in the administration and negotiation of partnerships will be increasingly important.

Thirdly, there are conventional information management skills which remain critically valuable when working at local level: in particular, expertise in identifying 'who is this information for?' – matching the information to the need, expressed or unexpressed, perceived or unperceived; and expertise in repackaging and transferring machine-readable data.

Finally, I would reiterate the principle that *the process of networking* – the interaction of a range of people from different organisations with separate but overlapping interests and agendas – is fundamental to information flow within communities; and therefore it is fundamental to the operation of local information services.

References

1   A fuller account of the nature of community activity and the way it complements the voluntary sector is given in Gabriel Chanan, *Discovering community action*, London, Community Development Foundation, 1994.

2   Recent research suggests that for some people on low incomes, feelings of powerlessness are closely linked to a culture of secrecy, and of not sharing or seeking information. Elfreda A. Chatman, 'The impoverished life-world of outsiders,' *Journal of the American Society for Information Science* 47(3) (March 1996), pp.193-206.

3   Submission in response to *The government and the voluntary sector: a consultative document*, HMSO, 1978, from the Joint Monitoring Steering Committee on the six VSU-funded resource centres, sponsored by the Gulbenkian Foundation. Cited in Marilyn Taylor, *Street level*, London, Community Projects Foundation, 1980, p.178.

4   Patrick Roach and Marlene Morrison. 'The place on the hill?' *The Library Association Record* 9(8) (August 1997), p.433.

5   Harris, Kevin. 'Freedom of access to information' *Informing communities*. Newcastle, Staffs, CSG Publishing, 1992, p.50.

6   Marcella, Rita and Graeme Baxter. 'Citizenship information and public libraries,' *Public library journal* 12(4) (July 1997), pp.73-77.

7   Horrocks, Ivan. 'Weaving the web: local government and the Internet', in *Assignation*, 15(1) (October 1997), p.32.

8   Moore, Nick and Jane Steele. *Information-intensive Britain*, London, PSI, 1991.

9   *The net result: social inclusion in the information society*, London, IBM UK, 1997, chapter 3.

10 *Ibid*

11 See for example Will Hutton, *The state we're in*, London, Jonathan Cape, 1995.

12 *The net result*, para 3.32.

13 Vickery, B, R Heseltine and C Brown. 'Interactive information networks and UK libraries,' *Journal of Documentation* 40(1) (March 1984), p.42.

14 UKCO, www.communities.org.uk

15 *The net result, op cit*, chapter 5.

16 Day, Peter and Kevin Harris. *Down-to-earth vision: community-based IT initiatives and social inclusion*, IBM and Community Development Foundation, November 1997.

17 For a full discussion of the role of community buildings, see Paul Marriott, *Forgotten resources? The role of community buildings in strengthening local communities*, York, Joseph Rowntree Foundation, 1997.

5

The role of information in developing policy

Sylvia Simmons

Introduction

Voluntary organisations are driven by a desire to change the world in which we live. An organisation's mission (that is, its common beliefs and the reason it exists) permeates all that it does; the desire to change wider attitudes in society is shown by the extent to which voluntary organisations carry out their campaigning roles and their success is defined by the specific changes in social and public policy to which an organisation is able to contribute directly or indirectly.

Policy work is driven by the underlying questions: What does our organisation want to achieve? What have we learned from the past, and how can we bring our agenda to a wider public policy forum? In the context of this chapter, policy means the activity which a value-led organisation is undertaking to achieve its goals via its internal policies or by influencing the wider social policy discourse. The formulation of policy is moulded, refined and catalyzed at these two overlapping and interdependent levels.

This chapter discusses the key role which is played by information and the information professional in supporting the strategic, operational and policy objectives of voluntary organisations, whatever their size or function. This role is essentially no different to that contributed by information units in other sectors – academic, commercial or industrial. There are, however, fundamental features in the culture, context and ethos of the voluntary sector which warrant specific consideration.

The information professional in the voluntary sector works in a dynamic, fluid and complex environment, gathering statistical, case history, policy, legislative and historical material. This requires staff who understand the wider context within which they are operating. Setting the voluntary organisation in context means identifying where it fits into the wider picture of:

- the voluntary sector as a whole (and the emerging trends within it);
- the sector within which the organisation operates (e.g. environment, mental health, child welfare etc.);
- the policy agenda and stakeholders which the organisation is seeking to influence.

Whilst not dismissing the need for traditional information retrieval and library management skills, information managers and their staff are being challenged here to undertake a detached, analytical review of the contribution they can make to their parent organisation to enable it to meet its aims and objectives. For their part, managers are asked to re-evaluate the broader contribution which information professionals can make at all levels of the voluntary organisation.

We refer extensively to the 'information professional' conscious that this term covers many realities: the solo librarian; the information manager with a small team of five staff ; the senior manager responsible for a multidisciplinary team of information and advisory service, library, research, and perhaps press, PR and communications functions. The essential point to be borne in mind here is not the information professional as an individual but rather the role that *information* can play in adding value to the identified function. More familiar to many in the voluntary sector is the one individual carrying at least three or four functions (but being paid for only one!) or several staff in posts none of which formally have 'information' in their title.

The very nature of the commitment and drive in a voluntary organisation may mean that not all staff are able to remain objective. Whilst organisational values must be cherished, the information professional has the special (and often difficult) task of sifting through what is sometimes subjective documentation. Information skills demand that they remain objective and ask, for example: Are we including only one perspective in this series of factsheets? Is there another approach to this policy issue? Which other organisations are committed to similar or diametrically opposed policies? Can we (or should we?) be referring to these?

Issues to be considered include:
- what information does the policy, research or campaigns department need and how should the information department provide this?
- what are the issues facing information and advice agencies and those who manage them?
- how does a voluntary organisation demonstrate need in a way which policy makers will listen to?

- how does an organisation monitor trends and identify significant emerging policy issues?
- what information does the media want from the voluntary organisation?
- what type of information is needed by legislators and parliamentarians?

These are not separate topics but much more of a web; this chapter does not offer one formula or set of guidelines for contributing to the formulation of policy (although examples from good practice are given where applicable). It does, however, seek to make information professionals and management aware of how effective information management can enhance the development of policy. This is a continuous cycle of information flow which is summarized in Figure 1.

The context

There is a rich, often unique resource of information within each voluntary organisation. Occasionally, there is a reluctance to admit to or identify an organisation's emerging competitors or to contemplate potential for collaboration. The library collection and information resource has usually been built up by dedicated staff who bring to the organisation or develop a strong commitment to what it is seeking to achieve. Over the past decade new constraints have arisen which impinge on the organisation from both an internal and an external perspective. This can surprise those who grew up in an earlier era of voluntary action when commitment, goodwill, and 'furthering the cause' were assumed to override all other considerations. But information in the voluntary sector – its use, value and potential – has undergone and will continue to undergo radical changes which reflect the revolution which has affected the sector itself.

How mature is the organisation?

Analyzing organisations at different stages of their development is best understood by considering the notion of life cycle, a model which suggests that organisations develop in stages. Periods of steady evolutionary growth are followed by periods of revolutionary development when everything seems to be changing at the same time, a behaviour pattern very common in third sector organisations. Not all organisations will move through a predetermined set of stages but the value of the model is that it helps set opportunities and issues in a broader context and this helps managers to understand their problems. The model suggests ways of moving on to the next phase of development. *(See Figure 2.)*

The Information Cycle in Policy Development: a suggested model for good practice

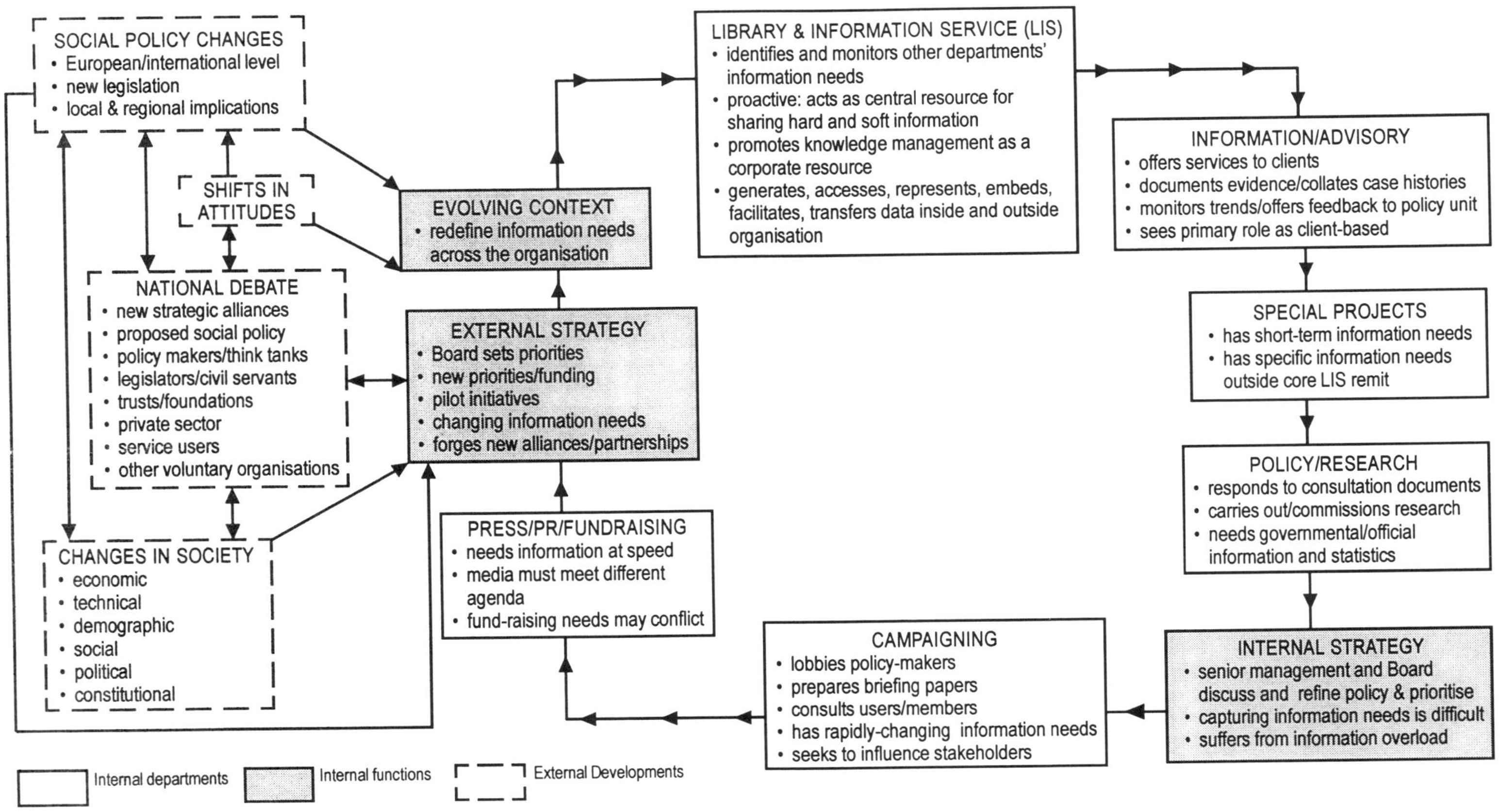

INFORMATION/ADVISORY
- offers services to clients
- documents evidence/collates case histories
- monitors trends/offers feedback to policy unit
- sees primary role as client-based

SPECIAL PROJECTS
- has short-term information needs
- has specific information needs outside core LIS remit

POLICY/RESEARCH
- responds to consultation documents
- carries out/commissions research
- needs governmental/official information and statistics

INTERNAL STRATEGY
- senior management and Board discuss and refine policy & prioritise
- capturing information needs is difficult
- suffers from information overload

LIBRARY & INFORMATION SERVICE (LIS)
- identifies and monitors other departments' information needs
- proactive: acts as central resource for sharing hard and soft information
- promotes knowledge management as a corporate resource
- generates, accesses, represents, embeds, facilitates, transfers data inside and outside organisation

CAMPAIGNING
- lobbies policy-makers
- prepares briefing papers
- consults users/members
- has rapidly-changing information needs
- seeks to influence stakeholders

PRESS/PR/FUNDRAISING
- needs information at speed
- media must meet different agenda
- fund-raising needs may conflict

EXTERNAL STRATEGY
- Board sets priorities
- new priorities/funding
- pilot initiatives
- changing information needs
- forges new alliances/partnerships

EVOLVING CONTEXT
- redefine information needs across the organisation

SOCIAL POLICY CHANGES
- European/international level
- new legislation
- local & regional implications

SHIFTS IN ATTITUDES

NATIONAL DEBATE
- new strategic alliances
- proposed social policy
- policy makers/think tanks
- legislators/civil servants
- trusts/foundations
- private sector
- service users
- other voluntary organisations

CHANGES IN SOCIETY
- economic
- technical
- demographic
- social
- political
- constitutional

Legend: Internal departments | Internal functions | External Developments

Figure 1

Classifying the organisation

Third sector organisations are normally classified by the types of activity they undertake (see, for example, the International Classification of Non-Profit Organisations) but they can also be classified by purpose:

* to provide services – e.g. housing associations, arts associations;
* to provide mutual support – e.g. trade unions, professional associations, self help groups;
* to campaign for change – e.g. Greenpeace, Amnesty International.

Potential conflicts

Our discussion examines these issues from several perspectives: that of the information and advisory staff and that of the research, policy and campaigning department, and asks what are the optimum ways of meeting corporate information needs? These perspectives should not be – but in reality often are – in conflict; for example, when time-limited special projects make heavy use of information unit time, personnel or resources, or when researchers fail to understand the sensitivity required in dealing with service users.

The role of information staff in supporting organisational objectives may, depending on the context, be met by:

* gathering national trend statistics;
* collating, sifting, editing and presenting case histories;
* monitoring trends over a period of time;
* identifying research reports and summarizing findings;
* gathering information on the scope, range and types of inquiries dealt with;
* gathering performance information data (for management committees and local authorities);
* drafting briefing and policy papers, and responding to consultation documents.

Who is providing information in the voluntary sector?

In a recent survey, the average running costs of organisations in the voluntary and charitable sector were estimated at £3.4 million, but a third of organisations had a total budget of under £150,000. 55 percent of organisations had library and information units which served 20 employees or less. They offered traditional, mostly reactive, services: general reference and inquiry (88%); publications (68%), document loan, literature searches, press cuttings, and some current awareness and online/CD-ROM searches.

The survey's findings on staffing are most significant when considering how the Information Unit might be more proactive and contribute to the organisation's wider aims. The manager of the Library/Information Unit was a full time member of staff in only 61% of organisations, was part time in 23% and in 16% was voluntary or unpaid. Of paid managers, 91% had responsibilities additional to managing the library/information unit. Nearly two thirds of managers (68%) earned £18,000 or less; only 3% earned over £27,000. The majority of post holders earned a full time equivalent salary of £16,000 or less. Only a minority had a library and information science (LIS) qualification; 76% had no LIS qualification at all.

Unsupported, often working alone and unrecognized, it is not surprising that information workers in the sector have turned to self help. The Voluntary Sector Information Workers Forum (VOLSIF), set up in the 1980s, aims to provide a forum for information workers to share information on skills, ideas and resources, to raise the profile and promote greater understanding of information work in the sector and help combat the professional isolation information workers often experience within their own organisation.

Voluntary action: an enduring and evolving role

Voluntary action remains relevant in our society; it pre-dates the state, is distinct from transactions that take place in the market, and is a major force in its own right. The findings of the Commission on the Future of the Voluntary Sector chaired by Professor Nicholas Deakin reiterate this, explicitly stressing that the sector also depends for its effectiveness on relationships developed over time with the other main forces in society. It is intimately involved with and closely affected by developments that take place within society as a whole, which influence both what it is and what it does.

The diversity of activity undertaken covers organisations of all sizes, with widely different objectives and characteristics. Some deliver services, others campaign; some exist for the mutual benefit or instruction of their members; others perform all, or none, of these functions. The growth and impact of the new 'social movement' is significant and predicted to grow. How will the information profession respond to this changing profile?

The sector, characterized by its dual 'mutual aid' and 'philanthropic' role, presents a complex picture, and its independence or its perceived independence is increasingly being blurred. Many organisations are reliant on ongoing local, regional, national or Lottery funding for the continuation of their core work or of specific projects. The voluntary sector does not exist in a vacuum; individual voluntary organisations need to recognize that to develop and thrive they must pitch themselves in relation to statutory service provision and other players in the not for profit sector.

The sector depends on and is closely intertwined with a number of other key players. To survive and flourish it must sustain working relationships with:

- central and local government and quangos;
- the corporate sector;
- trusts and foundations;
- users of services;
- the general public.

The voluntary sector cannot stand apart from critical policy debates currently taking place in society, but if it takes on a wider role, will it risk compromising its identity and values and who will make its case in these new changing circumstances? The future environment in which voluntary action will operate will be determined by wider economic, technical, demographic, social, political and institutional changes alongside shifts in attitudes and values.

A new paradigm is needed in which voluntary bodies are free to choose what they do best and are recognized as legitimate stakeholders with an independent voice to determine the content of their own programmes and the policies that affect them. The Deakin Review advances six principles for the future of voluntary action:

- public policy must recognize the unique qualities of the sector;
- a successful and equal partnership between voluntary and other sectors is essential;
- the sector is affected by the relationships it maintains with its members and users;
- voluntary bodies which act as partners with the state must be free to act as advocates, providing a 'voice for the voiceless' and campaigning on issues of public concern;
- the sector must learn sound techniques of management without stifling flexibility or innovation;
- access to alternative sources of funding is a guarantee of continued independence.

Three crucial contributions made by the voluntary sector to society are defined by Ken Young:

Representation – voluntary action has a wider, politically significant role beyond that of adjunct provider of social services alongside mainstream state provision. It contributes to the development of public policy, social integration and cohesion.

Innovation – the agenda for UK social policy has a strong history of voluntary bodies turning hitherto tolerated conditions into issues and policies for action.

Citizenship – the strength of the voluntary sector lies in its relationship to people who might otherwise be excluded from effective citizenship. Voluntary bodies as advocates of change owe much to their informal nature and are regularly consulted by government in a sophisticated democratic society.

Reviewing strategy

The well-managed voluntary organisation is involved in a continuous cycle of reviewing its strategy and services, both internal and external. Information professionals have a major role to play in helping to collate, sort and analyse the information gathered. 'Reviewing strategy is a process of monitoring changes in the external environment and development in the organisation to gain a deeper understanding of its strategic position which may involve reviewing an organisation's mission, objectives, strategies or a combination of all of these.'

The *external* strategic review needs to provide data on:

- relevant social and economic trends;
- political trends (e.g. in European legislation);
- technological development;
- trends in funding sources (e.g. contracting);
- the demographics and changing needs of the service user group;
- cultural trends within the organisation's specific sector;
- strategic developments in similar organisations (e.g. competition for funds or service users).

The *internal* review gathers information on:

- the overall portfolio of services and campaigns (e.g. trends in numbers of people assisted, campaign achievements, dependency of services on particular income sources);

The Role of Information in Developing Policy | 81

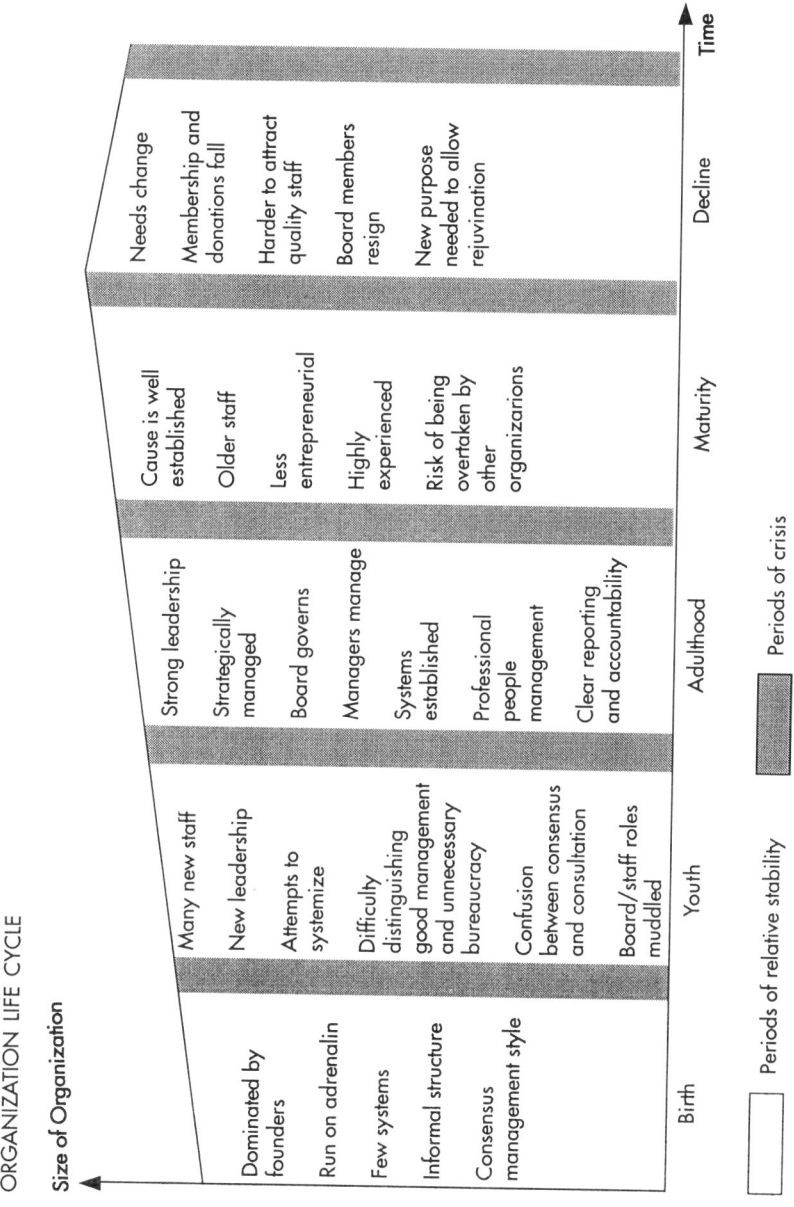

Figure 2 – Organization Life Cycle
Source: *Managing without profit: the art of managing third sector organizations*, by Mike Hudson. Published by Penguin Books, 1995.
Copyright Mick Hudson. Reproduced by permission of Penguin Books Ltd.

- the subsidy each service is receiving from donations not given to a particular service or campaign;
- the human, physical and financial resource base;
- intangible resources (e.g. reputation, contacts and goodwill).

These reviews generate a great deal of information and distilling this data is vital. It is important to focus on the information which will be most pertinent to the organisation's future development which will need to be monitored on an ongoing basis.

Service reviews should consider the following external and internal issues –

External
- the changing needs or rising expectations of service users;
- trends in the numbers of people requiring the service (including the potential numbers of those needing but not receiving services);
- competing suppliers and what distinguishes them (e.g. private and public sector organisations offering similar services; what is distinctive about each service);
- relevant legislative and political changes that will affect the service;
- trends in funding (including income from sales, government, donors, membership).

Internal
- current service users (individuals or organisations), segmented by criteria of need, age, socio-economic group and geography;
- how many currently benefit from the service, and projected trends in this area;
- benefits to service users (quantitative and qualitative outcomes of service);
- skills currently used and the identification of critical competencies required for the future;
- what has been learned about users and services and how this knowledge may be used to improve the service in the future;
- what skills and staff training are required and ways in which people's skills may be developed;
- service costs – overall subsidy required and costs and subsidy per user.

Changes and cultural shifts

Voluntary organisations are deeply affected by wider changes in public and social policy. The changes undergone by AIDS organisations offer a paradigm of this shift, with implications for the sector as a whole. Weeks et al demonstrate how the growth of the response to the AIDS crisis illustrates some of the tensions and contradictions facing such agencies as they sought to respond to changes in Government policy. Voluntary action rooted in community activism was central to the earliest responses to AIDS in Britain and the US, and resulted in the emergence of a wide range of community and nongovernmental organisations to alleviate the impact of the epidemic on affected communities. Central among the themes to emerge were tensions over service norms and the role of volunteers, between self help and altruism, informal versus formal organisational structure, political campaigning versus service delivery, national versus local needs, generalism versus specialism, and autonomy versus coordination.

The voluntary effort, based on a spirit of 'collective self help' had as its objective a massive change in social policy whose overall aim was to break through the prejudice, discrimination and fear that surrounded the dangerous new virus because of its association with a stigmatized community. But in the voluntary sector the effort at community mobilisation and AIDS activism hit a paradox. The prevailing social policy was opposed to expanding the role of the welfare state and was looking to that same voluntary sector to take on a new role as a part of a 'mixed economy' of social welfare. The resulting dilemmas and tensions which faced AIDS/HIV organisations illustrate the challenges which face the voluntary sector as a whole.

During the 1990s the voluntary sector was offered a more prominent role in the delivery of services via service contracts but this change had profound implications for the funding and mission of many voluntary organisations and particularly for the delicate relationship between community roots, campaigning, advocacy, service provision and charitable status which these agencies sought to sustain. Many have had to face up to sharp challenges: a shift in the organisation's structure, a widespread pattern of professionalization and a growing managerialism giving rise to internal conflict and cultural shift. A changing relationship between management, employees and volunteers and between organisations and the communities and client groups they relate to has led to a conflict between self help and altruism.

The growing collective assertion of formerly marginalized groups was a community response to the absence of government funded services. This grass roots effort proved to be a powerful, influential lobby whose values became embodied in the ideology of the new agencies which articulated the needs of a community. Diversification of services meant the direct link between the originating community and the organisation was weakened, with the emergence of distinctive 'client groups' breaking the continuity and earlier cohesiveness. It also posed difficulties for policy-makers – to whose voice do they listen?

Informal collective styles of working caused confusion for funders. The advent of paid workers was often a point of transition – 'We "the founding mothers" were the creative unconscious of the organisation ... a reservoir of information and resource which would bubble up and things would happen, and when we got paid workers this collapsed'.

As political aims became subordinated to service and funding priorities, there was less emphasis on campaigning and lobbying. Recent debates in the voluntary sector suggest the emergence of, on the one hand, voluntary campaigning groups, not funded by the state and 'free to pursue ideals, change and reform' and on the other, not for profit agencies, wholly funded through contracts and effectively agents of the state. Staff often feel they should be 'shouting a lot more and exposing the contradictions' but are afraid to do so for fear of losing grants. The shift from dependence on volunteers to service agency often means founders and early volunteers feel marginalized.

Implications for the information role

Finding the balance between satisfying the needs of clients in terms of ethos and running the organisation to meet the requirements of funders in an increasingly competitive climate has been difficult, but the pressure to be accountable should not be seen as entirely negative. Fewer resources, however, does mean a growing reliance on project funding, and a widespread sense of 'short-termism'. For information professionals charged with collecting data and monitoring policy in specific areas it can prove a frustrating task as they seek to respond to project-specific demands for information, whilst maintaining a core library and information service. Building up an in-depth collection for a two year project may affect other regular activities and budgets. Alternatives to be considered include 'buying in' information from a specialist organisation in an appropriate field or setting up collaborative arrangements with other voluntary organisations.

Negotiating detailed contracts, collating different information, responding to monitoring procedures and applying to a myriad of funding sources is an increasing burden on voluntary sector staff. The division between not for profit service agencies (which survive by competing with other providers for statutory funds) and the campaigning, perhaps militant, organisation which directs its energies against the more established organisations and government policies is likely to continue. The history of the response to AIDS suggests that communities have latent energies and creativity waiting to be mobilized. Collective self help has become a crucial component of social welfare.

Whose voice? – the role of new social movements

There is an assumption by government, local authorities and the general public that traditional organisations speak for the specific named users in their title. But whose voice is being articulated? Significant lessons relevant to the voluntary sector as a whole can be learned from studying user empowerment in disability organisations. The emerging disability movement can only, it is argued, be understood as a new social movement and not as a development within traditional voluntary organisational activity. One of the rationales for the voluntary sector has been its function as the vehicle through which new ideas emerge, are developed and put into practice. But many significant ideas about disability – independent living, civil rights, the social model of disability among others – have emerged from the social movement and not from the traditional voluntary sector which has been in direct opposition to these ideas, only later becoming reluctant converts. Organisations which have made concerted efforts to change the representative nature of their boards (including SCOPE and MENCAP) signal attempts to meet the challenge to the established voluntary sector.

To whom is the organisation accountable? We are concerned here not with legal or fiscal governance but the need to be democratically accountable to the organisation's main user group. The decision by chief executives of six of the larger organisations to issue a press release pledging themselves willing to work with the (then) government on the Disability Discrimination Act (1995) despite their commitment to Rights Now, a confederation of organisations pledged *not* to support the legislation, is an example of a 'mixed message' regarding purpose and commitment.

There are four criteria against which any social movement might be judged:

- whether any new political or economic changes have resulted from their activity;
- whether any specific legislation has resulted;
- what changes in public opinion or behaviour have been produced;
- whether any new organisations or institutions have been created.

The new social movements also have international dimensions and raise important questions in the emerging context of the global economy, opportunities for global campaigning, cross-cultural comparisons and the role of the Internet. Information is no longer restricted to national boundaries or legislation, bringing to the fore the role of a proactive information team, which seeks out similar organisations, exchanges information, policy documents and other published documentation. *(See also chapter 6 and case study 6.)*

Empowerment is a process by which those in society who have power can dispense some of this to those who do not have any. Many recent public policy developments have led to a general feeling of disenfranchisement which in turn has given rise to the emergence of new voices, groups of the unemployed, survivors of mental health services, and so on. A scenario for the 21st century suggests social movements will become stronger as the process of empowerment continues at local, national and international levels. The legitimacy of traditional voluntary organisations will continue to be questioned and lead ultimately to their decline. Up to now the 'old' and 'new' organisations coexisted in 'benevolent hostility' but as the social movement grows in strength and confidence, there will be increasing tension, as they compete for funds, resources and legitimacy in the minds of the public, government and statutory agencies. For the information professional, this means reassessing the range of information resources gathered and consulted, grey literature sources, journals and bulletins to be scanned and so on; the scope of this task will increase as more groups publish electronically.

The relationship between government and organisations supported will be predicated on showing how representative the organisations are of the groups they seek to serve and for whom they speak. The struggle will intensify and will coincide with an opening up of political institutions to include many individuals and organisations previously excluded from mainstream political discourse. The new voluntary sector will be concerned with giving voice to their constituencies within a newly emerging democratic and accountable ethos. Mike Oliver concludes that the choice for government in responding to these changes both now and in the future is therefore simple: do they want to continue supporting the past or invest in the future?

The function of information management

Presenting a case study on Citizens' Advice Bureaux in the UK, Myers and MacLean set out the basis for an information systems strategy and its role in knowledge management: 'To be effective, all organisations, including, not for profit and "caring" bodies require explicit or implicit processes to manage knowledge. These processes should enable individuals and groups to understand and share knowledge and practice, and to adapt and apply them to new situations'. This is particularly true of Citizens Advice Bureaux (CABs) whose advice workers 'dip into a shared pool of knowledge about rights, services, resources and procedures.'

'To empower the disadvantaged, knowledge is an important and valuable asset, and its management an important process … under information era economics, they [information professionals] have primarily to manage an exponentially expanding body of knowledge, that is, a new type of abundant and often reusable capital different in character from physical assets.'

The role of the information manager is pivotal: 'The most important aspect of the richness of information in any given organisation is not just what lies in the files. The real intellectual assets of an organisation go far beyond what can be produced on a printout. What counts in this new era is the ability to accumulate, share, interpret and apply knowledge efficiently from formal and informal sources.'

In a paper delivered to the Institute of Information Scientists at its 1980 conference, Myers, a former president of the Institute, underlines the need to capture both soft and hard data: 'In any organisation there is a reservoir of knowledge in the minds of the people who run it, and there is an informal grapevine which helps to ensure that matters progress reasonably smoothly. However, some of this valuable know-how is lost when people leave, and much useful intelligence can be missed if it is not captured for future use. One of the requirements for information systems is therefore to assist the organisation to collect, hold and make available when needed intelligence which could be of value in the future. At the same time, information systems should help to make the informal communication systems more efficient. If these requirements are to be fulfilled, the information system must fit in with the ways in which people in the organisation are willing to work, and its role has to be subservient to the prime objectives of the organisation.'

To be effective, organisations require processes to manage knowledge and best practice. The processes should enable individuals and groups to understand and share this knowledge, and then adapt and apply it to new situations. Six key approaches have been used by firms to compete more effectively within a knowledge- and information-sharing culture:

- tying in knowledge management to corporate strategy;
- developing a systematic approach to reusing and transferring 'best practice';

- capturing information on needs, issues and concerns;
- enabling and encouraging individuals to contribute to corporate knowledge;
- marshaling intellectual assets to improve performance;
- fostering innovation and the development of corporate knowledge.

The five steps to better knowledge management may be summarized as *generating, accessing, representing and embedding, facilitating* and *transferring* knowledge.

The value of information

Many organisations involved in advisory or casework fail to recognise the rich resources of data which they can use to inform social policy.

Why collect statistical information?
There are three principal reasons for recording information gathered in advice agencies:

- as a management tool and for planning an improved service;
- to provide insight into social policy issues and to offer evidence when responding to consultation;
- to submit applications to funders for additional resources.

Recording data enables agencies to provide a quality service and to turn information gained from individuals into a collective picture of the experience of the wider community served. *STATS*, a software package developed in response to research carried out by the Policy Studies Institute identified the need for a classification scheme which advice centres could use to record meaningful statistical information.

Managing an information and advice service and planning its development involves a complex decision-making process which requires consistent information. Statistical recording can help the planning process – for example, assessing whether equal opportunity targets are being met or which opening times are consistently busiest. Many advice agencies feel they keep abreast of this information because they are close to the community they serve. Whilst personal experience can be a useful indicator, it is not sufficient and cannot be trusted to be consistent. Agencies wishing to undertake social policy work need a statistical recording system which can supplement personal observations and provide insights into hidden problems and trends, exploring unexpected connections between different areas of work.

With the growth of Service Level Agreements, Franchising and Contracts, the need to provide statistical information is often a pre-requisite for further funding. Gathering such information should not be seen as unproductive and some funding organisations can be educated to alter the criteria and type of data captured. In the long term, they will be better informed about the agency's work and the range of issues encountered. Hard data can be used to support applications for additional funding and making the case for funding more credible. An agency which can demonstrate the quality and quantity of work handled will be in a stronger position to argue its case. Information gathered also contributes to the organisation's higher profile through well-documented campaigns, press releases and briefings supported by sound evidence.

Analysis of data
The response of an individual case or advice worker can vary across a wide spectrum of effort from a five minute telephone call responding to a client seeking a one-off piece of advice to the multiple debt client who requires six interviews, two court appearances and 35 hours of case work. The *STATS* system recognizes this and has developed parallel recording systems to reflect the real nature of the work that different approaches generate. Analysis can be carried out using broad headings, including, for example, accommodation, training, welfare rights, ethnicity, housing tenure, personal or employment status and so on. It can record and analyze by referral source, type of assistance provided (information, negotiation or representation) and so on. Data can be classified by subject, cross-subject (e.g. debt or discrimination), client profile and work profile. Individual agencies can modify these codes and create their own reports in addition to the standard reports and graphs or user profiles. When changes in social policy (for example benefits law) are introduced, there is a great deal of value in being able to demonstrate that 20 sample cases recorded over the last 12 months have involved the same difficulty for the individuals concerned.

Staff in advice agencies may be initially resistant to using a statistical recording system. Their reluctance may be based on technophobia, or an ungrounded fear that management is checking up on their work. But if data on casework is not recorded at source with crucial coding (but not necessarily data input) by the criteria that advice workers *themselves* feel are important, there is a greater risk of inaccurate analysis later on. Information needs to be collected on casework and it makes sense to do so in the most consistent, systematic, rigorous, time efficient way possible and to do so at source.

Monitoring demand and emerging need
The value of statistical information collected by an organisation's advice and information service is often perceived by funders purely in terms of accountability and performance monitoring. Many advice agencies and

law centres reliant on contracts have to collect information about the nature of their workload for just this purpose. Whilst this information can be useful for managing the contract it is often less helpful for the development of social policy. The data collected answers questions like how many clients interviewed, number of hours spent per client and so on. Voluntary agencies need to be wary of solely collecting information requested by their funding bodies.

To develop a coherent social policy and campaigning strategies, other tools, such as the software described above, are needed if the agency is to carry out its remit of identifying emerging trends. Here there is a need for ongoing dialogue between policy officers and advice and information workers. Tension can develop if the two groups of professionals are unclear what each is trying to achieve. In the mind of the advice worker, the agency exists to help the individual client but at a broader level and in the long term more clients can be helped if a coherent picture is built up on the range and scope of problems encountered. The information manager should seek to span the gap between potentially conflicting priorities and functions.

Within the National Association of Citizens' Advice Bureaux (NACAB) and other similar agencies, policy officers monitor work profile, client profiles and case loads. If they wish to track evidence on a specific issue, they may send out a request to be notified of exemplary cases, enclosing a standard form to be returned to the national office. Individual offices are encouraged to notify them of new cases which demonstrate policy implications. As more national organisations and federations of advice agencies develop electronic networks and intranets, this type of information sharing for policy monitoring will become easier, but the principles remain the same in a non-networked environment. To ensure continued cooperation, policy and research officers must ensure they feed back the results of any lobbying activity to the advice workers, showing how the latter contributed to the process.

Voluntary organisations must ensure that all the data quoted, its source and validity, is clearly set out in all published documentation. There is a big difference between asserting that '10% of the cases which have come to us over the last six months have shown that ...' and evidence from a national study with a carefully collected representative sample. However, given the time it takes for a lot of social research to get published, evidence collected locally and regionally may often be the only or the most recent and appropriate data to submit in evidence to policy-makers. Research officers can set the social policy agenda and must not be purely reactive to the latest proposed legislative change or consultation document. Working closely with advisory and information staff they can help the voluntary organisation in its wider campaigning role by monitoring the effect of changes 'as they happen'. They need, however, to remain sensitive to the issues of client confidentiality and be aware that not all service users will be willing or able to take on the campaigning 'mantle'.

Getting good media coverage

'Winning the hearts and souls of the public' is a key part of the voluntary organisation's role. Getting the message across to policy makers may not be enough on its own. There is a wider public debate.

'How do we get our story in the newspaper?' To be newsworthy, the story must be timely. Daily newspapers have three criteria for timeliness:

- recency – a story is based on new information;
- immediacy – which means that the story must be published with a minimum of delay;
- currency – meaning the story must be relevant to present concerns.

Voluntary organisations are deeply involved with issues and basics and rarely with the spectacular. Coverage of the sector generally fits two types: either goody-goody superficial stories … or scandals. A recent American study reported that 'nonprofits must get their stories into print to survive in an increasingly competitive market place. This competition is occurring as the nonprofit workload is increasing, while public funds are decreasing.'

Any media strategy will be unsuccessful if the voluntary organisation fails to understand the 'newsworthiness' of its information. Classifying stories about non profit organisations, Corrigan assigned news value descriptions:

- *significance:* emphasis on precedents, extensive changes and magnitudes (the unpredictable and unexpected);
- *vitality-conflict:* emphasis on death, violence and confrontation;
- *human interest:* the bizarre, the sentimental or hardship;
- *timeliness:* emphasis on the latest update in the continuing story (the press tends to follow stories already in the news);
- *prominence:* emphasis on well known or authoritative sources – news that is elite-centered;
- *consequence:* emphasis on specified effects on the publication's home town or a localized angle.

98% of all front page stories analyzed can be classified using these value codes. Based on his research, Martens recommends:

- when pitching a story emphasize the key news values;

- highlight the story's potential impact on a large number of people, or hook a famous person or institution;
- highlight any potential issue rather than information about the organisation or its funding;
- larger organisations with resource capacity should seek to sponsor news events but smaller ones should take advantage of existing events (e.g. public hearings);
- pitch potential stories at reporters who write analysis stories or have an interest in one's organisation or topic;
- talk to reporters about potential stories;
- trying to get a reporter too closely involved with your organisation may backfire as he or she may be prohibited from covering a story about your organisation;
- deal with reporters and editors, not publishers;
- reporting on results of voluntary sector produced studies, such as surveys of new data or trends, is likely to get the editor's attention (but make sure you know how the research was carried out);
- try placing a story that involves a local news angle on a national story;
- provide editors with information and sample stories for creating a voluntary sector focus.

Even with the growth of TV, radio and the Internet as communications vehicles, daily newspapers continue to shape the public's perception of the role of non profit organisations in society. Newspapers provide stories not only to their readers but to wire services, radio, TV and, increasingly, information providers on the Internet. Awareness of its newsworthiness will continue to be a critical element in the survival of many voluntary organisations.

Campaigning

Campaigning is a major activity of non profit organisations ranging from pressure groups like Shelter, Child Poverty Action Group and Greenpeace to those that are primarily service providers only occasionally involved in campaigning. For some organisations, campaigning may be their very raison d'être or evidence of their independence if they campaign against a government that also provides their funding.

Campaigning organisations vary in their degree of specialisation or expertise; some have dedicated teams and a wide range of support services and others small, uncoordinated, part-time volunteers who inevitably make decisions separately from each other. Yet they face common issues when trying to work out where they may have gone wrong.

Types of campaigning

Different types of campaigning activity can be defined:

Proactive – for a change in people's attitude or legislation (for example, Shelter at central government level).

Reactive – from knowledge or experience on the ground a local or regional agency can comment on the implication of a proposed change. To lobby effectively, a group of staff – information and advice workers and project workers in day centres – is brought together to gather documentary evidence. This process is not always totally positive – project workers often fail to understand the relevance. There are constraints on time, energy and resources to collate this information, and response to a consultative document needs to be fast.

Marketing – striving to position the organisation on the agenda of other stakeholders. All voluntary bodies are very dependent on funds, the battle for which is the main driving force. As is the battle in relation to other more 'popular causes' in the minds of the public.

Can campaigning be evaluated?

Campaigning organisations may use both internal and external criteria for reviewing any given campaign. *External* considerations include: changing public perceptions; changed circumstances that affect the objectives of the campaign or the strategy; forthcoming political decisions that provide campaigning opportunities; changing policies of each political party; and new coalitions required to make an impact on the issue. *Internal* considerations include: the specific objectives of the campaign; achievements to date; effectiveness in the use of people and money; learning about why some campaign objectives and not others have been achieved.

Despite the increased emphasis on service evaluation, little is known about how to evaluate policy campaigns; perhaps this is not surprising because typical campaigning situations are complex, 'customer' constituencies are hard to identify and may be in mutual conflict, and the relationship between activities and the impact of campaign management is uncertain. Campaigning is defined as 'any activity which is directed to influencing the decisions of others but not including activity simply directed to raising of funds for the campaigning agency' although some campaigns may have an (indirect) aim of both policy advocacy and revenue-enhancing objectives.

Performance in campaigns matters enormously. How does one evaluate the activity of a voluntary organisation in policy campaigning or advocacy? One can only determine success or failure against well-defined objectives, but in the voluntary organisation these objectives may be multiple and complex. Internal and external objectives may give rise to potential conflict between long and short term aims and can also reflect divergent departmental and stakeholder interests. Ideally, one would like to determine whether the outcome or amended legislation is a result of the organisation's activity.

Different campaigning objectives may be identified:

internal objectives: the explicit campaign demand (upheld by the whole organisation or the cause's main champions);

objectives relating to *different stages* of the campaign (building up goodwill, changing public opinion) leading to the key target stage of acceptance by legislators;

members, supporters and beneficiaries;

external objectives relating to organisational prestige or profile with target audiences (e.g. MPs);

external objectives relating to organisational profile in the eyes of donors ('How much more did we make on the appeal after we ran that campaign? 'How many column inches did we get?').

Measuring campaign effectiveness

Measuring campaign effectiveness is difficult. It is hard to define the relationship between the campaign, any given activity undertaken and the outcome. The complexities in the political process mean that attributing the achievement or non-achievement of outcomes to the ways in which campaigns are run is often impossible for practical purposes. Even getting usable data is difficult. When evaluating service provision, we can ask a sample of service users whether the service or intervention made any difference to the outcome. By contrast, in evaluating campaigning both the 'unwilling customers' (or target audience), and the 'willing customers' (the constituency of the campaigning organisation) may often behave strategically and misrepresent their views.

An organisation trying to evaluate its campaign work needs to identify:

- are the campaign's internal objectives politically and economically desirable and feasible?
- are the internal objectives consistent with the campaign's other objectives?

Campaigning has established conventions, norms and constraints. Seeking to amend a bill going through Parliament, one is bound by institutional conventions (for example, the ways in which amendments should be drafted and the parliamentary timetable). Other conventions prevent the government from reacting to an amendment, or restrict the minister's options for reacting to an amendment, or prevent ministers from inviting campaign activists onto the floor of the House of Commons for an instant bargaining session or to re-write legislation on the spot. Breaking conventions will by definition offend some traditional supporters, but may attract more radical supporters and is a crucial aspect of many 'outside' campaigning styles. There are constraints on direct action too, which, though they might help achieve the internal objective of the current campaign, will often forfeit goodwill with government which is necessary for 'insider' strategies of informal lobbying in Whitehall which may be necessary for future campaigns or even donors' goodwill.

Evaluating the campaign strategy
All voluntary organisations – no matter how small, embryonic or well established – operate within a complex environment of other similar organisations within the same sector. For example, no housing campaign in the UK can afford to ignore how it will relate to Shelter which predominates in the housing field. In a domain with highly competitive internal politics, the patterns of shifting alliances and competition need to be kept under constant review. There may be no single preferred strategy for doing this.

Game theory – a discipline which applies general models of rational decision making to situations in which payoffs to each player are affected by the actions of others – can be applied to the process of evaluation. Using game theory, Perri 6 and Julien E. Forder analyze in detail one example using tree diagrams and tables to trace the history of a campaign in episodes, weighting outcomes for each of the players in the campaign strategy of a lobbying consortium of non profit organisations. The campaign team has to understand the objectives and strategies of competitors and of the target constituency.

Game theory can be a useful tool in a number of ways. The campaigning organisation can use it:

- to assess whether they can estimate the preferences and best reply strategies of the other players;
- if not, to assess whether that information can be obtained at a reasonable cost;
- to estimate how strong the incentives of the other players are to change their strategies when faced with the best reply of the others.

Here again, the information role is pivotal. For how long does the information officer continue to collect information on one aspect or competitor before moving on to the next set of priorities? Keeping a clear head in shifting sands requires tenacity, as well as good records management skills.

Too much rationality?
Even in the most well structured campaign with good communication links, events do not run as predicted by a computer model. Telephoning civil servants, drafting and re-drafting amendments, sitting through consortium meetings and brokering between factions means in practice that campaigning is fuzzy and demands the need to react fast and with confidence in a messy world. Again, responsibility lies on the information professional to stand aside, dissect, analyze, find the correct piece of information, ensure it is well sourced, and keep accurate records which can be retrieved with ease and speed.

The key question remains: has the campaign group distributed its resources between planning and reassessment, activity delivery, and coordination of the campaign strategy with the minimum waste and maximum effort for the agreed level of priority? By working out at least some of the choices of campaign strategy and modelling the campaign, views on how its opponents will respond in each episode can be assessed and the organisation can see what the payoffs are likely to be from the strategy chosen for that episode.

Dealing with these issues in practice

Example 1
A charity, which works with the homeless in south west England, offers insights into some of the issues in practice. The voluntary sector has to work very hard to persuade the media of its case. The lingering problem of image remains: in many people's minds 'voluntary' still means amateur or volunteer. The sector is still not seen for what it is and for what it has become over the last few years – self help organisation, service provider, partner and part of the local statutory agency's plan for delivering services.

When targeting the media, it is important to differentiate between journalists who specialize in reporting social or health issues and generalists. It is still a struggle to portray the depth and complexity of voluntary sector issues and in the minds of the general public a ranking order in social issues persists. Homelessness – which overlaps with other traditionally taboo areas like HIV/AIDS, offending, mental illness – has to fight for space in local and national media.

It is possible to get a 'good story' published if the timing is right but the charity's staff still feel that getting what they perceive to be 'good coverage' is difficult and resent it when 'scandal stories' are published. The voluntary sector is often too reactive, but negative stories can be turned to positive advantage if the media are invited to 'see what we actually do'. A well-worded and well-timed press release may hit the right target at a low news period: for example, good publicity was gained on the launch of a directory of local homelessness services. Increasingly, the voluntary sector understands how it should approach the media and is aware of the media's different culture, constraints and timetable.

The organisation has an in-house researcher and a publicity and information officer who collect data. Reporting to the statutory sector to secure renewed grant aid has been expanded by the requirement to provide similar performance monitoring information for trusts and foundations. Regular surveys are carried out of service users, sponsors and donors to assess the extent to which each understands what the agency can provide. Other agencies surveyed regularly include all potential partners in the health authority, social services, probation and housing. Crucial to all organisational planning is the question: 'where do we place ourselves as an agency in relation to our competitors?'

Tracking trends and new policy issues is very difficult. A lot of information is collected across the organisation but analyzing it is not easy or assigned to one person. Dispersed internal information can be as vital as policy information in an agency employing 120 staff. Knowing which member of staff attends which local or regional inter-agency forum is essential; there are countless collaborative working parties on issues such as drug and alcohol abuse. Gleaning at a formal and informal level what each agency is planning is difficult, as is distilling the emerging policies which will affect the agency's development.

This 'soft' information is vital if the organisation is to re-position itself to meet changing circumstances, for example evaluating how the local Housing Department will react to a proposed new Housing Bill and developing the voluntary sector partner agency's response to service provision. National policy changes also affect the information and advisory service offered. The agency's senior management meets to share this type of information on a quarterly basis and 'trend information' is analyzed at annual planning days.

Legislators and policy-makers to be influenced are not all at Westminster. A regional agency must ensure it keeps local MPs informed, inviting them to open days, timing events to ensure they are able to attend, and sending regular newsletters. The agency publishes two bulletins a year to highlight current concerns, latest developments and burning issues. The opening of an emergency hostel by a local MP was an opportunity to circulate a briefing pack to local media contacts who are invited to all main events. Press releases include a local news story angle and staff and service users are briefed on the potential value of talking to the media.

Example 2: RADAR

The Parliamentary Liaison Officer at the Royal Association for Disability and Rehabilitation confirms that what the media want is informed comment from policy officers who have detailed knowledge of the issue under discussion plus the opportunity to personalize issues by highlighting the circumstances of individuals. Its policy and campaigns team maintain a regular two-way dialogue with the Information Department that is vital to gauge issues of concern and inform lobbying. Regular inter-departmental meetings are held and external correspondence is read by all relevant staff. Draft responses are circulated to enable them to submit an organisation-wide response, and statistics and monthly policy reports are considered by senior managers planning policy initiatives.

The Parliamentary Liaison Officer serves as Research Assistant to the All Party Disablement Group, which has 270 MPs and Peers in membership. They are sent regular summaries and briefing papers as required; whatever the complexity of the issue, briefing papers are no more than two sides of A4, with summaries and bullet points. More detailed background information is provided on request if an MP wishes to speak in a debate or put down an early day motion.

In Autumn 1991, the Department of Social Security's Benefits Integrity Project (BIP) was the focus of a concerted campaign by a consortium of disability organisations. A briefing pack about the initiative and its effect on individuals was prepared. Three people affected by the BIP were identified who gave evidence to the social security Select Committee. This evidence along with a lobby of Parliament, media coverage, submissions by the Disability Benefits Consortium and All Party Disablement Group combined the Government's admission that the initiative had been 'structurally flawed'. While pressing for further changes, disability organisations deemed this a victory for the lobbying process.

Conclusion

Information provision in the voluntary sector is at times demanding and frustrating; gathering, sifting, collating and analyzing hard and soft data in a shifting, charged environment can be hard work but it is ultimately rewarding. The intricate tapestry of statistics, casework, policy, legal and research data demands skilled weaving to produce a coherent, meaningful picture. Information professionals have a duty to consolidate their understanding of the sector's conflicts and concerns. Help and advice is available from information management consultants with sector-specific knowledge and experience of the demands of this sector, who offer impartial assessments and reviews of an organisation's information resources. An independent review assesses existing information resources, their potential for development and advises on the optimum development of the information function to meet corporate objectives. Senior managers in the voluntary sector need to recognize and harness the broad palette of the information profession's skills for the benefit not only of their own voluntary organisation but for the benefit of the sector as a whole and for social policy development.

> The author wishes to thank Sarah Blair, Agnes Fletcher, Jane Steele and Martin Vegoda for their comments and observations which informed this chapter.

Further reading and information sources

'Discover: Official Statistics' by John Birch, Ian Bushnell, Sarah Whiting & Mark Harris. *Managing Information,* April 1997. An excellent summary of printed and electronic information sources.

'Discover: Biomedical Information'. Supplement to *Managing Information,* September 1996.

'Discover: News & Current Affairs Information'. Supplement to *Managing Information*, October 1996.

Voluntary Sector Information Workers Forum (VOLSIF): contact Tracey Stiles at London Voluntary Service Council, 356 Holloway Road, London N7 6PA. Tel: 0171 700 8149

Notes

1. Hudson, *op. cit.*, p. 259
2. See L. Salamon and H. Anheier, 'A comparative study of the non-profit sector', in *Researching the Voluntary Sector,* London, Charities Aid Foundation, 1993 (cited by Hudson, *op cit*, p. 264).
3. Hudson, *op. cit.*, p. 265
4. *Survey of library and information units in charitable and voluntary organisations: final report*, London, Library Association, 1996
5. *Meeting the challenge of change: voluntary action into the 21st century.* Report of the Commission on the Future of the Voluntary Sector, London, NCVO 1996
6. Young, Ken. *Meeting the needs of strangers,* Gresham College, 1991 (cited by Hudson p.31)

7   Hudson, Mike. *Managing without profit: the art of managing third sector organisations*, London, Penguin in association with the Directory of Social Change, 1995
8   Hudson, *op. cit.*, p. 153
9   Weeks, Jeffrey, Aggleton, Peter et al. 'Community and contracts: tensions and dilemmas in the voluntary sector response to HIV and AIDS', *Policy Studies*, 17(2), 1996, pp. 107-123
10 Weeks et al. *op. cit.*, p. 113
11 Centris. *Voluntary action*, London, Home Office (in Weeks et al *op.* cit. p.13)
12 Weeks et al., *op. cit.*, p. 113
13 Oliver, Mike. 'User involvement in the voluntary sector: a view from the disability movement' in *Summary of evidence and selected papers*, pp. 42-55, prepared for the *Report of the Commission on the Voluntary Sector* (Vol. 2), NVCO 1996
14 Marx, G. and McAdam, D. *Collective behaviour and social movements*, Englewood Cliffs, NJ, Prentice Hall, 1994 (cited by Oliver, *op. cit.*, p. 46)
15 Myers, J. & McLean, J. 'Knowledge management for citizens' advice in the 21st century: an innovative IS strategy', in *Social Informatics, IRIS 20, proceedings of the 20th information research seminar in Scandinavia*, August, 1997
16 Darling, M. S. 'Knowledge cultures' in *Executive Excellence*, 14 (2), February 1997, pp. 10-11
17 Myers and MacLean *op. cit.*
18 Myers, J. 'Information systems for the future', paper presented at Info 1980 (IIS) Conference
19 'Emerging practices in knowledge management' in Myers & McLean *op. cit.*
20 *STATS* software, user guide and manual produced by London Advice Services Alliance (LASA) Computer Development Unit (88-94 Wentworth Street, London E1 7SA)
21 Martens, Thomas. 'The news value of non profit organisations and issues', *Non-Profit Management and Leadership* 7 (2), Winter 1996, pp. 181-192
22 Harder, W. P. et al. 'San Francisco Bay Area non-profit sector in a time of government retrenchment', quoted on Martens, *op. cit.*
23 Corrigan, D. M. 'Value-coding consensus in front page news leads', in *Journalism Quarterly* 67, 1990, pp. 653-652
24 Hudson, p. 184, *op. cit.*

25 6, Perri & Forder, Julien E. 'Can campaigning be evaluated' in *Non profit and Voluntary Sector Quarterly* 25 (2), June 1996, pp. 225-247
26 6, Perri and Randon, A. *Liberty, charity and politics: non-profit law and freedom of speech* (cited in Perri 6 and Julien Forder, *op. cit.*, footnote 19)
27 Wison, D. *Interest groups*, Oxford, Blackwell, 1990 (cited by Perri 6 and Julien Forder)
28 6, Perri & Forder, J, *op. cit.* p. 235 ff

6

International Perspectives
Carys A Hodges

Introduction
Although there are many common issues, information managers in international organisations have to face particular challenges which information managers in national organisations do not have to face. I shall draw on my observations and experiences of these throughout this chapter, highlighting the particular implications for information management within international organisations.

Why information is important
All voluntary organisations are having to become increasingly professional in their approach to their work as there is increasing competition for funds from the public, trusts, companies and official funders. Many organisations are also working increasingly with the members of the 'benefiting' community as partners. All demand a high level of accountability for which an organisation must be efficient and effective. Part of the process of becoming such an organisation is the identification of clear objectives, policies and procedures that guide and justify the value of the organisation's work. Many operational approaches are being revisited, evaluated and updated as the thinking changes and develops itself. Within this environment, an effective and competitive organisation must be prepared to look at how these changes affect its work. It must be prepared to evaluate its own experiences, recognise and admit to failures as well as successes. It should be able to identify and learn why mistakes were made and move on, improving its approach accordingly. To learn and improve, an organisation needs to create or have access to valuable information that is available throughout the organisation.

Information is usually obtained from learning tools such as books, documents, newsletters, videos, training courses, conferences, workshops and visits etc. It is very difficult to put a price on the value such material is to an organisation although various attempts have been made to establish this. Orna (1996) quotes from one such study that estimated cost values for reading a journal article to be $385, a book – $1160 and an internal technical document – $706. However, there is no guarantee that the information resources provided will be read by many members of staff. A survey of managers in business carried out by Best (1996) illustrates this: 69% of respondents complained that they and colleagues kept vital information to themselves despite the problems of paper overload; 61% found information hard to find, or not in the right form; 59% had to recreate information because they could not find it and 51% suffered from missing or lost information. An organisation needs to establish procedures and systems that take into account what information is accessible, how it is shared and how it is used to meet the organisation's objectives. In establishing these, it needs to consider what information should be managed, what systems should be used and what services should be provided. An organisation should also look at how these information activities will be reviewed and evaluated.

International organisations

'International organisation' is an umbrella term for organisations working globally on disaster and relief (International Federation of the Red Cross), international exchange (Voluntary Services Overseas), development (ACTIONAID, Oxfam, PLAN International, Save the Children), human rights (Amnesty International) or on a particular issue such as health (International Planned Parenthood Federation). They work in numerous countries across the world. Often the focus of their work are countries in the 'South' or the developing countries where work is organised locally through field offices and/or a country office. International organisations usually co-ordinate their world wide operations and raise funds through a headquarters. Alternatively they have a headquarters and several other overseas offices in the 'North' or the developed world, which between them co-ordinate operations and raise funds. The former organisations are often centralised, the latter are more likely to be decentralised. A centralised organisation has a large headquarters which is pivotal to all operations. A decentralised organisation is one where operations are functions of the whole organisation, co-ordinated by a small headquarters.

Information needs to be managed well in all agencies but this is particularly challenging in international organisations. If it is poorly managed, individual staff in the various offices will waste a lot of time trying to obtain information from others, especially from the country offices where the operational work is focused. There could be anything from one information manager to a whole team of information managers based at the headquarters itself. Other offices may also have one or more information managers. Their location will have a significant effect on their role.

In a centralised organisation we usually find a centralised information unit at headquarters providing a large, central store of information. This will service headquarters staff, especially decision makers, research, operational, marketing, public relations and fund-raisers. There may even be several information units in the headquarters which are servicing different departments. In this case the information manager in each unit should liaise with the others and make their different services clear to other staff. If there are several information units, one will usually be the main unit, servicing the whole of headquarters or even the whole organisation. It may focus on external information, or cover both internal and external information. Other units in the headquarters are likely to focus on a particular subject, just servicing staff in one department.

The headquarters of a decentralised organisation is likely to have fewer staff than that of a comparative office in a centralised organisation. The information unit is therefore servicing less staff who are in the office in which it is situated and its size will reflect this. Internal documentation on the field work will be particularly important but the central collection of material is no longer the core focus. The unit will be servicing staff in other offices. Services will be more diverse and the information manager's role is in more of an advisory capacity. The emphasis is on informing staff in the rest of the organisation about what information is available and where it can be obtained from. Thus, in a decentralised organisation, having an extensive collection of material is less important, but the 'outreach' services it provides are even more important than in the centralised organisation. This can be particularly rewarding if the information manager is keen to support the field work of the organisation as directly as possible. Unfortunately, the extensiveness of the services provided by the information unit in the headquarters of a decentralised organisation can be hidden to senior management and vulnerable to budget cuts. It is therefore important that senior management are kept aware of these services and how they are received by their recipients.

The information manager could be based at one of the branches of the organisation. Their responsibility will be to provide information to the staff in his/her office, to regional fund-raisers if he is in a fund-raising office or to field workers if they are in a country/field office. Much of the information will have been obtained from the headquarters or from other offices within the organisation based in other countries, as well as from other organisations. The information manager may also be responsible for providing information produced by staff in their office or elsewhere in their country, to other offices. He/she is unlikely to play a proactive role in disseminating information to the rest of the organisation. In that sense, working in this part of the organisation is more like working in a national organisation servicing one office or offices in one country.

Needs assessment

It is obviously important in all organisations to understand the organisation itself before trying to meet its information needs. The information manager needs to know the structure of the whole organisation, its mission, operational activities, the different divisions or departments and individual roles. In international organisations, especially decentralised ones, an information manager also needs to know about and understand the functions of the different overseas offices and roles within them. It is particularly valuable to know who is who across the organisation, although it must be remembered that staff move frequently. Some international organisations encourage this by giving short contracts to their international staff who are often the most prolific, and the most aware of the potential information available.

Many organisations will organise an induction programme covering most of these areas. Some of this information can be found in the latest annual report and publicity material. Interviews with staff are also recommended. If carried out well, these will enable the information manager to establish individual, team, department and office information profiles. Questions should cover what is currently obtained by staff themselves, what they rely on from the information unit, how useful the material is, what improvements can be made, what services are not used and why. The information manager should also aim to identify unmet needs and will often find that different members of staff are obtaining the same material, unaware that someone else also needs it, thus duplicating effort and spending resources needlessly.

The information manager in an international organisation needs to think about the countries of operation, communication issues, the different working cultures and languages. Again much of this information can be obtained at the headquarters but it is vital to interview staff from these other offices, or staff who have visited them. If possible, especially in a decentralised organisation, a selection of these other offices should be visited as much can be gained from first hand experience. It is easy to forget that even if English is the working language of the organisation, it is not the first language of everyone working in it. In some developing countries, especially in West Africa, email can take a long time to access and download. Relatively new offices may not have their own phone and particularly remote offices may only get post once a week or less. Equally, if you do not see or ask about it, it is easy to assume a country office's Resource Centre is rather more than the two shelf units of books which it actually is!

The movement of information and material between these offices and countries should be researched as part of the needs assessment. In a centralised organisation this tends to be to and from head office. In a decentralised organisation information flow is likely to be much more complex and harder to identify. Surveys or questionnaires are useful tools in helping to understand information needs, its use and establishing how internal information currently moves throughout an organisation. Of course information flows into the organisation from suppliers, customers, partner organisations, similar organisations, donors, multilateral organisations and the beneficiaries. It also flows out of the organisation to other organisations and the public, often from fund-raising, marketing and publicity departments.

The following are just some of the questions to ask with examples or a full range of the possible responses:

> Who the information is obtained from?
>
> What format it is in?
>
> What subjects are covered?
>
> Is the information essential or just desirable?
>
> How is it shared within offices?
>
> How is it shared between offices?
>
> What is actually useful?
>
> What is not useful?
>
> What format is desirable?
>
> What else would be required from whom?

It has already been suggested that voluntary sector organisations are subject to change. Ideas of good operational practice develop, organisational issues are re-examined, management and other staff change, and financial situations can be variable. It is important that the information manager remains up to date with these developments, adapts services accordingly and acquires appropriate material to support the changes. For this reason, it is advisable to reassess and evaluate the information services, asking similar questions every year or couple of years.

In the long term, enquiries and the feedback given to an information provider are an extremely rich source of information about users needs. It is a good idea to set up a system for gathering these which categorises similar requests together. An information manager may receive numerous requests of a similar nature that cannot immediately be met. Noting the requests down formally will not only highlight them but it will support decisions for reallocating resources to meet them. Recording comments received in appreciation of a particular service can support an information manager's intuition for the provision of the service and should resources become tight, strengthen a case for keeping it. Likewise, negative comments about a particular service or item can be used to support a decision to stop it in order for more valuable services to be adopted.

Relevant information

The information manager needs to be clear on the information for which he/she is responsible. This is likely to be the 'traditional' domain of an information manager covering publications, periodicals, articles and technical reports. It could include internal reports: annual plans, budgets, evaluations, reports to donors, press releases, case studies, photographs, videos etc. Nowadays it is also likely to cover electronic databases, CD-ROMs, details of Web sites. An information manager could have a more diverse role which includes the management of information on other organisations, contacts, events, seminars, courses, project information and even details of lessons learnt in the projects or field work.

The needs assessment should be used to prioritise information and decide what is important, what is desirable and what is unnecessary. The aim is to obtain a balance between not enough and too much information. The volume of information being photocopied or bought must be limited to minimise the cost of obtaining and physically distributing it and the staff time involved. This can be difficult for the information manager working in the headquarters of an international organisation. It is easy to send material out on a blanket basis to a generic group of staff like country directors. However, the information manager should avoid giving out far more information than staff have the time to read. Listen out for comments which imply that he/she is sending too much information. The information manager should ask if this is a reaction to this particular material, the timing or the overall volume of material that is distributed and then alter the system accordingly.

In an ideal situation the information manager would be an information specialist or librarian and be knowledgeable of the subject matter, countries or regions in which the organisation is working. He/she is often expected to share details of ideas, methodologies, policies and guidelines that are continuously being developed with all relevant staff. In this case an information manager who is also a subject specialist is a huge advantage. He/she should know which information is soundly based and who are the well established, reliable authors and organisations. Ideally, a proactive service should be provided, recommending material and researching aspects of the subject matter. Whether the information manager is a subject specialist or not, it is advisable to obtain feedback from the users. Ask them how useful an item was when they return it, if they would recommend it to others and credit them as appropriate. This will allow the end user to make an informed choice about what material they require. The user needs to be able to trust that the information provided is accurate and does not have to validate or consolidate a vast amount of information him/herself. Information also needs to be as up to date as possible or it will be ignored and users will look for more up to date information elsewhere. It is unlikely they will return to the information unit next time they require similar information.

The information needs to be appropriate to the users. It should be available at the right time, available to the right person, in the right format, appropriate to its use and complete. If the enquirer does not receive exactly what they want, the information manager will be blamed. Enquirers seldom explain what they want fully, but the information manager needs to try to obtain as specific a request as possible. He/she should always find out exactly when the information is required and what it is needed for. Is there a preference for graphs rather than tables, electronic information rather than hard copy, raw data rather than interpreted data? Remember, many words or phrases are open to misinterpretation, especially when exchanged by people from different countries. It is advisable that the information manager confirms what he believes the request is for before embarking on extensive research. Avoid providing incomplete information or partial information unless it is impossible or too expensive to fill in the gaps. If this is the case, it is important to explain this to the user as incomplete information can be as dangerous as inaccurate information. In international organisations, international and national standards may be needed and it must be clear which is which. It is also advisable to quote the sources used.

Information management systems

Information is passed on in a variety of ways. These may be paper based, verbal, electronic or a combination. Verbal information is very difficult to manage, yet this is often the most useful and interesting information. It is amazing how quickly the news that a director is leaving, a department is being restructured or other office gossip spreads throughout the most decentralised of international organisations! In stark contrast an evaluation report can take months or even years to find its way around an organisation despite numerous verbal and written requests for it! Unfortunately most information does not have the vitality of office gossip. The information manager should attempt to address the imbalance between formal and informal information. He/she should clarify what information should be shared and how, encouraging and facilitating the wider exchange of information.

Systems need to be clear and standardised so the information can be shared across the organisation. One of the first areas to look at is internal documentation. It is surprising how many internal documents leave out basic bibliographic information such as a date, author, or even the country where a project discussed is based. Although much of this can be gleaned from the content, this is time consuming and not always accurate. The information manager should try to push for a minimum standard of information, although in a decentralised international organisation this can be more difficult to influence. If the standard format can include a selection of key words or even an abstract then so much the better. The style or content is another area which could be standardised. If a researcher is looking for lessons learnt in evaluation reports, they should be able to turn to a certain section of the report so comparisons can easily be made and differences can be analysed.

Most information units in international organisations are computerised, although several are reconsidering the appropriateness of their system. In choosing or designing an information management database, it must be remembered that users will be from very different backgrounds with various levels of understanding of the English language. It is advisable that the same system is used throughout the organisation so that data can be easily shared. Different information units throughout the organisation could enter information into the same database which is collated at the headquarters. Alternatively, staff in other offices may have searching only access to the headquarters database. In some cases, the headquarters database will not be shared with other offices. Whatever the situation, the system must be simple to use, to search and have an easy printing facility. It should be a system in which the novice searcher can find material whilst the more practised searcher can perform more complicated queries.

If the database is used in different countries it is important to have a strong support person who can give clear, concise instructions to staff in other offices by phone, letter or email, as it is unlikely that they will be able to provide instructions in person. If possible the system should be made 'fun' to use. People are afraid of the unknown and many people are still nervous of computers. Most staff will avoid them unless they can see a clear advantage from using such a system and it is made to appear less frightening. It is relatively easy to prove and advocate the advantages of using the system through publicity material and word of mouth. However, getting across how simple it is to use is difficult, particularly in an international organisation where the information manager will not be able to physically show the system to all staff. A useful technique which will help is to create a personality for it. By giving it a name and a personality, using cartoons (if such an approach is acceptable in the organisation) to illustrate the system on publicity material or listings produced from it, it can become less frightening, more friendly and staff are more likely to use it.

It may be necessary to customise an information management system to the needs of the organisation so that it can include references to the organisation's projects, details of who recommended the material and full text of internal reports, case studies, lessons learnt or other items required. In particularly large international organisations where an international loan system would be unmanageable, it may be advisable to include supplier and cost details. If the system is going to be entered into by information managers in different offices, instructions for entering must be simple and clear. The system itself should also contain as many data validations as it can to ensure the consistency of data entered. Likewise, the classification scheme used needs to be chosen carefully. It needs to be simple, relate to the organisation, adaptable to potential changes in the organisation and if appropriate, relevant in all the offices. If it is going to be used in different sites, then it needs to be easy for staff with different first languages to use. Most international organisations have found it necessary to create their own classification scheme based around the regions or countries they work in, projects being worked on or the issues they work on.

> Many international organisations use simple systems which use a combination of letters or letters and numbers to indicate the subject or country, and the author or organisation which produced the item. In one organisation S/AGR/OXF will refer to a report on the subject of agriculture by Oxfam. In a second organisation this will be AGR/01/OXF – a report on many aspects of agriculture by Oxfam. In a third organisation it will be LIV/05/OXF – within the issue of livelihood, the subsection of agriculture by Oxfam.

A clear policy is required for recording and classifying material. In particular it needs to be agreed how material in different languages will be recorded. Most of the headquarters of international organisations are based in the United Kingdom, United States or Switzerland. Much of the information received will be in English, French, Spanish and a number of other languages. How these are entered will depend partly on the skills of the information manager, partly on the language skills of other staff and partly on how the information is shared across the organisation. If the information unit is servicing many offices and users are bi- or multilingual, then it would be advantageous to search on a keyword in one language and find material in a variety of languages. In this case the title and keywords are usually recorded in the main language of the organisation and the language of the document (where this is different). If most staff and information managers have limited language skills, and the information unit is servicing one office then there is little point in trying to work out the keywords of a document in several languages not widely used.

Data inputters should be trained on how to input data into the databases, preferably by the same person or at least by well established users. This may not be possible even if offices in different countries are using the same system. Simple and short manuals customised to the organisation's data are vital. Another useful aid is to customise the edit screen to include brief entering instructions. Validation lists which only allow certain data to be entered are invaluable and can save considerable time. It is important to explain the reasons why data should be entered in a certain way and the consequences if it isn't. Data inputters must know how to check their own data entering for consistency, particularly by viewing the actual data in the indexes. All users, especially searchers, must be instructed in how to get the most out of the databases and all that it can do. They will need reminding of this when appropriate, or features and information rarely used will soon be forgotten. When this rarely needed information is required, staff may have forgotten that the database can provide it and will recreate it elsewhere.

> In a country office of one international organisation, the information manager was using an English system which has a 800 page manual written in English. English is his second language so he avoided using the manual more than he thought necessary. Consequently he had not discovered how to check his data by viewing the actual data entered in the indexes, how to change the validation criteria to limit what data could be entered or how to design new reports. The data was therefore very inconsistent and he complained that he couldn't find all the data he had entered using keywords which should have been adequate. Other staff in the office were losing faith in his database, the system was blamed and they started to research other 'better' systems. Having been shown how to get the most out of the system, including how to check for consistency of data it was discovered that most of the problems had arisen be because of undiscovered typing errors especially in the English words. Once corrected, validation criteria were set up to avoid this happening again. The information manager and other staff became increasingly confident in the system and they decided it was perfectly adequate.

Ensure the information is secure, and safe from potential damage by bright sunlight, severe heat, damp and if in a tropical country, protected from infestation. Staff shouldn't be able to take material without the knowledge of the information manager and internal documentation should be classified as to whether or not it can be made accessible to an external audience. This may involve consultation with management, agreeing that the documentation and records of it are marked accordingly. Unless the software for the whole organisation is centrally purchased or arranged, offices will have different software. Even if they have the same software, they may have different versions. To exchange electronic files between offices successfully, agree to exchange files in a fairly old version which newer versions will be able to convert. When files are exchanged between offices around the world, virus protection is particularly important and all electronic files exchanged need to be checked using the latest anti-virus software. If viruses are found in a file the originator must be informed and if possible, the anti-virus software should be shared with them. If details of contacts or consultants are recorded, the system must be registered with and abide by data protection laws. It should also be clear what material and databases belong to the organisation or they could be lost or left unused/unshared if staff move on. Mark all material purchased accordingly, chase loans vigorously, ensure passwords and database access is shared before a member of staff leaves.

The organisation should maintain a balance between the accessibility of recently produced information and archiving material so the wealth of organisational memory can be easily drawn upon. Many international organisations now have their own archivists based at headquarters who will draw up record management charts. These guide staff on the length of time different internal documentation should be kept accessible, when it should be archived or even destroyed. An information manager should liaise closely with the archivist. Both need to be knowledgeable about the whole organisation from a similar point of view, both will be dealing with similar internal material, both will be recording bibliographic information, and both will be asking other staff for copies of documents. Even if an organisation hasn't yet thought seriously about archiving, it is likely that it soon will be. Usually the information manager is one of the first people consulted on this along with the finance manager who has to maintain certain archiving criteria for legal reasons. It is therefore advisable to consider retaining duplicate reference copies of internal material for an archive, making sure at least one copy of old material is retained, recorded and appropriately stored.

> Of five of the main international development organisations, two have full time archivists, one has an information manager who has joint responsibility for archives and the information managers in the other two have been asked to investigate the matter.

Accessibility

Information needs to be available in the appropriate format for all offices. It is no good providing information on CD-ROM, databases or intranets (internal Internets) that only work on high powered computers if the majority of overseas offices haven't got access to these facilities. The offices without these facilities are usually in developing countries, the parts of the organisation which are at the front edge of the organisation's work. They have the least access to information both from the rest of the organisation and other organisations so they need the assistance of information managers in developed countries the most.

In a large international organisation it is impossible to keep track of all staff, their interests, knowledge, projects they are working on and therefore the information they would be interested in. Yet circulation lists tend to remain fairly static and when new reports are produced they are issued to those thought of as stakeholders although they could be useful to others in the organisation. There is no way everything can be issued to everyone and it is unlikely that everything can be issued to every office in an organisation, so staff throughout the organisation need to know where they can go for information. Circulation or distribution lists must also ensure that information is shared across the whole organisation especially from a country in one region to a country in another region. Ideally this will involve management by staff who have some information management skills or are at least trained/instructed appropriately.

Material must be clearly expressed and presented in straightforward language. It needs to be easy to translate and not liable to misinterpretation in different cultures. A report should clearly state in simple language what it is trying to achieve, and how it aims to achieve it, and then follow through that commitment. Some international organisations will have an agreement that everything must be produced in one corporate language (commonly English) or more than one may be acceptable (often English, French and Spanish). Local languages will also be acceptable for some reports if their use is localised. Clearly there will be requirements to be met depending on what the report is produced for and who the audience is. All acronyms must be explained, especially as their meanings will differ in different languages.

Information services

As in any organisation, services need to be well targeted providing relevant, accurate and timely information but an international organisation brings its own challenges to information provision. The most obvious information service is the provision of a central information unit, resource centre or library. Staff from the office in which it is housed will be able use this like a local or academic library: browsing the shelves, researching, borrowing items, using reference material, making enquiries etc. In some international organisations the information managers have attempted to brighten up the atmosphere in the information unit using fairly low shelves, brightly coloured magazine boxes, plants and reading areas with comfortable chairs. These attempts to make the information unit a more enjoyable place to be and an escape from the usually busy atmosphere elsewhere in the office seem to be successful.

The information manager will have to process orders for publications and reports. It is advisable that the information manager is able to make his/her own decisions on these as he/she receives requests for information; he/she should be able to choose material to respond to such requests without referring elsewhere. Of course, the information manager should encourage and respond to suggestions and specific requests from other staff. The budgeting for these purchases will vary depending on how the organisation arranges its cost centres and whether the item is to remain in the information unit or with the member of staff. In some organisations the information manager will charge all books on a subject to the department dealing with that subject. It may only charge other departments if the material will end up in that department rather than the information unit. Alternatively, all publications may be charged to the information unit whether they are housed there or in other departments.

An often contentious issue in international organisations is whether the central information unit should order material for other offices. There is a high demand for this as many offices based in developing countries will find it hard and extremely expensive to pay suppliers, who are frequently in the developed country's, in the correct currency. In addition, they might not trust their country's postal system and prefer material to be forwarded to them via the headquarters. However, for the central information unit this can become a huge administrative task which is almost totally hidden from management and staff in the same office. It can cause budget problems too, as books will have to be charged back to the relevant cost centres. Although individual publications are relatively cheap, some organisations have a much higher minimum charge back value. If this is the case, the central information unit would have to absorb the cost of these publications. Before purchasing material for country offices it is worth investigating the alternatives as some publications produced by the World Bank, United Nations and other organisations are either free or cheaper to those in developing countries than the developed countries.

> Some international organisations have agreed that ordering for other offices should not be the task of the central information unit, others limit the orders to a manageable selection of material, other organisations have a policy of ordering anything requested by their country offices.

Journals can be even more of a problem to order for other offices. The central information unit staff have to make it clear to suppliers that the address on the order and processing payment is different from the delivery address, or all journals and newsletters for other offices would come to them for redirection. They also need to keep extremely accurate records as journal suppliers usually send the person who paid for the subscription as many as three reminders before deciding that the item will not be resubscribed to. The first reminder may come three months or more before the subscription runs out. If communication links between the information manager and the person who requested the item are slow, this can cause confusion.

The central information unit which collects copies of internal documents is an extremely valuable commodity to the organisation. In a centralised international organisation it will be policy to send these to the headquarters, or the documents themselves will be finalised at headquarters itself. They will usually go to the country or regional desks of the headquarters to be copied and circulated to stakeholders in the office. The information manager must be included on these circulation lists, ideally for two copies: one for loan and one for reference only. This should reduce the size of the circulation lists as many staff will be content to know there is a copy easily available to which they can refer. In a decentralised international organisation this may be more difficult as the whole philosophy is against centralising work, including reports. However, the information manager will still be expected by many staff to have these documents. It is possible to get around this by identifying just one or two core documents for central collection such as evaluation reports. Material could also be collected electronically rather than in hard copy. Lastly, the information manager should make it clear to others, exactly what his/her role is regarding internal documents. In both the centralised and decentralised international organisation, the information manager will be expected to provide copies of these. Again, this is easier if they are available in electronic format, but if not, this can be another time consuming yet hidden task.

> One information unit of an international organisation provides a bibliographic database of its own documentation to most of its country offices specifically to aid the exchange of internal reports. In another organisation current awareness bulletins which include internal reports are circulated to country offices from which copies can be requested. Elsewhere, the information unit focuses on internal evaluation reports issuing listings of these reports only and then servicing requests for further copies.

In an international organisation, the information unit should have a policy as to whether or not it lends material to staff overseas. The difficulty is in getting the material back, especially if something on loan to staff overseas is required urgently by a member of staff in the office of the information unit. The information manager will find it easier not to loan anything to anyone based in other offices. However, there will be pressure to lend things out, especially if the alternative to lending 20 or more internal reports is photocopying them all or buying as many new books! It is advisable to lend certain items, e.g. any material where the information unit has more than one copy, old material which has little demand, items which are quickly and easily replaced or resources which do not cover the 'hot' issues of the moment and are therefore unlikely to be in urgent demand.

Circulation lists are useful tools to ensure a good cross section of staff are aware of the latest material, usually journals or newsletters, received by the information unit. It is advisable to find out which members of staff wish to receive a particular item before drawing up huge circulation lists. When receiving a new journal, circulate a brief questionnaire with it asking staff if they thoroughly read the item, read some of it, didn't have time but would like to see other issues or do not wish to see other issues. By asking for this other information, valuable details are obtained to improve the individual information profile. The circulation list can also be tailored to prioritise those who thoroughly read the journal. It is unlikely that staff overseas will be included in the circulation of journals or newsletters. Depending on the policy for holding journals or newsletters and whether they are catalogued, it may be useful to forward a staff member overseas an item once it returns to the information unit. Circulation lists themselves could include a note asking if staff mind this happening or if they would prefer the item to be retained in the information unit. In centralised organisations the tendency will be to hold them for two to five years or possibly longer. In decentralised organisations, especially one without a central research department, this is less likely to be an issue. If this is likely to be a problem, it is advisable to include a note asking readers if there are any articles which they would like the information unit to copy to staff overseas and act accordingly.

Information profiles are invaluable to the information manager who would like to be proactive yet not swamp staff with information. By selectively disseminating information to staff in their own office and other offices, the information manager can soon establish a good reputation for information provision. This is not necessarily a time consuming role as the interests of many staff members will be obvious anyway – e.g. a Country Director is likely to be interested in anything on that country. In a centralised organisation this type of information may have to go through or at least be copied to a country or regional representative based in the headquarters. A very decentralised organisation will not have these staff so information can be forwarded directly without being duplicated.

The process can work both ways. If a member of staff is interested in a particular issue, the information manager knows that when they get a query about that issue, they could also refer the enquirer to the interested member of staff. Material they recommend could be marked as such in the database of the information unit to assist future enquiries.

It is important to keep staff informed of potential acquisitions so they can make decisions about purchases. Most publishers send catalogues of new books regularly. Again it is advisable to develop circulation lists for these, ideally marking the books already bought by the information manager to save staff time, possible duplication and to raise awareness of what is in the information unit. Those overseas, especially in developing countries, find these catalogues particularly valuable. Email is useful for sending quick summaries of new material or lists of different information resources especially as much of the information the information manager will distribute, can be extracted electronically from their databases and sent as an attachment thus saving time, paper and shipment costs. However, the information manager needs to also cater for countries without email or with poor access to email. One service which few international organisations provide for their overseas offices but staff in developing countries react very positively to, is the dissemination of relevant catalogues/flyers. These can be obtained from the suppliers in bulk for forwarding accordingly. That way the staff overseas have the full choice of what is available complete with ordering forms. The information manager could also write articles in internal magazines through which he/she can advocate the latest report or publication and even useful organisations, other resource centres, events, Internet sites etc. These will have a wide readership so it is important to choose the items accordingly. If it is a subject specific magazine it is likely that approval from the subject specialist in the organisation will have to be obtained before the article is written.

Current awareness bulletins are of course a vital way of informing staff what new material has been received by the information unit. If these are circulated to overseas offices, the reasons why it is being circulated to them must be clearly stated on the bulletin itself. Is it for staff to ask for copies of internal reports, books to be bought for them or merely as an information tool showing what the information unit has thought of as important enough to obtain? If the latter, it is advisable to include supplier details.

Many requests the information manager receives are for lists of material available on a specific subject. It is recommended that these requests are pre-empted and lists of valuable documentation on key issues are compiled and circulated at regular intervals to relevant subject specialists. Again, it is important to state the reason behind these but they are likely to be well received. If possible, they should include details of any staff member who recommended the item and include a note encouraging this sort of feedback. Other staff will have an interest in material in a particular format such as bought databases, CD-ROMs, email mailing lists and Internet sites. Again, these can be serviced through regular listings.

All information managers will provide some sort of enquiry service whether it is for the public and staff or just for staff. This will depend very much on where the information unit is situated in the organisation's structure. If it is in the marketing, communication or fund-raising department the information managers remit is likely to include responding to enquiries from the public. If the unit is based in the policy, research or overseas department it is more likely to respond to just internal enquiries. Although, if successful, the information unit will soon gain a reputation amongst external researchers, especially postgraduates in the area who will want to use the facilities, it is important to consider the implications of this for the storage of confidential internal reports and staff time. It may be necessary to open to external researchers just one or two specific days a week. Where internal requests are concerned, as in any other organisation, if the response will take time to research it is important to keep the enquirer informed of the progress made. This is especially important where enquiries from overseas are concerned as they may take days or even weeks to reach the information unit. It is advisable to reply immediately stating that the request has just been received and estimating how long it will take to process. This will avoid any misconception that the request is being ignored.

The databases of the headquarters may be shared with offices overseas. This is particularly likely in decentralised organisations. If this is the case, it has implications for the database and the information detailed in it. It also has implications for the information manager's time and budget. The database used may be one designed in house, alternatively some software manufacturers allow their system to be copied to other sites free of charge as long as it is only loaded on to hard drives. Otherwise sharing the headquarters information database may involve purchasing further licences and it must be clear at the outset who will pay for these. Copying updates of the actual data can also be a time consuming procedure. It might even be thought too difficult to clearly explain to overseas offices how to import these updates so the information manager may, for ease, resort to recopying all the data instead of just the new data. It is also very difficult to ensure the databases are installed and used once they are distributed overseas. Thus it is recommended that after a reasonable period, a brief questionnaire is circulated to all those who receive the database asking how easy it was to install, use etc. The number of staff who are then prompted to actually install it is surprising.

There are several networks for information managers in international organisations, some of which have been established by the information managers of similar international organisations themselves. They meet regularly to discuss information management issues that a number of them are interested in and maintain close links with each other to exchange ideas and where possible, documents or even databases. It is recommended that all information managers should belong to such a group and consider forming one if none exists as this liaison with his/her counterparts is extremely valuable. However, it can be too easy for other staff to ask the information manager to use his/her contacts to obtain information from the other organisations and for the relationship to become exploited. In this context it is especially important to maintain a balance of providing and asking for information. The information manager who is very demanding of others and gives little back in return will soon annoy their counterparts and may see a less enthusiastic response to requests as time goes on.

Encouraging the use of information

Improving the information resources and services in an organisation will gradually result in an increase in their use. However, if learning is not encouraged in the organisation, reading about best practice is low priority and thought of as a bonus to be done if time allows, the information manager should collaborate closely or even coerce members of staff, especially senior staff, for support. Most international organisations have now worked towards a shared vision, mission and strategic objectives. It is also advantageous to have cross departmental planning which encourage the exchange of ideas and knowledge, management and HR support for learning. Above all, staff themselves should want to learn and develop new skills. The more of these attributes an organisation has, the more the services provided by the information manager will be used, thus he/she can make a substantial contribution to the efficient running of an international organisation.

References

Publications

Best, David. *The fourth resource: information and its management*, Aldershot, Gower, 1996

Corrall, Sheila. *Strategic planning for library and information services*, London, Aslib, 1994

Institute of Development Studies. 'Knowledge is power: the use and abuse of information in development', *IDS Bulletin* Volume 25 No 2, April, 1994

Orna, Elizabeth. *Practical information policies: how to manage information flow within organisations*, Aldershot, Gower, 1990

Organisations

The Institute of Development Studies (IDS) is a research and teaching institute on development issues. It holds the British Library for Development, which is the most comprehensive development library in Europe, and runs Devline, an electronic information service.

Institute of Development Studies
University of Sussex
Brighton BN1 9RE
Tel: +44 (0) 1273 606261
Fax: +44 (0) 1273 621202
Email: *ids@sussex.ac.uk*
Web site: *http://www.ids.ac.uk/ids/*

Teaching Aids at Low Cost (TALC) is a charity that distributes subsidised books, slides and equipment on health to developing and needy countries.

Teaching Aids at Low Cost
PO Box 49
St Albans AL1 4AX

The International Development Research Centre (IDRC) is a public corporation created by the Canadian government to help communities in the developing world find solutions to social, economic and environmental problems.

International Development Research Centre
PO Box 8500
Ottawa
ON K1C 3H9
Canada

Networks

ELDIS: An electronic forum organised by IDS for organisations mainly aiming to harness new information and communications technologies to tackle the problems of information –
mailbase@mailbase.ac.uk

Information for Development Co-ordinating Committee (IDCC) is a network for librarians and information officers in governmental organisations, the voluntary sector, educational and research institutions which focus on other countries and/or development issues.

Information for Development Co-ordinating Committee
c/o June Stephen
Oxfam
274 Banbury Road
Oxford OX2 7DZ
Tel: +44 (0) 1865 313755
Email: jstephen@oxfam.org.uk

Child Rights Information Network (CRIN) is a global network of children's rights organisations seeking to suppport the efective exchange of information about children and their rights. Contact:

Becky Purbrick
c/o Save the Children Fund
17 Grove Lane
London SE5 8RD

Web sites

The Web sites in the United Nations system:
http://un.org/search/map/

A comprehensive list of the United Nations and its related agencies/organisations:
http://www.surfclick.demon.co.uk/global/nations/html

Oneworld on-line, a web site of over 150 leading global organisations, most of which are voluntary organisations:
http://www.oneworld.org/

Part B

Technical and Professional Issues

7

Managing the Library and Information Service in a Voluntary Organisation

Graham Bennett

Introduction

What does the 'voluntary sector' mean to you? For many people outside the sector, it conjures up visions of good deeds being done by hard-pressed and under-valued volunteers, battling to fill gaps in the services of statutory authorities on shoestring budgets. Or maybe it is just the rattle of the collection-box that springs to mind. As a voluntary sector worker, your view might be of an ethically-focused organisation of highly-motivated activists supporting community-based initiatives and confronting social or other injustices.

The truth is, as ever, much more complex than any of these visions. A key lesson I have learned in managing library and information services in the voluntary sector is the enormous variety of perceptions of the aims and objectives of particular organisations that exists. With academic or government or legal library and information services, there is at least a chance that the information staff and their users will be clear on the mission of the organisation; and therefore be able to orientate the library and information services to support that mission. There is one shared perception of reality concerning what the organisation is trying to deliver – though I am simplifying the picture for the sake of my argument. If you are to be successful as a manager of library and information services, you must learn to understand the organisational context, and the reality of this range of perceptions of what an organisation is about.

Managing in the Voluntary Sector: Organisational Structure

In the voluntary sector, there are as many realities of what the organisation's aim is as there are staff in the organisation; and these realities co-exist, sometimes quite happily, while the organisation is in good health, with new areas being developed and new services provided. This is the youthful stage of the voluntary organisation, where initial energy provides momentum, and where purposes seem clear (though these are often unstated; or if stated, then either very narrow or extremely vague). It is very common for voluntary organisations to be the product of the enthusiasm, drive and commitment of one (most commonly) or more charismatic, brilliant leaders, who have the vision and the drive to identify injustice or deprivation, and make a difference – to take up the challenge.

Amnesty International, for example, started in this way; the founder of Amnesty, Peter Benenson, was outraged by a story in *The Times* that students were arrested and imprisoned in Portugal for making a toast to freedom in a cafe. His reaction was to write to *The Times*, encouraging people to follow his example and send letters to the authorities in Portugal, demanding the release of the students. From that beginning has grown an organisation with one million world-wide members, and offices in sixty countries.

Yet the very factors which enable people to set up voluntary organisations and make a difference to the cause of their concerns have a flipside which returns later to highlight difficulties, especially in terms of clarity of aims and the degree of specialisation needed to keep the organisation effective and energetic.

But first, if a voluntary organisation survives its youthful stage and prospers, then it will move into its most effective stage of maturity. It has established its base, it has expanded its resources through fundraising, and it has a paid and volunteer staff who are committed, knowledgeable and focused on the mission of the organisation.

The organisation is growing, and confidence and competence increase. Resources have to be obtained to sustain the growth: but the organisation retains the energy and drive that makes it attractive to funders and to users alike. Very often the mission of the organisation will be enlarged, officially or in practice only, to encompass activities and areas which are further from the original core issue – reflecting the interdependence of so many of the causes to which voluntary sector organisations respond. This is classically the case with organisations which deal with poverty, where it may be the effects of poverty that are the initial focus. It is soon realised that the causes of poverty also have to be addressed, however, which leads the organisation into more directly political arenas. As a Brazilian Bishop remarked: 'If I give food to the poor, they call me a saint; if I ask why the poor have no food, they call me a communist.'

What happens in this stage of maturity will often govern whether the organisation will survive intact; but it will certainly face choices. Many of the original volunteers, who joined and sustained the organisation because of the service aspects of the organisation, may feel less committed or comfortable with some of the new areas or activities that accompany 'politicisation' – whether these be lobbying, advocacy or alliances with other organisations. At this stage it is often revealed that many of the staff and volunteers have widely differing perceptions of what the organisation is for, what role it should play, and who its users are.

Such issues may be addressed in creative and dynamic ways; but courage is needed. For example, an organisation may split into different strands, which may continue to cooperate at some high level, or even at grassroots, but may pursue different paths and develop different aims. This is often the case where an organisation has grown large, and has developed a bureaucracy and a high degree of departmental specialisation. The organisation may then split and give birth to dynamic and enthusiastic children, which may be far more effective than the mother organisation. This has been a strategy much used in industrial and commercial sectors; for example, in the break-up of multinational companies such as IBM and ICI into leaner and fitter components. Voluntary organisations have so far been less willing to pursue such paths; not least because of the job losses involved in such restructuring. The ethical framework of voluntary organisations, which arises from the work that they do and the people who form them, is much valued by staff and volunteers; but it can, perhaps, result in compromises in strategy between what is best for the users and what is best for the employees and volunteers. This is particularly the case when the voluntary organisation defines itself as democratic – not something that sits easily alongside an increasingly professionalised workforce, large resources and a complex mission. Yet this democratic framework protects the organisation's integrity, and helps to define the difference between it and a commercial organisation. One just needs to accept, when working in a voluntary organisation, that response to change may be slower, and that this brings some accompanying dangers.

Whether a voluntary organisation survives into old age depends on many of the factors above; and on others, including a changing environment and competition for resources with other, younger organisations. It often will need the 'retooling' that has been experienced so painfully by many companies in the 1980s and 1990s in Europe and North America. It will need to look at its organisational structure and decision-making processes; and, crucially, at its mission statement. If it does not have a mission statement already, then it surely will have one after it has called in one of the growing band of management consultants who specialise in the voluntary sector. The reason for this growth of consultancy in the voluntary sector is that many of the largest, most established charities and voluntary sector organisations in the United Kingdom have reached old age, and are finding that in many cases they are out of touch with the culture and environment of their users. How they respond to this will govern if they survive; and perhaps in some cases the right decision is to disband, because a job has been done and a situation has changed – hopefully, improved. But this is as difficult for a voluntary organisation to accept as it is for any company.

Organisational structure

Voluntary organisations will typically have a structure which has grown organically. The current trend in large voluntary organisations to restructure (for example, Oxfam in 1993, Amnesty International in 1994) following in the footsteps of industrial, commercial and some public sector service organisations, indicates that voluntary organisations recognise the need to develop a structure which will deliver the organisation's mission. The democratic nature of voluntary organisations, which may be more a principle than a practical reality, usually means there is a Board or Management Committee which is elected by the membership or users of the organisation, and which will include representatives from various parts of the membership. In smaller organisations, in particular, the Management Committee members may double as key volunteers for the organisation; resulting in an overlap or confusion of roles, which impacts in particular on staff.

For example, different members of the Management Committee may have different levels of contact with, and influence over, staff in the organisation – which may lead to ineffective decision-making and communication. Nevertheless, such a situation is common, and is a reality of working in a voluntary organisation. Below Management Committee level, there may be one identifiable Chief Executive or Director; or there may be a collective staff management group, which co-ordinates the activities of the organisation. Again, this may present difficulties in decision-making, communication and accountability.

The position of the library and information services within the structure is critical to how it is perceived, what slice of the resources it gets, and whether it will play a central, dynamic role or a peripheral, low-profile role. It is possible to transcend an unhelpful position in the organisational structure; but an appropriate position will certainly make the work of the library and information services much easier.

Larger voluntary organisations are typically subdivided into a number of standard divisions: campaigning; research; finance and administration; membership and public relations; and marketing. It is not unusual to see the library and information services situated in one of the latter three – but less common to see library and information services in campaigning or research where, ironically, many of the principal users will be situated.

Of course, situating library and information services with other services which have an organisation-wide scope (such as finance, office services, administration, human resources) has a logic; and may strengthen as a whole the services area, to the benefit of all the service departments. However, the political influence of the library and information services will be less, through association with less 'proactive' services, and without energetic leadership will result in the perception of the library and information services as isolated, out of the mainstream of the organisation. In my experience the library and information services are best served by close association with media, publications and public relations – functions that are seen as dynamic and outward-looking.

At Amnesty International in 1994, as part of our organisational restructuring, we experimented with some aspects of matrix management. This structural form – where, in essence, certain staff report to two different constituencies – is controversial and has been rejected by a number of organisations, including some in the voluntary sector. For the library and information services, this has proved very successful in one particular area – the library. The Library Team consists of six information officers, who were previously largely function-orientated; for example, a cataloguer and a United Nations documentalist. In the restructuring, we refocused the Library Team towards its main users – the campaigners and researchers in the five Regional departments – by creating Information Officers with regional specialisations (Americas, Europe, Middle East, Asia and Africa). The effects of this have been: a perception by the users that the library is more dynamic; increased job satisfaction for the library staff; a greater trust by the researchers in the subject knowledge of the librarians, which is matched by a real increase in knowledge; the librarians being included in a broader range of activities and communication from the regional departments, for example being included in email lists and being invited to regional department meetings; and generally a feeling in the library that the team is much more involved in the real human rights work of the organisation.

Structural change is worth considering seriously when taking over management of library and information services. Is the library and information services in the most strategically useful position in the structure; and if not, is there any possibility to change its structural position? Large-scale organisational change may also offer an opportunity to redefine the position of the library and information services; take the opportunity if it arises, though those who have experienced restructuring will attest to the way in which many staff view the process as threatening. However, positioning your library and information services correctly in relation to its users within the organisation is key to delivering successful services.

Decision-making in voluntary organisations

In any sector, consultation and participation are likely to deliver more effective and better decisions. The difference in voluntary organisations, arising from the organisational culture and the background and aspirations of many of the staff and volunteers, is that consultation will be expected. Consultation is part of gaining ownership and acceptance; though ultimately it cannot be used indefinitely as an excuse for not making a decision. Consultation in the voluntary sector is often more time-consuming, and more comprehensive, than in other sectors. This is certainly true for the library and information services; and especially when introducing change. The irony, in many ways, of the culture of voluntary organisations is that though they are perceived by others often as radical organisations, a great deal of personal conservatism can be present. This can slow the pace of change. When proposing changes to library and information services, carry out consultation with all the stakeholders: the library and information services staff who will implement the changes, and the users who will experience the changes to services provided. This may sound like good practice for any sector: it is. The key issue is that decision-making within the voluntary sector is often viewed, mistakenly, as a democratic process. In most cases – except where the voluntary organisation is truly a collective – this is not the case. There is a hierarchy, and one person is charged with the responsibility to make decisions, which can be unpalatable to some. Yet delayed decision-making, and fudging of hard decisions, seems often to be a root cause of conflict in voluntary organisations. It is hard to get the balance right.

The mistaken view that decision-making in voluntary organisations is democratic stems often from the early days of an organisation, when all the staff and volunteers could sit together in one room and discuss even detailed decisions. Like most organisations, those in the voluntary sector are now complex, hierarchical entities. What differentiates them from other organisations is not the process of decision-making, but the way that difficult decisions – for example, on cutting staff when facing funding shortfalls – are implemented.

The main lesson for library and information services managers is that your users are never so interested in your services as when traditional functions – for example, press cuttings – are mooted for replacement or phasing out in favour of more effective and appropriate solutions to the information needs of the organisation. In such situations, consult with your staff, gain their support, and consult with the users too. Make sure they all know they have been listened to; where you have not included their suggestions in the final decision, then explain why, even formally in a meeting or in writing. This ensures as much as possible that your staff and users feel they have participated, which is a key motivation for all those involved in the voluntary sector.

Management style in the voluntary sector

It is common in the voluntary sector to have people in management positions who view themselves first and foremost as activists – their key motivation in working for the organisation is the mission of the organisation. This situation mirrors that of some other sectors, such as health and education; but with a time delay in the voluntary sector. There are still many staff in voluntary sector organisations who believe that management is an unnecessary function; and perhaps too often the management has been so ineffective as to encourage this view, partly because they themselves believe it.

Again, the negative view of management stems from the origins of voluntary sector organisations – set up by activists, often to combat bureaucracy, and with abundant dynamism and energy – and with particular principles and ideals of democracy and non-hierarchical structures and decision-making. In many organisations, until very recently, the move to specialist managers has been resisted, even to the extent of avoiding the title of manager at all.

Times are changing. The challenge for the voluntary sector is to compete and thrive in a crowded market, while retaining the essential values that set aside voluntary organisations and engender such loyalty and commitment in staff. One common realisation is that professional managers are an increasing necessity; people skilled in human and financial resources management, who can motivate others, and who can develop the strategic plans and vision to ensure the organisation remains relevant in a changing world. There are now specialist management training courses aimed at voluntary sector organisations, and such organisations are increasingly recruiting specialist managers.

In my own experience, voluntary sector managers have much to share with managers from other sectors: the gulf is not as wide as some staff would wish to believe, in terms of what motivates staff in the workplace.

But voluntary sector staff have certain expectations of their managers which may go beyond expectations in other sectors. In particular, they expect participation and consultation, and an emphasis on openness in communication and decision-making. As a voluntary sector manager, you will find yourself working with highly articulate and committed staff, who are well briefed on their rights. This is how it should be; but it demands a participatory style, where you work as a manager very much with the staff, taking key roles in coaching and facilitating work. An authoritarian style will be unsuccessful.

This does not mean that voluntary sector staff do not need and want strong leadership. On the contrary, decisive decision-making is much valued by staff in the voluntary sector, where so often there is indecisiveness – a result of trying to be 'nice'. The key is to involve staff, to understand the mission of the organisation, and to recognise that the staff of voluntary organisations are your greatest resource – they are motivated, they are often poorly paid or volunteers, and they subsidise the organisation with the free time and commitment they give. They need to be part of the organisation in a very active way.

Attitudes of staff to management

In some voluntary sector organisations, the term 'management' is still treated with disdain or suspicion: or is avoided entirely. Many voluntary sector organisations start as the creations of small groups of highly-motivated activists, often operating with minimal formal structures and reporting lines – perhaps 'collectives', with decisions shared and reached with full participation.

Increasingly, as many voluntary sector organisations have developed into medium or large-scale organisations, with accompanying bureaucracies, administrative systems and specialisation of functions, hierarchies have developed, and there is need for greater coordination. The result, in most cases, is the creation of a management level, to provide the coordination, planning and leadership necessary for the organisation to maintain a clear direction and purpose.

The management level has typically been filled with promoted activists who may or not possess relevant management experience, skills and knowledge, and the interest in management to go with them. Voluntary sector organisations have been slow to address this issue, which is made worse by the lower salaries available for management level posts in the sector. It is hard to attract high calibre managers, unless they themselves feel highly motivated by the mission or ethos of the organisation.

Partly through a combination of natural suspicion of 'management' by the activists in the organisation, and partly through an ambivalence about developing a fully-professional management, many voluntary sector organisations have faced problems with poor management. An inevitable result is a lack of confidence by staff towards both the concept and reality of management – along the lines of 'we were better off in the old days'. Again the voluntary sector is not unique in this area; but we have come more slowly to accept both the need for professional managers, and the inevitable changes that come about in organisational culture when such hierarchies are introduced.

The suspicion of staff towards management in the voluntary sector is partly derived from the feeling that such hierarchies are in contradiction to the underlying foundations of such organisations; usually democracy, fairness and social justice. Voluntary sector managers, in the library and information service, as elsewhere, are therefore likely to face some challenges which are different from their colleagues in other sectors. In addition, as at Amnesty International and other campaigning organisations, staff are extremely articulate, highly-educated and assertive – they need to be able to carry out the important work they do on behalf of others. They are consequently equally forthright in putting their own views forward.

Such attitudes are not necessarily a problem, and can be part of the stimulation of working in the voluntary sector. Library and information workers may sometimes be slightly different in their attitudes than some of the staff; one reason being that they are usually professionally qualified in a specialised field and often have worked in other sectors. Many other staff, such as campaigners and researchers, may have spent all of their working lives in similar organisations – or even in the same organisation, since long-staying staff are a feature of the voluntary sector. Nevertheless, library and information staff in the voluntary sector may soon acquire a similar attitude to management, and this is a factor which incoming library and information service managers should be aware of, especially if they themselves are coming from a different professional sector of information work.

Multiculturalism/equal opportunities and cultural diversity

One of the most rewarding factors that I have experienced in working with Amnesty International, and previously with Voluntary Services Overseas (VSO), has been the opportunity to work with colleagues from a broad variety of backgrounds. At Amnesty, we have staff working in London from the Middle East, Asia, Africa, the Americas and Europe. The issue of equal opportunities and cultural diversity is a key one in an international organisation like Amnesty, and rightly so. In most voluntary sector organisations the issue of equal opportunities will be one that is strongly supported in theory – and hopefully in practice.

However, voluntary organisations, often through the absence of professional human resources staff and established practices and policies for recruitment, selection and staff development, may encompass existing practices of unequal opportunities in areas such as promotion and employment. One consequence, coupled with the long-staying nature of staff in the voluntary sector, is that professional departments such as the library and information services may have staff in professional positions who are not professionally qualified, and who may lack a key grounding in information management work. They may have many years experience, which is valuable; but sometimes they may be better at maintaining existing systems than in developing new ways of working – which has major implications for how you introduce necessary change. An understanding of the professional background of the staff you are managing in a voluntary organisation's library and information service is critical.

The diversity of background is critical to how you manage: for example, in running meetings and in communicating in general with the library and information staff. A flexible approach, within broad standards, is the best way to ensure that goals are achieved by taking advantage of the rich rewards that can come with having a diverse staff.

The other key element of diversity within the library and information staff of a voluntary sector organisation is that you may be managing volunteers. These may have greater experience and higher professional qualifications than the paid staff, which is a bonus if managed successfully. It is extremely difficult to make volunteers accountable in the same way as paid staff: they always have the option of leaving suddenly, or not appearing for work, though they are rarely this casual in approach. I have found that experienced and qualified volunteers, in particular, provide an opportunity to expand the human resources of the library and information service. The key is in providing volunteers with work that is matched to their interests, and which is (if possible) finite in duration – for example, a project to write a user guide to the library. In this way the volunteers are motivated; and damage is limited if they leave suddenly. If you spend a great deal of time and money on training volunteers to do high-level ongoing tasks, then you may find the time wasted.

There can be some tension between volunteers and paid staff – typically where they are doing the same level of professional work, one paid and the other not. This is all part of the challenge of managing volunteers. In addition, keep volunteers in the channels of communication – make them as much a part of the team of staff as they wish (recognising that some volunteers want to opt out of planning and other staff meetings; and have a legitimate right to do so).

Managing the Library and information services: specific elements

Designing the library and information service

As in all areas of work within a voluntary sector organisation, the key to success is understanding the culture and mission of the organisation, and setting out to consult and communicate with a broad spectrum of the staff and volunteers; and whoever else is a stakeholder. Aim to include, rather than exclude: how you consult with people is critical.

In many voluntary sector organisations that I have visited, as well as those where I have worked, the library and information service is typically struggling with reconciling widely differing perceptions of what service it is aiming to provide to users. The traditional services – especially book loans and news cuttings – may be what the library and information service is known and valued for. This may be in contradiction to the current areas into which the service needs to expand – for example, Internet use. Many voluntary sector library and information services will be poorly resourced, and will need to make real choices about what services can be offered.

In making choices about what services to offer, and how to deliver them, the key factors are: the mission of the organisation and what information it needs to achieve its aims; the specific functions of staff and their information needs; the size, complexity and physical/electronic dispersal of the organisation; and the resources available.

In most cases, as the manager of a library and information service, you are unlikely to be in the daunting but exciting position of being able to start with an empty room and no existing service (though I once had this experience, and would thoroughly recommend it as a way of finding out how broad your knowledge is of your profession….). In developing a picture of user needs as a first stage in designing services, a standard and increasingly popular approach is to create an information map of current usage. There are many interpretations of what this means, and many journal articles have been written on the subject. For myself, I have used infomapping as a practical way of building a pictorial representation of what the organisation is currently getting in terms of value and service for the resources it is investing.

In essence, infomapping involves identifying the services offered, finding out how they are used and whether they are valued (and by whom); and costing the services, in order to be able to make decisions about which services are most beneficial. It also provides data with which to make comparisons against new services and technologies. The results of such an exercise may often be very surprising to the staff of the library and information service, challenging existing perceptions of what is valued by users. The results of such infomapping exercises must be shared with the users: it is a critical part of the consultation process, and ensures that the users are deeply involved in understanding the choices to be made. It is important to give a context: the possible introduction of new services, perhaps as a result of increasing enquiries or even complaints, is an excellent starting point. My experience has been that, when users are involved at this level, they will develop a greater understanding and ownership of the services, and help to promote and support them later.

Strategic and operational planning

I have faced extremes in planning within voluntary organisations; from no systematic planning being carried out, certainly at the strategic level, through to the planning process becoming a nightmare feared by all the management. The two extremes can be relatively close in time. Planning is sometimes viewed as anathema to activism, a barrier to the energy and action of the organisation. However, it is few voluntary organisations, indeed, who would not carry out at least a basic level of planning; though this is more likely to be at the operational level, and relatively short-term (for example, one year).

The consultative culture of voluntary sector organisations is one factor leading to the other extreme, the long-drawn out planning process which seems to take as long as the projected planning period. Planning skills, perhaps, is a key area where voluntary sector organisations can learn from commercial organisations, since there is no doubting that planning the acquisition and use of resources within an increasingly competitive political, economic and cultural environment is fundamental to good organisational health.

Planning is not about predicting the future; it is much more about gaining an understanding of the environment in which the organisation operates, the actual and potential resources available, and the possible options available for achieving the desired goals. It is extremely unlikely that the desired outcomes will unfold in the expected way; but planning gives a deeper understanding of processes and possibilities, and enables flexibility later.

The standard period for strategic planning is increasingly taken as four years; and it is critical for the library and information service to look this far into the future. The starting point for strategic planning must be the organisation's goals: how can the library and information services add value to these? For Amnesty International, the aims of the organisation are clearly about human rights; and it is essential to trace the role of the library and information services in adding to the human rights work. This is a motivating factor for library and information services staff; but also places the work of the services in a context where its worth can be seen and understood by those whose work is more activist and campaigning.

Preferably, the strategic planning for library and information services should be part of the organisation's overall planning process, for true integration. The standard tools of strategic planning are applicable to library and information services: at Amnesty we have found SWOT analysis (identifying the Strengths, Weaknesses, Opportunities and Threats of the organisation and its environment) to be effective – it is a tool that involves staff and helps to provide clear contrasts in options, as well as recognising current strengths and past successes – always a good starting point.

In setting strategic aims, these must be achievable and clear, and with measurable end results. Making them too vague will be unhelpful, increasing the likelihood that your strategic plan will gather dust on a shelf, rather than being a working tool.

The strategic plan will translate into more concrete areas of work and tasks in the operational plan; which usually spans a shorter period, either one year or two. Each task can again be subdivided, and assigned to teams or individuals. This is how the plan becomes reality; and when it becomes most meaningful to most staff. The plan, if suitably and practically designed, can itself become the means of monitoring progress against end results, without the need to generate long reports.

Many library and information services may prove resistant to planning: it can seem very divorced from the day-to-day work, which may be difficult to conceive as discrete end results. However, if the plan, at various levels, is used as a practical tool by the manager, and is referred to when appropriate, then it has been my experience that staff develop a greater recognition of its importance. It can provide great motivation; even engender some competition between teams – though one hopes for cooperation and integration also. At the team level, the plan should contain the end results, which will be agreed with the manager, and which will show a clear link to the overall operational and strategic goals. However, the plan should not specify how tasks will be carried out, unless the means is specifically part of the standards for the task. It is for the teams, with their assigned resources, to best design and implement a process to deliver the end results. In this way the plan ensures what is to be achieved: but it does not dampen the creativity of staff, which can be a common misconception.

Two last factors in planning: do not make the process of planning long and boring; and involve the users. The most frequent complaint I have heard from staff is that planning takes too long: any enthusiasm can be dissipated by tedious, endless meetings. Get the staff to do the exciting parts: involve them in 'brainstorming' sessions, where any idea can be considered (and try to maintain the rules of such sessions; that negative comments against the ideas of others are kept back until all ideas are on the board, and build on the ideas of others). These sessions, if you have good process skills, can be very enjoyable for all: use the whiteboard or the flipchart – even if these seem strange to you at first, they are aids to putting ideas in the public domain and getting feedback. People like to see their ideas go up: it is a validation that they are making a worthwhile contribution.

And do not exclude the users from your planning. Even if the bulk of the planning is done within the library and information services, it is important to test out your ideas. Are you addressing the real needs of the organisation and its users – or just what you think they are? Use all the source documents that you can; the plans from other departments, or any other important strategy or policy documents. But also get the view of key users: your planning process will be much improved by such involvement.

Financial Planning and Management

The budget is the cost associated with putting the operational plan into action; and the plan is therefore the starting point for developing the budget. However, we deal in realities; and one reality is that the library and information service is unlikely to have an increasing budget, and will be under pressure to contain or reduce costs. The planning, therefore, must take account of the overall budget envelope – though creative thinking must be given space.

Once the plan is agreed, however, the budget needs to be planned. Library and information services managers in the voluntary sector need to have the standard skills in relation to managing a budget, and if they do not have them, to develop them. One factor which may differentiate the budgets of Library and information services from some other departments is that many areas – for example, journal subscriptions – may in effect be fully committed for the year. The only way you can afford new journals is to cancel existing ones, a factor which is difficult to put across to users. In other areas, demand may not be clear: online searching, Internet use, inter-library loans. The budget may be the determinant of demand. It is vital to know the unit cost of such services; something that is necessary for the infomapping exercise outlined earlier. It is also vital that staff, without being inhibited, are also aware of costs and understand the implications of unfettered expenditure on, for example, literature searches of costly company databases.

Responsibility for expenditure should be delegated to the appropriate level: as near as possible to the user. This may present a difficulty in some organizations, where all budget holders are at management level. However, where possible, put the decision-making authority into the staff of the library and information services, who know how to make the money work; it is the quality and effectiveness of your accountability systems, and your expenditure monitoring, that provide the safeguards in such a delegated system.

Maintain an overview of all expenditure: both committed and spent. Share the information with all the staff of the Library and information services: you can only benefit by spreading such knowledge and involving everyone, at some level, in the expenditure and the cost of running the Library and information services.

Managing staff

There are many theories on managing staff; and many existing books and articles to provide guidance or confusion, depending on your own outlook and experience. I have experimented with some of these; and have found, somewhat to my surprise, that some of the theories I read with deep scepticism during my professional education have real meaning and have helped me understand the complexities of staff management. An example, especially relevant to the Library and information services in the voluntary sector, has been the 'motivation-hygiene' theory (Herzberg, *The motivation to work*, 1959), which in summary is: improving the work environment can get rid of staff discontent, but it will not actually motivate people. No one is going to get very excited over a new desk or carpet in the library, but give staff real responsibility, perhaps in managing a key project, then you will get good results.

For library and information services, and other staff, in the voluntary sector, the major difference from other sectors lies in reward and motivation. The opportunities for reward are limited in any sense other than giving recognition and positive feedback. Other rewards, notably financial bonuses, are not available and are (in theory) not acceptable. This perpetuates the myth, as I see it, that staff in the voluntary sector are radically different from staff in other areas – perhaps morally superior in some way. I have heard voluntary sector managers say as much.

The truth is that staff in the voluntary sector do choose to work in that sector, and often because they do believe much in the mission of the organisation and the worth of the work; but this does not mean they expect to be without reward in any way. It is accepted that salaries will be lower, and often conditions of work will be less than ideal. Rewards, in general, will be limited. However, given this situation, it still discourages me to see how often that giving praise and providing recognition to staff is overlooked. Again, it may be related to the ethos of the voluntary sector: the assumption that doing your job well for a good cause is somehow reward enough in itself. Self-motivation needs to be complemented with positive encouragement by the manager, and between peers. And it doesn't cost anything.

As with rewards, so with sanctions. Again, perhaps, because of the ethos of voluntary sector organisations, allied with the absence of key staffing policies, there is often an unwillingness to take action against underperformers. With the increasing professionalisation of the voluntary sector, this will change; but at present underperforming staff can still provide significant problems. Managers get no credit for not tackling other issues; if you do not face up to problems of this nature, you can be sure that your staff will recognise this weakness, and your own position and standing will suffer. Recognise the unique nature of voluntary organisations, and that treating staff well and fairly is very much a part; but do not use that context to avoid dealing with staffing problems.

Staff development, too, can appear to be limited in scope within the voluntary sector, and especially in areas such as library and information services. A characteristic of the voluntary sector is that many staff stay for a long time; and opportunities to move up and be promoted can be severely limited. In addition, specialists such as library and information staff are often viewed only as librarians or archivists; though they may, through exposure to others within the organisation, and through their own interests, want to play a wider role in campaigning or other activist work. One means is to create chances for your staff to be involved in campaigns or other major projects: you will often have to be proactive in this, and stress to other managers the benefits of having library and information services staff directly involved in activist projects. I have lost some very good librarians to other areas of work in voluntary organisations; but I have counted this as a success for staff development, a small price to pay for having to carry out a recruitment to replace them.

Managing Technology

The area of library and information services is rapidly evolving; and technology is the key factor. The Internet, most clearly, is changing the nature of our work: such technology is now effectively used by intermediaries, bringing about a change in the role of library and information services staff to facilitators and trainers of end users. Many library and information services are caught, in terms of technological ability, between the users and specialist IT staff. However, in terms of making the best use of

IT for information management, library and information services have a vital role to play. The information centre can be the main access point for users to IT facilities such as CD-ROMs and public access Internet PCs. If the library and information services can manage these successfully, then such facilities will enhance the image of the department, and bring in users.

In bringing in new technology and managing it successfully, the main message is: manage IT, don't let it manage you. Make sure the technology is appropriate to its purpose; and make sure your staff are trained and can support it; and use the opportunity to examine your existing systems, rather than simply recreating them in the new technology. Your staff are the key to the success of IT introduction: involve them in decisions and planning.

Managing material and collections

In my professional experience in the voluntary sector, I have developed some heretical practices. These have sometimes come about through sheer lack of resources, but such experience has opened my eyes in some areas. I do not necessarily recommend what I have done, but my advice is to examine very closely what is really important and necessary – especially when starting in a new library and information service with many established practices, some of them long-cherished but no longer appropriate. Evolution may be better than revolution: it depends on the circumstances. But continuing to put resources into areas that do not contribute actively and obviously to the organisation's goals – and which gain recognition for the library and information services – may contribute to the marginalisation.

As examples: I have seen much staff time in the library and information services of some voluntary sector organisations spent to produce catalogue records to AACR2 standards. Why, when the book collection is often much less important than the journals and online sources, and where much of the information is redundant for the internal retrieval purposes within the organisation? I have also seen enormous time spent filing ephemeral material that will never be needed again. Make decisions about such material, and encourage your staff to do so: resist, when appropriate, natural library and information services inclinations, and fill the bins (or, preferably, the recycling bags); establish some strict retention schedules, and stick to them. I have also seen beguiling new library software packages encourage library and information services staff to implement loans packages in full; do not start sending overdue notices to all users just because you have the technology. If the pattern is that staff keep books out on more or less permanent loan, then support this practice if it reflects user needs. Make sure your collections, and how you manage them, are relevant to the needs of users.

Managing space

It will be rare indeed for the library and information services to have ideal space – for staff, collections or IT facilities. All the more reason to be ruthless in disposing of redundant material. You will never have enough space; so you must decide what is the most important factor in determining what you will put in it. The critical factor is how it appears to the users, and how it suits their needs. The appearance of your information centre influences how the service is viewed, rightly or wrongly, by the users in the organisation. It needs to be welcoming, professional, accessible, clearly-signed. With a little creativity, you can make many improvements at little or no cost. This is another area where you can get user input: what is the impression that you are creating, and does it match the impression you want to convey?

Marketing and promoting the Library and information services

All Library and information services managers have to be good promoters of their services. Working in the voluntary sector, where you may not be expected (at least yet) to generate income from your services, you are not excepted from this. You are competing internally for space, for budgets and for a key role in the development of the organisation. As part of this, you are competing for political influence: a key factor in the voluntary sector.

Discussions of marketing and promotion of library and information services tend to focus on designing good publicity leaflets and carrying out surveys of what the users want. These are fine in themselves; they are necessary, and can be very motivating for the staff, as well as having a degree of effectiveness.

Your main tools for promotion and marketing, however, are your staff and yourself as the manager. Well-trained staff, who offer a proactive and high-quality service, are the best advertisement for any service operation. With library and information services staff, you are often starting from the very negative and stereotypical point; but the good aspect of this is that it does not take much to make a positive impression if expectations are low. Even basic training – how to welcome users in person and on the telephone, how to establish exactly what they want – all of these contribute to the impression that the library and information services has an important and professional role to play. Make sure your staff get involved in what is going on in the organisation: others will then perceive them as playing a broader role, and the experience and knowledge they bring back will help in designing and delivering services.

But perhaps the most important promotional tool you have is yourself; both in terms of the leadership and standard-setting you show your staff and also in the role you have as part of the wider management of the voluntary organisation. It is critical to be aware of the major challenges and priorities of the organisation, and to make sure your staff know these. It is also important to use the opportunities provided by management team meetings or other fora to present the library and information services, to share successes, and to demonstrate how the library and information services can add value to the work of all aspects of the organisation. Develop your political skills: and use them to ensure the library and information services has the resources and influence it needs to fulfil its potential.

Working with a Management Committee or Board

Especially in smaller voluntary sector organisations, you are very likely to have contact with the management committee, usually composed of voluntary members drawn from different professions, but with two things in common: a commitment to the aims of the organisation and a belief that they know what is best for the library. In fact, when it comes to library and information services generally, most people have a view. As ever, such interest presents both opportunities and threats. The Management Committee may be a key political group to influence if you want to secure resources and profile for the services; the threats arise from not anticipating and entering this arena. Take the opportunities presented: if your organisation sends a summary report to the Management Committee on a regular basis, make sure the library and information service is represented in the report, preferably by contributing yourself with brief details of main issues and successes. In addition, if the Management Committee is discussing information management issues, then make sure you – and other key library and information services staff – are there in person to make your views heard. Consider proactively putting issues on the agenda of the Management Committee if you have good reason; and identify a contact within the Management Committee who has personal interest in the library and information services, and can act as a champion when you are not able to be present.

Managing change in the Library and information services

Many voluntary sector organisations, especially those which were established in the 1960s and 1970s and have reached maturity, are now facing the reality of a changed world where they must adapt to survive and thrive. Issues such as competition, anathema though they may be to many voluntary sector staff, are part of this changed world. One manifestation of this, for instance, is that library and information services are increasingly expected to charge for services to non-core users, generating income for the organisation. Another is that service quality systems and standards, such as ISO 9000, need to be adopted and followed. There is nothing, in essence, wrong with this, but the cultural adaptation for the staff may be difficult and painful, since such change can seem in opposition to the core values or main aims.

As the manager of the library and information services, you must lead the change. The impetus for change may come from the overall leadership of the organisation, with a major reassessment of the mission. You must ensure that the library and information services' perspective (information management) is represented in the thinking and in the implementation of changes in its own field. Alternatively, change may come as a result of a change of emphasis and thinking from within the library and information services; when it will be a key role to sell the change to the users. A third scenario is that change is enforced, perhaps through decreased funding.

In all cases, it is critical to bring staff on board with all aspects of the change. Firstly, the rationale: why is change needed? If this stage is neglected, then denial and resistance to the change will remain longer and cause greater problems. As ever, within the voluntary sector, staff will expect and demand a greater say in the changes; and as long as consultation is accompanied by good and timely decision-making, then outcomes will be improved.

Assume that staff, in particular, will find the prospect and reality of change threatening and stressful. It will mean changes in working practices and tasks, in the way work is organised and the way services are delivered to users. Many staff will fear job losses; and there may be job losses. The process will be stressful for all. Make yourself available to staff; talk to individuals, and take time to explain. Expect rumours; voluntary sector organisations are rife with them, partly because there is greater openness and more management decision-making is transparent. The problem is that, though transparent, it may not be clear. Adopt a communication strategy which means that all your staff, paid or unpaid, professional or non-professional, unionised or not, understand the change: acceptance has much more chance to follow.

The users also need to be involved, and change needs to be promoted with them. It may come through technological change, desirable or otherwise, but unavoidable. Hardcopy information sources disappear; more is available on databases and the Internet. This may not suit the users; they need to be convinced. A key way is to ensure that there is monitoring and evaluation of change: this needs to be scheduled as part of the change timetable. Throughout the process of change, keep the aims and objectives in mind, and revisit them when necessary to maintain the momentum and ensure you are following the plan. And do not be afraid to adapt as the change develops.

Large-scale organisational change offers both opportunities and threats for the library and information services. The opportunity is presented to adapt the services to the new mission of the organisation, and to be a focal point for information about the changes (in one organisational restructuring that I lived through – barely – the information centre provided internal and external papers and articles about organisational change, as well as a bulletin board and 'big picture' wall for staff to express opinions and ideas). This is your chance to ensure the library and information service is in the optimal position in the organisational structure, where it can best provide its services and remain relevant to the needs of the organisation. The threat comes if you do not embrace and understand the change; lead the library and information services, and make sure its staff recognise the opportunities presented to them to move towards a more proactive, exciting and fulfilling role. Lastly, before embarking on large-scale change, take advice: remember that many have taken that path before you.

Profile of the information manager in the voluntary sector

I have provided a brief overview of the challenges and tasks facing a manager of library and information services in the voluntary sector. As well as the formidable task of understanding and applying new information management technologies and techniques in a rapidly-evolving profession, the voluntary sector manager has the unique culture and atmosphere of such organisations within which to operate effectively. Such a combination demands a broad range of management and professional skills, knowledge and experience; these I have summarised in the form of a person specification below.

If you are new to management in the voluntary sector, then welcome: you will have an interesting time. You will face many frustrations, and you will work long hours. At times, you may feel that your own professional standards as a library and information services professional are challenged. But, ultimately, if you embrace the culture and learn to understand it (though not always to accept it), then the rewards will be great.

Library and Information Services Manager in the Voluntary Sector: Person Specification

The following are essential:

- Excellent communication skills (speaking and writing)
- Commitment to open and participative management style
- Experience of working as part of a team
- Thorough knowledge of latest developments in library and information services
- Strong interpersonal skills
- Ability to promote and market the library and information services
- Leadership and representational skills
- Understanding of the organisational culture of the voluntary sector
- Ability to manage change
- Sound financial management skills
- Ability to think strategically and plan
- Commitment to broader involvement within the organisation
- Commitment to equal opportunities and cultural diversity

Reading about management

My own reading about management, at least since university, has focused very much on the practical. I have used books (where appropriate) as sources of ideas to try out, rather than as a step-by-step guide to management. In this respect, I have found, in particular, that the series of commendably short 'Better Management Skills' books by Kogan Page is excellent. In addition, the book by Wilson listed below is the best I have found on that crucial area – the management of change. Key articles in newspapers are very useful, especially those in *The Guardian* and *The Financial Times*.

My favourite management book remains, however, the description by Ricardo Semler of the approach he took to management in an industrial company in Brazil. Colleagues in the voluntary sector have, on occasion, queried this choice, but to me it has been a reminder that risk-taking, and challenging the prevailing and accepted cultural norms of voluntary organisations, can be of great benefit – and lots of fun!

Recommended further reading

1. Handy, C. *Understanding voluntary organisations*, London, Penguin, 1988
2. Semler, R. *Maverick!*, London, Arrow, 1994
3. Wilson, G. *Making change happen*, London, Pitman, 1993
4. Tylczak, L. *Effective employee participation*, London, Kogan Page, 1990
5. Davenport, J & Lipton, G (eds.). *Communication for managers: a practical handbook*, London, The Industrial Society, 1993
6. Maddux, R.B. *Team building*, London, Kogan Page, 1991
7. Corrall, S. *Strategic planning for library and information services*, London, Aslib, 1994.

8

The National Children's Bureau Library and Information Services: User Services

Nicola Hilliard

> 'I was most annoyed and disappointed to discover that several crucial books and pamphlets were not available ... As a member, I feel that I should be able to have access to all books and pamphlets stocked by the National Children's Bureau's library'.

So wrote an aggrieved Bureau individual member after a visit to our Library in which she failed to locate all the references she needed to complete her dissertation. Whilst this was a thankfully rare letter of complaint it was a perfect example of the key issues faced by most if not all information providers and users: the provider has to know what the user wants and provide it and the user, knowing what he or she wants, wants to access it. Simple – that is, until you take into consideration the constraints of a limited budget, the potentially limitless number and variety of user and the impossibility of any library stocking 'everything'. Add to this an organisation's culture, its aims and objectives and in the case of the National Children's Bureau its dependence on and commitment to its membership and it is anything but simple.

Within this context, clearly there is neither a typical user nor a typical library but within the voluntary sector there are various similarities, at least in terms of certain key issues. Not least of these are the need for every information service to prove its worth, either within or outside the organisation – often, as in our case, both – and to show evidence of value for money. And this last point is crucial – information services are not known for their income-generating capabilities although many do contribute in various ways to their running costs. However, they contribute in numerous ways to the successful operation of an organisation – and critically to the way an organisation is perceived by the outside world. And the outside world, to a librarian, is the user.

What I propose to do in this chapter is to describe the Library and Information Service at the National Children's Bureau within the context of the organisation's development, its aims and objectives, its place in the market and its wide membership base. From this I hope to clarify who our users are, what we offer them and how we try to satisfy their needs as well as the needs of the organisation – these not always being coterminous.

The National Children's Bureau

Established in 1963, the National Children's Bureau is now one of the best respected children's charities in the country. It was founded to meet the need for closer cooperation between the increasing numbers of statutory, voluntary and professional groups working for children. Today, building on that principle of cooperation, the Bureau has become a major force in the development of both policy and practice aimed at improving the lives of children and young people. It achieves this by working in partnership with others, and encouraging participation between all agencies, across all disciplines. Its specialist knowledge on issues from early years to adolescent mental health, and from residential care to special educational needs, has contributed to key public debates affecting children, while its services for members – including the Library, probably the most extensive information resource on children's issues in the country – benefit thousands of professionals and practitioners every year.

The stated aim of the National Children's Bureau is to identify and promote the interests of all children and young people, and to increase their status in a diverse society. What makes the charity unique is that it looks at children's needs as a whole, across the full spectrum of services, including education, health and social services, rather than viewing each discipline in isolation.

Over the past thirty years, the Bureau has played an important part in advising policy makers at national and local level. It has helped many local authorities improve their services for children, as well as sharing knowledge and expertise on an international scale. In one year, the Bureau provided consultancy services in Hungary, South Korea and Romania.

An active research programme is central to the Bureau's work. The charity's first major project was the National Child Development Study, which provided a mine of valuable information, following the lives of a cohort of 17,000 children born in March 1958. Since then, the Bureau has published landmark reports on subjects such as planning for children in public care, social services for children from different ethnic groups, and linking school and home to support children and families.

The Bureau also has an active Policy Unit which works to promote informed debate on key issues relating to children and their rights. This Unit services the All Party Parliamentary Group for Children.

The Bureau is active, too, in seeking to improve practice amongst those working with children and young people. Our Practice Development Department aims to support professionals in identifying and learning from models of good practice in education, health and social services. As well as working in the field of child protection and family support, it also houses the Children's Residential Care Unit which aims to improve the lives of young people looked after by local authorities. This Unit is currently working with staff and young people in residential establishments to develop effective strategies for managing challenging behaviour and on national standards for the induction and training of secure accommodation staff. Another Unit within this department is the Organisation and Development of Services for Children Unit which supports authorities in creating child-centred services. Departmental staff are located both centrally and in regional locations ranging from Cumbria to Surrey, Essex to Berkshire.

Addressing the needs of very young children is another area of vital importance. The Bureau's Early Childhood Unit is a leading national centre for consultancy, training and information in the field of early childhood care and education. Its current work includes a project on the learning needs of very young children in early childhood centres across the country.

The Early Childhood Unit was instrumental in the setting up of The Parenting Education and Support Forum, a national forum open to organisations and individuals, which promotes parent education at local and national levels. The National Children's Bureau also has links with a number of Councils or Fora, which are based at the Bureau and come within its charitable status. These include the Council for Disabled Children, the Children's Play Council, the Sex Education Forum, the Forum on Children and Violence and the Drug Education Forum. In addition to these, the Inner and North London Panel of Guardians ad Litem and Reporting Officers is based at the Bureau. This is an organisation which provides independent social workers to represent children's interests in specified court proceedings. We also work in partnership with our sister charities, Children in Scotland and Children in Wales – a relationship which gives all three organisations the knowledge and resources to address children's issues across Britain.

Having built its reputation on the quality of its knowledge, the Bureau has increasingly become known for its expertise in disseminating that knowledge. For many professionals, their first contact with the Bureau may be through attending one of our conferences held across the country, or through buying a publication from a growing catalogue of books, reports and training materials. Recent conference topics have covered school exclusions, secure accommodation, inter-agency co-ordination and drug education. Similarly, our publications are wide ranging and have included child development, special educational needs and children and technology.

Membership of the Bureau is open to local and health authorities, health trusts, companies, independent and voluntary organisations, day care centres, schools, colleges and universities and individuals. It offers a unique opportunity to tap into a vast resource of information and expertise and a valuable forum in which to share experience and contribute to the shaping of future policy. There are a range of benefits available to members including regular mailings of information, a quarterly magazine, *Children UK*, factsheets and policy briefings, discounts on our publications and conferences and last, but by no means least, access to the Library and Information Service.

The Library and Information Service

The Library came into existence soon after the Bureau was founded and was initially staffed by one full-time and one part-time member of staff. Since then the staffing numbers have increased to five: three qualified information staff, an administrator and a part-time information assistant. We also have an additional part-time information officer funded by the Department of Health to manage and develop a resource on solvent misuse.

This is a relatively healthy increase in staff numbers but nothing compared to the enormous increase in the range and depth of the Bureau staff's professional expertise, the organisation's work programme and its diverse membership. From an initial staffing complement of about 20 staff back in 1963, the Bureau now employs over 100 people.

The Library and Information Service houses a reference library containing over 30,000 publications and approximately 300 British and international journal titles. The subject coverage reflects the full range of the Bureau's work as outlined above. This includes child protection, child and adolescent health, children's rights, disability and special needs, drug education, children in care, personal and social education, and young offenders.

Complementing the main Library Service are several information centres, located in the Early Childhood Unit, the Council for Disabled Children, and the Practice Development Department. Each of these has an information officer and the Bureau employs a total of 10 staff with a specific information remit. These separate collections are all electronically linked together so whilst they are physically separate their resources are all accessible via our computerised network. This is critical, not only to avoid duplication, but most importantly to ensure that users have immediate access to the Bureau's entire information base. These collections also provide specialist knowledge in key areas and provide valuable back up and support to the main library. They are a key resource for Bureau staff and members and the Early Childhood Unit's library, in particular, has become a highly regarded national collection attracting a wide specialist user group.

Our place in the market

It is as a unique national resource that the Bureau's Library and Information Service promotes itself, for whilst it is not the only child care library in the United Kingdom it probably has the most comprehensive collection and the widest usership, both actual and potential.

There are, of course, other national collections in the child care field, most notably the National Society for the Prevention of Cruelty to Children and Barnardos. NCH Action for Children and The Children's Society also have libraries and the Department of Health library has its own collection of child care resources. So what supports the Bureau Library's claim for uniqueness? Whilst in no way undermining the impressive collections of Barnardos and the NSPCC, these two charities both have a very large staffing complement based throughout the country and it is their staff who are necessarily their key target users. Their information services are therefore directed at meeting the diverse needs of their own staff to whom they lend books, provide back up and current awareness services and so on. Similarly, the Children's Society services the organisation's internal information needs and NCH Action for Children's library is crucial to their national training programme as well as supporting their staff. The Bureau's Library, however, makes it services available not only to our staff but to all our members, both national and, increasingly, international.

If the Bureau, the NSPCC and Barnardos all have similar collections why don't they pool their resources? This is an oft repeated question, usually from those with budgets to control, and of course quite valid. We do stock many similar titles and whilst the NSPCC's library is focused specifically on child protection and abuse it necessarily has a wider remit and we will have broadly similar collections to each other and to Barnardos. But the crucial difference is what we do with our collections and who they are for. Yes, we all might have a copy of a key government publication but how many people want to access it? We all lend books to our staff but our staff tend to be London based and there are no more than 30 to 40 active borrowers. NSPCC and Barnardos have many more staff who are based all over the country. So, clearly one copy of a book between the three of us is not viable. How one manages to stem the flow of requests for a new or particularly key text is an internal issue faced by us all and one that at the Bureau we try to overcome by making our collection for reference only. So whilst we do lend to staff, in the Bureau this is a manageable number and items can easily and quickly be retrieved. All users want their information immediately and prioritising demand is a constant headache. Maintaining the collection as reference at least ensures the collection is intact and, in theory, available to any and everyone.

The other major child care charities will have their own strategies for coping with the demands of their major users – their staff. At the Bureau, we are constantly looking at ways of not only serving our users but attracting more users, that is more members. Not an enviable position for an information resource with limited budgets and staffing levels. But this is what really makes the Bureau's Library and Information Service unique – yes, we count the organisation's staff amongst our key users but over and above that we have our members.

Bureau Membership

Membership of the National Children's Bureau is open both to organisations and to individuals – from local authorities, health bodies and independent and voluntary organisations, to day care centres, schools and colleges. Currently our membership includes 99 local authorities, 18 professional organisations, 190 voluntary organisations, 153 primary and secondary schools, 165 nurseries, 205 university departments, colleges and libraries, 47 health authorities, trusts and community health councils and over 700 individuals. The Bureau's aim is to support its members in their day-to-day task of meeting the needs of children and young people, as well as providing them with the opportunity to play an active part in shaping policies and practice.

Benefits of membership include quarterly mailings of information; factsheets on a wide range of subjects from foster care services to home-school support work, and from suicidal behaviour in children and young people to the role of guardians ad litem ; copies of *Children UK*, the Bureau's quarterly magazine; policy briefing papers on key issues examining such topics as Children's Services Plans and The Family Law Act 1996; and, as mentioned earlier, discounts on Bureau publications, conferences and seminars, as well as access to our Library and Information Service.

Increasingly, members are looking for value for money. Long gone are the days when local authorities would join the Bureau out of altruism – that is, the desire to support a good cause. They need to have a return on their investment, particularly since the purchaser/provider split has made their grant budgets particularly vulnerable to erosion. We have to offer them something they cannot get elsewhere and provide a service that supports their own aims and objectives.

In truth, we have to try to ensure that they need us as much as we need them. Whilst we joke that a library would be perfect if only we could keep the users out – no mis-shelved items, no lost books, no phone calls to interrupt us – in reality an information service is only as good as its users find it.

Who are our users? Who aren't our users?

This symbiotic relationship has to be tested of course. A common dilemma is how to attract the users you want and deter those you don't. The Bureau's audience is primarily professionals and practitioners and this has necessarily to be reflected in the services we offer. It is perhaps ironic that an organisation whose tag line is 'The powerful voice for the child' does not encourage children to use its library. But children are not our users – we work with the people who work with and/or for children. There are public libraries and school libraries and later college libraries to meet the needs of this important group. Equally, we do not actively promote our services to students even though much of our collection would be useful to them. Why so mean? Well, any student can use us if they are a member or if they are prepared to pay a daily visitors' rate. But they do, in theory, have information resources within their own institutions. The fact that these are often woefully inadequate cannot be our responsibility. We just do not have the staff or the resources to support a vast student population; nor do we feel it is justified to compensate for a cash strapped education service. We would, however, support those people working for a local education authority in membership – teachers, educational psychologists, early years workers and so on.

The dilemma for us is that we have so many users. The Library receives on average 800 - 1000 written and telephone enquiries a month. Not all of these are from members, because whilst we are a membership organisation all our services are open to non members; but we charge more to non-members and hopefully encourage them to join.

As has been described in some detail above, our users come from a wide range of disciplines and occupations and can include a social worker in a child protection unit, a health visitor, a college lecturer, a parent of a child with special needs, the manager of a residential home or a youth worker. Some ring for information that they know we'll have; others don't always know exactly what they want; still others preface their enquiry 'I wonder if you can help me?'. Whatever their approach, and whatever their level of need we aim to respond to their enquiry efficiently and professionally. If we cannot help we make sure we direct them to someone who can – it is such bad practice to offload a user onto another source which is ill equipped to help. Again, the public relations function of an information service cannot be over estimated. If you're going to be unhelpful at least be so in a helpful manner!

Of course we do also have another and very important audience – that is, our staff and again it is essential to offer a high level of service which supports them in their work. They too have differing needs and as has been described above Bureau personnel come from a wide range of disciplines and have equally varied remits, ranging from policy work to research, consultancy and training. We support the press office in its work with the media and work closely with our membership department. We provide all staff with a weekly current awareness service and since the organisation employs a relatively small staff we are able to provide an individual service. We know what their work interests are and can target them with items from the media and the professional press that we know will be of interest to them. It is very important to offer them a proactive service – again, we have to make ourselves as indispensable to them as to our members. As indeed they are indispensable to us – not only for the insight they give us into current professional and practice issues but also for their networks and outside contacts and their potential for 'selling' us to new users and potential members.

Services to Users

It is no longer viable to offer a reactive service. Whilst some of us might secretly hanker for the days of quiet study in dusky libraries, heaped with leather bound books and armchairs, these days are long gone although I believe such libraries thankfully still do exist. No, any library now has to sell itself in whatever market place it occupies. It is not enough to collect, catalogue and classify. Dissemination is vital – information has to be actively marketed. We cannot sit back and wait for the customer. Of course, the traditional services of lending books and providing reference and browsing facilities are important but today's users are more demanding – they want their information packaged and processed. However, to continue the supermarket analogy, they do not want unnecessary packaging nor should they be denied the opportunity to choose the way in which they want to digest their information. There are now so many different ways to present and publish information and users need to be given choices. Electronic publishing is dealt with in more detail elsewhere in this book and there is no doubt that it has provided a wealth of opportunities for information providers.

Dissemination of information is one of the key aims of the National Children's Bureau. Outside of the Library this is done via our extensive publications and conference programmes. In the library we are constantly looking at new ways of developing our services to users. To date this has involved the compilation of various printed publications and information digests.

Our most popular publication is a series called 'Highlights'. These are comprehensive summaries of key research findings on a wide range of topics with extensive bibliographies, or summaries of influential reports and legislation. Recent titles have included *School Effectiveness, Parental Psychiatric Disorder and Child Maltreatment, Health Promotion and the Family, School Food, Drug Education in Schools,* and *The Children (Northern Ireland) Order 1995.* All new titles are automatically sent free to Bureau members in our quarterly mailouts. Non-members are charged and there are differential rates for members and non-members for a complete set of titles.

Like many other libraries, we produce a series of reading lists on key areas of child welfare including 'Foster Care', 'Parenthood Education', 'Young Offenders', 'After Care' and 'Children's Mental Health'. These lists contain references to book and journal literature and again, members can purchase these at a reduced rate. We also produce listings of organisations which contain essential contact information about professional organisations operating in particular fields, including 'Child Health', 'Children from Minority Ethnic Groups', 'Play', and 'Family Breakdown'.

We also offer subscriptions to various information services. These include 'Conferences', which is a monthly listing of over 200 forthcoming conferences and major events in the child care field. These are events for all professionals and practitioners in health, education and social work and cover events taking place both in the United Kingdom and internationally during the next 12-24 months. Details include venue and contact numbers.

Two further subscription packages are *ChildStats* and *ChildData Abstracts*. *ChildStats* is a compilation of all statistical information on children and young people appearing in a variety of official and non official publications. These statistics have become increasingly difficult to collate, not least due to the fact that the government often discontinues a particular series or combines figures previously published separately. We also collect statistics that are published in *Hansard* and which are often unavailable elsewhere. *ChildStats* is published quarterly. *ChildData Abstracts* is a monthly publication and is an annotated listing of all new books, pamphlets, reports and journal articles which we have added to the library's database each month. Over 300 records are included per issue and they are arranged into broad subject headings. These two publications are offered either individually or at a combined, and cheaper, subscription rate – again with reductions for members.

Two years ago we launched *Children in the News*. This is a weekly abstracting service covering the key stories and major events relating to children, as reported in the national daily press. Press articles are collated on issues such as the family, education, legislation, truancy and school exclusions, young offenders, sexuality, and disability issues. Every morning, the papers are scanned and the most newsworthy and relevant items are collected and written up into a digest of social commentary, editorial opinion and reported event. Feature articles and law reports are also included. Each abstract is referenced to the original cutting and full newspaper contact details are provided. This service can either be posted or faxed to subscribers on a weekly basis and is delivered every week of the year, excluding Christmas.

A much longer running service is *Children & Parliament*. This is based on *Hansard* and published whist Parliament is sitting. It is the only information service exclusively devoted to covering all United Kingdom parliamentary business affecting children and young people. Coverage includes Questions, Debates on bills and motions, Petitions, Regulations and European Union directives. *Hansard* is scanned on a daily basis and all the issues affecting children are abstracted and arranged under broad subject headings giving full details of speaker, which House, column numbers and so on. *Children & Parliament* is available on subscription and, up until this summer, has been sent out to subscribers on a fortnightly basis either by post or fax. But like all publications the cost of production – printing, postage and so on – threatened to make it an unviable venture. We were having to charge an amount which whilst not exorbitant given the work involved was enough to deter some potential subscribers.

This provides us with a classic dilemma – how to offer a service for which there is a demand but for which there is also a high cost, not least in staff time? Since scanning *Hansard* is something that information staff would be doing anyway to inform their own and their Bureau colleagues' work and since the cost of *Hansard* is beyond the budgets of many organisations we felt we really ought to continue to produce this service but at a lower cost. We have been able to do this by putting *Children & Parliament* on the Internet and offering it to subscribers at almost half the original rate. Before we took this step we sent out a questionnaire to all current subscribers asking if they would welcome such a move and also offering to fax the publication to those not having access to the Web. We were gratified by the response and subscribers are renewing at a healthy rate.

What is more, by launching ourselves on the Web we have every hope of attracting more subscribers and hopefully future members and users of the Bureau and its other services.

We would hope in the future to offer more library services via the Internet and to make full use of the Bureau's recently launched Web site. We already publish our information in another electronic form; that is, CD-ROM. Four years ago we launched *ChildData* CD-ROM which contains five of the Library's databases – our catalogue database which contains indexed records of all the books, reports and journal articles that we have added to the collection since 1989; our organisations database, which is probably the most comprehensive directory of its kind with details of over 5,000 United Kingdom and international organisations in the child care and related fields; Children in the News, Children & Parliament and the Conferences listing are also included.

ChildData is published quarterly and once again we are able to offer Bureau members a substantial discount. This is very much the public face of the Library and Information Service and is an important source of income for us. As indeed are all our publications referred to above. It has been really important to show that the Library can generate income from the work that it is already doing and also that it can take on board new developments in this fast moving information age. We have to if we want to survive in a market where many of our users are far more computer literate than they were even five years ago. They are not going to have much confidence in an information service that does not take advantage of new technology.

As well as producing publications, we also offer our users an enquiry service. This is open to all via a dedicated enquiry line. We introduced this some years ago, primarily as a way of ensuring that library staff had some time in the day when they were free from interruptions. To this end, the line is open from 10.00 until 12.00 and from 2.00 until 4.00 from Monday to Friday. Apart from the odd disgruntled caller, we have not found that this has inconvenienced users and in fact I would argue that they now receive a better service from staff who are not overwhelmed by too many conflicting demands on their time. We always ask callers their membership status and explain to non-members that they will be charged more for our services. This also enhances the status of those callers who are members who are made to feel that their membership is being actively recognised. Visitors to the Library often join on a first visit; ideally if they are from an organisation not in membership they will encourage it to join.

The number of enquiries we receive each year has remained constant for several years now; charging for information has deterred some users and the enquiry line probably loses us a few unlucky callers who ring out of hours. We like to think that they would come back if they couldn't find the information elsewhere; similarly we hope that the majority of our users use us because they cannot get the information anywhere else.

Charging for information

Charging has become a key issue in recent years. Information is no longer, if indeed it ever was, entirely free. The Library has to be seen to be offering the Bureau's members a special service, something that makes being a member worthwhile. For example, members may visit the Library as often as they like for free; non-members are charged a small fee. Members are charged a nominal amount for computer searches, library subscription services and so on; non-members pay more. Members receive some Library publications for free and they get a discount on our CD-ROM.

All our Library publications are available on subscription. The debate about charging for information is a perennial one but today it is really very hard to justify the provision of a free service in an organisation constantly looking to make savings. Within the last year it is also becoming the norm to make charges for services within an organisation, so desperate are departments and cost centres to be seen to be covering their costs and providing a competitive service. For example, the library at the BBC charges the corporation's own staff and consequently many of their journalists are coming to us.

At the Bureau, certain core services have always been costed into the funding of new projects. The Library is one such service and until now the exact amount charged for its use has been subsumed under general overheads. This looks set to change in the next twelve months.

Until that happens, however, we continue to provide staff with all our services and publications for free. The only additional charge we do make is sometimes at the beginning of a new research project when the staff member makes an unusually high demand on our inter library loans service. Other than that, computer searches (no, not every staff member has succumbed to the benefits of being self sufficient in the use of our databases), printed accessions lists, *Children & Parliament* and all our printed information publications are provided free. However, to save money on printing costs and paper we now distribute many of these items electronically.

To our members and non-members we charge differential subscription rates. Again, this offers members a direct benefit. These different rates also apply to searches done on the database. There are some enquiries from members that we do not charge for when it seems politic not to do so. For example, we would not always make a charge for a relatively quick and simple search for an employee of a large local authority which already pays a considerable sum in membership. There is always a fine balance to be made when charging – it can often make good political and public relations sense to be seen to be giving extra value for money.

The Library now makes a not inconsiderable contribution towards its running costs and whilst I cannot see us ever becoming self financing it goes some way towards justifying our existence. Furthermore, if we can increase our subscription figures for our publications then we are guaranteeing more users and hopefully more members.

Evaluating services to users

So our users are made up of both members and non-members from all disciplines and professions. How do we know if we are offering them what they want and are their demands realistic? Are they in fact the users we want – or deserve? In a culture dominated by the purchaser/provider split it has become increasingly important to evaluate one's services with a view to ensuring cost effectiveness and the appropriate channelling of resources. Libraries have suffered greatly in recent years and the effects of expenditure cuts on public libraries are visible to all. As referred to above, academic libraries are also continually under threat and many students are suffering as a result. The voluntary sector is also no stranger to reduced resourcing and it is frequently the information service within a small, or even large, voluntary organisation that is the first to come under scrutiny. This is not to imply that libraries should not be evaluated; of course they have to be seen to give value. But it is not always easy to prove this – particularly since libraries are not renowned for making vast profits! Indeed, they are often regarded as a drain on resources – so many books to buy, so many over-priced journal titles to collect. Does anybody read them? Would they miss them if they weren't there? Couldn't we rely on the Internet – everything's up there isn't it?

How do you justify the expense? How can you atone for your profligate ways? Quite simply, you have to prove your worth; make your information service indispensable; ideally, make some income. Justifying the existence of an information service is not the remit of this chapter but I would argue that users are, in our case at least, a key justification for our continuation. As I have said, our users are primarily our members and the Library has to prove that it is a crucial element of the membership package. At its most basic, no library no users – and, we have to demonstrate, this would imply no, or fewer, members. However, we have to be able to justify this. Whether an information service is for members or staff or a specific user group, the issues are the same. How to prove that your service is indispensable – not only to its users but to the organisation?

It is really not enough to quote statistics of enquiries received, income generated, economies made and so on. Letters of thanks and generous praise, whilst encouraging, are not enough to convince a belt-tightening management board. At the Bureau, we are in the process of conducting a user survey – that is, users of the Library and Information Service – as a part of an overall review within the organisation. The aims of the survey are to give us a clearer idea of who our users are and to provide us with information to make sure that the information service is of the highest possible standard. We are sending out a questionnaire to a random sample of our members, to users who are not members and to Bureau staff. We are asking them to describe their professional status, which sector they work or study in, whether or not they are a Bureau member and if they have used the Library and Information Service. If they are a user, then we want to know what services they have accessed, which Library publications they subscribe to and whether or not they receive an appropriate, accurate and efficient response to their needs. Last, but by no means least, we are asking those in membership how important access to the Library was in their decision to join the National Children's Bureau. We live in hope that this last question receives the correct answer!

9

Developing New Products and Services, including Electronic Publishing

Mark Watson

Introduction – the need to develop new products and services

What role is there for the library, if any, in the new millennium? Are libraries, with their shelves of books and magazines and reference books, to be replaced with a global information superhighway offering access to a wealth of online computerised resources – a Virtual Library?

The future could be one that will be dominated by media mega-corporations led by the likes of Bill Gates and Rupert Murdoch, with PCs/webTVs permanently linked to the Internet with 'push technologies' and Java, 'search engines' and 'intelligent agents' continuously supplying personalised information to the desktop, enabling a direct relationship between the publisher/information provider and the end-user. In this scenario is there a need for assistance from 'intermediaries' such as librarians – for whom the threat of 'disintermediation' is being seen in some quarters as a serious one?

Libraries and librarians could appear to be an anachronism in the new Millennium when voluntary organisations can replace costly libraries with a modem and a £10 a month subscription to the Internet providing access to a global knowledge base.

Against this background, those voluntary organisations which still have library and information services (and there have been a number of notable closures and retrenchments in recent years) may be reviewing the provision of library and information services. Here are a few reasons why investment in those services and staff, and the development of new services may be worthwhile:

Information and Communication Technologies

Information Technology is becoming increasingly pervasive in our society. A majority of personal banking transactions which take place in banks are between customers and computers. The 'hole in the wall' cashpoint has become a terminal inside the bank, offering not only cash, but balance checks, statements, and other facilities. Some banks are taking a lead in allowing their customers to dial-in from their home PC to manage their own accounts.

Schools and colleges are investing heavily, with central government support, in Information Technology (it can be argued that this is being done at the expense of other resources – such as books and teachers/lecturers). Satellite and cable television, the World Wide Web, teletext services, and telephone information services are creating a society in which individuals are becoming used to getting the information that they want when they want it and via a screen.

The provision of 'traditional' library services has been based around visitors to the library and to members of staff on site:

- book loans;
- photocopying of journal articles in the library;
- reference services;
- current awareness services: abstracts of 'recent acquisitions' circulated to staff;
- newspaper clippings or journals circulated amongst staff;
- subject bibliographies and literature searches.

However, many libraries and information services are now concentrating less on providing material in the library itself (the 'just-in-case' model) to providing electronic resources such as CD-ROMs and access to the Internet (the 'just-in-time' model).

Over the past few years the development of high-speed telecommunications have brought about a new term: Information and Communication Technologies. These have revolutionised the potential for developing new library services and products:

- public access to library catalogues;
- electronic Table of Contents Services;
- CD-ROM and floppy-disk databases;
- World Wide Web sites and databases.

Such services and resources need not be restricted to the academic and commercial sector libraries – the voluntary sector can also exploit the opportunities that Information and Communication Technologies offer.

Profile

In the commercial sector most major companies have some kind of presence on the Internet. The voluntary sector is some way off this, but the World Wide Web in particular offers an opportunity to reach large numbers of people, on a local, national or international level, at relatively low cost.

Whilst the majority of the focus on the Internet is around the World Wide Web, email offers the voluntary sector the opportunity to exploit a key resource of the sector – the knowledge that staff and volunteers possess. [1]

Income generation

One aspect of the developing Information Society is the raised awareness of the need for information to support planning and decision making. Individuals and organisations are increasingly putting a premium on obtaining access to information, and are willing to pay for that access.

In the commercial sector, 'information' is big business, with many libraries and information services, and information brokers, making substantial income through supplying business-critical information about markets, competitors and trends.

The culture in the voluntary sector is somewhat different, with a belief that information should be free. There has been a marked reluctance to charge for library and information services, partly due to a feeling that charging for information is in some way in conflict with the values of the sector.

There have been changes in recent years, with a number of the larger social welfare libraries finding themselves deluged with requests for information. Some have taken steps to restrict access to non-members, and to charge for access. There appears to be an increasing problem caused by students approaching specialist libraries to access material which their university or college library can not supply.

The potential to generate income from library and information services should not be overlooked or underestimated. In an increasingly competitive marketplace, with large numbers of voluntary organisations vying for services, grants and other sources of funding, access to information about such resources can be crucial.

Aurelian Information Ltd, in addition to their range of books on the Internet, have developed 'Charities On-Line Express for Libraries' an online database listing thousands of charities and details of their charitable giving. The database is marketed as offering access to vital information, and a premium is accorded to that information: an annual subscription in the region of £200.

Examples given later in this chapter show how voluntary sector libraries can develop services and products which are greatly increasing the exploitation of the resources that the library holds.

Managing Information Overload and Exploiting the Corporate Wisdom

In 1995 Reuters published a report entitled 'Dying for Information'[2], which coined the term 'Information Overload Syndrome'. The report found that senior managers in the commercial sector were overloaded with information and suffering serious stress leading to ill-health and premature mortality in trying to make sense of that information.

Information and Communication Technologies having greatly increased the volume of information that is readily accessible – extracting and exploiting the most useful information is becoming more problematic.

The commercial sector, having embraced data processing in the 1970s, and Information Management in the 1980s, is now investing in 'Knowledge Management'. Corporate intranets are the latest technological craze and are seen as having a key role to play in exploiting the organisational knowledge base – what is being termed 'corporate wisdom', a frequently under-utilised resource. Such systems turn information into corporate intelligence for commercial advantage.

The culture of the voluntary sector may be somewhat different, but the approaches which commercial organisations are taking in order to achieve a market lead over competitors are no less important for the voluntary sector – who equally need to ensure that their services are meeting the needs of their users. The commercial sector is driven to manage and exploit information to ensure that products or services continue to meet the needs of the market place – products or services which do not will be swiftly in decline.

In the voluntary sector there is less of an imperative – service users tend to have fewer, if any, alternatives than consumers. This makes it *all the more important* that voluntary organisations manage their information needs properly to ensure that all their staff have access to the information they need to support their practice.

The 'information market' in many sectors is a well-developed, commercial one. Information is seen as a commodity, and information about the market, products, competitors and customers is seen as corporate intelligence. Librarians and Information Managers in the commercial sector will have key roles supporting staff throughout the organisation. Subscriptions to multiple databases and online hosts in order to obtain the right information at the right time are seen as a pre-requisite. Commercial organisations will see the maintenance of a comprehensively stocked and professionally staffed library and information service as a key element to their continued commercial success. Information supports research and development leading to new products and services, and feedback from customers into the product development cycle.

The latest issue of Gale's Directory of Databases[3] lists 5,900 online databases and 5,500 CD-ROM databases – the majority of which are only available commercially. Information and databases are big business in the commercial sector.

The situation in the voluntary sector is somewhat different. The library and information service is often seen as a luxury, and when financial cutbacks have to be made, it is the library and information service that is often the first to feel the pinch.

Information Needs not Information Technology

The need to address information needs in the voluntary sector was addressed succinctly some years ago in a CVS/NCVO publication 'Information Training for local intermediary bodies'[4]. The paper describes running a series of three pilot 'Information Training Days' which were aimed at providing information handling training for people working in the voluntary sector. These events took place in the pre-computer days of the voluntary sector, and are still worth looking at again at a time when more attention is paid to the likes of the amount of RAM needed to run software, client-server architecture and Java-applets, than the needs of the people using the software.

The publication outlined an 'information cycle' which underpinned the training days:

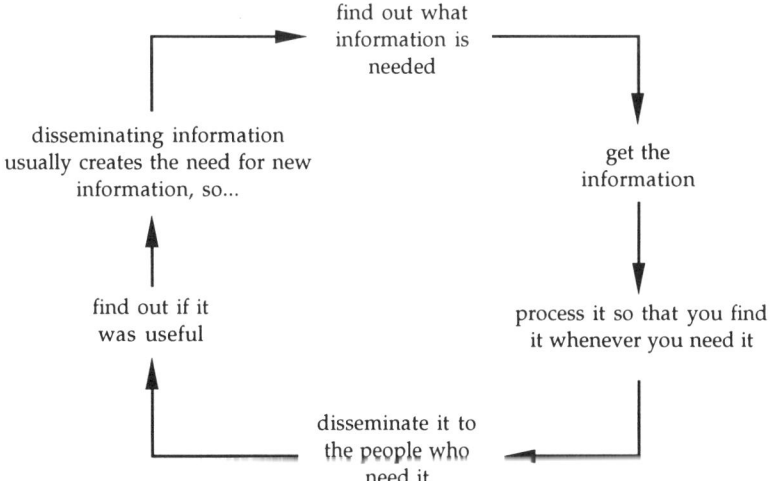

The need for services to be based upon assessed needs is crucial whether those services are social care services or library/information services. Too often the focus has been on the technology element of Information Technology rather than the information element.

This issue has been covered in depth in *Press enter: information technology in the community and voluntary sector*.[5] It remains a particularly useful guide to the processes which voluntary organisations should undertake when considering the use of information within their organisation:

Define mission objectives
What is the organisation 'about'?
↓
List and prioritise the kind of information required to fulfil objectives
↓
Specify the information channels – procedures and specifications for databases, memos, bulletins, circulation lists etc.
↓
Define the management responsibilities for the information and its channels
↓
Identify IT, training, support

The need to go through a process such as this which terminates with the analysis of Information Technology needs is also a key theme of the Type Help book *Formulating an information technology strategy starter pack*.[6] Too often the process starts with Information Technology and results in inappropriate systems being developed.

Exploiting the new breed of Librarians/Cybrarians

For many the stereotypical librarian, quiet, unassuming, and happily working away behind the scenes, would not appear to have a place in the high-tech world of globally networked resources. Librarians may have been guilty of doing their job just a little too well:

> It may be, however, that librarians have performed so effectively that they have made themselves invisible. Many professions – such as medicine or the law – make themselves appear indispensable by creating a mystique. A layperson cannot hope to attain the same level of knowledge as a member of that profession. By contrast, librarians appear to perform their jobs so well and unobtrusively that members of the public are often unaware that anything has been done at all. Books appear on the shelves by their own volition, catalogues are created automatically and exhibitions organise themselves. The librarian seeks to remove difficulties from the path of library users even before they

become aware of them, and is so self-effacing that they appear unconcerned as to whether its existence is acknowledged at all.

D.P. Wallace and C. Van Fleet, 'The invisible librarian', *RQ* 34(1) Fall 1994, pp.6-9.

The profession of librarianship has to a greater extent than many professions embraced Information Technology with open arms. Information Technology has removed a lot of routine manual systems, and enabled much more to be done with the information that is collected. And the stereotypical librarian is less appropriate then ever –

- In the health sector the move to 'evidence-based medicine' and the need for skilled librarians who can facilitate access to the expanding medical knowledge-base has led to projects such as the 'Librarians of the 21st Century Programme' at the Oxford and Anglia Health Authority (http://www.lib.jr2.ox.ac.uk/lldp.html). Librarians continue to have a key role in the dissemination of information in the health sector.
- In the United States of America a consortium of universities saw the need for their librarians to develop a new range of skills, and embarked on a training programme entitled 'How to Build a Digital Librarian' (http://www.dlib.org/dlib/november96/ucb/11hastings.html), which provided training in the increasing range of skills required to operate effectively on the Internet.
- In the United Kingdom academic sector, the Electronic Libraries Programme (http://www.ukoln.ac.uk/services/eLib) has invested over £15 million in a range of projects aimed at developing 'digital libraries'. In addition to projects which looked at making information resources available through the Internet, the NetSkills (http://www.netskills.ac.uk) project has developed a range of web-based tutorials, and delivered training courses and other materials aimed at assisting the HE community to make effective use of the Internet for teaching, research and administration. The EduLib project (http://www.hull.ac.uk/edulib) has done similar work to enhance the educational expertise and teaching skills in the higher education library and information services community.
- The Special Library Association in the United States of America has put together a series of competencies which their members feel are necessary for the future. The extract below outlines a range of competencies which most voluntary organisations could well benefit from:
    - 1.1   has expert knowledge of the content of information resources, including the ability to critically evaluate and filter them;

1.2 has specialised subject knowledge appropriate to the business of the organisation or client;

1.3 develops and manages convenient, accessible and cost-effective information services that are aligned with the strategic directions of the organisation;

1.4 provides excellent instruction and support for library and information service users;

1.5 assesses information needs and designs and markets value-added information services and products to meet identified needs;

1.6 uses appropriate information technology to acquire, organise and disseminate information;

1.7 uses appropriate business and management approaches to communicate the importance of information services to senior management;

1.8 develops specialised information products for use inside or outside the organisation or by individual clients;

1.9 evaluates the outcomes of information use and conducts research related to the solution of information and management problems;

1.10 continually improves information services in response to changing needs;

1.11 is an effective member of the senior management team and a consultant to the organisation in information issues.

(Competencies for Special Librarians of the 21st Century, Special Libraries Association, 1996. Web version at http://www.sla.org/professional/comp.html)

You will find that librarians will be found lurking behind a range of new and exotic job titles: Information Scientists, Information Managers, Cybrarians, Knowledge Engineers, and even (quite bizarrely) Knowledge Choreographers. Whatever their title, librarians have a range of skills and an aptitude for handling information that can be a major benefit to voluntary organisations.

Informing the development of new products and services

Against this background, there appears to be a wealth of opportunities open to the enthusiastic voluntary sector librarian who has senior management support, to develop a pro-active range of library and information services throughout the organisation.

Whilst the focus of this chapter is on developing new services, experiences from current services and the potential of those services to be further exploited should not be overlooked. The development of new services and products will inherently be more time-consuming and have a greater element of risk than building on existing services and users. Questions to be asked include:

- how successful are existing services in meeting the needs of existing users?
- how can existing services be marketed to new users?
- how can existing services have value added to them for the benefit of existing users and for new users?

Information Audits

The use of processes such as Information Audits is increasingly recommended as part of the Information Management task. The term audit is used to indicate that the process is similar to financial audits: finding out what information resources exist, their value, and who is responsible for managing and exploiting them.

One example is given elsewhere in this volume of an information audit in action. The information audit should be seen as a mapping process which brings together information about who the users are, what information they have access to (both from the library and from other sources), what their information needs are, and how the provision of information services can support those needs.

Peter Gillman[7] has outlined the use of information audits to identify about user needs, and he goes into some detail the rather thorny task of separating user needs and user wants.

Librarians are experienced in dealing with library users who will approach an enquiry desk or make a telephone enquiry with a very broad request relating to what they want – part of the librarian's (often unnoticed) skill is in helping the user to describe more fully what it is they really need. The user may state that they 'want' a copy of *Whittaker's Almanac*. This, after discussion, may be resolved into a need for a specific piece of information which the librarian can satisfy more quickly from some other resource in the library.

Similar problems can arise with an information audit, where there can be a reticence amongst users to state clearly what they need, and a temptation for the librarian to modify the expressed needs of users (rather than their real needs) with their perception of the needs of the users, based on existing resources and services.

There can be a strong inertia against taking forward any developments – services and products will be based on a 'we've always done it that way' or 'it suits us to produce it in this way' regardless of whether that meets the real needs of users.

It is also import to note that an audit should be seen as an ongoing process, rather than a one-off event.

Usage statistics

Analysis of statistics of service usage is perhaps the most straightforward method of collecting data in libraries. Statistics relating to book loans, photocopies, visitors and requests for information can be very useful in identifying trends over a period of time, and can be a useful resource for the librarian seeking senior management support for developments. It is the case that those statistics will relate only to current services, and only provide quantitative information about the delivery of services – not whether those services are meeting the needs of users, and will not give any indication as to non-users of services.

Enquiry logging

Logging enquiries of various types can be used to provide information about people who are approaching the library for information, what kind of information they are requesting, and whether the library is able to supply it. The logging of telephone calls, or visitors, can take place over a period of as little as a week, provided that week is typical.

In the example below, a grid lists types of enquirers on the horizontal rows, and the type of enquiry in the vertical columns. A simple five-bar gate system of ticking can be used to monitor each enquiry.

Such systems can also be used to monitor workloads, either for individuals within a team, or for the team as a whole. Carrying out the logging process two or three times a year can also help identify different usage patterns.

Questionnaires/interviews/focus groups

Postal questionnaires can be useful tools for obtaining information from users of services who are geographically distant from the library itself, or from potential users of new services and products.

Close attention should be paid to the design of the questionnaire, which should ideally be checked out on a small sample first to ensure that the questions are structured in such a way as to elicit the information which you require.

Date: 1.9.97 Time: 2-4 Initials: MW	*enquirer*	*quick reference*	*photo-copy*	*lit. search*	*used us before*	*not able to help*
Visitor						
staff	IIII	I	II		IIII	I
practitioner	IIIII I	II	I	II	II	I
student	IIIII III		IIII	IIII	IIII	
Telephone						
staff	II	II			II	
member	III	I	I	I	I	
student	IIIII III			IIIII		III
public	II					II

Table 1 - example of enquiry logging

Whilst questionnaires are able to gather information from a large number of people, there comes a point when interviewing individuals either by telephone or in person is necessary to explore in greater depth issues about their interest in new services. As Gillman has pointed out, one problem to overcome is that individuals will often only ask for what they think that they are likely to get in the way of services, rather than making a direct request for services that would really help them.

The use of focus groups in recent years has increased dramatically. Bringing together up to a dozen individuals in a group setting to ask focused questions and receive feedback can result in a useful dynamic in which individuals can exchange views and experiences in a way that provides information about attitudes to services and their particular needs which might not otherwise be obtained.

Ongoing feedback

The opportunity to obtain feedback from services currently provided is one which should be utilised on a regular basis. Whether sending out current awareness bulletins, book loans, photocopies or the results of literature searches, a short evaluation form can find out what prompted the request in the first place, whether the material supplied was exactly what was wanted and whether it was received in time, other sources tried and feedback on the service as a whole.

Added Value

One of the key issues that should come out of analysis of existing services, provided that analysis goes beyond a simple collation of usage statistics, is the extent to which modifications can be made to add further value to the service.

Taking as an example a current awareness bulletin, that service could have value added to it in a variety of ways:

- the frequency of publication may have been set many years ago and be based on the manual production of the bulletin using typewriters and have remained unchanged as it fits into the needs of the library, rather than the needs of the user;
- some users may prefer an email or Web version;
- the addition of address and telephone numbers of publishers, or the inclusion of ISBNs may be of great benefit to some users;
- the users may in fact want a more personalised service – rather than a monthly listing of dozens or hundreds of references they may prefer a weekly list of references on their particular area of interest.

New users

Whether new services and products are marketed to existing users and/or to new users also impacts on the development of those services and products.

Developing new services for existing users has the benefit of an established user-base with whom it should be relatively straightforward to enter into dialogue about their needs.

Developing new services or products for new users provides a double challenge in that in addition to the service or product itself, there will be a need for market research: what other services or products are available, who the competitors are, and the potential market for the new services or product.

Electronic Publishing: Databases

The remainder of this chapter looks at 'electronic publishing' of databases, and using the World Wide Web to provide information services.

The possibility of publishing a database might seem a strange one to many in the voluntary sector. However, it is a logical stage in the development of library and information services in the sector, and an option that is increasingly straightforward.

Library databases in the voluntary sector

The pace of change over the past decade can often be underestimated. Ten years ago there were few PCs in voluntary organisations. Libraries in those voluntary organisations were still typically using manual systems for recording book orders, book loans, and other routine procedures.

Card catalogues were the key to unlocking the contents of the library. Whether books should be organised by the Dewey Decimal Classification, Bliss, UDC or an in-house classification system was often a major debate. A great deal of effort was expended in the development of in-house classification systems.

As PCs became more accessibly priced during the 1980s generic database programs began to be used in voluntary organisations. Library catalogues were often seen as an 'obvious' choice for computerisation. The market leader in the mid to late 1980s was Dbase, a precursor in effect to Microsoft's Access database. The program was totally unsuited to handling text and for library management databases, but there were many systems developed using Dbase, often developed by programmers on the 'let's set up a database' principle, one of the key errors often made when a computer arrives in a voluntary organisation.

Other database software such as Cardbox and Inmagic offered a more text-oriented approach to database management. Cardbox, as its name implies, modelled itself on a tray of 5x3 index cards, and was sufficiently straightforward for many librarians to design systems themselves.

The Inmagic database developed a large market share in voluntary sector libraries as it offered a flexible text-management approach, and special add-on routines for library management operations.

Library management software aimed specifically at smaller libraries became available at this time – previously such software had been available only to larger academic libraries and public libraries. Library management software is special database software based around an integrated range of functions which support library routines – from book ordering to the issuing of books and the production of overdue notices.

A feature of such library management systems is that they also offer an OPAC facility – an Online Public Access Catalogue: a menu-driven, easy to use, 'front-end' enabling library users to search the library catalogue themselves. Such easy-to-use search facilities can be missing in generic database software.

The vast majority of libraries in the voluntary sector are now using either databases such as Inmagic, or library management software, for both their own use and to offer easy access to the library stock for their users.

The benefits of offering access to the library catalogue to users of the library are substantial. Whilst there are training and awareness issues which need to be addressed, most library users will be able to carry out a search of the computer system and retrieve references to material on the shelves in a fraction of the time that it would have taken previously. Time saved on manual searching through card catalogues can be spent on reading the material that has been identified and located.

Having a library catalogue on computer also greatly increases the potential for further exploiting the information held on that catalogue – there is an increasing range of current awareness bulletins produced by voluntary organisation libraries which can output the previous month's/week's additions to the catalogue with little effort.

During this period of change within voluntary sector libraries, there were also changes in the external environment which have had a major impact on the provision of information services.

Online hosts and CD-ROM – changing the library/information sector

The process of locating literature prior to the development of computer databases was a tedious one. Card catalogues offered one route into the contents of a library, with classified subject indexes and author indexes. Printed indexes and abstracting services such as the British Education Index and the British Humanities Index had hefty annual cumulations with subject indexes.

During the 1980s an increasing range of databases were made available 'online': accessible on a subscription basis via a modem. Rather than having to subscribe to a range of individual databases, 'online hosts' such as Data-Star, Dialog and ESA-IRS 'hosted' a wide range of databases. A subscription to an online host enabled the user to choose from those databases and only pay for those searched – for access time and records downloaded or printed. For many libraries this enabled access to a wider range of sources than could previously have been afforded by annual subscription to the printed versions.

Librarians were the major users of online hosts as their search interfaces were difficult to master. Each host had its own search interface and command system, requiring the user to make reference to handbooks and manuals prior to carrying out a search.

The slow telecommunications at that time also made the process of searching a laborious one. Words appeared singly on the screen, which would scroll down painfully slowly. If a lengthy number of references were identified, these would be printed off centrally and posted to the user – in many cases it was cheaper to have these printed off at the online host somewhere in Europe and delivered by post.

Databases such as the London Research Centre's Acompline and Urbaline databases, which had useful information for the London voluntary sector, were only available through online hosts.

VolNet and the voluntary sector get online

The VolNet database made pioneering steps in the late 1980s and early 1990s. A joint initiative of the Community Development Foundation, the Volunteer Centre, Barnardos and the National Youth Agency, the library databases of these four organisations were made available on a dial-up basis through the University of North London's mainframe computer.

Software was provided by Head Software International, and the database was made available for a relatively low annual subscription (less than £100 for small voluntary organisations).

CD-ROM and the voluntary sector

In recent years CD-ROM has offered an opportunity to publish databases using user-friendly software and enabling access to a large group of users. University libraries will typically have a range of CD-ROM databases accessible both in the library and networked throughout the campus.

The initial CD-ROM databases were typically large databases such as Sociological Abstracts. However the voluntary sector began to make use of CD-ROM during 1993 and 1994. The VolNet database was published on CD-ROM, followed by the National Institute for Social Work's Caredata CD, the National Children's Bureau's ChildData, and the Centre for Policy on Ageing's AgeInfo database. More recently the Stationery Office has published a full-text database of Department of Health publications as Health-CD. These databases are aimed at the library/organisation market, with subscriptions costing several hundred pounds per annum.

There are also an increasing range of smaller databases being published:

- the Cochrane Library CD-ROM provides access to a large database of systematic reviews and controlled trials, one of a series of major developments in the health sector;
- Social Trends – the first 25 years on one CD-ROM;
- Family Process: the full text of every article from the 35 years of a key American journal on family therapy;
- Homoeopathy: a library on CD-ROM – over 20,000 abstracts and a range of other key homoeopathy resources.

Publishing a CD-ROM database: options

There are a number of options available in publishing a database which the organisation can choose between depending on the nature of the project, skills available in-house (IT and marketing) and money available for development costs. For example, a multi-media CD-ROM with video, audio and the need for attractive graphics and design will require more support to develop than a straightforward text-only database.

The extent to which an organisation is able to handle the various tasks involved will need to be looked at in a similar way to when the organisation looks at publishing a newsletter, an Annual Report, books or reports, or in setting up a Web site.

Even when the organisation has a well-developed database running on software which enables the distribution of search-only versions with a minimum of modification, there will be issues to be considered with regard to the consistency of data. Whilst the database is used in-house there may be a tendency to ignore some data inconsistencies, spelling errors and other 'nuances' of the system which the one or two regular users of the database are familiar with. Once the database is published, paying customers will not expect to have to face such issues and these will have to be resolved prior to publication.

The production of user guides, help text and other publicity materials will need to be addressed as part of the publication process.

There are essentially three main alternatives when looking to publish a database which relate to the extent to which the nuts and bolts of publication are handled by the organisation itself or an external publisher:

i) a publisher takes your database and they publish it

Overview
Under this option you will have no involvement in the technical side of the production, or the ongoing marketing and management of subscriptions. Under this model you should receive several copies of the database, and income from sales of the database.

Description of publishing process:
- you provide a one-off/monthly/quarterly/annual download of data to the publisher;
- several copies of the database appear on your desk in a number of weeks – (ensure that your agreement specifies the number of copies that meets your needs!);
- marketing/sales and subscriptions are managed by the publisher (you can input into this).

Examples:
- ChildData, published by Head Software International, although quite clearly marketed as being the National Children's Bureau's database. The Bureau have a role in promoting it, and their members receive a small discount on the subscription rate;
- VolNet CD-ROM, also published by Head Software International, although the organisations providing the data (National Centre for Volunteering, Community Development Foundation, Barnardo's, National Youth Agency) appear to have less involvement in the marketing of the database.

Advantages:
- little or no involvement in the technical aspects;
- low or no set-up costs;
- you receive royalties per sale and a number of free copies.

Disadvantages:
- royalties per sale as a percentage of total sale price could be lower than expected;
- you may feel a lack of 'ownership', or have a limited involvement in the design of the database and lack of involvement in the promotion, and the database might not end up quite as you envisaged;
- negotiation around prices/royalties and so forth may be time-consuming.

ii) in collaboration with a publisher

Overview
Under this model you will have much more involvement in the design of the database, and can choose to manage marketing and subscriptions yourself, or jointly with the publisher.

Examples:
- Caredata CD – published by the National Institute for Social Work, using Head Software International's HeadFast software;
- AgeInfo – published by the Centre for Policy and Ageing, using Head Software International's HeadFast software.

Description of publication process:
- you provide one-off/weekly/quarterly/annual data to the publisher;
- a master CD-ROM disk is returned by the publisher (their input can stop here);
- the master CD-ROM disk is duplicated by a commercial CD-ROM replicator;
- duplicated copies returned, despatch, marketing/sales and subscriptions handled by yourself.

Advantages:
- you should have the final say in the design of the database – within the constraints of what the software can and can not do;
- you can deal with marketing and subscriptions and ensure that the database is seen as your product;
- most of the technical side is dealt with by the publisher.

Disadvantages:
- you will have to pay the publisher royalties from your sales income for using their software, annual software licence fees, and pay charges for modifications to the database – these reduce net income from sales;
- negotiation around pricing/royalties may take some time;
- you may have to pay set-up costs at the beginning of the project.

iii) in-house

Overview
Database software such as Inmagic's DBTextWorks and Microsoft's Access now have search-only (also referred to as 'run-time') versions which enable you to publish databases and distribute versions using their software without paying licence fees to them. In the previous two models the

negotiations over licence fees for software and royalty payments are potentially time-consuming.

The availability of CD-RW recordable drives for considerably under £500 offers the opportunity to produce a master CD-ROM for replication entirely in-house at extremely low-cost.

Replication of 200 copies can be done for around £500, enabling 200 copies of a CD-ROM database to be produced for a total capital outlay of only £1,000 – only £5 a CD-ROM. With CD-ROM databases being sold at anything from £20 to £1,000 each, the potential for generating substantial income is apparent.

Example:
- the National Institute for Social Work, in conjunction with De Montfort University produced a floppy-diskette database, Learning for Caring, using DBTextWorks for the Hampshire Care Homes Association. The second issue will be published both on floppy-disk and CD-ROM.

Description of publication process:
- fully working version of database is set up in-house;
- database is copied to CD-Recordable drive to produce a master CD-ROM;
- master CD-ROM is duplicated by a CD-ROM replicator;
- duplicated copies returned, despatch, marketing/sales and subscriptions handled by yourself.

Advantages:
- you retain total control over design of database (within software constraints);
- you retain all income.

Disadvantages:
- you need to be able to press your own master CD-ROM for replication;
- you will have to handle all technical processes and user support.

	Advantages	Disadvantages
Published by the publisher: *i.e. the design, production, distribution, marketing and subscriptions are dealt with by the publisher*	• you will spend a minimal amount of staff time and money on developing and selling the product • few risks taken by yourself	• database not necessarily being seen as your 'product' • you will receive royalties per sale – the exact % to be negotiated • you are not likely to have the final say in design, marketing etc.
In collaboration with a publisher: *i.e. the technical side of producing the database is dealt with by the company, the marketing, subscriptions etc. handled by you*	• you can concentrate on marketing, subscriptions etc. • you should receive a greater proportion of the income than in the example above	• you will probably have to pay for initial set-up and design • having to negotiate with the publisher about changes/developments and costs for them
Published entirely in-house:	• all income comes to you	• you are responsible for everything – design, production, marketing, support

Table 2 – summary of publishing options

The final decision on which of these routes to take should be based on careful thought, costings from various sources, and advice from other organisations who have experience in these areas.

Web sites: an information and communication channel

A lot of the attention that the World Wide Web has received has been with regard to it being as a source of information – perversely, there has been little focus on using it to provide information. And if organisations are not providing information on the Internet, then others will not have much success in finding information on the Internet.

One of the advantages of the Internet over other methods of publishing and communication is that it is a relatively low-cost means of reaching a potentially large audience. For as little as £10 a month a voluntary organisation can maintain a Web site that can match those of much larger organisations provided that they are able to provide some useful content.

However, for many organisations, how their Web site looks is given a higher priority than what the Web site actually contains. Some Web sites are little more than glossy brochures, at best akin to annual reports – not particularly useful to many people.

The major drawback in putting material on the Internet is that unlike books and reports, training resources and so forth, generating income from sales is not at present a straightforward process through the Internet. There is a conundrum to overcome – how to put useful information on the Web which could otherwise bring in income through sales of traditional products (newsletters, journals and reports).

Some organisations who through their funding situation are able to provide information freely do not have this problem. The Joseph Rowntree Web site makes available full versions of their Findings series. An increasing amount of central government publications are now available on the Open Government Web site (http://www.open.gov.uk) – White Papers, reports, Press Releases, Circulars: material which previously was difficult to keep up to date with, and which would either have to be paid for or ordered through HMSO or other sources.

Other voluntary sector organisations have attractively designed Web sites which look particularly nice (ignoring the fact that their large graphics take a long time to load) but little information. Other voluntary organisations are either conspicuous by their absence or have a disappointing web presence.

There are various options in approaching the Internet with a view to providing information –

- The 'shop-window' approach: using a Web site to provide brief details of various products and services with a phone number or fax number for them to place an order.
- The 'loss-leader' approach: making available some material which you normally charge for, in the hope that the users of this material will be impressed and purchase a more comprehensive product.
- Password-controlled: most web-sites will have the facility for restricting access to part of the web-site to password-holders. The National Children's Bureau's *Children & Parliament* digest of parliamentary proceedings which refer to children and youth is available through their Web site (http://www.ncb.org.uk) on a subscription basis.

- Advertising-led/sponsored: the major search engines on the Internet such as Yahoo operate through income from advertising.
- Saving money: savings on printing and postage costs for various publications, current awareness bulletins, briefings and so forth can be substantial, particularly if large numbers are distributed.
- Providing a 'free at the point of delivery' service through charging others: there would appear to be a potential for voluntary organisations to produce listings on their Web site of new books, or forthcoming conferences or other resources in their particular area. Publishers of books and journals and conference organisers are used to paying to publicise their wares.

Databases on the Internet

To conclude this chapter, a few notes on the Mount Everest of the electronic publishing world: publishing a database on the World Wide Web.

In the early days of the Internet a range of academic library databases were made available through the slightly cumbersome text-only 'telnet' function, which has now to a large extent been replaced by the Web.

The larger online hosts, such as Dialog (http://www.dialog.com) have moved rapidly to provide access to the majority of their databases both on the Web and through direct dial.

SilverPlatter, previously a leading CD-ROM publisher now has a hybrid CD-ROM/Web service marketed under the Electronic Reference Library label, with databases accessible both on CD-ROM and via the Web. The Encyclopaedia Britannica, with sales of its printed version falling dramatically, has cut back the sales force for the printed version and is looking to its Web version (http://www.eb.com) as being the future.

Web services such as UnCover (http://www.uncover.com) offer credit-card access to a wide range of journal articles using search software which is a lot easier to use than the text interfaces of the online hosts.

Whilst large, well-resourced corporations such as these are able to publish databases on the Internet are there any opportunities for the voluntary sector?

Both the VolNet database (http://www.cdf.org.uk) and the Centre for Policy on Ageing's AgeInfo (http://www.cpa.org.uk) have Web versions hosted at the University of North London. Both are subscription-access only, although a subset of each database is freely searchable.

The Institute of Development Studies (http://nt1.ids.ac.uk/eldis/eldfull.htm) at the University of Sussex is one of a number of Web sites on the Internet using the Web version of DBTextWorks to publish databases, and they offer to host other databases for organisations within their sector. The Oxford and Anglia Health Authority are currently hosting a social care research database for the National Institute for Social Work.

There is a clear opportunity for voluntary organisations who invest in a relatively straightforward database package costing under £1,000 to produce their own databases, either on CD-ROM or diskette, and also have them mounted on the Web through a university willing to host their database.

The opportunity is there – take it!

References

1. Watson, Mark. 'Email and the voluntary sector', *Voluntary Voice*, No. 113, April 1997, p.9
2. David, Lewis. *Dying for information*, London, Reuters, 1996
3. *Gale directory of databases*, 1998 edn, Andover, Gale, 1997
4. Orna, Liz. *Information training for local intermediary bodies*, London, Councils for Voluntary Service National Association, National Association of Voluntary Organisations, 1984
5. Harris, Kevin. *Press enter: information technology and the community and voluntary sector: report of the IT and communities working party*, London, Community Development Foundation, 1992
6. *Formulating an information technology strategy: starter pack*, London, Type Help, 1996
7. Gillman, Peter. 'Clear away mirages and spot mutants: what information audits tell you about user needs' in Foreman Lewis (ed.) *Virtual libraries – information for tomorrow's organisations*, London, Stationery Office, 1997.

10

Acquiring and Organising Material

Frances Tait

Because of the nature of the voluntary sector many of the information services operate on a shoe string budget. Also because of the nature of the sector much of the literature is either ephemeral or grey and does not appear in regular bibliographies. These two elements have major effects on the acquisition and organisation of material.

It is a considerable advantage if there is a clear mission statement, aims and objectives or development policy established for the Library and Information Service (LIS) itself, as well as for the organisation as a whole. This should be decided in conjunction with the major users as this can guide what is selected for stock and how it is used and organised. It is not just a question of what is kept but also it can help to decide what to exclude, or subjects that you can rely on other people and external sources to cover for you if they are marginal to your organisation's main interests.

The first part of this chapter covers the selection of material and how to handle monographs – reports, books, etc. and the second part is on other types of material. However, many of the principles discussed in the first section also apply to the second. When a 'record' or 'catalogue entry' is referred to it means the written, or computerised database, details of the publication or other material as listed within the voluntary organisation's LIS system.

Subject coverage

In most charities and other organisations it is primarily the management and other paid staff who are main clients of the information services rather than the volunteers. Obviously, up to date information on the main subjects covered by the voluntary organisation is needed by most staff, and there are the practical areas of major importance such as fund-raising and volunteers, and the legal and accounting issues governing charities. Other staff may be lobbyists and publicists for the particular cause of the organisation, either within the country where the organisation is based, or on a world-wide scale for those working in the international field who need to influence world leaders and the UN. Then there are those involved in the formulation, development and carrying out of policies for the organisation, publication editors and journalists, all of whom have to be backed up with thorough information research.

Consequently all these topics have a bearing on the selection of material for the LIS. The staff of the LIS need to look out for, and decide whether or not to obtain, anything that will inform the decisions, policy making and running of the organisation. The International Planned Parenthood Federation (IPPF) Information Resources Unit has to cover all aspects of their main areas of interest which are family planning and sexual and reproductive health world-wide: social, ethical, religious, medical and demographic angles, international developments, and relevant detailed information on all countries, especially the less developed. The decision about whether or not to purchase an item will depend on the budget, whether or not you already have sufficient material on that subject or if this adds something new, and above all on whether or not you can risk being without the item, i.e. is it absolutely essential?

Whether or not you have a primarily monograph based collection or a mainly journals based collection will depend to some extent on the subject and how fast it changes – journals usually have the most recent information. Basic research reports on more obscure issues or rarely researched geographical areas may not be repeated for a long time and the information will still be relevant. Other topics such as medical research or management techniques may be constantly changing and being superseded. The materials purchased will be almost entirely based on what the staff need. The specialist collection amassed may then be one of the most valuable and most focused research collections on that subject in the country.

Depending on your budget you may decide that you are going to follow the concept of 'Just in time' rather than 'Just in case'. In the latter you collect material systematically 'Just in case' it is needed, and then you will have it in stock when the need arises. However, you may be spending time on acquiring publications that are never needed. Alternatively you may be much more selective about what you get and then rely on obtaining anything else you need 'Just in time' and only when it is asked for. This inevitably involves delay in providing the item, but cuts down on wasted expenditure and all the attendant costs and time spent on cataloguing and classifying stock that is never used. It is also a risk as it assumes you will be able to get what is needed in time. In fact most libraries run a mixed system, although the trend is to go more for 'Just in time' especially when budgets are tight. This is tending towards the 'virtual library' where most of the information required is in electronic form and called up on CD-ROMs or on line when needed. The practicality of this depends very much on how much of what you need is available electronically, but there is still only a fairly limited amount in many voluntary sector areas.

What's available?

Most libraries work in a small specialised area and therefore it is not cost effective to subscribe to published general bibliographies of recent books such as the *British National Bibliography* and even the weekly *Bookseller,* which lists new books, is beyond the budget of most. Therefore selection of new material has to be done from other sources. Most libraries have to rely heavily on what comes in anyway to find out what has appeared, so you need to make full use of what is received, e.g. journals, newsletters etc. A key source is incoming periodicals, newsletters and newspapers: these need to be scanned through for announcements and reviews of new material or references to older publications of importance. Sometimes the first you will know of new publications will be a request or recommendation from staff or their contacts. Announcements of new books from specialised publishers known to be working in the field are useful, so getting on the publisher's mailing list is a good starting point.

You will probably find that many of the publications you need are from other similar organisations to your own, both nationally and internationally; often these will be reports or information leaflets that are not listed elsewhere. Keeping in touch with their publishing output is vital: this can be done either from their mailing lists or you can check their journals and newsletters if they publish any. The Internet has become a useful source of information on an organisation's publications. You can check the Web pages of your key sources regularly for updated information on publications or ask to be emailed about new publications.

If you are fortunate you will find publications coming into the organisation for free, addressed to all manner of people, but probably not the Library. These might be items a publisher thinks should be reviewed in your publications and so sent to the editor of your journals, items sent to a particular staff member because of their known interests or high profile in a particular field, or as a result of their committee work. You should try and encourage them to give them to you (to save your budget), or at least tell you about these publications as you may not find out about them in any other way. In one way this can almost be a problem as you may find there is a considerable quantity of unsolicited material, particularly reports. Therefore you need to make it clear to colleagues that if they send you things you have the final say on what you keep and what you discard as not being essential to your library.

You can regularly check specialised commercial databases in your field to find out what has just come out although this can be expensive. You may decide to have a weekly alerting service of new references from these if you can define your subject interests fairly narrowly so that you are not overwhelmed with references. The British Library Document Supply Centre (BLDSC)'s *Sigle* database of 'non-conventional literature' lists reports, theses, dissertations etc. issued informally in EC member countries. An alternative is lists of new additions of articles and books to library and information services working in relevant fields. These may be free or available for a fee, or you may be able to exchange if you issue a similar list. Two examples of well produced and comprehensive lists that are useful for selection purposes are the UK Department for International Development's *Development Index and New Books List* and the Health Education Authority's *Journal Articles of Interest to Health Educators*.

Obtaining material

If the request for a publication originates from a colleague always ask where your requester heard of the publication. It helps to give you an idea of how available it will be if you know that s/he saw it referred to in an article published ten years ago or if s/he heard about it through talking to the author at a conference last week – in the latter case it may well not be out yet.

You can order books from the publisher or from a bookseller although large commercial publishers may not always be willing to supply one-off copies or may make a surcharge. It is advisable to have an account with a large bookseller for the more commercially published, and readily available, material. This cuts down administration as some of the bills will be consolidated and you do not have to send any money in advance. The Royal National Institute for the Blind (RNIB) buys direct, but the IPPF and Age Concern England (ACE) buy commercially published books through a bookseller. There are two different kinds of bookseller – stock holding and non-stockholding. You need to know which one you are dealing with as this will affect their response time. The former will have books on their shelves and may be able to supply what you need straight away, the latter will always have to order it from the publisher and this will inevitably incur delays as publishers take varying lengths of time to respond – from days to weeks. Some booksellers will give you a discount depending on the size of your account or on what you can negotiate with them. There may be an advantage to you in using stock holding booksellers who may not offer a discount for a small scale account but who have most of your book requirements in stock, and who may also provide a daily delivery service to your office.

If there is a bookseller specialising in your subject area it is also a good idea to have an account with them too for material which the large general bookseller may not stock. If you need many government publications you should also have an account with The Stationery Office if this is economic (check their discounts and surcharges); if not order through your usual bookseller. There are also some booksellers on the Internet who may be able to provide what you want, but you may prefer to build up a more personal relationship by phone with a regular supplier. It's up to you where your priorities lie and what you can negotiate.

You need to give your book supplier as much information as possible about the item you want. At least try and provide author, title, publisher, year and International Standard Book Number (ISBN). This will help the bookseller to order quickly from the publisher and they will not have to waste time searching for the details. It is always wise to check the existence of a book before ordering unless your enquirer has given you full and realistic looking publication details such as publisher and ISBN. A few minutes spent checking in whatever reference sources you have, ringing a bookseller or looking at the British Library or other catalogues and booksellers on the Internet can save a great deal of wasted time and to-ing and fro-ing between you and your bookseller. This is particularly important if the book is required urgently. In this case it is sensible to contact the publisher to make sure it is currently available (and not out of print, or not yet published as is quite often the case when your enquirer has heard about a book on the grapevine). You can report back to your enquirer on how long it will take to get it, or let him/her know quickly if it is not going to be possible to obtain it. Many librarians have ordered urgently needed items in the usual routine way without initial checking and it then transpires, some weeks later, that they are not yet published, or out of print either temporarily or permanently. It is much better to give a negative answer quickly.

However, ordering through a bookseller is often not appropriate for publications from organisations, as opposed to commercial publishers, such as voluntary organisations and other institutions which are not in the mainstream of publishing. Not only is a bookseller likely to have problems in identifying the publisher and their address, but often the bookseller is not able to obtain a discount for themselves, so you will probably find you have to pay a surcharge to make up for this. In this instance it is best to go direct to the organisation yourself. Most organisations, including charities, now charge, if only a small amount, for publications and/or postage and packing. Unfortunately many no longer operate an invoicing or even a proforma system and will only accept cash with order or a credit card payment. So a 'company' credit card, if you can obtain one, is by far the most practical way of obtaining material from these sources. A credit card also enables you to obtain commercially published books needed urgently from booksellers who have the item in stock, but with whom you do not have an account. If you are unsure about order procedures from an organisation, check their catalogue if you have one, phone or try the Internet. An organisation in the United States called Women, Law and Development International (http://www.wld.org) in Washington DC has a Web site that gives brief details of their publications – author and title, how much they cost, the postage in the USA and overseas, and how to order and pay.

The Internet is becoming a way of obtaining a printout of some of the smaller publications directly online or quickly getting extracts from sections of larger ones, for example from organisations such as the World Health Organisation, the United Nations and IPPF. If they are online it saves ordering them in the usual way and sometimes they are free, but watch out for any copyright restrictions (see Chapter 13). This is often the fastest, and most efficient and most satisfactory way of dealing with special requests. It is also possible to order publications online through the Internet or email but this is not totally reliable – possibly because the recipient organisation has not set up a satisfactory method of dealing with Internet requests for publications but this will no doubt improve. It is probably preferable to fax or write if there is time or, if speed is of the essence, to telephone to ensure that the request is dealt with quickly and the publication is actually available, and to check about payment methods.

Some material published by small organisations is free if it is produced for advocacy, informational or educational purposes. Even if it is not free they may be prepared to set up a 'free' exchange arrangement with your organisation whereby you agree to 'swap' journals or monographs. It is usual not to worry too much whether the prices actually match exactly or if in theory someone 'owes' someone else, provided the cost roughly approximates. However, this can be rather unreliable as personnel and publication distribution policies can change in both your own and the exchange organisation, and even long established arrangements are then forgotten.

If you have any doubts about whether a publication is worth buying, try and borrow it first from another library such as the BLDSC , or you can ask your bookseller to supply it on approval so that if you decide not to keep it they will accept it back and give you a credit for it, provided it hasn't been marked in any way.

Recording of orders

You should give each order a unique number which provides a unique identifier for the bookseller and helps to avoid confusion when a book you receive is published with a slightly different title to the one you ordered it under. It also acts as verification of your order and is a useful element in the audit trail. Apart from details of the item itself you should also record the date of your order, who you ordered it from and any subsequent messages that you receive from your supplier about the progress of the order, e.g. not yet published, out of stock and/or reprinting in six weeks.

When the book is received, note the date of receipt immediately against your order record to indicate that it is now in the Library, and all the details of the invoice such as the invoice number and date, and price you paid. Again, this helps with the audit trail and if there should be queries about non-payment of the invoice. Unless the supplier insists on prepayment do not pay for a book until it is in your possession – you may never receive it. A LIS should have its own budget for stock ordering, so you will need to keep a check of how much has already been spent, how much is outstanding on orders placed but not yet paid for, and how much remains.

Recording material

In voluntary organisations, as staff time is usually limited, the quickest and simplest method of recording material is best. Some small voluntary services use a card catalogue as at Mediation UK. In most situations the cards are arranged by author, but there may also be duplicate cards under subject, title and classification. Although there is nothing wrong with this method if it suits your particular situation, it is an advantage and more practical to maintain a catalogue on computer, even if it is decided that all that is needed is a simple word processing system using something like Microsoft Word. At least this is word searchable when looking for a half remembered reference, a subject, an author or fragment of a title. You can also produce printouts by author, title or subject. However it is advisable, if possible, to invest in a database system designed specially for libraries. There are several suppliers and these can be bought and then adapted to the local situation. The adaptation can take a varying amount of time depending on how comprehensive and complex a record is to be, and what the supplier provides as a base. Some of the library computer systems, such as Inmagic DBTextworks used at IPPF, also have a User Group which meets regularly, so pooling of ideas becomes possible and leads to useful contacts including those with similar problems.

Each organisation needs to decide what level of cataloguing is needed in their own particular situation. Whether on computer or cards, or in some other manuscript form a cataloguing record should be designed that has all the elements in it that are needed by your own information service and a field allocated to each one. For monographs in most cases the very minimum will be author, title, and shelf location. It is useful to have the year, publisher and place of publication in the basic record as this gives information about the type of book without having to go to the actual publication. It will give some guidance on how authoritative or relevant it is, i.e. is it from a well known publisher in the field or is it up to date? If you know from your catalogue the place of publication, e.g. if it is British, American etc., it tells you immediately if it is written from a particular country's perspective. It is also usual to include the number of pages because not only will it indicate how comprehensive it is but when you come to start looking for the item on a crowded shelf it is sometimes helpful to know whether you are looking for a thick book or a small pamphlet amongst all the others. If you work in a multilingual environment, such as at the IPPF, it is well worth recording the language of the book so that you can quickly pick out those in French, Spanish or Gujarati when the need arises.

In a voluntary organisation it is wise not to get too hung up on the strict and formal rules of cataloguing that the British Library or a University Library might use. If you know the official rules you can use them, but otherwise just decide what you are going to do and try to be consistent. For instance this applies to the author's name. If a book has four authors you can decide never to list more than the first, or maybe the second as well. If the publisher is an organisation which looks as if it could be thought of as an author by some people, or it is likely to be asked for as if it was the author, put it in the author field if it will be helpful to you and your enquirers even if is not standard procedure elsewhere. Always put the various elements in the same order, usually author, title, place of publication, publisher, date, pages.

It is remarkable how much material appearing in the voluntary sector is published without a date – even from quite important international bodies. Always check this and make sure you write in the publication date when you think it was published. If it is missing you can use '1997?' if you are uncertain. One way of ascertaining the date is to see if there is a bibliography and assume that the date is either the same as the latest reference cited or the year after. You may know at the time that you acquire the publication that it has just appeared but in a couple of years time you, or your successor, will have forgotten, or not know, in which year it arrived or was published unless you have noted it initially.

You should probably catalogue your own organisation's publications in more detail than those produced externally. This particularly applies to listing all the authors, not just the first, and comprehensive subject indexing. It can be very embarrassing if you do not know, or remember, that you have published something yourselves and you haven't realised you can answer an enquiry from your own publications.

What to catalogue

You also have to decide whether or not everything that you receive needs to be catalogued. If there are serious time constraints this will affect not only how much detail you go into but also how much cataloguing you can do. It may be that you decide that some items will not be catalogued at all. This might apply to small reports, pamphlets, brochures and journal articles. In this case you can have a pamphlet box, lateral or vertical file in which these items are filed under the classification number or subject as an 'Information file' or 'Documents file'. This system is in use at the IPPF.

The disadvantage of not cataloguing something is that you do not have a full picture of what you have in the LIS, and you will find yourself regularly going through the subject boxes or files to check whether or not you have a particular publication. This is not too much of a problem when you are answering an enquiry when you just want to find any useful material that you have in stock. However, it can be rather frustrating when you are trying to decide whether or not to order something and you have to check through the various information files to see if you already have it – especially if you are not sure which subject it has been filed under. So the advice is to catalogue everything if possible, as at the RNIB, even if very simply, but this will always depend on the time available, and a mixed system is perfectly feasible as at the IPPF.

Identify every item as yours, whether it is catalogued or not, with the Library's stamp on the title page and elsewhere in the book. It is advisable before putting the book on the shelves to stick in a loan date label; this helps with ownership identification and also makes lending it quicker as you do not have to keep someone waiting while you find a label; and stick it in. It would be useful to have a bar-coding system for each book and each borrower but the small size of most voluntary sector libraries makes this non- essential although it will save time in lending if you can fund it.

Information files

Many organisations maintain information files and some rely heavily on these files as their primary source of information. This applies particularly to those with 'Helplines' and dealing with particularly current information. The files or boxes will probably contain a selection of pamphlets, articles, cuttings, reports, bibliographies etc. as at Age Concern

England. BACUP include reviews, information on clinical trials, unpublished research and enquiry research. At the Centre for Alternative Technology they have one series of files on their subject areas and another on relevant companies, and at ACE in addition they have a sequence of files on organisations, arranged alphabetically by the name of the organisation and containing policy documents, annual reports, leaflets and other miscellaneous material. The files can either be classified using the same scheme as the rest of the Library or arranged alphabetically by subject or corporate name. These files might be in boxes or in lateral or vertical filing cabinets.

Classification

Classification schemes can range from non-existent to very specific, depending on the size and scope of the Library. However, most organisations will have a relatively detailed classification scheme. In common with most specialised collections of whatever size, the broad standard schemes such as Dewey Decimal Classification used in public libraries, are not usually appropriate as they are too broad and not broken down into sufficient sub classes for a special information service's needs. UDC (Universal Decimal Classification) may be detailed enough if the relevant section has been updated recently but it is a complex scheme to use and probably too sophisticated for most voluntary LIS. Sometimes you can find a specialist published scheme that is suitable. At BACUP, the cancer support service, they use selected sections of the US National Library of Medicine classification.

If you are starting up a new library, or need to change a classification system in a voluntary organisation, do not go ahead with devising your own scheme until you have checked thoroughly that one does not exist already that you can either use as it is or adapt. It is a mistake to assume that nobody else can possibly have worked out a classification for your subject. Specialised libraries have been in existence long enough for there to be a reasonable chance that one already exists. You can save yourself a great deal of time and intellectual effort by asking people working in related subject libraries if they know of anything or by checking the library indexing and abstracting sources.

Many, in fact probably most, libraries in this sector have developed their own schemes although some may be quite old. The main subjects do not change a great deal over the years although some will expand, others become less important and some new ones will appear. The IPPF has a classification scheme compiled specially by a consultant in 1975, which is based on numbers for the main sections and uses decimal points for the subdivisions. It has been regularly updated since 1975 to take in new topics. Although it is over twenty years old its base is still sound but, now that the catalogue is on a computer database, keywords are used in the catalogue entry instead of the previous selection of multiple classification numbers. Previously all these numbers had separate cards in the catalogue and all needed to be filed individually. The UK Family Planning Association has adapted, and considerably simplified, the IPPF scheme for their own needs. The RNIB's classification originated in 1958, is very detailed and flexible, and uses letters for the main subdivisions and then numbers. If you cannot trace a scheme you can use you can devise a very simple, but detailed, scheme using either single or double letters or numbers or a combination.

For subject keywords you will need to build up a 'thesaurus' if one is not already available in your subject area. This is a listing of the subject terms you have used in the catalogue, in what context, and helps to remind you which term you have decided on if there is a synonym. As with classification schemes, before you start compiling your own thesaurus list of subject keywords, check whether a suitable one has already been devised by someone else – either published or unpublished. If you are unsure, contact other people working in your field in LIS and ask them if they know of any or check with the Aslib Information Centre/Library which maintains the national collection of thesauri. The IPPF uses the thesaurus published by Johns Hopkins University Population Information Program in the USA in connection with their *Popline* database. It is fairly comprehensive, but additional terms are added as they come into use or because they are appropriate to the UK, where the IPPF Library is based, or because they are on a subject relevant to IPPF but not to Popline. A thesaurus can be as simple or as complex as you choose: it can be a straightforward list of words or can include cross references to broader or narrower terms and scope notes about how and when you use the term.

Shelf arrangement

If you only have a small collection of books, a hundred or so, you can arrange them in whatever way you think is the most useful – usually author or subject or, less often, title. Mediation UK have a subject arrangement under just three sections: Criminal Justice, Community and Education, supported by a simple card index of authors and subjects.

In larger libraries the main class number from the classification scheme is normally used as the filing order on the shelves. The IPPF Library, with 5000 monographs, is strongly international. General books on a subject go under a fairly narrowly defined subject classification but books that refer to one specific country are shelved under the country classification and then subdivided by the subject because, being an international organisation, there is a major requirement for all the material on one country to kept together.

If possible, keep all material on one topic as close together as possible to cut down on time taken in going to two or more different places for similar information. For example, if you have books and use A4 pamphlet boxes for non-catalogued material, these can be co-sited on the same shelf. It is easiest to keep track of where things should be on the shelves if you stick a small label at the bottom of the spine to indicate where it goes. This is worth doing even if you only have a smallish collection with few subdivisions and use colour coded labels. It means that you can see at a glance if something is in the wrong place and if it gets on someone else's shelves they can spot it quickly too as being an LIS book.

Periodicals

There will be a number of essential periodicals which you will need to obtain for your organisation and the simplest and most reliable way of doing this is through a subscription. You can use a subscription agent who will handle all your orders and bill you once a year or, if you only have a small number of titles, you can buy them direct from the publisher. If your organisation is a periodical publisher, you could also try to set up an exchange agreement with others that are non-commercially published titles. Whether periodicals come on subscription or exchange you need to record the receipt of each issue to make sure that you have received all the issues and chase up any that are missing. As with books, you need to keep a record of invoices, the name of the supplier and, most importantly, the period that the invoice covers, i.e. volume numbers or year. The title and holdings information can be included in the main catalogue or in a separate database or list.

In some voluntary organisations a welter of unsolicited periodicals arrives which the publishers think you should see or might find useful. They may come addressed to the Library, but most will be sent to the organisation as a whole or to named individuals who then send them on to the Library either immediately or when they get round to it. Whatever the case, the regular receipt of these titles cannot be guaranteed – hence the need for a formal paid subscription order for key titles to ensure they arrive.

The non-subscription titles can either be disregarded altogether or, if time permits, they can be filed and/or scanned for relevant information. It can be useful to list the titles that come in on an ad hoc basis as someone may need a particular title. Also, if you have already noted what you do with that title, e.g. file, scan, throw away, it saves deciding every time it arrives, or trying to remember what you did with it the last time. This is particularly helpful if the registering in of receipt of periodicals is done by different people so that they then know immediately what happens to it and do not finish up with a large pile of queries. Periodicals can be arranged on the shelves in a broad classification or, more usually, just in straight alphabetical order of title, as often the subject content is quite broad in scope.

If there are some titles which are marginal to your interests, possibly because they are too general or too specific or they are just too expensive for your budget, you can consider getting just the contents pages of these. There are several ways of doing this. The British Library and several other companies and agents have a subscription service for contents pages. You can find some on the Internet either by checking the publisher's or other supplier's Web site page regularly, or by asking the publisher to email them to you as they appear. In the latter case they do not always have full information in them, such as authors and page references, but if you need a specific article the publisher or supplier will then send you the article for a fee. Occasionally you may find it is available free in full text on the Internet site. Alternatively, you can acquire the article through sources such as the BLDSC or other commercial document delivery services.

If journals are received by the LIS there are various ways of making use of them. There is scanning for new notices of reports, books and other items, articles you may want to index or take for your information file, and there is notifying staff of interesting items. You can do this by circulating the whole journal to those who are interested in the topic, or you can just circulate the contents page and then supply a copy of any specific news item or article they need, depending on the copyright regulations.

Periodical articles

Whether or not you are keeping the periodical issues you may want to extract useful articles from them and put them into your information file or catalogue for future use. Some voluntary organisations scan journals and index or abstract relevant articles and publish a list of recent items as at ACE – this applies to books as well in the form of an accessions or 'new books' list. At BACUP the nurses on the staff and working on the Helpline advise the LIS staff and help them to decide which are the key new articles and references which should be kept and/or listed for future reference.

These article references should ideally be put into the catalogue or database, as at the RNIB, and be identifiable and searchable as a separate set when appropriate. It does not usually matter to the enquirer where the information they need has appeared, whether in books or journals, so in this way articles are accessed as part of any information search in the catalogue. Full abstracts or very brief descriptions of the contents of the articles are useful if there is time, otherwise even author, title and some keywords may be better than nothing. But often there is no time in a voluntary organisation other than to tear out the article, or photocopy it, and put it in an information file.

Integrated records

Always try and use records of material as efficiently as possible. Whatever system you use, try to enter the details of a publication only once and then build on that record to save time. For example, the first record will normally be at the point of order when the basic information will be recorded – at least author, title and publisher. You can then reuse that same record for cataloguing by adding additional information when you actually acquire the book such as full publication details, subject keywords and classification or location. You can either have a combined orders and catalogue file or you can keep them separately by copying the order record into a catalogue file and then adding the classification and other information. If you want to you can have a combined catalogue for different formats of material – monographs, videos, articles, posters etc. But you should then have a field that identifies the type of material so that you can search just for videos if necessary.

The value of a computerised catalogue is that if the organisation is networked it may be possible for users to have direct access to the catalogue from their own PCs, and this sometimes results in saving the librarian's time in answering enquiries and requests for publications. Another option may be to provide outlying libraries or non-networked users with a copy of the catalogue on disc, if it is small enough. It is worth bearing these options in mind when selecting a system.

Whether you have a manual or computerised system you can integrate your loans record with your catalogue record. If it is a small card catalogue just note on the card who has it on loan and when it's due back, and cross out their name when it is returned. This works well for the small collection of books available to the staff and volunteers at West London Community Counselling. If you have a computerised system you will want to have a database of the LIS users' names, addresses and phone numbers for lending purposes.

You can also use your user record to build up a list of which subjects everyone in your organisation is personally interested in so that you can notify them of new publications in their field. You can also ask them if they will let you note their specialisms so that if you have an enquiry that you are having difficulty with you know whom to ask for help.

In many organisations there seems to be a considerable amount of material held in individual offices. It is almost impossible to say that everything must be in the Library as often people genuinely need something at their fingertips every day to refer to, but you can try to persuade them at least to let you add it to the Library catalogue so that if anyone else wants to refer to it you know that it is there. You may also be responsible for buying any books and journals that are needed in offices, in which case again they can be catalogued and the location noted.

Non-text material

This is probably the most difficult section of material to organise as it comes in such a variety of forms, from posters and videos to photographs and maps. In the catalogue you should have a field or section to indicate the format of the item if you want to have a catalogue that integrates everything in the LIS. Tracking down this material has the same problems as mentioned earlier, but there are some additional factors in organisation and recording although the basic format and principles used for monographs is still appropriate.

Posters

Posters are often needed, and collected, in voluntary organisations. They may be published by your organisation or by another. They are frequently used as an information source or explanatory diagrams on office or waiting room walls to help explain procedures and policies to clients, for publicity purposes, or even to liven up your organisation's stands at exhibitions. Posters can be recorded in the catalogue, if you have time, giving title, publisher, country of origin and description. Check if there is a date on the poster somewhere (there usually isn't) and if not make sure you write at least the date of receipt on the back to give you some idea of its age for future reference. Also put your ownership stamp on the back, otherwise you will have no evidence of who it belongs to; it is best to put it on the back as putting it on the front might detract from the impact of the design.

The main options for storing posters are either rolled up, flat or vertical. A 'plan' or 'map' chest or special vertical poster holder trolley is the most satisfactory way so that you can glance through them quickly and easily. Otherwise you find yourself rolling and unrolling posters if you are trying to find one on a particular topic. Posters can be classified in much the same way as books or, as there are likely to be only a limited number, they can be arranged by broad alphabetical subject term. Of particular importance are the posters produced by your own organisation, for which you will often have an archival role and may need the fullest cataloguing record. At IPPF examples are stored of posters produced by their member Family Planning Associations around the world and these are filed under country of origin.

Video and audio tapes

Video, and to a lesser extent audio, tapes have an important role to play in voluntary organisations. The organisation itself may produce them to publicise a particular campaign or for training staff and clients. Alternatively they may be purchased from other organisations to provide background, for training purposes or just for information.

Recording the content of videos or audio tapes can be very time consuming. When you catalogue a monograph you can glance through it quickly in a few minutes and index the key subjects rapidly. However, with video or sound, if you want detailed information, you have to actually sit down and watch or listen to the tapes all the way through, making notes about what you see and hear and then transferring the details to the catalogue. Clear decisions have to made about how much detail is really necessary in the catalogue to retrieve what you need. Remember that when you want to check the content of a video or tape, e.g. for particular stories, pictures or words, you will have to watch it through unless you have already listed some of the detail in your catalogue, with time codes telling you whereabouts on the tape the item you want is located. This is very time consuming compared with quickly flicking through a book to see if it is relevant to your enquiry.

A short cut to watching or listening to the tapes for cataloguing purposes is to look out for any printed information already provided and copy it into your record as this may be sufficient. For instance, a publisher's notice or a review often gives a reasonable amount of information which you can use – check for this when you are ordering. There may be a booklet accompanying the tape which gives you a good outline of the content and you can also use any other material with the video such as training manuals or booklets to quickly get the gist of the contents. You can just use short abstracts or descriptions of the content in your catalogue if you do not need to go into great detail.

You may have to treat internally and externally produced videos in different ways. It is probable that you will need considerable detail about the internally produced ones. At the IPPF, for the videos they produce themselves, the need is often for information about what shots have been used and where it was filmed. This is because the video is their copyright and therefore they can make the pictures available to other filmmakers or broadcasters, or they may want to re-cut it for their own use later.

Video and audio tapes can be kept in classification order or, as happens quite often, in accession number order. You can put them on the shelves with the books or keep them separately on narrow shelves or in filing drawers as this is the most efficient way to use space as they are smaller than books and cannot be browsed on the shelves in the same way. For tape cataloguing it is usual to assign subject keywords in the same way as you would a monograph or article, but you may also need to include the names of the producer, the narrator and other people taking part, such as the interviewees, as this is often what people remember. You also need to note the format of the video, e.g. BETA or VHS, as these will be required in different circumstances, i.e. the former is for good quality broadcast purposes and for the master copy, the latter is often sufficient for training or home viewing. Information on the copyright in a video is important because sometimes they can be used without restrictions or payment of a copyright fee for educational purposes – this can be particularly useful in a voluntary organisation. The copyright announcement usually appears in a statement at the beginning or end of the video and can be included as a unique field in the catalogue.

CD-ROMs

CD-ROMs might be purchased – e.g. directories, dictionaries, reference manuals, business information or abstracts and indexes. These are worthwhile if you use a particular one a great deal and the investment is cost effective against buying the printed version or you need the more advanced searching facilities offered by an electronic version. However, if your use is sporadic, then online use is usually more cost effective and also makes a wider variety of sources available. If you have CD-ROMs consideration should be given to networking them across the organisation, for instance key databases, dictionaries, directories etc. Catalogue CD-ROMs in the same way as books but make clear it is a CD-ROM in the format field and its location as you will probably be storing it in a disk file somewhere either by title or subject.

Photographs

Photographs may well be another type of material kept in the LIS. They may be pictures from field trips that staff have made, or pictures taken for publicity purposes and used in your publications. As always, the ideal is to catalogue as much detail of photos as possible. An alternative is to arrange them by subject, but they are often of more than one subject, e.g. a mother in a refugee camp in Rwanda raises the question of how it might be needed next time – by someone studying refugees or someone writing about Rwanda. So which of these subjects do you file it under? Here a subject index is advisable either on cards or computer, unless you have time to look through the stock each time you need a visual reference. Lateral or vertical files can be used for storing actual prints of photographs, and for storage of 35 mm slides you can get specially designed folders for hanging files. There are several computer storage systems for photographs on the market with indexing facilities.

Library procedures manual

As you will have gathered, there is a great deal to be done in acquiring and storing material in a voluntary organisation library and information service. You will find you are continually making decisions, for instance how to handle particular types of material, what level of cataloguing and classification you aim for, how to order books, what to do with periodicals and numerous other instances. As a result you should have a library procedures manual so that you do not forget what you have decided, or waste time thinking it through again, or make contradictory decisions the second time round. This will also ensure that if you have part-time colleagues or a high staff turnover or if you leave there is a point of reference for procedures. It does not have to be complicated but should be comprehensive enough to produce a systematic and consistent approach. Ideally it should be maintained in computerised format so that it can be updated easily.

Conclusion

There is plenty of scope to adapt the selection, recording and organisation of material in the LIS to your own needs. The advice to anyone working in this area is to be pragmatic and flexible, do not worry too much about formal librarianship and information science rules as long as you are consistent in your approach. Every decision has to be based on what is needed in your situation and what staff are available – even if you know what you would ideally like to do given infinite resources.

Further reading

Aitchison, J., Gilchrist, A. and Bawden, D. *Thesaurus construction and use: a practical manual*, 3rd edn, London, Aslib, 1997

Aslib handbook of special librarianship. Most editions have relevant chapters. Latest edition: 7th edited by A. Scammell, London, Aslib, 1997

Beenham, R. and Harrison, C. *The basics of librarianship*, 3rd edn, London, Bingley, 1990

Chapman, I. *How to catalogue: a practical handbook using AACR2 and Library of Congress*, 2nd edn, London, Bingley, 1990

Fothergill, R. and Butchart, I.C. *Non-book materials in libraries: a practical guide,* 3rd edn, London, Bingley, 1990

Hunter, E.J. *Classification made simple,* Aldershot, Gower, 1988

Marcella, R. and Newton, R. *A new manual of classification,* Aldershot, Gower, 1994

Rowley, J.E. *Organising knowledge: an introduction to information retrieval,* 2nd edn, Aldershot, Ashgate, 1992

Webb, S. *Creating an information service,* 3rd edn, London, Aslib, 1996

11

Library Automation for Voluntary Organisations

Jacqueline Cropley

The challenges for automation in the voluntary sector are many. It can be the way to expand upon scant human resources, or operate as an alternative where no information professional is present. It may involve updating old systems which were previously either good or inadequate. It can add capacity when an earlier system no longer copes with the volume or diversity of activities. The existing system may work well for the librarian, but does not fit in with the organisation's technology direction. Several bodies may have come together, and technology which was adequate for one no longer fits the needs of the enlarged organisation. This could be because of size or range of activities, but also because of technical incompatibility with systems arriving from other parts of the new organisation. Alternatively, a stand-alone in-house system may need to be changed to handle the distributed requirements of devolved, outsourced or geographically scattered activities. Whether the need is to build capacity to create new opportunities for the organisation or to deal with the management issues of an ongoing process, there are basic principles for automation, which this chapter explores.

Planning

The stage of the project most often neglected is planning. This should always be taken seriously. Although it is possible to modify an original outline, and some system changes may appear extremely simple, the difference between a well implemented, successful automation project and one which is problematic or fails to serve the purpose, is a result of the assiduity of the planning process.

People often gauge the magnitude of a project by the cost of the software. An expensive installation needs extensive justification. Many library solutions are relatively low in software cost, so do not require much authorisation. Expenditure may be within the authority limits of a single line manager. This does not mean that the decision to go ahead should be taken lightly. New software can have a substantial impact on an information unit's operations. A wrong decision has major implications. Small or large, automation projects need careful planning from start to finish.

Potential for change

There are two different approaches to library automation. The first is to take the traditional view, to plan to install a system which will operate for a number of years, up to five, without major change. The more recent option is to take advantage of the many new database software products coming on the market with information or document management capabilities. They can be adapted for library needs. Some people use these for short-term applications, switching software regularly, perhaps once a year. This allows them to take advantage of rapid advances in technology and avoids dangers of systems grinding to a halt as they become overloaded.

With the first route, the choice of system sets how the library will operate for a considerable period into the future. Thought must be given to what will be required in the later years, so the project can be scaled to fit forthcoming demands. Most organisations change over time. Few librarians will find themselves dealing with exactly the same issues throughout the working life of the system. If the potential for change, and its likely direction, are not properly taken into account, library staff will find it hard to adapt their working methods to new demands, because the system holds them back.

If a series of short-lived applications is the chosen route, planning must incorporate a longer-term view. Otherwise the advantages of adapting quickly can be overtaken by the dangers of switching from one improperly thought out system to another, always living with the consequences and compromises, and perhaps perpetuating design flaws from one implementation to the next.

Once a library system is installed, it is rarely easy to make more than a few simple changes. This is because the procedures involved are usually complex. For example, loan records for books may relate cataloguing data on a book to copy numbers, and to a specific borrower and personal details, length of loan and transaction reporting. Alternatively, there may be a number of steps involved in a process, such as identifying a journal, logging its receipt, producing the routing slip and labels, combined with links to checking processes such as which issue is expected, has the right number of copies arrived, the subscription status, whether the circulation details are up-to-date, etc.

It is no wonder that trying to amend an operation can cause malfunctions, such as extended delays or full-scale software errors, as the new task affects processing in another part of the system. A catalogue and loan system may slow down unacceptably when interfaced with a new acquisitions and accounting component. A simple database product for serials control may have trouble with merged titles or too many special issues. Upgrades to new hardware because of volume increases or malfunctioning equipment, for example a server or printer change, cause problems if integrated software commands need amendment as a consequence.

Issues like these cause systems to age before their time. Computer constraints prevent libraries adapting to new challenges, and lock them into repeating activities and processes which no longer meet needs. The consequences can be particularly troublesome in the voluntary sector, where there is a prime requirement to operate efficiently. Resources are scarce. The organisation itself may be going through structural and procedural changes. Planning must meet the organisation's present and future requirements.

Identifying priorities

It is important to have a clear view of what the new system is required to do, and what in particular is to be achieved. For most voluntary sector work, the prime focus must be how the automation is going to assist the people who benefit ultimately from the organisation's activities, rather than staff working in-house. Unless the activity is very simple, it is important to make an accurate assessment of priorities and requirements. Most software has multiple features and capabilities. Many of these are never used. They get in the way of smooth running of the prime functions. At the other end of the scale, aspects of the system which appear to be present may be rudimentary and inadequate. Suppliers make high claims for the multi-functionality of their software. However, no system performs every function equally well. This applies as much to modular systems as to single interface systems connected to a number of back-end processing suites.

Outline requirements for different capabilities or system modules

The following represent sample requirements for various library applications. Not all features in each category will be needed. Some conflict with one another. The potential for conflict increases where two or more applications have to operate together.

1. *Cataloguing:*
a. Public access catalogues and online public access catalogues (OPACs)

Clear interface

simple and expert access strategies

single interface for different parts of the collection, e.g. books, serials, videotapes

multiple locations

subject or keyword access

relevance ranking and combination searching, e.g. Boolean operators: and, or, not

list handling, sorting

browsing facilities

link to printer for screen, item or list printing.

b. Catalogue features for cataloguing staff:

Most of the features for public access catalogues, plus:

machine readable cataloguing (MARC) standards, at various levels

multiple entry

entry of repeated data, e.g. publisher, series

quick checking

authority files

cross-referencing

thesaurus linking

links to standard catalogues

remote access, e.g. Internet, Z39.50.

2. *Acquisitions:*
Electronic ordering and receipt

differential delivery

part receipts

multiple orders

supplier details and preferences

links to supplier systems

authorisations

chasers

workflow and item tracking

reports

accessioning

labels

donations
fund and budgeting information
discounts
multiple currencies
financial reports
audit trails.

3. *Serials:*
Many of the elements for Acquisitions, plus:
rapid entry
allowance for missing or supplementary issues
multiple copies
multiple suppliers
differential pricing
forecasting
late arrivals
consolidations
title changes
binding
archiving
replacements
routing
contents processing
links to current awareness
links to catalogue.

4. *Circulation and loans:*
Rapid transaction processing
issues
returns
renewals
reservations
authority
charging and accounts
funds
fines
transaction alerts and traps, with annotation
item transfers

inventory
demographics
record sorting
self-issue
remote transactions and renewals, including voice response
bar coding
optical character recognition (OCR)
wands
labels
readers
reports.

5. *Management information and reports:*
Straightforward report production
printing
graphics
manipulation facilities
automated report generation
routing
automated updating
links to other systems, e.g. word-processing, accountancy packages, desktop publishing.

6. *Information retrieval:*
Automated searching for current awareness
selective dissemination of information (SDI)
alerts on current information
ad hoc searching
set searching, storage and retrieval
saved repeat searches
relevance ranking
lists and newsletter production
links to other systems, e.g. electronic mail, word-processing
hyperlinking
annotation
remote access
list management
links to multiple databases.

Statements of requirements from libraries often contain one of two main mistakes. The first is to be too vague, and encompass anything which appears to serve the purpose. For example, to select any systems with integrated acquisitions and cataloguing elements, regardless of detail. The other is to request a great range of facilities with no priorities set, to go for a fully functional automated library system carrying out all kinds of tasks, many conflicting with one another.

Some examples demonstrate the need for clear priorities –

- A busy lending library with many personal callers wants fast processing of loans. Numerous audit trails running on the circulation system slow down the procedure of issuing the book. Checking the borrower's authority to borrow is a prime requirement. Other activities delay the transaction, for example counting the number of times that book has been borrowed for stock control purposes, or online reservation checks.
- Searching a catalogue may involve large quantities of data. Automated sorting of items retrieved before the initial list is returned can cause lengthy delays.
- Checking in serials requires fast data entry and production of routing slips. Extended records showing all available information about the serial take longer to retrieve, even where data entry fields are arranged efficiently.
- A catalogue system with automated checking for existing similar records runs slower than a simple data entry system.
- A telephone enquiry service needs fast data entry and response times. Data logging for statistics purposes causes delay.
- Many systems which look good on-screen have difficulty in formatting printed reports. Changes to standard, default layouts can be hard.
- Reporting and auditing requirements slow down processing.
- On-screen graphics slow down display.
- Fast numeric processing is slowed down by complex text processing.
- Too many features make screens confusing and tasks cumbersome.
- If a computer is processing several tasks at once, everything runs more slowly than it should. If a complex task fails completely, the computer may be prevented from carrying out any subsequent activity. Tasks may be extensively delayed or data lost.

Compromises are needed. A correct assessment of priorities helps control these decisions. There must be a balance between what is actually on offer from suppliers, or what can be adapted, the ability of the computers to carry out the processing, and, most importantly for user acceptance, an appropriate interface and features which are practical and appeal to human beings.

Allocation of time

Reinforcing the need for planning is the fact that voluntary sector information staff never have spare time to spend on unnecessary automation. Putting in a new system, whether from scratch or to replace an existing one, takes a great deal of time. Planning, detailing requirements, justification, investigating options, making the choice, developing the system, modifications, training, data loading, evaluation, and many other issues, have to be fitted in alongside normal day-to-day work. Time spent at the planning stage can substantially cut the amount of time required later. It reduces wasted effort and the need to revisit areas or make compromises. The time and effort which is necessary can be put to more productive effect. Even if the librarian is fortunate in having additional project or consultancy help, time spent on planning produces an end result nearer to what is required, much more quickly.

Although the aim of computerisation is to do more and to be more effective, it should not be undertaken lightly, because of the increase in workload while bringing in the new system. It is unwise to keep pace with fashion changes, unless there is real benefit for the users.

Some of the essential planning gives library managers the chance to take a medium- to long-term view of what is important for the service, and how best this can be delivered. Discussion about user requirements, expectations and attitudes is invaluable. Most other activities in the project are tasks that might not otherwise be done. These take time from other jobs with greater short-term benefits. The librarian may need to spend long periods away from the service point, meeting with advisers and suppliers, visiting exhibitions, and evaluating products.

It is rare for library automation to be a simple upgrade of existing processes. Requirements change rapidly, and if a long-term perspective has properly been taken into account, the new system should involve different procedures and functions from before. It should allow for new activities and products. Consultation on these issues is essential for system acceptance, unless the service is a one-person operation without regular users. Time should be devoted to discussing the options and effects of procedural changes. These may be guided by the technology to a certain extent, but the exact workings must be properly thought through, and users' views and concerns thoroughly addressed. Computer systems are useless if people are uncomfortable with them. Poor interfaces put off librarians and library users alike. Staff bypass the computer if it makes their work more difficult, or threatens their job security. Unhelpful reports mean the computer generates reams of paper never read. Involving the people whose work will be changed identifies procedural problems and unexpected elements. Early identification of these issues makes finding a solution quicker, easier and cheaper. The discussions also make the system more familiar to people when it is finally installed.

Because people are mesmerised by the technical complexities and requirements of a project and the resulting changes in working practices, all effort may be directed towards simply getting the system in and working. These are major activities in themselves. However, none of this will be to much purpose if inadequate time is allowed for training and practice for staff and users. It is imperative that this is properly dealt with. Even the most straightforward software requires initial effort to learn, and there will be many future occasions when it is not obvious how a task is carried out, or how to deal with a new complexity.

As it is unlikely that normal day-to-day library activities can cease while the automation is going on, allowance must be made for the increased workload. Extra help may be needed. This can be additional staff, volunteers, consultants, or outsourced assistance, such as market research for user requirements. Alternatively, non-essential activities may be put to one side or abandoned. It can be expedient to spend money on assistance, rather than incur other costs or difficulties caused by activities not being carried out or performed inadequately. Overtime payments, if appropriate, are not cost-effective if the extra hours worked cause undue strain on staff. These considerations mean that librarians must be realistic about time demands. To underestimate them leads to loss of confidence by management and users, and resentment among staff.

It follows that over-optimistic expectations should be tempered. The organisation may propose an inadequate time-frame, simply because the manager does not realise how much work is involved. The librarian should discuss this and agree a more acceptable deadline. Equally, the librarian must be clear that the time spent, and the consequent distraction from other activities, are worth the effort. A major project for small gain is best left to a later date, when greater benefits may redound, unless there is a compelling external reason, such as a one-off allocation of funds or rare availability of expert technical help. As always, the librarian must have a clear idea of who and what the system is needed for and what is to be achieved.

Time-consuming tasks

Data loading can be very time-consuming, particularly when retrospective conversion is required. When moving from a manual system, substantial data input is unavoidable, even if the decision is taken just to automate new transactions or records. For example, each purchase processed by an acquisitions system needs to be linked to supplier details. For a service which obtains large amounts of grey literature from multiple suppliers, this can mean entering full contact details for numerous suppliers. A new catalogue means that authority files and subject and keyword entries have to be entered from scratch. Adding new material is slower than selecting from previously entered choices.

Where previous records are held in electronic form, care is needed to transfer data across properly. The old and new structures need to be mapped to one another accurately, and some manipulation is necessary. Transferred data should be checked. Sometimes there are so many problems in converting old data that the best option is to re-key it in its entirety, and the retrospective conversion is a major undertaking, probably the largest part of the whole project. This may be particularly necessary for historical research collections, where the new cataloguing system is expected to process records collected over many years. Some could be manual records, others may reside in a number of different databases, perhaps employing different technologies. It is likely that the cataloguing standards adopted throughout this period vary, so that records need to be brought into line.

An incremental approach is possible for some transaction systems. For example, an enquiry monitoring system can be built gradually from a particular date, yet still provide meaningful data. Most other aspects of library automation need a database of reasonable size, critical mass, to be effective. An acquisitions librarian will find it difficult to process a batch of books received if some of the orders are on the new system and others on the old. Incorrect identification is easy. As the new system probably controls the fund and accounting allocations, all expenditure details must be included if the reports are to make sense.

Some libraries use the automation project as an opportunity to update their records in conjunction with user and stock checks. This allows the system to reflect the collection and its usage accurately, and means that money and effort are not spent on creating out-of-date records. Obviously these activities are time-consuming. Although they are desirable, and important for major, fully-funded projects, trying to do this at the same time as everything else may be too much for a unit with few staff, unless volumes are low.

Finance and justification

For all projects except those which are small and use low-cost, off-the-shelf software, a statement of financial justification is needed. This explains the purpose of the system and the timing, as identified in the planning phase, and relates expenditure to the benefits to be gained.

Costing the system is well defined. There are a number of elements to include, which the financial controller expects to see. The cost-benefit analysis must show benefits which make the expenditure worthwhile. Principal elements of the costing statement are capital outlay, start-up costs, and ongoing, recurring costs.

1. *Capital costs:*
    Hardware, processors, terminals, personal computers (PCs), servers

    storage media, magnetic discs, tapes, optical disks

    cabling and power, networks

    software

    licences, per user, concurrent users, site and multi-site licences

    lighting and methods to reduce reflection and glare

    furniture and equipment, fireproof storage, anti-magnetic and anti-static devices

    building works, especially cable trunking.

2. *Start-up costs:*
    Development

    customising

    installation

    commissioning, ensuring the system works under all volumes of activity

    implementation

    data conversion

    parallel running until the new system is proven or fault-free to an acceptable level

    staffing

    consultation

    documentation

    training.

3. Recurring costs:
These can be the most important. Running costs often outweigh the initial cost of installation. A system which looks fairly cheap to implement may prove expensive in the long term.

Processing

security

backups and backup equipment

consumables, tapes, diskettes, paper, labels, input devices such as light pens, printer cartridges

power, uninterrupted power supplies

environmental controls, air-conditioning

administration and operations

insurance

training

documentation

hardware and software support, help desks

maintenance

communications, telephone charges

licences

development, modification and customisation

upgrades.

Although hardware and software tend to become cheaper over time, this is not always so. Specialised library systems may not follow this trend. Most other costs do increase. Allowance must be made for this in the recurring cost projections. Projects sometimes fail because running costs rise sharply after the first couple of years, as modifications are needed, volumes grow, and equipment has to be replaced. Licence and support costs should be watched particularly.

One ratio to check is to make sure that 5 to 10 per cent of the overall project cost is allowed to deal with human factors, such as training, good documentation, comfortable workstations, appropriate lighting, heating and ventilation. As noted before, it is acceptance by staff and users which is all-important, and in particular anything which makes the system more usable and useful for the library's patrons is money well spent.

Applications and systems

Once the choice of automation for libraries was fairly straightforward. A wide range of specialised library systems were on the market, and selection was generally determined by size, cost and appropriateness for the purposes of the purchasing library. As this was a specialist sector, directories and advisory services were able to supply all the information required. The library system was considered independently of other technology within the organisation. Library priorities defined the choice.

Now every type of activity is automated. Most librarians do not have the luxury of choosing the best system for their purpose, but must select something which matches the operating environment of other systems within the organisation. Few organisations take an all-pervasive view of their systems strategy, though a librarian working for a very small body may be able to exert sufficient influence to have the library's requirements properly taken into account. Too often, the first major system to be installed determines the operating environment. As this is frequently an accounting system with efficient number processing and batch report production, the system structure may not be very supportive of a librarian's need for high levels of interactivity and large volume text processing.

Office systems have received major attention from software manufacturers. They set up-to-date standards for appearance. Many perfectly functional library systems suffer from looking old-fashioned against these, and therefore meet user resistance. It is proving difficult for some library system suppliers to produce interfaces that give a Windows look and feel, or which integrate simply with Windows office systems or Internet services. Windows and graphical user interfaces (GUIs) also run more slowly than traditional command-driven or menu-based library systems. This affects productivity. There is additional price resistance, as office systems may be cheaper than library systems because of high volume sales, though the library software may come with better after-sales service.

Within the voluntary sector, librarians may need to share computers with other workers. The software has to co-exist with other functions, such as word-processing, marketing and membership databases, publishing software, inventory controls and specialist database and online packages, which are not part of the librarian's remit. If not loaded on the same PCs, these products often reside close by on a network, along with other core administrative software, such as accounting and personnel systems. Key concerns for the librarian are that the software does not conflict with other applications, and can link with it. For example, the organisation's membership records and the librarian's user details might be a shared database.

Technical conflict is a constant problem. One PC may absorb new software without difficulty, while the next simply stops running. Consequently, installing and upgrading the library's software is becoming more complex, particularly in comparison with single use central processing, and remote dumb terminal systems.

Library management systems

Most systems from library suppliers automate traditional library tasks. Some concentrate on one or two areas, others cover a range, often on a modular basis. They focus on management and administration tasks, with the OPAC as the main customer-facing product. Some library management systems are closed-state. They are self-contained and do not link with other software. Others have only limited inter-operability. These systems come in turnkey form, with hardware and software provided. Apart from some standard customisation, they can be installed in their entirety and run as delivered.

Several more recent entries to the market, and some rewritten versions of traditional products, have made a point of being open systems. These run alongside other software and link to it. They operate on the purchaser's existing hardware, or compatible equipment. Many suppliers have chosen UNIX as their sole open platform. It should be noted that these systems are not fully open, as they do not run in other environments. Some computer environments are unable to cope with adding UNIX to their architecture, because of protocol stack problems on the user terminal, which cannot handle the extra UNIX layer. This is a fundamental problem, which is not solved by increasing the size of the PC. UNIX exists in many forms. Not all inter-relate easily. However, many organisations do use UNIX, and their libraries have a good range of library management systems to choose from. True openness is rare.

Library management systems are particularly good at controlling processes. As there is great similarity between fundamental procedures in any type of library, suppliers have been able to program their products to follow these precisely. If the priority tasks for the purchasing library are procedural, a library management system can prove the easiest route.

Acquisitions software is an example of the procedural approach –

- A purchase requirement is identified and the details are entered on the system, or electronic book information sent from a book supplier can be selected from, and the details transferred to the library's order records.

- An order is generated and sent to the book supplier, either electronically or by post.

- The projected cost is added to the funding file, showing the amount of expenditure which has been committed but not yet paid. If payment is made with the order, the cost is deducted from the balance in the fund.
- An acknowledgement of placing the order may be generated and sent to the person requesting the book.
- Any reply from the bookseller is entered on the records, again perhaps electronically if the two systems are linked.
- The system monitors the date the order is placed and the presence or absence of responses. After pre-set periods, chasers are generated if the publication is not received as expected.
- Once the book is received, the record is amended to show receipt. Incorrect details may be altered, for example title and price.
- The invoice details are completed, and the cost is deducted from the fund.
- Payment may be direct, or the invoice is passed to the Accounts department for settlement. Any necessary reconciliation between the two systems is carried out.
- The software may generate routing information to accompany the book through accessioning, processing and cataloguing.
- Accesssioning procedures may be incorporated as part of the Acquisitions process, or may operate separately.
- If the Acquisitions software is stand-alone, the process ends. Otherwise the system may continue controlling the progress of the book until it reaches its destination.

Although the software has other functions, operating for example as a database and a source of statistics and reports, its prime characteristic and main use are that it governs a procedure. As a word of caution, the librarian may wish to limit this procedural control. In particular, systems which generate frequent chasers and reminders may be unwelcome. They can provide more tasks for consideration by the librarian than he or she needs.

Another excellent feature of library management systems is their ability to deal with complex database requirements. In particular, catalogue requirements are well handled, because of the in-depth experience of the software suppliers. As well as the database of bibliographic data about the items in the collection, the software handles such aspects as multiple copies in multiple locations, and open and closed entries. Data can be segmented or combined, for example to give separate catalogues by location as well as a union catalogue. Thesauri and authority files are linked in.

The third key attraction of library management systems is that many do cover most of the traditional library activities, particularly those that are book- and serial-based. They permit links between related tasks, such as acquisitions and cataloguing, or accessions and loans, so that shared data is entered just once, and alterations are kept in line.

Although library management systems come in all sizes, voluntary sector librarians may find that they do not reflect the principal activities carried out. The processes determine that the library is the centre of activity. Other tasks are subservient to this. The library is treated as a collection to be managed, rather than a dynamic information resource to be exploited. Information retrieval, SDI, enquiry handling, research and analytical work, newsletter and information sheet production, tend to be less well served.

The option of using a specific library package may not be available for technical reasons, or it may be inappropriate. Fortunately, there are other software choices. There used to be little point in amending other software to suit library purposes when specialist software already existed. Now, modern alternatives are often readily adaptable. They can be more flexible and better suited to specialist needs, particularly if there is a strong requirement to operate with other hardware and software.

Text retrieval software

This has been adopted by librarians in special libraries for many years. It combines many of the features of cataloguing systems with advanced searching and indexing capabilities, sometimes with flexible output options for the production of newsletters and information sheets. Text retrieval systems process large volumes of text efficiently, and cope with field-based input and free-text searching. Thesaurus features may be part of the software package, or the system may link to a separate thesaurus application. As thesauri require complex hierarchical relationships, and text retrieval needs good indexing, two pieces of linked software may be the optimal solution if thesaurus capabilities are required. Each application can then be tuned individually.

Text retrieval software is the ideal route if there is a large amount of unstructured free-text data to be processed, though it is often used for straightforward bibliographic details as a catalogue. Even here, the software can additionally be used for rapid processing of analytical entries. The software works well where the full text of material is entered, such as the complete content of internal reports. Extended abstracts can be created and searched.

This software is regularly used by commercial publishers for electronic publishing. Some suppliers facilitate linking their material with the librarian's in-house holdings. If publishers which are important to the library offer this or intend to in the future, a strong case can be made for adopting the same software, or extending the use of the publisher's offering.

Document management systems

Closely related to text retrieval are document management systems. This software was designed to control word-processing, and to make it easy to find previously typed documents, even if they have been filed or archived away. The software also supports version control, so that separate drafts of a document and the final version can be readily identified. Because all the in-house work product is searchable, the software operates as a modified text retrieval system, though it rarely offers all the search, retrieval and manipulation capabilities of fully functional text retrieval.

If document management is used elsewhere in the organisation, the librarian can adopt the system in several ways. Firstly, internal documents needed for the information collection can be identified. This may be done automatically, with certain categories of documents routed electronically to the librarian, for example when the final version is produced. Alternatively the librarian can search for material meeting appropriate criteria, and copy it into the collection or link to the original document so that it is retrieved when the collection is searched. Conversely, items from the librarian can be made directly available to users in their own working environment.

Workgroup software

This allows documents to be accessed by all members of a working group. The group can be defined in any way the users wish. It could comprise in-house contributors such as researchers together with external users. It is useful for research or expert communities, where, if so desired, anyone may add comments to material present on the database, so that an expanding area of knowledge is built up. For example, doctors may report experience of medical cases referenced in journal articles, or sociologists can debate a highlighted topic. Workgroup software operates over multiple sites, so fosters virtual communities. It is a popular tool for knowledge management.

Databases

Many database products are suitable. These range from simple field-based database systems, which are cheap in stand-alone form, to sophisticated relational database packages.

Some relational databases operate in conjunction with text retrieval and other office software. Very powerful multi-functional systems can be built. If the information requirements are extensive, and require high volumes of text processing over multiple sites, with interfaces to other applications, such as membership, marketing and publishing, these may be the most effective choice. The large, relational database-driven systems offer the greatest flexibility. The software undergoes regular development in a competitive market, so constantly moves with the times. Especially in its integrated form, this software is useful for information sharing, information research, text retrieval, SDI, report, newsletter, list and information sheet generation, as well as conventional database functions such as cataloguing. It is less helpful for procedural and transaction processing, though links to workflow are possible.

Integrated systems suitable for libraries are not available off-the-shelf using these components. It would require a major project to build a fully integrated system. Development is costly, though it may be worthwhile if a large community of users benefits from it.

At the small, cheap end of the scale, PC and networked relational databases are readily available, and are often bundled as part of an office software package with hardware sales. Relational databases can usually handle free text as well as structured information, so can be used for catalogues, acquisitions, databases or information retrieval systems. They can be adapted to provide some procedure control or transaction processing, but these are not their strengths. They are a viable option where information retrieval and enquiry handling are prime concerns.

Small relational databases are relatively easy to set up, and it is possible for librarians to build and modify their own systems, with fairly straightforward training. Low-cost consultancy is available if expert help is needed. Although there are some capacity limitations on smaller systems, they should be adequate for a small to medium-size information unit. If there are concerns about growth, the answer is to pick a database which can be scaled up by transfer to a larger system, for example by moving from a networked PC package to a related client/server product. This should create sufficient capacity.

Workflow software

Workflow software follows the same principles as library procedural systems. It is often found controlling accounting procedures or regular practices such as applications and claims. Normally the systems supplier works with the librarian to identify procedures, and builds each step into the automated process. These systems cope especially well with controlling the routing of an item such as a book or invoice, and with generating supporting documentation or checking authorisations.

Office automation systems

There are many products available as part of office automation systems which can be useful for librarians. Imaging software creates indexed databases of facsimile records, so that a picture of the full text of a document can be viewed or printed out. All diagrams, photographs, graphics, layout features and annotations are included. These systems organise collections which are not predominantly text-based.

Optical character recognition can be used to create databases of machine-readable data. These systems can stand alone, or may operate in conjunction with text retrieval. In the latter case OCR software captures the text, which is then transferred to the text retrieval package. OCR software is effective where absolute accuracy of input is not required, as all OCR systems create errors in interpreting text. If the prime purpose is to identify and locate relevant documents, it is usually adequate. It will not suffice without checking and some re-keying if verbatim duplicate records are required. Text validity increases if standard input forms are used, where information is precisely laid out in pre-set parts of the document.

Virtual libraries and the Internet

Perhaps the most useful development for the voluntary sector is the prevalence of Internet technology. This allows services to be delivered far and wide with minimal outlay. It is becoming an invaluable method of reaching widespread and scattered communities. The voluntary service can use the Internet to advertise its wares, and to exchange information with interested parties. Where electronic distribution used to mean setting up a physical means of communication, via networks, telephone connections, or sending out discs and CD-ROMs, now links can be established to anyone with Internet access.

Internet browsers can also be used to access internal databases and create standard interfaces, replacing the need for detailed technical development for many straightforward database or information dissemination activities. Using this technology internally on intranets allows the librarian to set up links to external resources alongside in-house material. This has the joint result of extending the range of readily accessible material and avoiding the need to build up some parts of the collection in-house and keep it current.

With this approach, care is needed that the linked external material is of fit quality for the service's purposes. Also, browser technology is still limited. Search and display features are currently not sophisticated, and unskilled or partly skilled users can be misled by it. Nonetheless, capabilities are improving rapidly. Pressurised information units should give serious consideration to the Internet, intranets, and closed user group extranets, which include external contacts, to see if this technology replaces the need for many of the traditional ideas of how a service should be set up and run.

It provides a simple means of organising data, particularly in conjunction with Windows databases. It is excellent for dissemination and communication, even more so if combined with workgroup technology. It is a cost-effective method of publication, and can draw in interested parties from a wider area than conventional methods, not least because of serendipity as well as targeted use.

Advice

Faced with all the technical options, the librarian may feel that it is impossible to work out what should be done. There are a number of consultancy and advisory services specialising in these areas, and early discussion with one of these is strongly recommended. Key contact points are the Library Information Technology Centre (LITC)[1], Aslib's consultancy contacts [2], Informed Business Services [3], or INFOmatch's consultancy contacts [4]. For word of mouth recommendations, it is worth checking with comparable information units, or discussing requirements with people who have set up something which appears to be suitable. Most librarians are willing to share invaluable practical experience.

Once a direction has been taken, it is recommended that the librarian has frank discussions with people who have similar implementations. This helps to set supplier and broad-based claims in context. Suppliers usually have reference sites for consultation. These are not entirely biased in their favour. Other users can be identified from system user groups, and from information directories which list technology used.

To make sure the best information is gleaned from advisers and informal referees, it is important to revert to the planning process and draw out the most important issues for the project. It is easy to become enthusiastic about a system because it works well elsewhere. Preparing the questions based on the key priorities verifies that no prime features are missing or inadequate.

Directories and publications

There is a good range of published information, on library systems in particular. Directories[6-8] give system, evaluation, and contact details. Library and information journals publish articles about information software. Accounts of user experience are particularly helpful, though may understate difficulties.

Exhibitions

Exhibitions offer quick overviews of systems capabilities. They should not substitute for proper research. The two most focused events are Libtech International [9] in March, and Online Information[10] in December. Vendors exhibit at many other library and information events. General computer exhibitions tend to show a low return on effort, but specialised document management, imaging or Internet shows may warrant a focused visit.

It is advisable to have a basic knowledge of the system capabilities beforehand, so that just the most relevant services can be inspected. It may be useful to be accompanied by a technology adviser, less at this stage for more complex technical issues as for general awareness.

Approaching suppliers

Ideally, these investigations lead to a reasonably short list of suppliers to approach. Depending on the library's requirements, there are two categories of organisations which may be involved. The first are the vendors themselves. They provide the products, and arrange everything from pre-sales through purchase, to implementation and support. Other suppliers work through or with systems integrators, who take the product and adapt it to meet the user's specific requirements. Systems integrators are especially necessary where different systems have to work together, for example linking imaging input software to a text retrieval system, or moulding different types of database software into an integrated system. This work may be done by an in-house technology department, but there are many advantages in buying in expertise from people who are familiar with the products to be integrated.

The way that suppliers are approached does much to facilitate smooth selection and implementation of library automation. It is best to work in depth with just a small number of possible vendors. This saves the librarian's time and makes the most of the supplier's capability. They are able to give more time and thought to situations if they have a 30 to 50 per cent chance of winning the sale, than if they are one of a dozen or more suppliers on a long list. To shorten an overly lengthy list, a letter or series of telephone calls covering a handful of key questions is the best way to make a preliminary selection. For example, if the operating system is unusual or an important requirement non-standard, a quick check on whether the supplier's system can handle these issues determines whether further investigation is worthwhile. This approach is much more effective than sending a broad range of suppliers an extensive list of all the requirements of the desired system, with a vague request for a response. The time for detailed checking and evaluation is when the short-list has been reached.

Unfortunately, for practical reasons, vendors cannot travel widely to display their wares on site at the preliminary enquiry stage, particularly if they are offering inexpensive systems. It is best to work first through any documentation that the vendor can send, supplemented by demonstration software, CD-ROMs or videotapes, and telephone conversations with the vendor or referees. It should be noted, though, that while demonstration software may give a flavour of the operation, it is often truncated, and may not display all features or give reassurance on volume issues.

If the librarian can travel to the vendor's location or display site, a clearer view is possible. To make this more meaningful, many vendors will load test data supplied by the librarian, if this is compatible and sent well in advance of the demonstration. Familiar data is particularly recommended if the librarian is accompanied by users when viewing the system.

The world of library automation is small. Good working relationships with vendors are important. Most suppliers are very knowledgeable about the market and other implementations, not just of their own product, but of the competition. Rather than install an ineffective system, they are honest about their capabilities. Some will even recommend others to approach if it is clear their own product cannot help. If the librarian establishes a professional relationship with them whether they obtain the contract or not, it is an opportunity to represent one's information service positively to an expert and influential group. Furthermore, no system has a working life much beyond five years, and a previously rejected product may prove ideal at the replacement stage. Building harmonious relationships each time helps the transition.

The one area which is different is where non-specialist off-the-shelf packages are selected, such as some of the standard PC database products. Here the amount and quality of support varies. Products are purchased from a reseller who may or may not have a broader relationship with the librarian's organisation. In this case, magazine articles (most often from the computer press) and references from other users may have to carry more weight.

System trials

Before making a final decision, it may be possible to test one or two packages for a trial period. These may be in truncated version, but the assessment is useful for librarians and users to obtain a feel for how the system works in practice. Testing with a small amount of data, running volume tests, or setting up a trial application, give good insight before final commitment.

The opportunity to familiarise people with the product before implementation is also helpful.

Supplier suitability

Software capabilities should govern system selection rather than a preference for one piece of hardware over another. However, there is one other consideration which can be overriding, and which is sometimes overlooked until too late. The technology market is crowded and competitive. The vendor may be required for maintenance, support and upgrades after purchase. It is essential to select a supplier who can keep this up. A financial check should be made on supplier viability. It is important also to ascertain the planned direction of business. Vendors make firm decisions about the sectors they work in, and a voluntary sector librarian whose vendor concentrates mainly on other markets may find co-operation dwindles after the initial sale.

Services for the users

Some librarians have genuine choice about whether to automate or not. Simple tasks may be carried out manually to great effect. A personal touch can bring flair to some products which computerised solutions cannot match. For most other automation decisions, the question is more how to carry out activities effectively. Time-consuming processing tasks are usually amenable to automation, and many librarians look to these as the point to start. The theory is that if these activities are left to the computer, then staff can spend time on more important jobs. Nevertheless, as computerisation is time-consuming and costly in itself, it may be a long while before the effort devoted to this is made up in increased benefits.

The librarian should look most closely at services to the user. Computerisation provides many user benefits, such as direct delivery of information, better communication, and a broader range of products. User needs, expressed or unexpressed, are where real improvements reside. Saving librarians' time comes later. Installing systems which do nothing for users is old-fashioned. Automation is not an end in itself, though its complexity diverts attention from the real aims. By retaining the principle of creating user benefits firmly in mind, the librarian should be able to work through the many planning and decision points to best effect. A clear view of the ultimate goal helps all the staff and users deal with the extra workload and disruption until the system is in and finally delivering the chosen benefits.

References

1. LITC. South Bank University, 103 Borough Road, London SE1 0AA. Telephone: +44 (0) 171 815 7872. URL: www.sbu.ac.uk/litc/
2. Aslib, The Association for Information Management. Staple Hall, Stonehouse Court, 87-90 Houndsditch, London EC3A 7AX. Telephone: +44 (0) 171 903 0000. URL: www.aslib.co.uk/
3. Informed Business Services. 41-47 Old Street, London EC1V 9HL. Telephone: +44 (0) 171 282 1900. URL: www.informed-ibs.com/
4. INFOmatch. The Library Association, 7 Ridgmount Street, London WC1E 7AE. Telephone: +44 (0) 171 636 7543. URL: www.la-hq.org.uk/
5. Wood, Joanna. *European directory of software for libraries and information services*, Aldershot, Ashgate, 1993
6. Wood, Joanna and Moore, Caroline (eds.). *European directory of text retrieval software*, Aldershot, Gower, biennial
7. Leeves, Juliet. *Library systems in Europe: a directory and guide*, London, TFPL, 1994
8. Leeves, Juliet. *Libsys.UK: a directory of library systems in the United Kingdom*, London, Library Information Technology Centre, 1995
9. Libtech International. University of Hertfordshire, College Lane, Hatfield, AL10 9AD. Telephone: +44 (0) 115 967 7706. URL: www.herts.ac.uk/libtech/
10. Online Information. The National Hall and Olympia Conference Centre, London. Learned Information Europe Ltd, Woodside, Hinksey Hill, Oxford OX1 5BE. Telephone: +44 (0) 1865 736354. URL: www.online-information.com

12

Knowledge Management: Why Get Involved With the Internet?

Emma Hallam and Mark Walker

'We stand on the threshold of a revolution as profound as that brought about by the printing press.'[1]

Internet technology, often perceived as a communications and networking tool of the future, is here now, and no organisation competing in today's political and economic climate can afford to ignore it. Despite fears that it will create a society of information 'haves' and 'have-nots', new technology can act as an important leveller for any organisation which is subject to financial pressures and limited resources.

Technology is not in itself the model solution, however, and its use can only be truly effective for those organisations which have clear objectives and coherent strategies for their communications management and development. This chapter discusses:

1. What is Voluntary Sector Information?
2. The Communication of Voluntary Sector Information and Electronic Networking Opportunities
3. Internet Tools
4. How Internet Tools can be Used to the Benefit of Voluntary Sector Knowledge Management
5. Improving Opportunities for Collaboration
6. Greater Visibility for Voluntary Sector Organisations and Their Activities
7. How Electronic Networking can Lead to Greater Visibility
8. Conclusions

1. What is Voluntary Sector Information?

The voluntary sector is dynamic and diverse, made up of a wide range of organisations which differ hugely in their subject interest, size and resources. There is a also a wide diversity of roles played by voluntary sector organisations, from social clubs, to support groups, to campaigns, to practical help and advice-giving. Its growth is largely random and often stimulated by people's individual interests and life experiences. This inevitably means that the information needs of the voluntary sector are complex and diverse, presenting specific challenges to effective communication of that information.

As a starting point, voluntary organisations and groups can be divided into two basic categories:

- groups which have developed locally;
- groups which are part of a national organisation.

Voluntary sector information can also be divided into two basic types:

- formal information;
- informal information.

Both categories of information will be used by both categories of voluntary organisation. To explore the information needs of voluntary organisations more fully, voluntary sector information can be divided into the four categories shown below:

i) Basic Information

Formal in nature, and often specific to a local area, this information is useful to members of the public and employees of organisations from every sector. It is often found in local directories of voluntary sector organisations, and usually consists of a brief introduction to the organisation, what it does and contact details. Whilst most pieces of basic information should remain correct over long periods, others can very quickly become out-dated, such as names and addresses of key contacts, details of specific services, etc.

ii) Advice and Information Relevant to the Organisation's Beneficiaries

This information may be of a formal or informal nature and is typically provided directly by the working members of a voluntary organisation to its beneficiaries. Such information is often collated from a variety of different sources, including public, private and voluntary sectors organisations. Indeed the information may also be provided to other agencies in other sectors.

For example: the National Association of Citizens' Advice Bureaux, in working with its local offices to provide advice to the public, needs to keep abreast of changes in government legislation and guidelines relating to benefits. It can collect and collate basic information from a number of national sources, but also needs to update its own systems to reflect local needs and services. In addition, the National Association performs a consultative role to the Government on relevant social issues.

iii) Advice and Information Relevant to Other Organisations

In order to maintain and develop their expertise, workers in any voluntary organisation need to communicate effectively with each other and manage their information pool effectively to facilitate efficient and accurate retrieval. This requires formal measures within the organisation, such as expertly-designed database systems with sophisticated search facilities.

It is also necessary for voluntary sector workers to keep up-to-date with external developments. No single organisation can possibly have all the information it may need without consulting other organisations, which highlights the need for information sharing and communication and collaboration between organisations from all sectors. This can be of both a formal and informal nature, although encouraging informal communication is an important way of facilitating information flow generally.

iv) Information Necessary to Operate an Organisation

This covers a huge range of information, such as employment law, management resources, financial advice and details of funding opportunities. This information will not usually be of direct relevance to the beneficiaries of an organisation, but in an increasingly competitive environment the importance of a proactive approach to seeking information and opportunities cannot be emphasised enough.

For example: A voluntary organisation has successfully registered as a charity and an initial marketing campaign to increase donations has been moderately successful. It is recognised that the organisation cannot rely on existing donors and a member of staff is asked to investigate funding grants and sponsorship currently available to voluntary sector organisations. Many published sources are available, including electronic databases, at varying costs and of varying use. Access to the published information alone is not enough – the worker must use his or her skills and experience to identify the most effective way of gathering and using the information. Any advice or guidance available from other fund raisers will add considerably to their ability to achieve this.

2. The Communication of Voluntary Sector Information and Electronic Networking Opportunities

It is the diverse nature of voluntary sector information which gives it its unique strength: one which could be further developed through structured communication and networking: 'We believe that the vastness and diversity of the sector, the quality and depth of its content harnessed on a central service provides not only strength in numbers and cohesiveness but an unprecedented opportunity for the sector to be at the forefront of the emerging information society.'[2]

Highly regarded for their co-operative and communicative approach, organisations in the voluntary sector have traditionally employed a range of different methods of communicating their information, both internally and externally. It is still difficult for voluntary groups to keep track of what others are doing, however, which creates gaps in information and service provision and leads to duplication of effort. Opportunities for communication offered by the Internet, could change this aspect of voluntary sector activity forever: 'For the first time, voluntary organisations can publish information, electronically and directly, to a mass audience without incurring high production and distribution costs, and perhaps more importantly, be able to do so without interpretation by the media.'[3] How does this relate to individual voluntary organisations in their everyday activities and operational requirements? The communication concepts of voluntary sector activity will be examined first.

i) Communicating Basic Information

Directories of basic information, often compiled by a local umbrella organisation, are a useful reference point for those wishing to find out about voluntary sector activity in their locality. However, traditional paper-based directories are relatively expensive for local community centres and libraries to produce and very difficult to keep up to date once published without replacing the whole publication altogether. This is a long-standing problem for holders and publishers of such directories, especially when the audience for the information is unlikely to be able to pay for expensive updates or regular reprints.

Many voluntary sector organisations now prefer to use and share electronic databases of basic information, as these are far more flexible to up-date and simpler to duplicate and distribute. However such databases are not usually available for the public to browse, and where not part of a network can only operate as a single source of reference, often requiring reference to further more detailed sources.

All such information often relies on data drawn from a variety of sources, which may not always include the holder of the information itself. A small playgroup may offer a different number of free places for each school holiday, for example. Because the data available in local directories is supplied once a year via the local council's play worker the quality of information in the database relies on the quality of the communication between the group and the play worker.

ii) Advice and Information Relevant to the Organisation's Beneficiaries

Newsletters and mailings are often used to keep beneficiaries and supporters up to date on an organisation's progress, including new developments in its particular field of interest, information about new services and notices of events. Although the mailing and production costs of a newsletter may be covered by a subscription fee, they are still an expensive resource for the organisation to produce. No matter how often they are produced they are also subject to the limitations of any printed communication: they can rapidly become out-of-date and are difficult to update and distribute cheaply.

Sharing such information by post costs the same amount for each item posted – the per item cost of a mailing may fall as the quantity increases but this does not reduce the total cost to the organisation. This can create a tension between an organisation's wish to communicate with a wide range of audiences and its ability to afford to do so.

For advertising events and activities, notice boards, in libraries and community centres, are popular, cheap and effective. They too, have their limitations, however, for those people unable to get to their library or community centre, or who do not visit regularly and find out about an event too late.

Less formally, attendance of events, meetings and activities enables people to keep up-to-date with progress and communicate directly with representatives of the organisation. Informal word-of-mouth communication can work very well, particularly in organisations operating on a drop-in basis, such as support groups and advice centres. Follow-up contacts, whether by telephone, meetings or letter can prove expensive, however, and without a coherent and well-resourced communications structure to support it the networking and information benefits of such informal communication can be lost.

iii) Advice and Information Relevant to and From Other Organisations

Different organisations and different branches of a national organisation may use a variety of methods to communicate developments and expertise with each other. Whether on an organisational or individual basis it is natural for networks of particular interest to evolve, as a means of providing mutual support and sharing specialist information.

This goes beyond simple information provision as it is a two-way process of communication – being able to ask questions and share expertise within a specific field. Whether formal or informal any network will usually provide two main benefits to its members:

- a chance to meet as a group; and
- individual contacts to be used as required.

Events – such as training workshops, conferences and seminars – can provide voluntary sector workers with a chance to meet, communicate and share ideas by word of mouth. They also provide an opportunity to make contacts which will be of use after the event.

However, despite best intentions, most groups of people will tend to lose touch between events, concentrating instead on one or two specific contacts for individual queries or information. Familiarity and mutual understanding is difficult to sustain with large numbers of people through telephone or written contact and, in general, a lack of regular group contact and established networking will tend to limit the potential communications benefits of the events themselves.

As well as direct contact with other organisations, structured, shared databases of relevant information – such as VolNet UK, which contains thousands of references to research undertaken by voluntary agencies – are vital to the management of voluntary sector knowledge and expertise. Well-managed resources such as these enable voluntary sector workers to draw on a pool of specialist information as well as allowing them to contribute to a growing body of specialist knowledge.

Networks of email messages can spread quickly and easily amongst large numbers of people. Messages shared by email are easily passed on to others and subjects can be discussed in a way which encourages input from everyone. This can help enhance the quality of information available within a group and promote more effective use of meeting time as people will be better informed before attending events.

iv) Communication of Operational Information Within an Organisation

Meetings play a major role in the communication within any organisation and are used to share ideas and formulate solutions to problems, as well as to communicate new developments and thus keep staff and volunteers up-to-date.

As with any organisation, staff time is perhaps the voluntary sector's most valuable resource and effective communication with staff members is of paramount importance. Regular meeting attendance may be problematic if the majority of the staff are voluntary and/or part-time, and an organisation with several branches may find that the cost of travel prohibits jointly-held meetings. Keeping minutes and circulating them to those unable to attend can be time-consuming and expensive, and where information is changing rapidly, may even be out-of-date by the time they are circulated.

Internal newsletters or memos are also used, mainly by larger organisations, to provide up-dates on organisational changes and external developments affecting the organisation's work. Once again, however, the inflexibility of newsletters once they have gone to print, and the cost of producing and distributing them may outweigh the benefits.

For example: An important aim of an organisation's newsletter is to boost staff morale about the organisation's progress. The organisation has successfully won a local campaign, but details of this are not added to the newsletter as it has already gone to print. The newsletter is printed every two months, so by the next edition the victory is old news. Most staff have read about it in the local newspaper and the newsletter, costly to produce, has failed to achieve an important aim. Email and/or Web pages provide a way of producing more timely information and sharing the good news with people both inside and outside the organisation.

3. Internet Tools

The Internet is a network of computers which provides a physical link between any two computers on that network. Over the past five years the use of the network has developed at an incredible pace and there are now millions of computers connected in every country across the world. Using those connections it is now relatively easy to share information and communicate with millions of other people using a standard personal computer.

The purpose of this chapter is not to look in depth at how the Internet works, but to examine what it can do. A reasonable working knowledge of a computer is required for anyone wishing to make full use of its capabilities, but most people who can use a word processor should find the transition to the Internet relatively straightforward.

The language of the Internet is the digital code used by computers. This means that anything which is produced on a computer can be shared with any other computer on the Internet, whether word processing files, pictures, sound or video. Paper and pen is still a common means of recording and transmitting personal information, but more and more communications already involves the use of a computer.

i) What can the Internet do?

There are two common ways of using the Internet to enhance the quality and convenience of communications:

Electronic mail (email):
Typed messages can be sent between any two points on the Internet, in most cases almost instantly. It is a cost-effective, simple means of communication which is convenient to use alongside existing tools, such as the telephone, fax or post. Most significantly, because of the way the Internet works, any message to anyone in the world costs the same amount, and it is only slightly more expensive to send the same message to one hundred people as it is to send it to one person.

The World Wide Web:
A new way of accessing and publishing information through the Internet. The Web enables any computer on the Internet to see specially prepared 'pages' of information stored on another computer on the Internet. Web pages are similar to the pages of a word processing document, but can present information in a number of different ways. One of the most significant is the ability to link into information held on other computers on the Internet, allowing the user to follow particular strands of information published from many different sources. Allowing for the barriers to actual use of the Internet – such as cost of hardware, lack of expertise and ongoing telephone charges – it is relatively simple to publish a Web page. It is this which encourages many voluntary organisations to consider using it as part of their communications strategy.

Other applications of the Internet include video-conferencing, live chat systems, file sharing and Internet-based telephone calls, all of which provide opportunities for more effective communication and information-sharing.

Email and the Web are the most common basic applications, however, and examples included in this chapter particularly relate to their use.

ii) How to get online

As with many new applications and tools, the only sensible way to learn more about the Internet is to have a go. No amount of words can replace the experience of composing and sending email or 'surfing' the World Wide Web. It is also difficult to imagine the potential of new technology without some concept of how it does what it can do.

There are two routes to finding out more: using a publicly accessible Internet connection, such as a cybercafe or library, or having access via the home or office. Using someone else's computer and getting them to give you a guided tour is great way of finding out more about the Internet's capabilities and becoming familiar with terms such as 'email' and 'Web Page'.

Anyone wishing to access the Internet to send emails and use the World Wide Web, would probably need the following:

- A minimum of a 486 IBM compatible PC;
- A modem connecting the computer to a phone line – the faster the better;
- An Internet Service Provider (commonly referred to as an ISP) who will provide access to the Internet and email facilities for a monthly charge or a fee calculated by the time spent online (many offer the first month free as a trial);
- The relevant software (provided by the ISP) to use the Internet and email facilities on the PC;
- A telephone line – it is possible for all but the most frequent user to share with an existing fax or phone line.

The above is not meant to be prescriptive as standards change all the time. However, it is frustratingly slow to access the World Wide Web on anything less than a 486 computer and it may prove cheaper to share a machine or pay in advance for access via a local cybercafe or library.

It is important to recognise that the Internet is a tool. There is no need to be at the cutting edge of technology, especially when most people spend most of their time using email, which will work on slower, older and cheaper computers. It is the use of the tools which is valuable, and the concepts which underlie them which provide the enormous potential for communications and information sharing.

4. How Internet Tools can be Used to the Benefit of Voluntary Sector Knowledge Management

The Internet tools described above can be applied to voluntary sector activity to help cut communication costs and develop new services. However, the effects of the new technology are more far-reaching, in the light of political and economic change:

> The work of voluntary agencies is becoming increasingly information-intensive. This reflects a general social trend, but can also be attributed to government policies which have placed greater reliance on market forces and principles in the area of social policy; and a more general trend towards decentralising public responsibility for economic development and human services to the local level. Arising from these national policy changes are strong financial pressures on the community and voluntary sector, and a growing emphasis on public-private sector partnerships, which have necessitated higher levels of efficiency, flexibility and competitiveness.[4]

If Internet tools are embraced by all voluntary sector organisations, networks of communication can be developed which have not previously been possible. Amongst other outcomes this would further raise the profile of this diverse and dynamic sector in society.

This could lead to further voluntary sector activity, by building on and developing the many strengths of the voluntary sector, and enabling closer co-operation with similar public and private sector agencies. Such co-operation could further minimise duplication of effort and facilitate a greater focus on gaps in service provision and the changing needs of society.

Amongst the tools which could prove useful are:

i) The World Wide Web

Information need only be published on the Web once, and need never be duplicated or copied for circulation. Web pages, comprising links to other pages and other Web sites, enable the user to follow his or her own path through the information available. This allows greater freedom to follow particular strands of interest, rather than predetermined pathways through static information.

For example: A mother who was experiencing difficulty in breast feeding her Down's Syndrome baby, found little information locally about her highly specific problem, after her midwife was unable to advise her.

Finding relevant organisations' sites on the Internet linked her to the information she needed, and also put in touch with other mothers of Down's Syndrome children, enabling her to form supportive and understanding friendships.

Web-based directories and databases, such as Poptel's Grey Pages and Information Directory[5] can form an integrated part of a highly interactive information system. This could also include direct email contact to the organisation in question, bulletin boards and even chat facilities as some of their links. These interactive features may be used on a variety of different levels, from encouraging feedback to gauge user satisfaction, to actually providing an advice-giving service online.

For example: Manchester Community Information Network has incorporated an interactive Citizens' Advice Bureau site, which also contains answers to 'Frequently Asked Questions'. This is more than a list of telephone numbers and opening hours: if the person looking through the Web Pages finds that their question is frequently asked it will be immediately answered, with links set up to lead to further helpful information. This has benefits for both the users of the system, who may not be able to access the CAB when it is open, and for CAB staff who can answer more queries. The provision of Internet access in the office acts as a further source of guidance alongside their library of printed materials.

Particularly dynamic information can also be consigned to specific pages, headed with a title such as, 'What's New', enabling regular visitors to up-date themselves about new developments quickly and effectively, without combing through previously scanned material.

Links to relevant sites of other similar organisations are also possible, creating a network of references and interactive information on a particular subject supported by cross-sector and international organisations.

For example: GreenNet is a major Internet Service Provider for voluntary and campaigning groups, and includes contacts, through links, to International Womens' Organisations, and reports from United Nations and Non-Governmental Organisations.[6]

ii) Mailing Lists and Bulletin Boards

Mailing lists take advantage of how simple it is to send an email to more than one person at a time. They come in different forms but the simplest it is a list of email addresses put together by the person sending the message. When sending a message it is possible to include as many addresses as required, with almost no additional cost incurred for each one.

For example: Sussex Community Internet Project (SCIP) sends out regular announcements about its monthly meetings. Over 100 are sent via email.

Once the message is composed it is sent in about 25 seconds to all 100 people on the mailing list, which incurs the minimum BT charge of five pence. Another eighty letters are then printed, photocopied, put in envelopes and posted, at a cost of approximately 20 pence each (second class). The email is available to most people within ten minutes – a second class letter may take two days and is more expensive to SCIP.

Members of any mailing lists can actively participate in discussions by sharing their thoughts on whatever topics are raised by other people on the list – sending their reply to everyone else, or taking up specific points with particular individuals. Or they could simply 'lurk', keeping an eye on messages as they are sent out but not actively contributing directly.

Bulletin board systems are a forerunner of the Internet and are still popular as a way of providing a 'managed' interactive space for contributions on subjects of mutual interest. Involvement requires a computer, modem and appropriate software (which is usually free). An Internet account is not necessarily required and, whilst relatively simple to use, the whole system must be set up by someone with some technical expertise.

Although largely superseded by the advent of the Web, bulletin board systems are still a great way to link up people to share electronic information. Individual organisations' Web sites may include links to a bulletin board system specialising in their area of expertise, and save duplication of effort in publicising information of interest to other like-minded individuals and organisations.

As with the World Wide Web, bulletin boards allow a single 'posting' of new information to be immediately available to everyone with access to the board. This highlights the fact that bulletin boards and the Web are subject to the same limitations as traditional notice boards – they are only effective if people look at them and keep them up to date!

iii) Private Email

Messages can be sent electronically to another individual, in the form of simple text, and their privacy is protected by password access. Copies can be sent at the same time to other people within the organisation, and files attached and instantly sent. This can be useful for circulating minutes to meetings or sending reports, for example. Where a report needs to be sent which is only available in paper form it may be converted into a computer file using a scanner.

This form of message need not be restricted to internal use within an organisation, but can be sent to anyone, in any organisation, provided that they have an email address. As research shows that there is a 20%

chance of actually getting through to an individual by telephone during a working day, email use can be a far more effective use of staff time.

As the connection charge to send an email is at the rate of a local telephone call, it can be a far cheaper option for national and international communications, with obvious benefits to charities working with other organisations spread over a wide geographical area.

For example: a twinning association in a British town is trying to organise a celebratory event with towns in France and Germany. Each town will be sending its mayor and leading business figures to promote local products, as well as local artists to contribute to an evening's entertainment. As the event draws nearer there is more and more to organise and the twinning association is having to rely increasingly on the telephone, which is expensive and has caused several linguistic misunderstandings. Most of the telephone calls could be replaced by email messages, at the rate of a local call, and printed for clarity and easy reference, to avoid misunderstandings. Internet services are also beginning to emerge which automatically translate messages en route to their destination.

Email contacts in organisations, provided by direct links through an organisation's Web site, immediately make that organisation more accessible, and encourage communication with its members. Unlike letters, email can be very informal, which may be far less daunting to an individual contacting an organisation for the first time, especially if it is regarding a personal matter. People who feel anxious about making initial contact may find it easier to prepare a written message than to speak to someone.

For example: Samaritans has pioneered an email service for people wishing to contact them for support, which has proved very popular.[7] Anonymity is maintained using a simple re-mailing system and since its launch in 1996 it has grown in importance in the organisation. Users are usually found to be more articulate about their needs in an email message – probably because they have the chance to work through their 'letter' before sending it. Because of the current profile of regular computer users the Samaritans has found that it is now reaching more young men than before, and a higher proportion of students. One spin off has been the introduction of a postal service for Samaritans!

Email not only enables voluntary sector organisations to be more accessible to those they serve, but also enables the development of new services to make all aspects of society more accessible to people otherwise marginalised.

For example: A charity in the South West, Disabled Young Adult Centre (DYAC), provides a service enabling disabled people in rural areas to undertake training courses of their choice, ranging from NVQs to degrees from Cambridge University. After a visit to assess their needs, each client is set up with an individual programme and an email account, in order to study remotely. This is also an excellent example of cross-sector collaboration, as the charity uses Exeter University's email network.[8]

iv) Chat Facilities

These offer the chance to communicate 'live' to many people at the same time, rather than just one person, thus creating the opportunity for live discussions online. This can make organisations more accessible, and enables their membership to communicate with each other, without physically having to meet. This is particularly important for organisations whose members are scattered over a large geographical area.

For example: an individual with cerebral palsy comes across a support group for people with cerebral palsy with a chat facility. She meets several people, and regularly chats and plays games online with them. Thus, she learns about medical developments in America from the patients' viewpoint, and develops some lasting friendships. She also hears of a friend who collapsed while playing chess online in Britain. His partner in the States, noticing a delay, successfully alerted the English emergency services, who arrived in time.

5. Improving Opportunities for Collaboration

Collaboration – whether between voluntary sector organisations or cross-sector – has traditionally been challenged by the cost of travel and meetings, and telephone conferencing.[9] However, Internet facilities, offering the opportunity to communicate effectively and cheaply without the need to physically meet, offer the voluntary sector new, economically viable opportunities for collaborative efforts.

For example: The 'Mental Health Handbook', on Cambridge Online City's community network, offers a totally comprehensive guide to mental health, useful to members of the public, volunteer workers and professionals alike. The information is provided by two organisations, 'Lifecraft', a voluntary organisation run by users and ex-users of mental health services, and 'Directions Plus', an independent organisation funded by social services offering information to all people with any kind of disability or illness, including mental illness.[10]

This could easily have been created remotely by geographically separated organisations. The ability to attach files of information to email messages enables instant and cheap communication of large quantities of complicated information, as well as remote editing of items such as reports (NB this chapter has been circulated by email between editors and other contributors).

The pooling of operational information resources can benefit organisations in all sectors, and avoid duplication of effort in individual organisations by encouraging a sharing of responsibilities.

For example: 'Meeting Venues' information on Manchester Community Information Network comprises a list of all types of meeting venue available in the city, 'from large hotels to small community centres', including details of the level of disabled access.[11] A variety of organisations can contribute to the information held online, with occasional meetings used to update on policy and share feedback on how to develop the information.

The benefits are multiple – not only can existing services be improved by collaboration, but new services can be created that could not be provided by organisations working in isolation. This may be particularly useful for highly specialist organisations, such as a support group for people with a very rare illness. Such an organisation might feel isolated in their local area, and wish to join forces with another, like-minded organisation.

Smaller voluntary sector groups on tighter budgets can also use collaborative efforts with larger organisations from other sectors to create a presence for themselves online, thus increasing their visibility in the local community and the visibility of their cause in society as a whole.

6. Greater Visibility for Voluntary Sector Organisations and Their Activities

Greater visibility for voluntary sector organisations and their activities has obvious benefits in an increasingly competitive environment, both for the particular causes that they serve, and from an operational viewpoint. These are examined in more detail below.

Greater visibility means better public support and boosts membership
Obviously, the higher the profile of a voluntary organisation, the greater the level of public support it will receive – an issue recognised in November last year by the British Legion, when they used the Spice Girls to help launch the latest Poppy Appeal Campaign, in an attempt to raise its profile with the younger generation.

Greater visibility increases an organisation's chances of attracting volunteers
The higher the public profile enjoyed by a voluntary organisation, the more likely it is that individuals thinking of offering their time will remember its name.

Greater visibility means improved access
Not everybody goes to the library to find out which local voluntary groups and organisations reflect their interests, concerns and hobbies. Many people find out about voluntary sector activity purely by chance and the greater the visibility of an organisation's activities and staff members, the greater the chance that they will find it.

Greater visibility of an organisation can support funding applications
Voluntary sector organisations need to look for sources of funding other than members' subscriptions and individual donations from the public. Once a possible source of sponsorship money or grant has been identified, competition is usually fierce. Greater visibility for an organisation can lead to greater understanding of its work. By helping to underline the value of what it does it may prove easier to secure funding.

Greater visibility creates opportunities for work with other organisations to develop projects that might not otherwise be possible
Greater visibility and wider public recognition also mean that interested parties and like-minded organisations will be more aware of an organisation's interests and activities. A snowball effect can be started when an organisation answers another organisation's query. It may lead to regular communication of ideas and problem sharing, which could eventually lead to a joint project being established to bridge a gap in existing services. This in turn generates even greater visibility for both organisations, as well as further contact with other organisations.

7. How Electronic Networking can Lead to Greater Visibility

Electronic networking enables an organisation's visibility to be developed by helping to improve the effectiveness of existing channels of communication. For example, people with similar interests and expertise can be introduced to relevant voluntary sector organisations through email news groups and mailing lists.

Visibility of voluntary sector activities and concerns can also be developed in completely new ways. For example, messages shared on an email mailing lists enable organisations to communicate with people with whom they do not normally have contact, which is not possible with more traditional communication methods.[12]

Email can also improve access to an organisation, as anyone seeking information can browse an organisation's Web site and follow up particular queries by contacting key workers by email. This contact can take place at the convenience of both parties – a message may be sent during the evening and answered at the beginning of the next working day, to be collected again that evening.

i) How to Achieve Greater Visibility

Electronic networking is a tool which most voluntary sector organisations cannot now afford to ignore. As time goes on more and more people will have access to similar technology – in much the same way that the telephone and fax came into common usage. As the number of people online increases it will become ever more critical for any organisation to examine its use of new technology, both in terms of the quality and the cost-effectiveness of its communications.

Electronic communications tools must also form part of an organisation's overall communications work. Simply adding a Web site and having email isn't going to deliver greater visibility. It is necessary to also look more thoroughly at the audiences you expect to be reaching through these media and what messages you wish to share with which audience. Use of the Web and email must integrate with print, meetings, events and other forms of communication

ii) Greater access

Many voluntary organisations are recognising the need to tackle issues of social and economic exclusion faced by those without the money or skills to access technology such as the Internet. The provision of public Internet access points in community centres and public libraries can help ensure that anyone, regardless of status, has access. 'Community centres make ideal public access points – because they are often the hub of existing social networks. [Internet Communications Technology] can be used to reinforce these social networks by strengthening existing and developing new relationships between community groups and individuals.'[13]

Several community information network projects have striven to achieve this, such as Manchester Community Information Network[14] which has provided twelve different public access points across the city so far.

The BEON Project in Bristol, funded jointly by BT and ICL, provided two million pounds' worth of computer equipment to schools in the Hartcliffe and Withywood areas. Despite scepticism that the computers would be stolen, 21 months later the truancy level has dropped by up to 90% and parents are going into school to learn IT skills from their children.[15]

Access to IT facilities for voluntary sector organisations can be provided by establishing partnerships to develop local community networks, as is the case with Cambridge Online City and Manchester Community Information Network. Both of these joint ventures involved voluntary sector organisations as partners in the development process, trading their human resources and expertise for computers and online access. Sponsorship is also available from a variety of sources, such as the Lottery Fund and the European Union.

iii) Training

Without access to the technology, many people have not developed the requisite IT skills to take full advantage of electronic networking. Initial training workshops, to promote the benefits of electronic networking to the voluntary sector and encourage its use, would help overcome people's reticence and fear of the technology, especially if these included demonstrations and practical experimentation.

These could be followed up with IT training sessions, which could be internally organised, or a collaborative effort between organisations, to enable voluntary sector workers to use the technology. Support for people on a steep learning curve could then be offered in the form of mentoring by those more familiar with the technology. Once trained, voluntary sector workers could also support public use of online information at access points.

8. Conclusions

Internet technology provides many potential benefits to voluntary sector organisations, and offers new tools which can be used to improve the quality and effectiveness of communications and information sharing. The needs of the sector are many and varied, and it has traditionally been slow to take up new technology. Resources are naturally focused on meeting existing needs, with little experience or expertise in developing IT-based solutions to information and communications needs.

Many organisations are developing their use of the Internet, however, and resources are available to encourage others to join them. The costs of being online continue to fall and there is increasing awareness amongst the general public that the Internet is not exclusively the domain of traditional computer users.

The tools available on the Internet – especially email and the World Wide Web – offer new ways of meeting internal and external information and communication needs. Greater collaboration, more cost effective and open communication and greater visibility can be achieved through focusing on how to use those tools to meet a specific organisation's needs.

The challenges facing voluntary sector organisations wishing to get online are recognised. It is still far from cheap, and not especially simple for a computer novice. But, like other challenges faced by the voluntary sector, this is not insurmountable. Funding for facilities is available, and savings on communication costs using email can be achieved.

Furthermore, the technology encourages and underpins partnerships with other organisations, which is an ideal way to develop information and communication networks within local communities which can bring the benefits of the Internet to everyone.

References

1. Labour Party Views and Policy
   http://www.labour.org.uk/views
2. Voluntary Organisations Internet Service (VOIS)
   http://www.vois.org.uk/vois/html/content.html
3. Ibid.
4. Community Development Foundation. *Press enter, report of the IT and Communities Working Party for the Community Development Foundation: information technology in the community and voluntary sector.* Research Policy Paper No.16, 1992, p.1.
5. Poptel (0171) 249 2948
   http://www.poptel.org.uk
6. GreenNet (0171) 713 1841
   http://www.gn.apc.org
7. *http://www.samaritans.org.uk*
   Their email addresses for those needing help are as follows:
   jo@samaritans.org
   samaritans@anon.twwells.com
   (for those wishing to email anonymously)
8. Disabled Young Adults Centre (DYAC) Clarke House
   Southernhay East
   Exeter EX1 1PQ
   01392 202273
9. Grunwald, Terry. *Making the NetWork: online strategies for community-based organisations.* Published in the UK by Communities Online, 1997, pp.44-45.
10. *http://www.worldserver.pipex.com/cambridge/mhealth/intr12.htm*
    The Cambridge Online City homepage is available on
    http://www.worldserver.pipex.com/cambridge
11. *http://www.poptel.org.uk/mcin*
12. Grunwald, Terry. *Making the network: online strategies for community-based organisations.* Published in the UK by Communities Online, 1997, p.11.

13 Day, Peter. *The Community benefits of electronic networking*
   http://www.partnerships.org.uk/articles/day1.html
14 *http://www.poptel.org.uk/mcin*
15 More details are available from the South Bristol Learning Network:
   ICL House
   Redcliff Street
   Bristol BS1 6NS
   0117 9279995
   Website: *http://alice.cs.bris.ac.uk/SBLN*
   Email: *100335.3033@Compuserve.com*

13

Copyright and Information: Issues in Protection and Liability

Jeremy Phillips

Introduction

The information industry is rightly concerned with two major issues which lie at the heart of its operations. The first is the extent, if any, to which the copying, downloading, editing, rearrangement and transmission of information-bearing materials is restricted by copyright and other intellectual property laws. The second is the extent, if any, to which legal liability may be incurred where the use of any information-bearing material constitutes an infringement of copyright.

The information professions are disadvantaged in their consideration of these issues for the following reasons:

- Copyright protection is a phenomenon which is couched in legal terminology, much of which bears no direct correspondence to terminology employed within the industry sector. This means that, to the information profession, it is not always apparent that a particular activity carries consequences which extend to the question of copyright liability.
- While copyright does not protect information *per se*, and addresses itself only to the issue of wrongful unauthorised uses of the form in which an information-bearing work expresses its content, the professional user of that information – notwithstanding the fact that it is not protected by copyright – may find that his/her use of the information for purposes quite unrelated to exploitation of the copyright nonetheless constitutes an infringement of that copyright.
- The manipulation of information-bearing materials very frequently takes place in a context in which it is not cost-effective for the information manager to obtain professional legal advice.
- In many sectors of the information industry those who seek to reproduce or transmit information have become unduly dependent upon the statements made by groups or organisations of copyright owners with regard to what may actually be copied.

- Copyright owners have become greatly sensitised to the risks and dangers of copyright infringement damaging their businesses. This has often caused them to be vigilant in policing uses of the materials they publish. It has also caused them to operate increasingly through the medium of industry or special interest groups (for example the Business Software Alliance, the Federation Against Software Theft, the Copyright Licensing Agency). Users of materials which are protected by copyright are generally less sensitive to the possiblities of copyright infringement and are accordingly less vigilant. They also tend to be units, rather than hunting in packs, which makes them easier to pick off one by one.

This chapter does not purport to offer legal guidelines as to what information may be copied, transmitted or otherwise exploited in any given situation: this requires specific legal advice. It does however seek to review and summarise some of the principal issues relating to the treatment of information as a by-product of copyright protection and to examine some of the difficulties which arise from the notion of information as 'property' in a legal sense.

The legal status of information

Copyright

There is no copyright or other enforceable legal monopoly right in individual items of information or fact. The protection which is accorded by copyright extends only to the form in which information is expressed, not the information itself. Accordingly, individual items of data such as bibliographic references, Web site addresses, telephone numbers and items of fact such as the identity of a person or the date of a battle fall outside the scope of copyright protection.

Where a copyright infringement is alleged and the owner of the copyright seeks an injunction to stop the alleged infringement continuing until such time as a full trial can take place, the court has to form a swift opinion as to whether the copyright owner has made out a *prima facie* case that his/her copyright has been infringed. In such circumstances the courts have inferred, from the fact that information contained in the plaintiff's work has also appeared in the defendant's, that a copying of the plaintiff's work has occurred. This does not mean that the courts have accorded a proprietary status to the information.

Confidential information

Information which is not generally known and which is not publicly available may enjoy the protection of a complex body of laws which protect and respect the confidentiality or secret nature of information, whether this information consists of items of data, intentions, opinions, business plans or anything else. These laws may operate so as to prohibit or restrict the publication or dissemination of information, to provide for criminal sanctions when that information is so treated or to enable a person who enjoyed the right to control that information to obtain compensation for its wrongful dissemination or use. Those same laws do not however provide explicitly that information is a form of legal property in the manner in which, for example, copyright is.

May another's information be used?

The main categories of law which must be considered before determining whether and how information may be used are as follows:

Statute law
There is no one body of statute law which governs the secrecy or confidentiality of documents, but there are many statutes and statutory instruments which address this topic in one form or another. The best-known law on the subject is the Official Secrets legislation, which greatly restricts the use to which information in the possession of the government and its organs may be put, whether that information is available from other sources or not. The Patents Act 1977, which provides that inventions may only be patented if they were not made available to the public before the date of their patent application, presupposes the existence of a legal means of preserving secrecy in inventions for which no application had yet been made. This Act also specifies that, in a case in which an inventor owns an invention and wishes to patent it but to do so would make public information belonging to a third party, the third party's right to the confidentiality of his/her information overrides the inventor's right to file for a patent. The Copyright, Designs and Patents Act 1988 also impinges upon the control of information which may be of a confidential or restricted nature, by specifying that the dissemination of a work, or of copies of it, to the public is a copyright infringement.

Contract law
Where information is supplied by one party to another, either in the form of raw data or in the licensing of the use of a copyright work, the provisions which are contained in the contract govern the use to which that information may be put. This is so, notwithstanding the provisions contained in the copyright legislation or elsewhere, since explicit contract terms override the provisions of the Copyright, Designs and Patents Act 1988. It is important to remember this point when contracting for the supply of online information services or for the use of information contained on CD-ROM or other solid state formats, because even the

provisions of the law which provide for the making of copies of works may be usurped by contract law.

Equity
Even where copyright law does not apply in respect of a proposed use of information, and even where there is no contract between the party which seeks to control the information and the party which intends to use it, the law of equity may be relevant. Equity law is an imprecise but important body of case law which endeavours to provide justice in an individual case even though the law does not strictly speaking require it. For example, where information is communicated to a person in circumstances in which it would be unfair for him to make use of it (for example, information contained in a press release which 'embargoes' the use or publication of that information before a particular time or date), the law will restrain any seemingly unfair use of it, even if there is no contractual or copyright restriction upon the use of the information in question. The principles of equity are rarely capable of being invoked successfully in any situation in which information which owes its value to its being secret has lost its quality of secrecy.

Database right
This right (discussed below), which became part of United Kingdom law at the beginning of 1998 following the implementation of the EU Database Directive 96/9 of 1996, restricts the extent to which items of information may be removed, copied or otherwise 'extracted' from a protected database. It would appear that, while the large-scale or systematic small-scale extraction of data from a database will infringe the owner's right, the accessing of a protected database in order to obtain and subsequently use individual items or small quantities of information will be permitted.

Copyright in authors' works

Where a number of individual items of fact or information have been assembled or collated into one work, that work may be protected under the law of copyright as a 'compilation', notwithstanding that none of the items contained within it is a work which is entitled to copyright protection. Thus a dictionary or a collation of officially sanctioned European Union acronyms will be entitled to copyright protection even though none of the individual entries in it may qualify for copyright protection.

Where a copyright work is used as an information source, the law provides that information may be extracted from it and subsequently used without restriction. However, in extracting that information the person who seeks to use the information contained in the work must satisfy himself that the copyright work has not been copied, downloaded or otherwise reproduced in its entirety or in 'substantial part'. What constitutes a 'substantial part' has long been a point of uncertainty and will remain so, since Parliament has left it to the courts to determine what is a copying of a 'substantial part' in any given case. This makes it difficult for members of the information professions to predict the extent of their entitlement to make copies without first seeking permission.

A further complication is that both the 'compilation' and the works contained in it may be works which are protected by copyright. For example, there is copyright both in an encyclopaedia and in its individual entries. To download or photocopy a single entry from an encyclopaedia will not normally be capable of being be regarded as the copying of the whole or a substantial part of the encyclopaedia, but it will inevitably be the copying of the whole of that entry, the copyright in which may vest in the author or photographer who has licensed its reproduction in the encyclopaedia. Likewise, where an abstract of an article or data concerning the physical characteristics of chemicals is obtained through an online subscription service, the data provider's aggregated stock of available sources is a 'compilation' but each separate item held within that compilation may also be a separate work.

No review of copyright law as it affects information would be complete without a mention of two joined cases which came before the European Court of Justice in 1995. In both the *Magill* and *Time Out* cases, magazines sought and were refused licences to reproduce lists of forthcoming television programmes. In each case the television company refused to license the use of the lists because it would damage sales of its own television programme magazine. This meant that, in the United Kingdom and the Republic of Ireland, viewers had to purchase more than one magazine in order to get a full appreciation of the week's viewing. *Magill* and *Time Out* both objected on the basis that the refusal to license them to reproduce the programme listings was an abuse of a dominant market position which constituted a breach of Article 86 of the Treaty of Rome. The European Court of Justice agreed. Since the real reason for refusing to license the copyright in the television programme listings was to stop *Magill* and *Time Out* using the information contained in the lists, the television companies were using their power as TV companies to prevent the magazines from satisfying consumer demand for an omnibus programme magazine in the European Union. This was indeed an abuse of monopoly, which could not be tolerated. The court's conclusions are of the greatest significance to the information industries and professions, since they sound a clear warning to copyright owners that any attempt to use copyright in order to restrict the use of information which is wrapped up in it will run the risk of contravening European competition law.

Protection of databases under the Database Directive

From 1 January 1998 a new and broadly similar regime for the legal protection of databases should have been implemented not only in the United Kingdom but in all 15 European Union jurisdictions. The source of this harmonised approach to database protection is the Database Directive 96/9 of 1996. This Directive seeks to compel all European Union Member States to adopt a binary system for the protection of collections or compilations of information.

Where a database is capable of being viewed as the product of an author's individual creation (for example where it consists of a bibliography of learned publications on nineteenth century French porcelain or an annotated catalogue of postage stamps), it will be continue to be protected by copyright law. Its protection will be analogous to that of other 'literary works' under the Copyright, Designs and Patents Act 1988, which means two things. First, an extremely lengthy duration of legal protection will be enjoyed by the owner of copyright in it: copyright will not expire until the end of the seventieth year from the author's death. Secondly, the wide range of defences to copyright infringement, including fair dealing for the purposes of research and private study, criticism, review and the reporting of current events will continue to apply to it with only slight modifications (at the time of writing it has been proposed that the use of a copyright-protected database for the purposes of profit-making research should not be permissible). Since United Kingdom law already conferred copyright protection upon databases, the implementation of this part of the Database Directive may make little impact on the current understanding and practices of the information management community. According to some commentators, the copyright protection of a database will extend only to the 'structure' of the database and will have no relevance to the copying of items of information contained within it; others, however, observe that the Directive does not explicitly state this and that the Directive's intention of protecting the database but not the works contained within it may be understood in many different ways.

In addition to copyright protection for databases which are the result of an author's creative activity, a new *sui generis* right is introduced which now protects any database which is of a non-creative nature and does not reflect the author's individual creativity. Such databases may be taken to include, for example, an alphabetical list of subscribers to a telephone system together with their addresses and telephone numbers. This new *sui generis* right will protect the database owner against unlawful copying of his/her database but – unlike copyright which subsists for life plus 70 years – has been given a duration of only 15 years. The extensive web of defences to an action for copyright infringement will not avail the unauthorised exploiter of a database which is protected by database right, though s/he will be able to extract and use information from a database if s/he is careful not to do so on a systematic basis.

In countries such as the United Kingdom the substitution of database right for copyright may be viewed by database owners as a regressive step, since copyright has been the traditional vehicle by which such works have been protected against unauthorised copying. But in countries such as Germany and France, where the requirements of a work's originality have been sufficiently high to preclude lists of raw data from enjoying copyright protection, the new database right represents an increased level of legal protection.

In reality, whether a database is protected by copyright or by database right will make little or no difference to the information manager. This is because (i) the ability to extract and utilise individual items of information will exist in each case (though probably to a different extent, since the law uses different terminology in each case) and also because (ii) where a database is subject to substantial updating or upgrading on a regular basis, each revision of it will constitute a fresh work, to be protected for a new period of life plus seventy years, or 15 years, respectively.

The future of the database right at international level is a matter of dispute. In December 1996 the World Intellectual Property Organization (WIPO) hosted an international diplomatic conference on the protection of databases, hoping to establish norms which would be accepted globally before the majority of the world's copyright-protecting nations had eatablished their own database protection regimes which would then be too firmly entrenched to be easily amended. Unfortunately WIPO did not receive any support from the United States, one of the jurisdictions with a great interest in database protection and long experience of protecting it. The United States demanded a 25 year term of protection for databases instead of the European standard period of 15 years. When it became apparent that this demand would not be met, the Americans withdrew from further discussion and refused even to state their negotiation position. The conference was thereby deprived of the opportunity to reach any consensus.

Information, the Internet and intranet

The basic provisions of copyright law which cover the old, paper-based technologies will also govern the making available of information and its transmission and downloading on the Internet, unless there is some clear legal ground for establishing the contrary. It may be safely assumed that any copyright owner who places information on a Web site has consented to that information being spread and used without limit, unless the Web site is a controlled site in which access is limited to subscribers or other recipients. This is so, notwithstanding the fact that copyright protects the creator of a web page against the unauthorised reproduction of that page in whole or part (where reproduction is specifically permitted or implicitly encouraged, no copyright infringement will however take place).

An interesting problem, which was canvassed in the Scottish case of *Shetland Times v. Wills*, relates to the legality of hypertext links as a means of leading a visitor to one site to information contained on another. On an application for an injunction to stop the defendant making hypertext links from the plaintiff's electronic newspaper to his own, the judge in that case was prepared to assume that the copying of headlines from the plaintiff's pages to the defendant's constituted an infringement of copyright, though the matter was not fully argued. This assumption is correct only if (i) newspaper article headlines are literary works which enjoy copyright protection or if (ii) newspaper headlines constitute a 'substantial part' of a newspaper. A further point considered by the judge in that case was whether the provision of an electronic newspaper constituted the provision of a cable transmission within the meaning of the Copyright, Designs and Patents Act 1988. This too the judge was prepared to assume to be the case.

As to information which is made available to users of an intranet system, it is safe to assume that the use of that information will be principally governed by whatever conditions are laid down by the entity which controls the intranet for its use by permitted users only. There is not yet anything which can be said to be a recognisable body of intranet law, so normal principles of contract, copyright and breach of confidence law may be expected to apply.

Both in respect of the Internet and with regard to intranet systems which cross national borders, difficult jurisdictional issues exist. The difficulty arises from the fact that Web sites, electronic noticeboards and information held on servers may be accessible from, and therefore in, several countries. If a Web site is physically stored on a server in the United Kingdom, its physical presence there is of no consequence whatever to the person who is accessing it and downloading material from it. However, it may be that it is the law of the country in which the server is located which governs questions of copyright liability for that Web site. If this is the case, an action to have an offending Web site 'seized' or destroyed would have to be commenced in the United Kingdom if the server was located there, in France if it were located in France, and so on. Alternatively, it may be law of the country in which the internet service provider is located or domiciled which governs the action, even if the Web site is physically elsewhere. And what of Internet users who have downloaded material? Is the downloading of materials in infringement of copyright actionable in the country in which the downloading party is domiciled? Informed elements within the legal profession are agreed that there should be a common approach to these problems which should be accepted by all countries, but debate still continues as to what that approach should be.

The high level of interest in the use of the Internet for commercial purposes has generated a high volume of speculation as to how, without over-regulating or stifling use of the Internet, the legitimate interests of copyright owners and information users may be balanced. The European Commission has yet to make any formal proposals in this field; nor has the World Intellectual Property Organization. The Commission's principal concern is to preserve the integrity of trade, commerce and professional services within the Single Market, while WIPO's has been to identify a frequently elusive area of consensus between information-owning and information-consuming nations. In the light of the desire both of the Commission and of WIPO to establish a solution which is of general applicability, it is unlikely that any initiative will be taken by the United Kingdom at a purely national level.

Liability for false or damaging information

The provision of information is a potential ground of legal liability, where the information is false and the provider knows that the person to whom the information will be provided will rely upon it but nonetheless fails to take reasonable care in providing it. A substantial body of case law has established that the recipient of the information need not be the person to whom it is supplied, so long as s/he falls within a class of persons who are reasonably likely to acquire that information and rely upon it to their detriment. This liability is additional to any liability which may attract to the provision of information which is defamatory or which constitutes an infringement of copyright.

In some cases an information provider will be insured against some or all of the risks inherent in the supply of false and damaging information, but it sometimes happens that s/he will be unaware of this fact. Any provider of information which is likely to be relied upon to the detriment of its recipient should examine the possibility of gaining suitable insurance cover. There are also circumstances in which it is possible for the information provider to exclude liability by issuing an explicit disclaimer as to the currency, efficacy or reliability of information provided, particularly where that provider is not the originator of the information, is not able to verify it himself and where the recipient is not an ordinary consumer but a business. Legal advice should in all cases be sought before seeking to exclude liability in respect of the provision of information.

On the subject of liability in respect of copyright infringement, any person who suspects that s/he is at risk of committing an infringement should be careful to ensure that his/her conduct is demonstrably in good faith. In the case of most other legal wrongs, the wrongdoer is obliged only to pay such damages as will put the injured party in the position s/he would have been in if the wrong had not been committed. Since most copyright infringements are small-scale, casual activities which individually make little or no impact on the copyright-owner's position, one might imagine therefore that the level of liability for copyright infringements will generally be low. The situation is however quite different. Copyright is one of a very small number of legal rights which, if infringed, entitle the injured party to claim not only compensatory damages but also 'additional damages'. These damages are in effect penal. They reflect the flagrancy of the infringing act and the conduct of the infringer. It is only in the most rare and unusual cases that these additional damages are sought, but they can be most considerable.

Further observations

In terms of professional priority, great importance is placed upon the speedy identification, location and delivery of information. Notwithstanding the fact that copyright does not protect information, but ostensibly guards only against the wrongful use of the form in which information is couched, the very existence of copyright acts as an inhibition, if not an obstacle, to the information manager's discharge of his/her information functions. In particular:

- It may be impossible (as in the case of pictures or photographs), difficult or highly inconvenient to separate out an item of information from the form in which it is embodied. A supplier of information cannot realistically be expected to waste time paraphrasing or editing copyright-protected material in order to avoid technical infringement.

- Since there is no copyright register, there is no convenient means by which copyright clearance may be sought when it is desired to reproduce, transmit or store electronically a work which contains information but where the current owner of the copyright cannot be identified or contacted.

- The laws of copyright appear to the layman to consist almost entirely of details and exceptions, at least in the form in which they exist in British statutes, rather than to state clearly the general prin-

ciples by which they operate. A perfect example of this is the set of rules which governs the very simple question whether a library may make a single copy of a work at the request of a library user.
- Because British copyright law is so complex, it follows that the terms under which the provision of information is made are also likely to be complex, at least to the non-lawyer. Many contracts which provide for access to online information services and blanket licences for the photocopying of newspapers and educational materials bear this out.

In the light of these observations one might be forgiven for expressing the sentiment that some sort of Information Users' Charter is long overdue. There is little likelihood of this eventuality ever coming to pass before two things happen. First, Parliament will have to overcome its preference for drafting copyright laws in terms of absolute detail and face the challenge of drafting in terms of relative principle. Secondly, copyright owners will have to be satisfied that their own needs and interests are not placed under threat by the needs and interests of the information community and that, in many cases, they are actually served by them.

14

Records Management and Archives in the Voluntary Sector

Rodney Breen

Records Management and Archives

In the typical voluntary organisation, archivists and records managers are to be found in the same section as librarians and other information professionals. This is not an unreasonable arrangement. All of these people are concerned with information – gathering it, ordering it, and making it available to anyone who needs to use it.

However, there are important differences between the work of records managers and archivists and that of their colleagues in the information professions. The most fundamental difference is that the information they deal with is generally produced within the organisation and cannot be replicated from elsewhere. The records they deal with cannot be catalogued according to an externally defined system in the way that books or periodicals are often catalogued, but must be approached in a unique way that stems from the individual character of the material.

Furthermore, while archivists and records managers themselves have much in common, the two jobs are actually quite different although closely related. The records manager is concerned with the here and now, with the day-to-day business of the organisation and its efficient organisation. Their interactions are with the staff of the organisation doing their routine work; the records they deal with are owned by the people who created them; and economy and speed of response are key elements in convincing the users that the service they provide is a worthwhile one. The archivist, on the other hand, is concerned with older records; the material they deal with is owned by the organisation, not just one section of it; the users they serve are as likely to be outside the organisation as inside; and the work they do usually takes them away from the day to day running of the organisation. Even though, in practice, in voluntary organisations the two roles are typically held by the same person, they require different skills and modes of thought and the individual concerned has to become adept at switching between one hat and the other and making compromises between the two jobs.

The existence of the trained professional records manager and archivist is quite a new phenomenon. Many voluntary organisations have had archivists for many years, but these have in general been untrained, and even though they often did a good job and knew the organisation well, their lack of training could create problems. In many cases, the archivist was a long-term member of staff appointed as a volunteer or given the job in the years before retirement. The advantage was that the individual concerned knew the organisation and its history well and could make sense of records going back over many years. The disadvantage here however is that the untrained archivist may not be aware of essential principles and facts which the trained professional archivist will be familiar with. Furthermore, a volunteer with extensive knowledge of the organisation may well be too close to the material to make a reasonable assessment of its worth where an outsider will see it in a different light. In all but the smallest of organisations it is worth having trained staff to do this job where possible, and the number of professional archivists in the voluntary sector is growing.

The voluntary sector: specialist problems

The problems that beset the records manager/archivist are pretty much the same in most organisations, and there is not a great deal that is different where voluntary organisations are concerned. But there are some particular aspects worth considering. For one thing, there is always the pressure from supporters to keep expenditure on administration to a minimum – and archives tend to fall into the category of administrative costs. The culture of voluntary organisations tends to be frugal, and however highly regarded the archives may be, it is often very difficult to ensure the cost of proper archive storage and management is met realistically.

The cost argument is not such a problem for records managers, who can usually justify their existence in terms of better use of space and rapid access to vital documents. But they in turn face another characteristic of voluntary organisations: the culture of voluntarism. Because most such organisations have begun working on a voluntary basis, and depend to a substantial effect on various types of voluntary support, there is often a casual attitude to systems and procedures that can undermine even the most enthusiastic records manager. Even though many voluntary organisations now have professional staff, there is often a resistance to systematic and businesslike approaches, and that can be highly frustrating.

Records management and archives as part of an information strategy

It is fair to say that, where information specialists are concerned, archives and records management has traditionally been an under-regarded area. One excellent book on setting up an information service has no mention of archives in its index, and under the heading 'records' it says: see 'administration/stationery'. This is by no means untypical; and yet information is essentially what archives and records management is about. Any organisation which sets out to have an information strategy without having its archives and other records as a key part of it is missing out an absolutely vital element.

Records Management

The function of the records manager

The function of the records manager within an organisation is to ensure that the information created in the process of the organisation's work is accessible for as long as necessary and as quickly as possible. Given the readiness with which the modern office creates paperwork, a very important part of the process lies in ensuring that information that is not essential is destroyed as soon as possible. And a key factor in the management of the organisation's records is that of making sure that information which is not immediately required is stored out of the office while remaining readily accessible.

The job of the records manager, in principle, is to manage this information throughout its entire life cycle. It is important to realise that is not just a question of physical management – the logistics of storage and retrieval – but also the 'intellectual control' of the record series. A basement full of files, however well preserved, is completely useless without certain key pieces of information – who created it, when, and for what purpose. Most of all, it is essential to keep together all papers that were originally created together. For the records manager, and for the archivist, the context of a paper is every bit as important as the content.

One simple way of describing the records manager's job is the 'life-cycle' concept.

According to this approach, every document – and this may be a form, a letter, a computer file, even a photograph – has a natural life-cycle. This life-cycle is composed of three parts:

The active phase
The first part of the cycle is the active phase – when documents are created and are used on a regular basis. This usually means that they will be placed in a filing system and accessed regularly by the user. This phase will probably last for about one to two years.

The semi-active phase
The second part is the semi-active phase. The files are not referred to very often, but need to be kept available in case they are needed. Usually this means they are placed in some sort of storage system from which they can be quickly retrieved. This phase can last for anything from three to twenty years. Of course, a fair number of files do not even make it to this phase and will be discarded rather than stored.

The archival phase
Finally there is the archival phase. When the files have come to the end of the semi-active phase, they are no longer needed by the people who created them. A great many files will fall by the wayside at this point, and be discarded. But some will be retained and transferred to the archives for permanent preservation. (The expression 'archiving' is sometimes used to refer to the process of transferring semi-active papers to storage. This usage is liable to cause confusion and should be avoided.)

In practice the role of the records manager is often limited to managing the semi-active stage. But the more input that is available in the active phase, the easier the job becomes in later periods. A good filing system for active documents will make the job of managing the material in the later stages of its life-cycle so much easier.

Raising awareness

The job of records manager is not one with which most people in an organisation are familiar. A very important part of the job, therefore, is that of making people aware of what records management is and what a records manager does. Given the rapid turnaround of staff in modern organisations, this is an approach that has to be constantly repeated.

Having support at the highest level is important. If senior management is aware of the function of the records manager and the benefits in principle of having a records management policy, the easier the job will be to justify to others.

Communicating how records management works is not easy. The most obvious approach is to explain the more obvious benefits of a good records management policy: less clutter in offices, and the freeing up of valuable space for other uses. The danger of this is that it could end up leaving an impression that a records manager is nothing more than a glorified furniture consultant or warehouse manager.

This is where it is important to stress the information approach. The key thing is to shift people's attention away from files and storage boxes to what is contained within them. Try to get them to consider how easy or difficult it is to find information from their own filing systems. How much time do they waste on a regular basis, trying to find a piece of paper they know is 'in there somewhere'? How easy would it be to find out about something that happened five years ago? If the organisation were faced with a lawsuit, and they had to produce all the relevant paperwork on a particular item, how would they cope? These sorts of questions will help to focus their minds on the potential information disasters that lie in wait for the disorganised.

Getting the message across is not simply a question of what is said – how it is said is also extremely important. All the effort required to convince the user that they are being offered a professional service will be completely wasted if the supporting materials do not present a professional image. It is worth taking time and effort over this. Forms and documents should be clearly and thoughtfully designed, by professionals if possible. Boxes, and storage areas, should be clean and bright and well-presented. In many voluntary organisations, there is a temptation to skimp and use cheap or second-hand materials; in the long term, this is likely to be a false economy.

Finally, while the culture of voluntary organisations may seem frustratingly casual and informal to anyone experienced in other circles, it is necessary to work within it, and it can sometimes be an advantage. Attempting to impose formal and compulsory approaches is a recipe for disaster; it will be necessary to compromise and explain, and an awareness of the values and language of the organisation can often be put to use. There is no reason why a records manager cannot also be seen as 'facilitator' and 'empoweror'.

The records survey

The first stage in the records manager's approach is usually the records survey or audit. This involves visiting individual sections and discussing with them what work they do, how their records reflect that work, and any problems they may have had with using these records. The aims of the records survey are:

- to introduce yourself to the staff and explain what you do;
- to find out about the organisation and how the various sections operate together;

- to identify problems that currently exist with record-keeping and promote solutions to them; and
- to gather information to draw up a retention schedule and make long-term plans for storage options.

There are obvious similarities between the records survey and the information audit that other information professionals may be planning. The information gathered may be different, but there is a potential degree of overlap and it makes sense to check what others may be doing. You may wish to share notes, and certainly to arrange it so that your visits do not clash. You may even find it convenient to make a joint visit. Do not, however, accept an offer to do a survey on your behalf – the personal visit is an essential part of the survey.

A good survey begins with good preparation. Get a senior manager of staff to send a memo to say that you will be visiting; get a structural plan of the organisation, so that you can see where each section fits in; and make an appointment to visit at a convenient time. Once there, introduce yourself and ask them to explain their work and how it fits in with that of others in the organisation. Have a look at their filing systems and how their records are physically stored. Quite often, a visit by you will prompt them to look at documents they have been storing for ages and you will be able to advise them how to dispose of them. Try and find out how these records relate to their work and identify problems that can be dealt with.

It is important to keep a good record of your discussions. It helps to have a survey form drawn up on which you can enter details as you speak. This will record the name of each series of records ('day files', 'customer correspondence', 'invoices', etc.) along with the dates it covers, the area of space occupied, and the length of time they want to keep it for.

Filing systems and management of current records

Users often perceive the job of the records manager as beginning only when they have files to be placed in storage. The process can begin earlier than that, however. A good filing system makes it easier to share and transfer information, and by making that information more accessible to the user can produce clear gains in efficiency.

In organising a filing system, the important thing is flexibility. There is no point in creating a complex and sophisticated filing system that people will find impossible to use. It will eventually be abandoned and they will end up having their own private files in addition.

There are a number of ways of designing filing systems. The simplest is a numeric, tree-based system, like the directory system used for computer files. The easiest way to create this is to ask the user to break down their job into sections, and then into subsections and then if necessary into further subsections. This system is known by the acronym FAT – for Function (the first level), Activity (the second level) and Transactions (the final level).

For instance, a manager might have several functions, one of which is managing staff. This might be broken down into several activities, such as appraisals and recruitment. Each of these can then be further broken down. The filing system might then contain files such as:

    2.3.1: Staff Management – Appraisals – J. Smith

    2.3.2: Staff Management – Appraisals – Y. Patel

    2.4.1: Staff Management – Recruitment – Application forms

    2.4.2: Staff Management – Recruitment – Interviewees

This system is logical, and at the same time organic; it allows the user to add new branches as functions grow or change, and ensures that each piece of paper has a natural and logical place in the system. This makes misfiling less likely and enables someone not familiar with the system to find a document easily. It also means that even after years have passed, the process of deciding which files should be retained and which can be discarded will be much easier.

Most organisations will have some form of internal induction and training programme for their staff, and it is worth getting to know the people responsible – offering to do some training on filing, for example, is a good way to sell your services.

Another area where the records manager can offer advice is in the organisation of storage in the office. In essence, this will usually mean advising against four-drawer filing cabinets in favour of open-fronted cabinets, which hold more files in the same area of floor space.

Retention scheduling

One tool which many records managers are enthusiastic about is the retention schedule, also known as a destruction or disposal schedule. This is essentially a list of the different types of records series in a particular office or section, with details of how long they need to be kept for and what should happen to them at the end of that period (e.g. destruction, archives). This can be very useful for planning future storage needs. Retention scheduling is very common outside the voluntary sector and is popular with records managers because they see it as an intelligent tool for controlling the retention of documents. There is certainly a case for the use of retention scheduling with regard to financial records, for example, where the retention of documents is subject to clear legal requirements. It is also useful in relation to technical documents in fields such as pharmaceuticals and engineering. In the voluntary sector there are often specific legal requirements and codes of practice, in relation to issues such as child protection and patient care. It is important to be informed about these particular requirements.

Beyond this, however, the effectiveness of the retention schedule can be limited. Any survey should be followed up with a draft retention schedule to which the surveyed staff can respond. They should be encouraged to use it as a basis for managing their files. A copy should be retained on file by the records manager and consulted when that section comes to place its material in storage.

Storage options for semi-current records

When decisions are made about the management of records within the organisation, one of the most important questions is what to do with the number of old files that are in the building. It is only when the last basement room is almost full that organisations tend to decide that something ought to be done about them.

There are two possible solutions to this; commercial storage and setting up a records storage area within the organisation. Other solutions that are sometimes suggested are (a) throwing material away, and (b) microfilming it. It is worth looking at these first.

Throwing material away is an excellent approach if it is done in an informed and systematic way. The likelihood is that a large amount of material in storage is useless and can readily be discarded. However, this does require careful examination by the records manager and this will take time. This time can be avoided in the long run by having a good retention schedule.

Microfilm is often seen as a cheap way of storing documents, but this is far from the case. There are situations in which microfilm has uses, but simply using it to save storage costs is not one of them. For one thing, the material may not need to be stored; for another, to microfilm it will require staff time and effort in preparation work, as well as the commercial costs involved and the necessity of having indexes and machinery available to consult it. It is unlikely to be cheaper in the long term than having a well organised paper storage area combined with good retention policies.

Storing those papers which need to be kept can be done in-house or it can be done externally. The external option is usually costly and where cheap operators are used, the result is often poor service and low reliability. It should only be considered when no adequate space is available on or adjacent to the organisation's offices. However it can be an effective way of saving office space if it is used intelligently. There are a number of options available; one is to simply hire an area and shelve it for the organisation's use. Another option is to use a company which specialises in the management of stored material.

Questions that should be asked of a commercial storage provider include:

- What does it cost to deposit material in the first instance?
- Can material be deposited in existing boxes, or does it have to be transferred to new boxes?
- How are boxes separately identified and tracked?
- Is the cost of storage calculated by shelf space or number of boxes?
- What is the cost of retrieving files, and at what frequency?
- How quickly can material be retrieved in an urgent situation?
- Does the cost of retrieving material include the cost of returning it?
- Are there any arrangements for consultation on site?
- What arrangements exist for destruction of material, and what does this cost?

It will generally be found that if there is adequate space for storage within existing premises, or on premises that can be rented nearby for the purpose, this will be the cheaper and most convenient option. It is important to scrutinise potential areas carefully before accepting them, and to be prepared to refuse unsuitable storage.

The requirements for a good storage area for semi-active records are similar to those for archives, although the standards need not be as high since only a small proportion will be kept permanently. The storage area should be clean and dry, secure against intruders, with a temperature between 13° and 18° Centigrade and with a relative humidity of 55 – 65%. Within this range, there should be as little variation as possible. Other media, such as microfilm, photographs, films, and magnetic tape, require different conditions and may need to be kept separately. Papers should be stored in good quality cardboard boxes on sound metal shelving.

If a large amount of shelved space is available, it is possible to provide areas and allow sections to deposit their material in their own separate area. However, this encourages bad habits and if the area fills up quickly – and it almost certainly will – results in highly inefficient use of storage space. One way to use storage effectively is to use mobile shelving, in which shelves can be moved on tracks and opened when needed for access. This saves space but is expensive and requires a heavy floor loading, and is more suitable for archival storage. Another approach is to use a random shelving system in which each box is numbered and boxes are allocated to the user at random around the storage area as the space becomes available. This is a much more effective way of using the space, but it often requires a lot of explanation to get people to use it properly.

A records storage area will also need an area where records can be consulted without taking them out of the building. A table and chair and a light will be needed.

If a storage area is set up, it is likely to prove popular very quickly. It is important for the records manager to retain control over what is deposited there, and even more importantly, what is not stored there. Nothing but semi-active records should be allowed on the shelves, and then only when they are accepted in keeping with an agreed retention schedule. There should be no question of other materials such as books or publications being stored there, and certainly not machinery, paint, cleaning equipment, or anything else that presents a hazard to safe and proper storage of papers.

One of the functions of semi-current storage is to allow material to be retrieved rapidly when required. Ideally, a records store should have its own staff to do this, but in practice, in the understaffed voluntary organisation, retrieval will usually have to be carried out either by the records manager or by the staff from the creating section. In most cases, the latter is to be preferred because retrieving and returning other people's files will take up valuable professional time and helps to reinforce the image of the records manager as warehouse operator.

Security issues

The security factor is an important question that arises in relation to storage. Much of the material you have to deal with is confidential and needs to be managed with security in mind. In work with children, for example, social work case files are often kept and need to be retained confidentially for many years. Any records to do with personnel, and with donors, needs to be kept secure from accidental disclosure. It is important, when setting up a system for storage, to ensure that the contents of boxes are not immediately obvious from the outside. It is also important, when disposing of records, to ensure that nothing confidential is thrown away in the normal manner. It must be shredded, either on site or by a company that specialises in this type of work. Where documents are stored by a commercial company, they will usually offer a destruction service when the documents are no longer needed.

Disposal of records

A very important aspect of the storage of records is that of ensuring that they are not retained beyond the point where they are no longer needed. This is achieved by insisting that every item that is stored is given a review date, at which point it will be decided whether they can be destroyed or not. This date can be worked out as part of the survey and retention schedule. However, it is normal to consult with the depositor at the time when the review takes place, just in case the material actually does need to be retained for longer.

The review date is usually, for practical purposes, given to a whole box, and the whole box will be looked at when the date comes up. The process by which material is looked at to decide what should happen to it is known as *review* or *appraisal*.

In many cases, review is a simple process. A good filing system will make it very straightforward, enabling decisions about what to keep and what to dispose of to be made quickly. A lot of material, such as accounting records, can be automatically destroyed once the legal time limit has been reached. But in other cases the process can take a considerable time. There is no real alternative to simply sitting down with the files and reading through them in order to come to a judgement as to whether they ought to be kept or not. This process needs space, peace and quiet, and time. If the files are very old, it may be necessary to do some research to find out about the situation that existed when they were created in order to make sense of them. It may be necessary to check whether the same material has been duplicated in a different department. Once those files that no longer have value have been discarded – and this will normally be the majority of them – the remainder will be passed to the archives for permanent preservation.

Electronic records

One important area in the future of records management is that of electronic records. Although computers have been around for many years, the explosion of electronic information in the form of networks, email, intranets and the Internet, has meant a revolution in the way information is generated within organisations. At the same time, the traditional information paradigm probably still holds true. For the most part, especially in voluntary organisations, it seems to be the case that key documents – policy statements, records of decisions, etc. – are generated on paper, or printed out on paper. Whether this will remain the case for a long time remains to be seen. Certainly records managers need to keep an eye on developments in this field. Organisations with Web pages should certainly attempt to capture them on a regular basis.

Disaster planning

Disasters, of course, can strike at any time, and they do not just strike records and archives. If there is a disaster plan in existence for the organisation, the records manager should ensure that archives are included. If not, it is important to have one. Other materials can usually be insured and replaced, but the records and archives of an organisation are unique and irreplaceable.

The most likely dangers are fire and water. Fire risks should be minimised by having proper alarm systems and testing them regularly. Electric wiring should be checked and electrical equipment in or near the storage area should be avoided. Remember that even when policies are in place to prevent disasters in normal situations, it is the unexpected situation that may present a problem. Building works and renovations are a particularly dangerous time when normally safe conditions can become dangerous – a spark from an electrician's drill can create a huge amount of damage in a short period.

Water from flooding is another potential danger, and the risks are often the same because water damage cause by fire hoses is usually the most serious consequence of a fire. Where papers become wet, the greatest risk is that of mould, which can appear very quickly and do lasting damage. The best response is to air dry or freeze wet records.

A basic disaster plan must contain a list of staff who can help in an emergency, with home addresses and phone numbers. It is especially valuable to have the assistance of experienced archives and records personnel in a disaster, because they will be aware of the particular problems involved in handling records in this situation; salvaging papers will be useless if intellectual control is lost. For this reason, it is useful to make a reciprocal arrangement with other archives and records professionals who can help out in a disaster.

The plan should also contain maps of the storage area and lists of vital records which are to be salvaged as a priority; an inventory of emergency supplies; and the telephone numbers of freezer storage and disaster recovery companies. There are several companies which specialise in disaster recovery and it is possible to make prior arrangements with them. The cost of salvaging documents, which can be enormous, can be met by insurance if it is possible to arrange this. Finally, it is important that a disaster plan is updated regularly, updates are distributed to all staff involved, and a copy of the plan is kept outside the building – usually at the archivist/records manager's home.

Archives

The value of archives

Any organisation's archives are among the most important information resources it has. But they differ in several important ways from any other part of the information environment. The information they contain is unique, and irreplaceable. Their value does not diminish with age – in fact the opposite is usually true. And while most information resources are employed almost exclusively within the organisation, the archives are likely to be at least as much in demand by outsiders as by those on the inside.

The archives of an organisation are valuable in several ways. They are a cultural artefact of value to the community in which they were created. The history of voluntary organisations throws an important light on many other aspects of history – health, education, race relations, social action, women's studies, and so forth. Unfortunately, in the frugal environment of the typical voluntary organisation, this is rarely enough to persuade trustees to spend money on maintaining an archive. The archivist needs to make the case for archives as a resource for the organisation itself.

Exactly what an organisation's archives contain will depend on the organisation, its work, and its history. However, it will include all key documents relating to the creation of the organisation, its policy and decision making processes, legal agreements, files relating to its project work, its financial operations, and its communications with the external world.

Archives as a fundraising resource

If organisations make use of their archives as a resource, it is likely in the first instance to be for fundraising. Anniversaries are an especially popular occasion on which to hang a fundraising initiative, and the archives can be drawn upon to assist this. In the present competitive fundraising environment, any organisation which has been around for a long time will want to draw attention to the fact, both to create an occasion to ask for donations, and in a more general way to benefit from the prestige of being long established and having a good track record. In recent years, for example, Save the Children with its 75th and the British Red Cross with its 125th anniversary both used their archives as part of a fundraising campaign.

The fundraising use of the archives does not end there, however. There are many aspects of history which offer a fundraising angle. Photographs and artefacts – uniforms, badges, collection boxes – provide visual material which newspapers are always hungry for and which may make the difference in getting publicity. Items of interest from the past can often be used as an excuse for a similar event in the present: local supporters, for example, can be invited to repeat a fundraising exercise (such as a 'mile of pennies') from years ago, complete with historical costume. Particular events in history can provide a special angle with organisations or corporate supporters. Save the Children's early relief work in Vienna, for example, was a helpful peg for setting up a fundraising concert by the Vienna Boys Choir.

Archives as an organisational resource

On a very basic level, the archives have an essential function. Even the smallest voluntary organisation needs to know when it was founded, and where, who its supporters were, and what work it has done since then. On a more general level, the archives are an important way by which an organisation maintains a sense of itself, its objectives, and its values. Over a long period of time, any voluntary organisation will go through many phases of change, from the excitement and enthusiasm of its foundation to later periods of consolidation, reappraisal, and renewal. As with any individual, an awareness of its history is an important part of self-knowledge, and the archives can often provide a perspective on the nature of that history. Where the need to change established patterns of action creates difficulties, it is often useful to look back at how long these patterns have existed. In explaining to its supporters why it is moving away from operating its own projects in developing countries towards working with existing organisations in those countries, for example, Save the Children has found it helpful to be able to point out that that is exactly how the organisation worked in its earliest days in Europe in the 1920s. Similarly with Oxfam: 'Lunchtime showings of 16mm films for staff', the archivist, Chrissie Webb, explains 'have been useful in provoking discussion on Oxfam's direction and strategic planning – what our attitudes and outlook were, say, twenty-five years ago, how things have changed or not and how they might change in the future.'

One way of promoting the use of the archives as a resource for the corporate history is by the regular induction sessions for new staff. In Save the Children, this includes a questionnaire – presented by the archivist – in which a series of questions about the organisation's history are asked, and the answers are found to reflect many of the key issues which currently drive the organisation's policy. A series of quotations from the founder, Eglantyne Jebb, has also been produced, and these quotes regularly find their way into policy documents to support one argument or another. It is certainly true to say that the organisation's current policy is very much informed by an awareness of its past and its history.

Acquisitions policy

As an archive becomes successful, it will grow. Apart from archive material that will be discovered in the course of records surveys and as a result of promoting the archives, there will be a regular accession of material as a result of the appraisal of stored files. There will also be the offer of materials from others. Quite often supporters or former staff members will offer material they have collected. This will often prove to be of little value, with duplication of existing files, and will need to be dealt with tactfully, but often material acquired in this way will be extremely valuable. Apart from covering gaps where files were simply discarded without consideration of their potential value, the papers of individuals can provide a perspective on the history of the organisation that cannot be found from the official record. This is true also of oral testimonies which can be recorded on tape and transcribed. Much of the work of voluntary organisations is unpaid and unrecorded. The individual worker or volunteer on the ground may have much to say about the history of the organisation, but this will not find its way into the archives unless an effort is expressly made to do so. The business of oral history interviewing is a specialised and time-consuming one, but if it helps to enliven the history of the organisation, and preserve a record of otherwise unheard contributions, it is well worth pursuing. In this case, it is often best to engage the services of a willing volunteer.

Storage and preservation of records

The storage of archives is a very important part of an archivist's job. Most documents which end up in an archive were intended to be used for a fairly short period of time, and yet in the archive they are expected to last, in principle, for ever. The physical environment is full of potential hazards which may prevent this preservation from being successful. The storage of archives is intended, therefore, to ensure that these hazards are minimised. But this means that proper archive storage, to a professional standard, is comparatively expensive.

There are several basic requirements for good storage of, archive documents. There is a British Standard, BS 5454, which outlines recommendations for the storage and exhibition of archival documents. In broad terms, the needs of storage of archives are similar to those for semi-active records but the standards need to be higher. In particular, documents need to be kept in acid-free boxes of an appropriate size. It is essential to ensure a constant temperature and humidity with as little variation as possible. Non-paper materials require slightly different storage conditions, and in the case of films it is probably better to deposit these films with the National Film Archives. Video copies can be made beforehand to ensure that a record copy is available for researchers.

Conservation of archive materials is an important issue. Professional archivists will have a knowledge of conservation materials and techniques, but it may well be worth calling on the services of a specialist conservator.

Archives resources

The archivist/records manager in a voluntary organisation is normally a person working on their own with minimal resources. They will usually have the assistance of other information staff such as librarians, but the archive profession has a lot of specialist requirements which cannot be met from within the organisation.

One important resource that is useful is the support of other archivists/records managers in the voluntary sector. An organisation called CHARM – the charity archivists and records managers group – was set up in 1996 and meets four times a year to discuss issues of common interest. It is quite informally organised, but new members are always welcome, and membership is not limited to those with a qualification in archives or records management.

An organisation willing to offer advice to those interested in setting up an archive is the Royal Commission on Historical Manuscripts. Other useful organisations are the professional organisations within the field, chief amongst which are the Society of Archivists and the Records Management Society. Each of these has regular meetings and publications, and joining either or even both is well worth considering as a means of keeping in touch with current developments and thinking in the field. For those interested in the history of voluntary organisation, the Voluntary Action History Society has regular seminars. Details of these organisations, and other reference sources, can be found at the end of this chapter.

External deposit or internal storage?

Although it is clear that every organisation needs to have its archives organised and available for research, and will gain considerable benefits from doing so, it is also the case that storage of archive material, to be done properly, is costly and uses space that may very well be used in other ways. Given the pressure on most voluntary organisations to limit their costs, this often means that the option of depositing files with an outside body is one that must be considered.

The advantages of external deposit are considerable. Adequate storage can be assured; properly trained archival staff will be available to manage and conserve the material; specialist resources for researchers will be available; and the archive material will be placed in a location where other, usually related, material is also to be found for researchers. Finally, this can all be achieved with minimal cost to the depositor.

There are also, of course, disadvantages. One is that finding an organisation willing to accept the deposit of materials is not always possible. All archives have some sort of acquisitions policy, and the material may not fall within its limits. (In practice, small collections are usually fairly easy to place and local record offices are often willing to accept such deposits). Equally, archival repositories are always wary of accepting 'accruing series' – a collection from an ongoing organisation which will continue to generate material. Furthermore, there is inevitably a certain loss of control over the material, even though it is usually possible to negotiate a detailed agreement over access to the archives and the uses to which the archive materials can be put.

However, the key question is the extent to which depositing the archives with an external body will in fact separate the organisation from its history. Depositing archives externally must not be seen simply as a cost-saving exercise, because this is bound to cause problems in the long term. For one thing, it runs the risk of making the organisation lose touch with its past and the benefits in terms of fundraising and identity that come with it. Secondly, organisations that deposit their files outside usually do not have an archivist, and thus lose the benefits of having someone who understands the value of archives. Worse, since the archivist is also usually the records manager, they lose the benefit of a good records management policy, and when they come to deposit a further tranche of archive material they may well find that the repository may be unwilling to accept all the material they want to get rid of. In this case they may very well have little control over what is kept in their own archives.

Making the archives available: searchroom services and finding aids

A major function of the archivist is to make the archives available for researchers to use. The easier the process is, the more likely it will be that the archives will be used. External researchers are normally used to primary sources, and have the skills and experience to extract information from them; but internal users are likely to be intimidated by archive material and considerable efforts have to be taken if they are to be persuaded to use them at all.

The experienced user will want as comprehensive a list as possible of the archive holdings. Unlike a library collection, every archive has to be approached as a unique set of information, and the method of listing will be entirely unique, attempting to reflect the organic nature of the material – how it came to be created, the place the records had in the functioning of the organisation, and the subsequent history of the collection. This process is a key part of professional archives practice. Sorting and listing an archive collection is a specialised job, and needs to be done in a thorough way, with a sound understanding of the history and context of the papers.

This then has to be presented in a way which is meaningful to the external researcher.

A good finding aid, then, will not just contain a comprehensive list of the collection, but also background information on how it came into being and the situation of the organisation at the time it was created. Given the nature of the voluntary sector, it is quite possible that many of the people concerned will be unknown outside the organisation and a list of personalities, with background information on them, will be particularly useful. For the less experienced user, especially the internal researcher, the most useful documents are likely to be the annual reports and serial publications, journals, etc.

While many archival collections are still listed on paper in the traditional manner, there is also an increasing use of electronic databases for storage of the information. While this can be very useful for searching purposes, it does require considerable work in listing the material, entering keywords, and so forth. Not all researchers are comfortable in using databases of this sort, and in practice it is usually the archivist who will end up doing the searching.

The most important thing is to have a good introductory guide to the archives, explaining as much as possible about the background to the material, and drawing the attention of the researcher to important documents and items which might otherwise be overlooked.

It is also of course important to establish clear rules of security for visitors; they should be placed in a well-lit and clearly visible area, they should not be allowed to bring in bags, nor should they be allowed to eat, drink, or smoke anywhere in the vicinity of the archives. Ideally they should also be required to use pencils instead of pens. What they must definitely not be allowed to do is to browse the shelves themselves.

Raising awareness of the archives

An essential part of the archivist's role is that of making people aware of the existence of the archives and the value of the material contained within. Of course, an archivist with a valuable collection of material will want to ensure that it is actually used, and will want any potential users to know what it contains and how they can use it. However, it is important in another way as well, which is that of ensuring the survival of the archives and the supply of the necessary resources for their upkeep. In the frugal fundraising climate of the modern voluntary organisation, an archive needs not only to be useful but to be seen to be so.

The archivist, then, needs to be a good communicator and a good networker. Few people will seek out the archives for themselves. It is necessary to drum up support. Good people to get to know are designers, journalists, researchers, and anyone who has to make a speech or presentation. A quotation, fact, or image from the archives is just what they need when they are facing a deadline and have run out of ideas. Managers who appreciate the value of a gem from the archives in spicing up a speech are always worth cultivating. Having a stock of photographs of key events and personalities handy will make the archives a regular port of call with fundraisers, press officers and anyone who needs to use an image to make a point.

Archives talks and exhibitions are often popular as well. Most people find history an interesting subject if it is presented to them in a lively and entertaining manner, and the archivist who is a good communicator will readily find a willing audience. Good illustrative materials – photographs, posters, and above all old films – will be especially welcome.

One important thing to have is a leaflet which tells the history of the organisation, using archive materials. A well-designed history leaflet, which can be given to supporters of the organisation as well as to journalists, job applicants, and general enquirer, is an excellent way of placing the history of the organisation in the forefront. It should also contain lots of interesting facts and details which people can use in talks, articles and press releases. The Children's Society, founded in 1881 and whose mission statement is 'Making Lives Worth Living', has a history leaflet entitled *Making lives worth living since 1881*.

Finally, every organisation wants to present a good image to the public and a good way of doing so is to have a bright, visual archive display in the reception area which visitors can see as they wait. This has the added advantage of ensuring that everyone who works in the organisation is confronted, on a daily basis, with images from the archives!

Useful organisations

CHARM (the Charity Archivists and Records Managers group), c/o Nicholas Malton, Archivist, NSPCC, 42 Curtain Road, London, EC2A 3NH, UK.

Records Management Society, Mrs Jude Awry, Administration Secretary, Records Management of Great Britain, Woodside, Coleheath Bottom, Speen, Princes Risborough, Bucks, HP27 0SZ, UK.
Tel: +44 1494 488599
Fax: +44 1494 488590
Email: rms@awdry.demon.co.uk

Royal Commission on Historical Manuscripts, Quality House, Quality Court, Chancery Lane, London, WC2A 1HP, UK.

Society of Archivists, 40 Northampton Road, London, EC1R 0HB, UK.
http: www.archives.org.uk/main.html

Voluntary Action History Society, c/o Dr Justin Davis Smith, The National Centre forVolunteering, Carriage Row, 183 Eversholt St, London, NW1 lBU, UK.

Useful archive sites on the World Wide Web

Archive and Archivists:

http://www.angelfire.com/oh/harlanjohnb/archives.html
(this includes details of the Archives listserv, which has a strong US bias but does have valuable discussions and information)

British Library:

http://minos.bl.uk

Conservation Online (CoOl):

http://palimpsest.stanford.edu/

The Records Management Society of the UK

http://www.rms-gb.org.uk/

Royal Commission on Historical Manuscripts:

http://www.hmc.gov.uk (this includes the excellent site, ARCHON, which has a list of archives online and other archives links)

Bibliography

BS 5454: 1989 *British Standard recommendations for storage an exhibition of archival documents*, London, British Standards Institution, 1989.

Cook, Michael. *Archives administration: a manual for intermediate and smaller organisations and for local government*, Folkestone, Dawson, 1977

Emmerson, Peter (ed.), *How to manage your records: a guide to effective practice,* Cambridge, ICSA Publishing, 1989. The chapter 'The problems of particular organisations' includes a section on charities.

Hare, Catherine and McLeod, Julie. *Developing a records management programme*, London, Aslib, 1997.

Penn, Ira, Morddel, Anne, Pennix, Gail, and Smith, Kelvin. *Records management handbook*, Aldershot, Gower, 1989

Suppliers of archival storage and conservation material

Conservation Resources Ltd, Unit 1, Pony Road, Horspath Industrial Estate, Cowley, Oxfordshire, OX4 2RD, UK.

Preservation Equipment Ltd, Church Road, Shelfanger, Diss, Norfolk, IP22 2DG, UK.

15

Staffing Issues in the Voluntary Sector Library

Lynette Cawthra

This chapter will cover the skills and work experience which may be required in the library; selection, recruitment and induction of new staff; team management in the voluntary sector; alternative ways of working, such as job-sharing and volunteering; solo librarianship; the importance of 'networking'; training issues; managing people at times of change; working for a manager from another discipline; securing organisational recognition of the library's work; and continuing professional development and career development. Some of what is written is more applicable to the larger library or information unit, some aimed more specifically at the one-person operation.

Skills and experience required

Clearly this will depend on a range of factors, such as the size of the library team (or if one is instead the only information worker) and where the library sits within the wider organisation (is it seen as part of the policy-making function or attached to the helpline, for instance?). Alongside organisational abilities, adaptability in what will inevitably be a wide range of situations, and 'traditional' library skills in enquiry work and the collection and proactive dissemination of information, the following experience could also be relevant:

- editing and layout – if responsibility for publications falls within the library's remit (as was the case for 66 per cent of respondents to the Library Association (LA)'s 1996 survey of libraries and information units in the voluntary sector);[24]
- marketing – again of publications, but also more broadly if the library sits within or contributes to a charity's fund-raising or PR function;
- counselling – if the library is closely linked to a helpline which receives calls on sensitive issues;
- archival – if, for instance, a collection of photographs or client records forms part of the library;

- detailed IT knowledge – database construction and management, knowledge of relevant software, maybe statistical packages, digitisation (e.g. of photographs);
- Web page creation/editing – if the organisation's Web pages are the library's responsibility, or if one wishes to persuade others that they should be!
- research – for example if the library is close to the organisation's policy-making or lobbying function;
- training/teaching – for user orientation, and the proactive dissemination of information skills particularly in an online environment.

Omission from the above list of the phrase 'relevant subject knowledge' may seem surprising. However, an information professional's training should equip them to transfer their skills of information gathering, organisation and retrieval from one subject area to another. Information training is much more relevant, in most cases, than subject knowledge.

One of the aspects of working in a voluntary organisation most commented upon in the professional literature is that of the 'value-based' culture. Many people come to work for charities because they believe in the organisation's aims, and are therefore highly committed. The 1996 report of the Commission on the Future of the Voluntary Sector[6] points out that 'pay for staff in the voluntary sector is between 20 and 30 per cent below that of the commercial sector at all levels, and fringe benefits are fewer. Staff ... tend to be committed to using their skills to benefit others and accept that they gain other than monetary benefits from their work'. However, the Commission goes on to warn that while staff are a valued resource, 'they are not, except in a few special cases, the reason for the organisation's existence ... They also carry a responsibility to strive to improve the quality and cost-effectiveness of services to users'. This sense of commitment, then, can have its downside. Staff may be reluctant to take change on board, for instance, if it does not tally with their own priorities. Handy[16] talks about 'strategic delinquency', and the danger of putting 'the ethos of the place in front of the goals to be achieved'. Staff must learn to distinguish between their personal values and their organisational responsibilities.

Leat[21], interviewing managers who moved from commercial to voluntary organisations, found that some of them queried the effectiveness of commitment as a source of motivation. Some also took the view that internal politics and jealousies may be just as important a factor as in for-profit organisations, but that these may take more subtle forms which are more difficult to address, particularly given the collaborative and decentralised approach to management often found in voluntary organisations.

Selection and recruitment

It is good practice when recruiting for staff to have not only a job description but also a person specification drawn up in advance of the selection process. The latter lists skills, experience and qualifications required in the post (possibly in two categories: essential and desirable). Shortlisting criteria should be agreed by members of the interview panel – they must agree, for instance, on whether library and information skills are to be viewed as more relevant than experience in the organisation's subject area – and shortlisting of candidates should be undertaken by more than one person. Both these practices help to ensure an even-handed approach to the selection process. Those shortlisting and interviewing should themselves have received some training in these skills. Jago[20] has written that 'recruitment and selection equal other important management activities such as strategic planning, budgetary control and marketing of the service, and the results usually have an immediate impact on the quality of the library/information service'.

For many voluntary organisations, the concept of user involvement is key. Some disability organisations practise positive action towards people with a disability in their employment policies. For others, user involvement in the recruitment process is essential.

The interview itself should follow equal opportunities principles, with all candidates answering a standard set of questions. This does not mean it has to be an over-formal or monotonous process; as long as all candidates are asked the same lead questions, they can be asked different follow-up questions as a result of their responses. Those interviewing should decide in advance how they are going to choose between candidates – perhaps using a grid system to note how each matches the person specification – and the most important characteristics to look out for.

Induction

It is important before the new member of staff starts to have a structured work programme in place, so that both they and the manager have a clear picture of what is expected of them in their first couple of months. Once they arrive, an induction programme should be ready, involving information about housekeeping matters as well as what they need to know in order to do their job, including any training requirements. However much experience they bring to a new job, staff providing an information function will need to absorb a lot of detail early on about what information the library holds, how the organisation deals with enquiries, and so on. Their training requirements may include specific customer care skills, telephone skills, and technical briefings on the library's classification scheme and its database.

It is also very helpful if the organisation produces a core induction programme to cover general points which all new members of staff need to know.

Health and safety is an essential and sometimes overlooked issue, and all managers should be aware of the responsibilities both of the organisation and the employee under such legislation as the Health and Safety at Work etc. Act 1974, and the Health and Safety (Display Screen Equipment) Regulations 1992.

Managing a team

Assuming that the library/information service has more than one member of staff, what management issues are involved? Many are not peculiar to the voluntary sector, but the realities of life in a charity may add a particular slant. The issue of confidentiality – for instance the importance of having a private place for one-to-one discussions – is given an added twist if the team is working in cramped surroundings in an unsuitable building. Communication within the team needs particular consideration if the team contains part-time workers or occasional volunteers.

The team may be a very varied one in other ways: it may contain a mixture of professional and non-professional library staff, or people from different professional backgrounds such as advice work or research. Managing such a team, which may have quite disparate work goals as well as personal objectives, can be a challenge. One important key to meeting this challenge is for the manager to hone listening, questioning and observational skills, in order to be aware of individual and team motivations, strengths and weaknesses, as well as tensions both stated and implicit. Group dynamics should be analysed to ensure that all team members can contribute to its work, and are not prevented from doing so by lack of confidence or by others' dominating behaviour, or by prejudices such as racism or sexism. An awareness of different learning styles and learning preferences is also important.

Another practical point is that job descriptions should be clear, with professional boundaries made explicit. If the team contains library and helpline staff, is it part of the librarians' job to cover for helpline staff when they are away from the phone? If it is, this must be made very clear in the job description and must have been taken into account in drawing up the person specification; there are also potential training needs to be noted, relating to telephone skills and confidentiality in the above example.

Staff working for voluntary organisations may well, as has already been noted, have a strong commitment to their work. However, different people will have different motivations, and the manager must be aware of these in order to get the best out of each individual (just as it is important that the strongly committed are appropriately managed so that this commitment does not lead to overwork and eventual burn-out). Involvement of staff in departmental decision-making and in the production and delivery of departmental publications and presentations can help build teams and motivate individuals.

Good practice in staff involvement was exemplified in the King's Fund Library (before the author joined the organisation) when the job descriptions of three Library Assistants needed revision. Their managers invited the post-holders communally to decide for themselves what changes needed to be made. Since they inevitably knew much more than their managers about their jobs' daily content, it is not surprising that they did this most effectively. They also made a request that their job titles be changed to Information Assistant, to reflect what they wished to see as their broader role in helping people find and exploit information resources, alongside their role of maintaining those resources. Later – and again with their managers facilitating the process – they organised between themselves their joint work flow, with the particular aim of streamlining library procedures such as the booking in of new issues of journals. Again, the new system showed clear improvements.

Teams in whatever environment function best when they have:

- a clear corporate role;
- distinct objectives which are felt to be worthwhile;
- effective work methods;
- creative strength (including encouragement of new ideas from individual members or from outside);
- commitment from individuals;
- the ability to examine team and individual weaknesses without personal attack;
- appropriate leadership.

In a voluntary sector setting, a highly directive management style is unlikely to be appropriate if always used, although it needs to come into play at moments of crisis. An emphasis on coaching, on giving other team members the opportunity to exercise leadership in situations where their skills make this appropriate, is likely to sit better in the participatory and consensual voluntary sector culture.

Alternative ways of working

The voluntary sector has many **part-time workers** (including 'term-time' workers and others). In the LA's survey of the sector's libraries, for example[24], 23 per cent of managers were themselves part-time and the same was true of 57 per cent of clerical support posts and 17 per cent of other professional posts (this should be viewed alongside the statistic that 69 per cent of organisations had *no* other professional post). The process of ensuring that part-time workers work as part of the wider team can be aided by good communication, including clear notes of meetings and other activities which take place outside such workers' hours. Ideally, joint activities, such as team briefings, should happen wherever possible *within* those hours, although it may be possible for part-time workers to come in at a different time from their usual once a month in order to participate. It is good practice to put important messages that all the team needs to see in writing to part-timers, rather than relying on someone remembering to tell them. They, for their part, must undertake as part of their job to keep up-to-date by checking messages, email boxes and, increasingly – at least in larger organisations – the news sections of the organisation's intranet. Part-timers should not be excluded from training opportunities. This includes external courses, despite the added complication of these potentially again falling outside part-timers' hours, and also having cost implications if the number of part-time individuals is high.

Job-sharing is another popular option, representing 10 per cent of the posts reported to the LA in its survey. The importance of both post-holders thinking along similar lines about the library's remit and objectives must not be under-estimated. However, one of the particular strengths of a job-share is the opportunity it gives to prove the adage that 'two heads are better than one'. Ideally the two people will *not* approach an issue the same way, but will give each other (and their manager) different ways of viewing it, and thereby a more rounded picture. Complementary interests and experience often mean that particular library routines may be undertaken by the person with more enthusiasm and/or knowledge: one person may have superior cataloguing skills, for instance, while the other is experienced in stock selection. Having said that, the stock selector should be able and willing to catalogue if their partner is away. One of the selling points of a job-share to a manager should be that, unless both post-holders are ill or on leave at the same time, some sort of library cover will always be maintained. As long as both partners are happy with the split of duties the two people should be allowed to work out their own *modus operandi* without interference from the manager.

Communication between the two people in a job-share is essential; both parties must be committed to sharing all relevant information, with the aim of making the library service as seamless as possible to the outside world. This may be particularly difficult in the voluntary sector, with its emphasis on informal sources of information and knowledge-sharing networks rather than formal enquiry procedures. Job-sharers must work hard to ensure that users of the service experience continuity of service between the two partners, and that other members of the team do not end up covering for gaps in their knowledge. A handover period between the two post-holders must take place regularly, ideally every week. This should be a long enough time to allow some joint working on longer-term projects when this is needed.

Another flexible form of working found in the voluntary sector – infrequently at present but with potential to increase as electronic access becomes more widespread – is **teleworking**. Indexing/abstracting and Web site management, for example, are activities which may be particularly suited to this sort of work.

Links with public library services may offer alternative uses of a charity's information staff and resources. Disability advice services, community information sessions and reminiscence projects with older people are possible examples.

Charities which now need to bid for local authority contracts to provide services, where once they might have had grants, may offer fixed-term rather than permanent **contracts** to staff on the grounds that their own funding is dependent on the same fixed length of time. Particularly if the contracts are renewable as often as annually, staff turnover is bound to be affected, with employees constantly on the lookout for another job. Good candidates may not even apply for a job if the contract is short-term. Recruitment via an agency is one possible answer, though this will have cost implications.

Consultants may be brought into the voluntary sector library or information unit to advise on new projects, such as buying new library software, or setting up a Web site or helpline. They can also advise on methods of working, or even act as facilitators in a situation of conflict. It is important to make use of their expertise without the manager or anyone else in the team feeling that their own skills are being questioned. The consultant should be given a clear brief at the outset, and at the end of the process should ascertain whether the manager and team are comfortable with any changes to systems or working practices which they have suggested.

Volunteers

63 per cent of respondents to the LA's survey had used voluntary help in the previous year. The LA's own detailed guidelines on the use of volunteers[23] state that the LA is opposed to this if it is 'an attempt to compensate for the reduction or withdrawal of services caused by redundancies ... or inadequate staffing'. This statement should be emphasised to an organi-

sation's management if any suggestion is made that volunteers could take on tasks previously undertaken by paid staff, as a cost-cutting measure. At the same time the LA specifically mentions, as an example of where use of volunteers may be appropriate, 'helping a small charity that does not have sufficient funds to pay for staff'.

The Children's Society has a volunteer policy which states that, since practical work forms an important part of pre-, mid- and post-course information/librarianship training, volunteers can be taken on but only if they are qualified librarians or are working towards such a qualification. The charity also states that volunteers should only be used on specific projects which enhance operational activity but which the paid staff do not have time to do, for example dealing with a processing backlog or indexing a collection of annual reports. The tasks undertaken by volunteers must have clear parameters to avoid them doing work being undertaken by paid staff.

Age Concern Leicester has worked towards good practice from a very different starting point. The Age Concern Library has been run jointly since 1984 by Leicester City Libraries (which pays for the librarian's salary and the bookfund) and Age Concern Leicester (which pays for the heating and lighting of the library space, which is housed within their building). One professional member of staff is assisted by a team of no fewer than 27 volunteers, in teams of three. Their role is to assist the librarian, particularly with tasks such as loaning books. Although in the past they were left on their own if the librarian had a meeting to attend for example, she has more recently managed to recruit a part-time experienced library assistant from the City Libraries to add extra supervisory cover.

The librarian offers training sessions for volunteers three times a year, on topics such as using reference books, setting up book displays and a Volunteers' Charter. Since the sessions are optional, not everyone attends: this flags up the importance of the volunteer selection process, and the need for a job description which sets out what is expected of the volunteer. At Age Concern Leicester, all new volunteers are given a volunteer's handbook, and an initial training sheet which they go through with the librarian after three and six months to ensure knowledge of the full range of tasks. Social events help the volunteers feel part of the organisation: the main motivation for many of them, they freely admit, is company. This is, indeed, another form of user involvement.

Volunteers may be a source of innovation, bringing fresh thinking into an organisation. Hampson[15] has outlined the benefits both he and the organisation gained from his time as a volunteer with Living Options, an advocacy group in the Wirral for people with disabilities which is staffed entirely by volunteers. He was able to offer information skills, which led him to create a newsletter, and IT skills with which he set up Web pages for Living Options. He also developed new skills, in advocacy, fund-raising and communication. As he says, 'it should be a win-win situation in which the volunteer achieves personal goals and developmental aims whilst contributing to the objectives of the supporting organisation'.

Not every case history is a success, however. Managing volunteers can take as much time as managing paid staff. Unsatisfactory performance (loss of motivation, unreliable time-keeping) can be difficult to handle, and there are certainly hidden costs such as training time. The Commission on the Future of the Voluntary Sector[6] reported that 'key factors in motivating volunteers and in improving the quality of their performance, are: the substantiveness of the job (in other words, volunteers don't respond to being given dead end tasks); the degree of autonomy within the organisation and, most important of all, the level of feedback volunteers receive on their work'.

Secondments

Secondments take the form of the temporary placement in a voluntary organisation of an employee from a commercial firm, or even from another voluntary organisation. They offer benefits to both parties: specific skills to the charity, and for the secondee the chance to see a different organisation at work, to learn to work with people with different experience, and to innovate. The placement should be part of an employee's training and career development, not an excuse to shunt someone into a backwater. The voluntary organisation must be clear what it wants and expects of the secondee, induct them accordingly, and ensure that its own staff are fully briefed on the secondee's role.

Solo librarianship

In many voluntary organisations the main staffing issue will be that the librarian is working either entirely on their own or with just a little clerical assistance. The International Planned Parenthood Federation (IPPF) librarian, who works in this way, pinpoints prioritising and time management as the keys to success in such a situation. Given an ever-increasing flow of incoming information, and no-one else to help manage it, being very clear as to priorities – and as to what one cannot even start to deal with – is essential. Decisions must be made quickly (the principle of handling a piece of paper only once may come into play here) and, if a similar issue is likely to come up again, should be recorded in some way. Clear guidelines on procedural matters may not be written down in some one-person libraries, because all the relevant information is stored 'in the librarian's head'. However, the production of guidelines has a particular value in a one-person library since they can be followed by someone else if the librarian is ill or on leave.

The need to be clear who one's users are is particularly crucial in solo librarianship. It has yet further resonance in the charity sector where the librarian will often be used to juggling the demands of students doing project work, journalists wanting statistics for a story, and internal colleagues with their own urgent deadlines. The library must set out, and gain firm management support for, guidelines on who has the right to use its services:

- internal colleagues only?
- bona fide researchers?
- students but not schoolchildren?

It is particularly important to renegotiate such boundaries if the library becomes a one-person operation as a result of organisational cuts. Once such guidelines are established the librarian's reference and 'networking' skills (discussed later in the chapter) come into play, as they establish other relevant information resources to which enquirers can be referred.

Other skills significant to the success of a one-person operation are self-sufficiency, adaptability, political awareness of how the organisation functions, and a willingness to take the initiative to ensure that the library is not forgotten by managers but is involved in new ventures and potential projects.

Time away from the library – on a training course, at meetings, on holiday – can be particularly tricky for someone working alone. The IPPF librarian's view is that as long as colleagues are given plenty of warning, and the library phone is diverted so that it is at least answered somewhere in the organisation, it may well be better to do without holiday cover unless the leave period is a long one. The library's holdings will inevitably be specialist, and therefore she feels that the validity of calling in a non-specialist from an agency, with all the training implications that involves, is doubtful. (One should bear in mind that this particular post is a job-share which has the advantage, noted above, of continuation within the job even when one of the partners is away.)

The IPPF librarian is also used to tapping/buying into outside sources, rather than trying to do everything herself. For instance, no indexing of articles is done in-house; rather, library users are given access via CD-ROM to abstracts on population, family planning and related information from the Popline database. If a special project is to be undertaken, can extra help be brought in on an *ad hoc* basis, either to cover everyday work under the librarian's supervision or to initiate the project? In the IPPF's case, a librarian taken on to do everyday tasks during the construction of an in-house database proved so adept at IT that he ended up setting up the database (at, it was pointed out, far less than consultancy rates!)

'Networking'

Creating and maintaining formal and informal links with other professionals is crucial to the continuing professional development of the voluntary sector librarian. Bryant[5] describes this as the 'invisible college'. One obvious starting point for people working alone is Aslib's One-Man Bands Group, which produces a quarterly newsletter as well as arranging activities which, to quote their Web page (www.aslib.co.uk/sigs/omb), 'reflect the special needs of its members for management, promotional, organizational and presentation skills at an early stage in their careers and at a more specialized level than their counterparts in larger organizations'. Other professional groupings of potential interest include Aslib's Social Sciences Information Group (ASSIG), and the Community Services Group, Health Libraries Group (which also has a Community Care Sub-Group) and Career Development Group of the Library Association.

Developing a network of contacts within one's own organisation will mean that there are people around with whom to discuss new ideas, or who can provide support at a stressful time (quite apart from adding to the information professional's knowledge of key developments and potential projects, something which is crucial to the job). Age Concern England offers a 'buddy' to new staff, someone (deliberately *not* another member of their department) to whom they can turn with queries about the organisational culture, 'the way things work around here'. Although the relationship officially lasts only for six months, the contact usually continues on a less formal basis.

'Mentoring' is mentioned below as a training aid, but it is equally valid as a longer-term developmental tool, whether for coaching purposes or specifically to reduce professional isolation. Nankivell[25] writes that in a formal mentoring relationship, the partners must get on well together and be committed to making the idea work; the structure of the relationship must be agreed by both (how long will it last? how often should we meet?) and be subject to regular review; and each person's objectives in participating must be clear to the other.

Email lists and online bulletin boards and newsgroups are, if one has an email address (and, for online groups, Web access), a way of communicating with information and other fellow professionals without needing to leave the library. Just a few of the many possible groups of interest include:

- the mailing lists attached to VOIS, the Voluntary Organisations Internet Server, at www.vois.org.uk, offering news of non-profit use of the Internet;
- the newsgroup soc.org.nonprofit (though this is heavily North American in its postings);
- volsec-research-arvac@mailbase.ac.uk, an open news and discussion list for those involved in research in, on and about the voluntary and community sector in the United Kingdom;
- some of the many bulletin boards on environmental issues hosted by GreenNet at www.gn.apc.org/gn/info/conf/index.html. These are available for a monthly fee;
- various community development discussion lists accessible via UK Communities Online at www.communities.org.uk;
- lis-medical@mailbase.ac.uk, a very lively source of news for health/welfare (not just medical) librarians, including Web site and searching tips, offers of duplicate journals, and useful digests of North American mailing lists;
- lis-listen@mailbase.ac.uk, set up in 1997 to focus on issues around continuing professional development for librarians.

Details of Mailbase, which was set up to provide electronic discussion lists for the UK higher education community, and of how to subscribe to its lists, can be found on the Web at www.mailbase.ac.uk

Training

Staff need training in order to retain their enthusiasm for the job, to continue their personal and professional development, and to maintain a high quality library service. The National Council for Voluntary Organisations's *Good employment guide for the voluntary sector*[8] states: 'Although there is no legal requirement for an employer to train and develop their employees, it is only through such a commitment that an organisation attains a highly motivated workforce working at maximum effectiveness and the fulfilment of overall objectives'. Some developments in the service, such as the installation of a new computer system, have training implications for all team members. It is equally important to assess individual training needs, and this can often be done as part of the appraisal process outlined below. An analysis of training needs enables staff to outline areas of their job where they feel most and *least* confident, and should encourage them to focus on specific 'learning outcomes' rather than general, vague expressions of need 'for computer training' or similar. People should also be aware of their preferred learning style (watching a video? reading? learning by doing?) to get the most out of training.

Constraints on training – costs, time, even geographic availability – are an obvious issue in the voluntary sector. There is often a lack even of recognition of the need for training, let alone a strategic approach to training across the organisation as a whole. A 1996 publication[7] presents evidence from the Industrial Society that spending on training in the United Kingdom was among the lowest levels in Europe, at 3.28 per cent of a company's salary bill, and that in the voluntary sector this went down further, to 2.84 per cent. The LA survey of voluntary sector libraries found that staff in only 57 per cent of organisations had undergone any training in the previous year. There are perhaps particular issues around training part-time workers – should they be paid or receive time off in lieu, for instance, if the training takes place outside their usual hours?

However, training can take many forms. It does not have to mean attending an expensive external course. It could mean:

- working co-operatively with other departments or indeed other organisations to provide joint training, externally or in-house, either on a one-off subject or as part of a communal developmental framework. Even buying in an experienced trainer can be cost-effective if sufficient staff attend;
- using self-instruction manuals or videos, or computer-assisted learning. (Customer care is one library-related skill base which could be developed in this way). Again it may be possible to centralise such resources within, say, the Personnel Department, or purchase or hire them in tandem with another organisation with similar requirements;
- more formal processes of distance or open learning;
- matching a member of staff with a mentor, either internal or external, who can offer advice and informal 'coaching' based on their own knowledge and experience;
- involvement in cross-departmental working groups, or project work;
- secondment, job swaps or, lower-key, job shadowing, either within the organisation (e.g. to learn marketing skills or gain particular IT experience) or in another organisation;
- even 'incidental learning' from experiences within a job, if time can be taken to step back after completion of a project and work out what has been learnt during it.

A 1991 survey of voluntary sector training needs[17] suggested that, as a matter of good practice, voluntary agencies should start to build in to their budgets a 'training overhead', to help training to become viewed as a necessary part of the effectiveness of the sector as a whole, rather than as an expensive luxury for a single organisation to bear.

A range of work-related qualifications is also available to individuals, of which perhaps the most relevant in the library context are National Vocational Qualifications (NVQs). There are three levels of NVQ developed by the Information and Library Services Lead Body:

- level 2, intended for people undertaking a range of work in the library, and probably with job titles such as Library Assistant or Clerical Assistant;
- level 3, intended for people with more autonomy and responsibility in their jobs;
- level 4, intended for people working across a broad range of complex work activities with considerable personal responsibility and autonomy. (This is the highest level Information NVQ; beyond this, one would perhaps be looking at undertaking a level 5 Management NVQ).

All are work-based and involve collection of evidence of competence in different elements of library work. (Some of the modules are also used in other NVQs such as Customer Service and Administration). This 'evidence', which may take the form of pieces of work, or 'witness statements' from colleagues and others confirming satisfactory performance, are drawn together into a work portfolio for checking by the assessors who will also have directly observed the individual at work over a period of time, and questioned them to check knowledge and skills.

Whereas a level 4 NVQ may seem to offer validation of skills which people have already proved by possessing a professional or educational qualification, levels 2 and 3 provide non-professional library staff with an excellent opportunity to receive formal organisational recognition of the quality and range of work they are undertaking. The work-based nature of NVQs overcomes many of the potential objections about the cost and time factors of training in the voluntary sector, and provides a potentially less intimidatory approach to learning for people who are unused to formal educational methods such as the writing of essays. This is because the work done for the NVQ (barring the putting together of the portfolio) is almost entirely work which is being done anyway in the course of the person's daily working life. Even the drawing together of the 'evidence' enables the person to see connections between library tasks (e.g. the same skills used in performing different routines) and thus take a more rounded view of their role. Courtney[7] also suggests that the structure of the elements which make up the NVQ units may help an organisation in drawing up or revising job descriptions and person specifications.

For professional library staff, the Library Association's process of 'registration of Associates' – chartering – in most cases means following an LA-approved one-year training programme, and then

- writing an evaluative 'professional development report', or
- compiling a portfolio of evidence of professional development along the lines of the NVQ portfolio, or
- completing a 'professional development proforma' and undergoing an assessment interview.

The training programme must be supervised by an experienced Chartered Member of the LA. The LA's Professional Qualifications Department can help match a candidate with an external supervisor if there is no-one suitable in the candidate's own workplace. This makes it a particularly valuable way for the professional who works alone to maintain links with the wider library world and ensure their own continuing development. The programme must develop professional and management skills, make candidates aware of the objectives of the library and the wider organisation, and cover topics such as communication, professional awareness and assessment of training needs. These areas must also be covered in the report or portfolio, along with an evaluative account of the professional work undertaken in the post.

If the organisation as a whole wishes to prove its commitment to training and development it can work towards attaining standards, perhaps

- Investors in People, which is based on principles such as an organisation's public commitment to develop all its staff in such a way as to achieve the organisation's objectives (two of its main advantages thus being that training is linked to the organisation's aims, and is included in strategic planning); or
- ISO 9000 (formerly BS 5750), which offers a framework for accountability (including user feedback) and systematic review of services, by specifying and documenting the processes by which those services are delivered.

Being in a position to announce that the organisation is working towards or has achieved such standards, and therefore is clearly serious about training and development issues, may help in attracting high calibre recruits and reducing staff turnover.

Training must, of course, be evaluated to assess its effectiveness. Again, staff must be clear about the expected outcomes of the training before they undertake it; they should also report back to the manager on its effectiveness in meeting their development needs (rather than whether it was simply interesting), and prepare a list of specific action points resulting from the training, progress on which can be reviewed over the next couple of months, perhaps as part of an appraisal process.

A formal performance appraisal or staff review procedure 'helps to ensure the delivery of a quality service by giving staff a framework of knowledge and practical support'[12]. The more that staff are collectively involved in developing and refining such a procedure, the better its chance of success. A developmental scheme of staff appraisal should never be viewed as part of an organisation's pay, promotion or disciplinary procedure. Instead it is an opportunity for a manager and a member of staff to spend time in a confidential, honest two-way discussion about jointly-agreed objectives for that person; these objectives should be specific, measurable, within the control of the individual to achieve, and aimed positively at improving performance within the job (in other words developmental, not proscriptive). Developing in staff the confidence to analyse, and then share with their manager, a realistic evaluation of their own performance is potentially a training issue for the manager in itself; but if this can be achieved, the value to the individual of diagnosing problems for themselves and developing their own solutions will often outweigh attendance at an expensive course covering the same ground. Other forms of appraisal, such as peer appraisal, self-appraisal and upward or 360 degree appraisal are also possible, and may seem more in keeping with the culture of one's particular voluntary organisation.

By focusing on genuine training needs, on learning outcomes, and on evaluation of what has been learnt, the manager will have the issue of quality always at the forefront of their thinking. Since a voluntary organisation will stand or fall on the quality and effectiveness of its staff and/or volunteers, this is crucial.

Continuing professional development and career development

When the Library Association launched its Framework for Continuing Professional Development (CPD) in 1992, it did so with the intention of nurturing in its members a career-long personal commitment to professional development. One of the areas where this proof of continued development is potentially most useful is the voluntary sector. Many librarians are, as has been said, working for a manager who has no other links with the library and information world, and possibly only the haziest of understanding of what an information qualification entails. A completed CPD framework document, outlining as it does in an analytical way the skills and competencies an individual brings to their work, can be presented to such managers as an introduction to the librarian's job if the manager is new, or as the starting point for an appraisal, even as the basis for a regrading claim. Many information professionals, after some years in a particular voluntary sector job, feel that they have become so specialised in their field that career advancement is impossible. It is, however, possible for imaginative leaps to be made even in the career of a voluntary sector librarian with no obvious upward move in sight. The CPD Framework, in encouraging an analysis of changing areas of work, development needs and personal priorities, can spark off this process.

It may also begin to offer thoughts, to the non-librarian manager as well as to the individual, on the 'transferability' of many of the skills outlined: on secondment to an IT or a communications/PR environment, to a managerial role, to a working group looking at setting quality standards across the organisation, to a project setting up a Web site. Indeed, looking at career development in its broadest sense, Farmer et al [10] suggest that information professionals' 'transferable skills' make them well placed to move into IT, communication and general management positions; with reference specifically to health, they mention jobs in contracting, budgeting, business planning and the setting of quality standards.

The Library and Information Commission's '2020 vision' for the future of United Kingdom library services[22] emphasises 'connectivity, content and competences', and the third of these elements promotes the concept of equipping individuals (and organisations) 'to play their full role in a learning and information society'. Personal development can help this process, whether it is achieved by

- reading widely in the professional literature;
- committee work;
- visits to other libraries and information units, not just in the voluntary sector;
- writing an article for the charity's bulletin or the professional library press;
- learning a new IT-related skill; or
- starting a formal part-time postgraduate course for voluntary sector managers.

At a time when the phrase 'information overload' is as frequently heard in the voluntary sector as elsewhere, information professionals who can locate and disseminate high quality information, and teach others how to do likewise, will ensure that their charity becomes 'a learning and information organisation' ready to tackle whatever changes lie ahead.

Managing change

The voluntary sector is used to constant change – from a successful Lottery bid to the non-renewal of a local authority contract – but is not always good at *managing* this change. Planning for change, and including the wider library team in the process, is an important aspect of staff management.

Reasons why team members may resist change include:

- a lack of appropriate information;
- the feeling of having no involvement in or control of a situation;
- it being contrary to their own values (and their perception of what the organisation's values should be) or personal agenda;
- diffidence or inhibition on the part of those presenting the change.

It is essential to foster a culture of good communication, of as much involvement as possible in decision-making of those who may be affected by changes, and of positive feelings towards the possibilities offered by change. One way of encouraging such a culture is to get the library team together at least once a year to contribute to the compilation of medium- and long-term aims and objectives for the service, including an assessment of what has changed and what is likely to change in the foreseeable future. This takes on extra importance for managers of the information function given the strategic need for awareness of potential change in the larger organisation, and of possibilities of proactive change in the library which will enable it to remain as – or move to become – an integral part of the organisation.

Working for a manager from another discipline

The likelihood is that the voluntary sector library manager will be managed by a non-librarian. This probably means having to adapt to a different approach from the manager, and certainly necessitates being constantly alive to the politics of the situation. The picture may be especially complicated because many voluntary organisations, particularly smaller ones, are managed in a participatory and consensual way. Sometimes the structure of authority is not clear-cut. There may be a management committee and/or assorted working groups and project teams as well as a structure of line management. In any event, the librarian is likely to have to be aware of the manager's different 'starting point' and put extra effort into explaining basic library needs: the importance of cataloguing and indexing may not be immediately apparent, for example, so requests for temporary staff to assist with a cataloguing backlog will have to be explained with some background explanation of the importance of such tasks. Any tendency to use 'library jargon' must also be curbed.

A major advantage of having a non-librarian manager is the opportunity for a heightened awareness of the library's context in the wider organisation, of 'the broader picture', and for developing lateral networks within the organisation. Another advantage is that the manager, once they have grasped the importance of the library's objectives, can make a powerful advocate for the library service.

Securing organisational recognition

The LA's survey of voluntary sector libraries found that 91 per cent of paid managers had responsibilities other than managing the library or information unit. To what extent this was through their own choice was not ascertained. However, in terms of securing organisational recognition of a librarian's range of expertise, 'branching out' into other areas can score highly. The librarian can legitimately 'market themselves' as:

- a trainer (in the effective use of information. Offering Internet skills training can be a high-profile way of bringing the relevance of search skills to a wider audience);
- an expert in customer care, and in eliciting the information needed to find a satisfactory answer;
- an evaluator of quality, being experienced in evaluating information resources;
- an advisor on implementing new ways of handling information. At Age Concern England, the library team offered to help colleagues reorganise and plan their filing systems;
- a 'knowledge mapper' for the organisation (understanding the need to log knowledge and expertise in colleagues' heads, as well as paper and electronic information resources held by the organisation);
- a research analyst with wide-ranging knowledge of the sector and excellent presentational skills, and who is able to locate high quality information amidst vast quantities of paper and electronic resources;
- a guide to the plethora of technological possibilities for the organisation;
- a manager of change, an innovator, a proactive and flexible professional.

The above may sound like a series of arguments in favour of the librarian getting a salary upgrade. They could indeed be used as such, but principally they relate to many voluntary sector librarians' need to 'sell' to their organisation's management what the information professional can do and should be doing. If the director sees the library simply as the storage place for information – or even as the storage place for information *which they don't need* (while what they think they do or will need stays in their own filing cabinet) – they may not turn to the library when they decide the organisation needs a Web site, for example. Even library skills which professionals take for granted, such as organising an SDI (Selective Dissemination of Information) service, can make a difference to the wider work of a voluntary organisation. It is up to the library manager to be proactive in volunteering their own skills and those of their team, in being upfront about their professional status: to be on working groups or special project teams, to train colleagues, to train *themselves* up to deal with new technological possibilities.

Bryant[5], writing specifically about the solo librarian, could be speaking to all voluntary sector librarians when she talks of needing 'to understand the purpose and culture of their organisation, so they can define the value which the information service can add'. The librarian must be looking to use information resources strategically within the organisation in innovative and creative ways. It is incumbent upon them to show the contribution the library can make to the organisation, and in particular to the improvement of the core functions provided by the charity. This requires a clear understanding of how the organisation currently works, and a determination to make one's voice persuasively heard within it, outlining practical methods by which the library can contribute to the wider organisation's strategic vision.

Thanks to Christine Goodair, Margaret Speak, Frances Tait, Mike Chambers and colleagues in the King's Fund Library for their help and input.

Bibliography

1. Abell, Angela. 'Ready to move centre stage?', *Library Association Record* 98 (5) (May 1996), pp. 35-36
2. Adirondack, Sandy. *Just about managing?: effective management for voluntary organisations and community groups*, London, London Voluntary Service Council, 1998
3. Armstrong, Michael. 'A charitable approach to personnel', *Personnel Management* 24 (12) (December 1992), pp. 28-32
4. Billis, David and Harris, Margaret (eds). *Voluntary agencies: challenges of organisation and management*, Basingstoke/London, Macmillan, 1996
5. Bryant, Sue Lacey. *Personal professional development and the solo librarian*, London, Library Association Publishing, 1995

6. Commission on the Future of the Voluntary Sector. *Meeting the challenge of change: voluntary action into the 21st century: the report of the Commission on the Future of the Voluntary Sector*, London, NCVO, 1996
7. Courtney, Roger. *Managing voluntary organisations: new approaches*, Hemel Hempstead, ISCA Publishing, 1996
8. Dyson, Joy (ed). *The good employment guide for the voluntary sector*, London, NCVO, 1997
9. Elkin, Judith. 'Personal development: looking at further opportunities', *Assistant Librarian* 90 (9) (October 1997), pp. 139-144
10. Farmer, Jane, Campbell, Fiona, Wilson, Kay and Williams, Dorothy. 'A framework of the transferable skills of information professionals', *Library and Information Research News* 20 (65) (Spring 1996), pp. 17-22
11. Farmer, Jane and Campbell, Fiona. 'Information professionals, CPD and transferable skills', *Library Management* 18 (3) (1997), pp. 129-134
12. Gann, Nigel. *Managing change in voluntary organizations: a guide to practice*, Buckingham/Philadelphia, Open University Press, 1996
13. Gosling, Paul. 'Making the most of secondments', *NCVO News* (June 1991), pp. 9-10
14. Goulding, Anne and Kerslake, Evelyn. 'Flexible information workers: training and equal opportunities', *Librarian Career Development* 4 (2) (1996), pp. 5-12
15. Hampson, Andrew. 'Personal development in the voluntary sector', *Assistant Librarian* 89 (6) (June 1996), pp. 90-91
16. Handy, Charles. *Understanding voluntary organisations*, London, Penguin, 1988
17. Harris, Margaret, Davies, Gill and Lessof, Carli. *Training and education for the voluntary sector: the needs and the problems*, London, London School of Economics and Political Science: Centre for Voluntary Organisation, 1991
18. Hope, Philip and Pickles, Tim. *Performance appraisal: a handbook for managers in public and voluntary organisations*, Lyme Regis, Russell House Publishing, 1995
19. Hyatt, J. 'Outsiders inside: the use of consultants by voluntary organisations', *Assignation* 13 (1) (January 1996), pp. 15-18
20. Jago, Alison. 'Selecting your team: how to find the right people', *Librarian Career Development* 4 (3) (1996), pp. 27-31
21. Leat, Diane. *Challenging management: an exploratory study of perceptions of managers who have moved from for-profit to voluntary organisations*, London, City University Business School/VOLPROF, 1995

22. Library and Information Commission. *2020 vision*, London, Library and Information Commission, 1996
23. Library Association. *Guidelines on the use of volunteers*, London, Library Association, November 1997
24. Library Association. *Survey of library and information units in charitable and voluntary organisations: final report*, London, Library Association, 1996
25. Nankivell, Clare. 'Essentials of a good relationship', *Library Association Record* 99 (10) (October 1997), p. 545
26. St Clair, Guy and Williamson, Joan. *Managing the new one-person library*, London etc, Bowker Saur, 1992
27. Siggins, Jack A. 'Job satisfaction and performance in a changing environment', *Library Trends* 41 (2) (Fall 1992), pp. 299-315

16

Marketing the Information Service in Voluntary Sector Organisations

Diana Grimwood-Jones

Introduction

The marketing of information services within organisations has become a routine area of concern for the staff who have to provide such services, and not simply within a commercial environment. Over the past several years, there has been an increasing need for 'libraries' (however defined) to justify their existence: sometimes quite literally, by having to recoup some of their costs, sometimes in recognition that unless they can raise their profile internally and 'sell' their own benefits successfully, they are liable to be axed as an inessential fringe support service, made redundant by the private collections of 'must have to hand' texts set up by individuals or departments and end-user access to electronic information (increasingly the Internet), which fulfil immediate information needs.

The growth of office networks, even in quite small organisations, and the increasing emphasis on sharing information and improving 'knowledge management' across the enterprise ought to have highlighted the importance of information activities and enhanced the role of those who provide them. Unfortunately, this does not appear to have been the case, and information staff can find themselves confined to traditional reactive 'library' duties of buying and issuing books and journals and reshelving them, with perhaps occasional searches on CD-ROM to add excitement. A good marketing programme (which can be scaled up or down to suit the size of the organisation and the resource it has available) offers opportunities to turn this around – by determining the nature of the information service that really is required by users, whether internal or external, scarce resources can be reallocated to better effect all round.

Another common problem information staff have faced in trying to implement a more market oriented or customer focused approach is that user expectations of the service can be surprisingly modest. The library has also tended to suffer from a lack of management support – or indeed management ignorance about what information staff actually do, what the nature of their expertise is and how it can best be harnessed to support the needs and goals of the organisation. Lindquist observes (1993: p.268) that one of the difficulties in marketing information is that a lack of it is not always apparent. Even when users claim to have a high opinion of the service, they often don't know how it works or what exactly it offers, and have little real contact with staff.

But how necessary is active marketing within a voluntary sector organisation where everyone knows where the library is, and has at least some idea of the services provided? With resources already stretched to the limit and the need for close accountability, isn't it all a bit of a luxury? And what *is* marketing in this context? The usual definition quoted by most UK writers is that of the Chartered Institute of Marketing: *Marketing is the management process which identifies, anticipates and supplies customer requirements efficiently and profitably.* Even if the last element is inappropriate for the voluntary sector, the rest of it makes sound sense. As to what can be marketed, de Saez (1993: p.4) points out that marketable commodities can be much broader than the basic goods and services: organisations, people, physical buildings or locations, social issues can all be 'sold' to raise both awareness and customer numbers. The selling of social issues will be familiar to voluntary sector organisations – but how active a contribution is the information service making to campaigns, and is that contribution recognised? This kind of recognition, and a clearer view at the top of the actual or potential contribution made by information staff to the organisation's aims, should be one of the main aims – and chief benefits – of marketing activity. Put another way, 'Successful special libraries, located in either profit or nonprofit organizations, effectively increase organizational opportunities by discovering and delivering information that is really needed' (Powers, 1995: p.478). The penalties of failure can be heavy indeed: 'Without strategic marketing planning, many special libraries may be isolated from organizational objectives and eventually eliminated' (Powers, 1995: p.492).

There is not much guidance in the current professional literature specific to voluntary organisations, though Guy St. Clair's occasional marketing articles in the newsletter *One Person Library* provide useful tips for smaller units. Coote and Batchelor (1998) offer practical and accessible advice for both first-time and more experienced marketeers. More detailed guidance, with lots of examples which can be tailored to voluntary organisation need, is the workbook by Keiser and Galvin (1995). The case study by Evan-Wong and de Freitas (1995), though not set in a voluntary sector context, is a good example of the benefits of a structured marketing approach by a small unit with limited staffing, and demonstrates that such an exercise need not be a complex or expensive process. (See *References* for details of all of these publications.) For the purposes of this chapter, we will consider marketing to be seeking to answer the following questions:

- What is the broad environment within which we operate?
- Who are our customers (actual or potential), and where?
- Which of our services are used, and what for? Who are heavy users, and who are non users who ought to be users? What is the nature of the competition – if people are not using our services, do we know how are they getting their information?
- What are our Strengths, Weaknesses, Opportunities and Threats?
- What do our customers actually say they need, and how do they want it delivered?
- How do we measure the effectiveness of what we're doing?

The stages in this process (which can be taken as a sequence of actions or as discrete elements) will be:

1. Environmental analysis
2. The information audit
    2.1 The SWOT analysis
    2.2 Usage analysis
    2.3 Budget/Resource review
3. Information needs assessment
4. Marketing Plan
5. Evaluation.

1. Environmental analysis

The purpose of the environmental analysis is to provide a context and a framework for marketing activity. The analysis will need to take account both external and internal factors. Externally, what influences are likely to affect the future development of the information service? As de Saez points out (1993: p.22) the variables are complex and dynamic. They are usually grouped in terms of PESTs– Political, Economic, Social/Cultural and Technological contexts, and their relative importance will vary depending upon the nature of the organisation. The uncontrollable – and indeed unexpected – nature of these for the voluntary sector can be illustrated by two quite different recent examples: the impact of the National Lottery and the death of the Princess of Wales on the pattern and scale of charitable donations and the emergence of 'fashionable' causes. What effects are these in turn having on information service provision in the sector? Internally, there is a need to define the library's context within the wider organisation and how marketing as an activity is carried out. Where does marketing fit into the organisation and what is its marketing 'culture'? Some valuable lessons can be learned from this. One difficulty of marketing an information service within voluntary organisations (assuming there are no cultural objections to the concept of actively promoting, in a planned way, what is a support role) can be identifying what the information service actually is and where it sits: is it a discrete unit, with a dedicated staffing level, or a part of general administration, where library duties such as journal circulation are carried out as and when time permits? Which wider department is it attached to (put another way, to whom does the information officer report?). How many 'hats' does the information officer wear – helpline manager? bookseller? Events organiser? There is a particular need to look closely at the organisation's corporate mission and objectives: to which ones does the library actually or potentially make a contribution? Look at the library's own objectives: how closely do they mesh in with wider organisational ones?

The outcome of this stage of the marketing exercise should be a short document recording key external factors which might impact on the service; a list of corporate objectives and the library's contribution; the library's own objectives and any questions relating to them which may have emerged from the contextual investigations.

2. The information audit

The term 'information audit' is used in different ways by different people, and can be employed as a blanket term to cover a range of activities including a user needs assessment. For the purposes of this chapter we have separated out the needs assessment from actual usage. The information audit as thus defined will document, in a systematic way, the usage made of the different categories of service provided, and examine how the resources expended upon those different services map against use.

2.1 SWOT analysis

At the beginning of any review process it is worthwhile carrying out an analysis of Strengths, Weaknesses, Opportunities and Threats (SWOT) in which the first two will relate to the organisation itself, and the latter two to the external world, picking up points from the environmental analysis. It can be useful to plot these on a 1-page matrix (Evan Wong and de Freitas, p.125, gives an example), with up to half a dozen points under each heading (there will seldom need to be more).

Strengths, particularly in a voluntary sector context, will commonly include the expertise of information staff and their depth of personal commitment to the organisation's aims, or the richness (or indeed unique nature) of information resources in a particular subject area. However,

Strengths can also include factors such as strong management support for the information function or good geographical location, situated close to key departments. Human nature being what it is, staff find Weaknesses all too easy to identify. Inadequate resources, which permit only a skeleton service, out of date reference material, inadequate technology and poor internal communication are all popular candidates. The informal, non-bureaucratic approach to processes and procedures which characterises many voluntary sector organisations may provide evidence of both Strength and Weakness. Apply some lateral thinking to Opportunities: might there be scope for collaborating with another organisation in the same sector to produce a new product or service? Will a new piece of legislation provide openings for extending or developing the service in new external markets? Threats can be the converse of Opportunities (e.g. will recent or proposed legislation have an adverse effect on the organisation, and by extension on the service). Weaknesses may be partly under your control. What are their root causes? How might you minimise their effects? Are there weaknesses which could be turned into Strengths with some tweaking?

2.2 Usage analysis

A vital stage for any marketing programme is to identify and quantify the actual or potential markets within the organisation (and indeed the non-markets). It will be seeking answers to questions such as the following:

- Who exactly *are* our users?
- How similar are they in what they need and use?
- How many are 'self service' users – frequent visitors but only to browse current journals – and how many address real queries to the staff?
- What sort of competition does the library face – e.g. from individuals or departments building up their own information collections, or subscribing to their own external information sources?

Successfully marketing your services will depend on how well you can gauge levels of interest in different services by different groups, and target these accordingly. This will of course assume a thorough knowledge of the organisation, its structure, culture, how it communicates, how it sees its future and who the major players are.

Look at the way your organisation is structured, and where the information service fits in. What is the organisational breakdown in terms of function, and the staff numbers for the individual departments? Are there geographical factors (e.g. regional offices) to take account of? Are demographic factors (e.g. age, gender) likely to be significant in terms of the service or its delivery? Quantification of the total internal potential market is straightforward enough – you will know how many people there are in Fundraising, Membership, Press and PR and so on and how many of these are in management, professional or clerical roles. Quantifying your potential external market, which may include such diverse groups as medical staff, academic staff and students, volunteers, sufferers and their families, journalists, lobbyists, consultants and the general public will be more difficult, but it should be possible to derive some 'order of magnitude' figures from usage statistics. Which of these groups you will want to target as priority customers, and which not, will feed into your Marketing Plan. Keiser & Galvin (1995: p.17) point out that each user group has a different, identifiable force which drives it; knowing what this is will enable you better to market your product or service.

Having obtained a global figure for your genuine potential customers (with some indication of which information is critical to them) you will be in a good position to map type of use, and level of intensity, against each of the services you offer. Does a particular group use you mostly for rapid enquiries, current legislation, what other voluntary sector bodies in the same field are doing? Is a disproportionate amount of time spent satisfying high volume but low priority demands, such as students doing project work? What impact do the organisation's marketing campaigns have, from the point of view of internal or external demand – can you plot blips in usage patterns? Are there services which are resource intensive, and which you feel should be of wide benefit (perhaps a current awareness service) but which are scarcely used? What percentage of your users are personal callers, as opposed to telephone callers? Is the use of email overtaking both as a means of communicating requests to the library?

2.3 Budget/Resource review

Your work on market segmentation – analysing your user groups and their information gathering behaviour – and your SWOT analysis will have given you a clear picture of where you are now, with some indication of how you might develop: you will know who your heavy users are, how many of your low users are potential high users, and the kinds of use made of the different services offered by the library.

You now need to plot, on a service by service basis, how all your resources (financial, staffing, technological and even the space you have available) are being allocated, and thereby give you a snapshot of what your current priorities for service delivery are – whether these are planned or otherwise! This process should generate a number of questions about the resource justification for individual services, and whether your resource allocations accord with the demands of your priority users. It may be an illuminating experience to follow Eddison's advice (1990: p. 115) and examine your library service and processes just as you would if you were asked to function on a complete cost recovery basis.

By the end of this phase, and armed with your three documents: the SWOT analysis, Usage analysis and Budget review, you are well placed to begin to identify what your user needs really are.

3. Information needs assessment

The core of any good service delivery programme is to find out what your customers want and need in such a way that you can judge how far you are delivering the required service in the most beneficial way to the customer, and in the most resource efficient way to the organisation. As you will have discovered, 'consumer analysis' is an activity which to an extent you are doing subconsciously all the time: even before your systematic analysis of usage, you will have had a good idea of what your customers ask for, how they gather information either individually or on a departmental basis, and possibly individual preferences as to how the information they need is delivered to them. The User Needs Assessment stage of the marketing process built into your marketing activity will allow you to clarify perceptions (theirs of the services you are offering, yours of their needs) identify trends, ideas for new services (or indeed pointers to scrap existing ones) or new delivery points and methods – in other words a clear view of *needs* rather than *use*.

No matter how small or how large the organisation, make sure that the data you collect provides you with a representative picture of your user base at a particular point in time. There are many ways of doing this:

- short structured personal interview, separately arranged or conducted during a user's library visit;
- a questionnaire survey;
- a focus group of interested individuals.

They are not mutually exclusive, and which you select will depend upon the size of the organisation and what is appropriate in terms of the way you work. All three will follow the same broad structure; what you will record is:

- what an individual's job is, and how the main areas of activity break down;
- the kinds of information needed to carry out that job and what the most important categories or sources are;
- where they get this information from (the library? colleagues? their own resource collections?);
- how quickly and how often the information is required;

- what format they would like information delivered in;
- current difficulties or problems in getting the information they want;
- ideas they have for resolving the problems, or improving the service; what would their ideal service be like? Can they suggest one single improvement which would make a real difference to their working lives?

For a personal interview, it is advisable to stick to a small number of key 'open' questions, and to give your interviewee scope for free evaluative comment. If the interview is to take place in their office, let them have the main topic heads beforehand, so that they can be thinking about a response – no-one likes being questioned 'cold'. If you intend to approach users with a clipboard whilst they're in the library, alert them in advance to what you're doing, and why (so that you can deliver a service more closely targeted to their needs) and ask for their positive support. Keep it brief (10 minutes for a library interview, 20-30 minutes for a formally arranged one, unless the interviewee has lots to say).

A printed questionnaire, which can be mailed or emailed to remote sites or selected external users, will allow large or scattered organisations to collect a good cross section of views on user needs and how far users themselves believe these are being met. A covering note or introductory paragraph should explain the purpose of the questionnaire, emphasise how quickly it can be filled in (take the time taken to drink a cup of coffee as a guideline!) to whom it should be returned, and by when. (If the covering note is on a separate sheet, make sure the return information appears at the end of the questionnaire.) Here are some ways of ensuring a good rate of return:

- Keep it short: no more than 10-12 questions. A good format is the 4 x A4 pages, photocopied double sided onto A3, where page 1 gives the introductory and return details, pages 2 and 3 the quantitative or quantifiable questions, and page 4 allows some space for free text comment on the information service, suggestions, ideas, or general moans and groans;
- Keep it simple: offer features like boxes to tick (e.g. for services used; to respond to questions such as 'which of the following statements most closely expresses your opinion on service X'), a rating scale for importance or degree of satisfaction (three or five points are common, but they allow respondents to sit on the fence and tick the middle option for everything; giving them four will force them to be actively for or against); yes or no answers;
- Make sure your terminology is understandable to the recipient (e.g. don't ask if they use the SDI service without any further explanation if they are unlikely to know what it is);

- Make sure each question only asks one question, and asks it unambiguously;
- Make the questionnaire easy to return – by enclosing a stamped addressed envelope, or arranging for batch collection at remote sites;
- Allow people enough time to fill in the questionnaire and return it, but not so long that it will be forgotten. Two or three weeks is about right. (It goes without saying that you won't send out your survey in mid-summer or mid-December …)

A little thought will give you a good rate of return (depending on numbers and location, 30% can be good and over 60% excellent) and give you the means of building up quite a complex picture of user needs and perceptions. Questionnaire design looks deceptively easy: it isn't. You will be well advised to pilot yours around a small sample to make sure that gaps can be spotted or ambiguities ironed out before the full mailshot goes ahead.

Depending on how large the survey is, you may like to code up elements of it so that you can analyse the returns in a variety of ways: department or function; type of user (e.g. internal vs. external, or by user category); geographic location (are there specific regional requirements or problems?). If you need to carry out a thorough, large-scale survey, and the resources are available, you might use consultancy assistance for part or all of the Needs Assessment. De Saez (1993: pp.102-103) offers advice on how to get the best out of a research supplier and stresses the need for information staff and researcher to be equal partners in a dialogue: you need to make sure they understand the context in which you are working (and are not labouring under some outdated image of what libraries are), be clear about what information is essential to collect, not merely desirable (the more you collect, the more it will cost), allow sufficient time for planning, and make it clear how you want the results reported back to you. Grimwood-Jones (1996) gives some general advice on choosing and using consultants.

The results of your survey will give you pointers on how you might rework your service provision so that your effort and resource is used to best advantage, and those users who should be the focus of your best efforts are getting a service which is more closely tailored to their actual needs.

Focus groups can be an excellent way of getting 'live' feedback, with the benefit of interaction and discussion (sometimes argument!) amongst members of the group. They can also strengthen your relationship with your users. Each group will involve around half a dozen people (ideally from different departments) who will discuss a small number of key topics for a set period (about an hour to an hour and a half). The group can be facilitated by an information person or an external consultant can be brought in to facilitate a 'closed' session. (The use of an external consultant may be expensive, but views expressed are likely to be more open than if the information manager is present.) Either way, key discussion points need to be recorded, so if you are doing the job yourself arrange for a colleague to act as 'rapporteur' whilst you chair and facilitate the discussion.

4. The Marketing Plan

You are now entering the policy making phase, whose aim is to establish priorities for your main user groups, the allocation of various library resources to them, and what it will all cost.

A customised marketing plan needs to be prepared, setting out its own clearly set goals and ways of monitoring their effectiveness. Traditionally, plans have included the 'marketing mix' of variables: Product, Price, Place and Promotion, known as 'the four Ps'. De Saez (1993: p.39) suggests replacing this *'seller's'* paradigm with a user paradigm of 'the four Cs' developed by the American Philip Kotler, an expert in the marketing of not-for-profit organisations. In Kotler's system, Product becomes Customer value, Price the Cost to the customer, which includes the time and energy required by them to access the service, Place translates into Convenience (of delivery point or delivery mechanism) and Promotion into Communication. Such a shift of emphasis from provider to recipient may be considered by many information staff in the voluntary sector to be more appropriate for the services they provide. Powers (1995: p.486) notes a variety of marketing strategies which are viable in the special library context: market segmentation strategies (offering a new service to existing clients), market development strategies (developing new clients), market penetration strategies (increasing use of services by existing clients), diversification strategies (new services to new clients) and distribution strategies (new ways of information delivery). Which of these are the most important to you will depend upon your own priorities.

A good marketing plan will be simple, straightforward and practical, providing a day-by-day operating guide to activities for the set period (a year is the maximum recommended). Essentially, the plan will cover:

- An overall statement of purpose;

followed by, on a service by service basis:

- What the service objectives are, in SMART terms: Specific, Measurable, Achievable, Results oriented (i.e. focused on the outcome) and Time-related;

- How these will be achieved in terms of the four P's (or four Cs), by when, and how their effectiveness will be monitored;
- The resources of all kinds required to deliver the objectives.

This last is clearly of supreme importance: to be achievable, your plan must be realistic. There is no point in planning in (for example) longer opening hours if staffing is already at minimal level (though if this is a stated requirement you can revisit how much it is used at present and whether different opening hours may achieve a higher rate of satisfaction at the same staffing level, or indeed whether the library needs to be staffed at all times to be usable) or arranging to deliver services electronically if the required technology only exists at present on a wish-list – though it can strengthen the case for implementing the wish-list. The resources required to achieve the various objectives can be pulled together to form a resources plan which will detail all cost elements including staff effort across the services provided during the period of the plan.

Product or Customer value

From your investigations you will have discovered which of your services are most highly valued by your priority customers, and which may have outlived their usefulness. Some little-used or little valued services may be considered for axing, to allow development space for others, but it is important to be sure why they are little used: the problem may be in the way the service is perceived, or that too few people know about it and it needs to be publicised in a more effective way. At the other end of the scale, you may experience a problem common within voluntary organisations, concerning not a high priority group, but a low-priority one which causes a disproportionate amount of staff effort: the schoolchild or student doing a project. A way of making space for your real customers is to put together for such groups an information pack based on their frequently asked questions.

Price, or Cost to the Customer

This may be literally a 'price' that you have to set, either for external customers or for internal ones with whom you have a Service Level Agreement. How you go about it will depend on a number of factors: how far are you attempting to cover your costs; is the main purpose of charging cost recovery or a control or deterrent to unwanted numbers or non-priority groups? Will there be differential charging for different categories of user? It may be worthwhile to try to find out what similar sized organisations (or organisations in the same sector) are doing. Charges for handling in-depth enquiries are probably most easily calculated on a time basis – there may need to be a period of experimentation with price levels and mechanisms, assessing their relative effect (including user perceptions of 'value') before you arrive at a workable conclusion.

Taking a broader view of 'cost to the customer' will involve a consideration of how much time and energy your users have to expend in getting the information they need. It can involve any number of factors:

- is the library positioned in the most convenient location for your heaviest personal users?
- how long do people have to wait for the telephone to be answered/ an email or postal request to be acknowledged and dealt with/a short or long query to be answered?
- can personal visitors find things easily, in the catalogue or on the shelves?

Place or Convenience

An aspect of information service delivery too often ignored by architects, planners and senior management is that there is a direct relationship between the distance a user has to travel to the library and the use that will be made of it. All too often, in resource centres in all sectors, the library is put in the odd corner deemed unsuitable for offices: in the basement, in awkwardly shaped areas, in areas with no windows or having other poor 'environmental' features. In an existing building, there may be little you can do about physical relocation. However, it is worth assessing how you 'sit' in relation to your priority user groups, and how far your location affects their patterns of use. Are they building up competitor private libraries because you're two floors away? And what can you do about it?

One approach is to view the 'Place' question in much broader terms of convenience, or how easy it is for anyone to use your services. Other factors linked to convenience will include the availability of the service, and the methods of delivering information or results. Improving these two may offset to an extent the disadvantages of poor location.

First, availability. Do users know what your opening hours are? As de Saez points out (1993: pp.46-47) it is better, given scarce resources, to have an information service that is known to be consistently available within restricted hours than one where availability varies according to capacity. How far do you need to have 'opening hours' at all? In McCarthy's opinion (1992: p.291) 'the percentage of people who will actually steal from an in-house library is very small, so we should not make the rules to cope with them but to suit the majority'.

Delivery is all about being flexible. Email offers a time-efficient method of transmitting results of short enquiries or sending file attachments where appropriate (and indeed receiving the initial enquiry in the first place). A networked CD-ROM can permit instant access without the need without the need for library intervention. If it is difficult for users to come to you, is there scope for you to go to them, perhaps by offering to deliver books or photocopies requested, or to give brief sessions on getting the most out of the Internet in your sector? As Powers (1995: p.484) observes, 'the real barriers to place are often in the cultural and philosophical thinking of place as an object rather than a process. Place is often the process of delivery, is often dynamic, and is often active'.

Promotion

However good your services are, there is no point in providing them unless people are using them, know that they're available, or indeed what the services are – a common but dangerous assumption. Your campaign can be about general awareness raising – a reminder to your users and non-users of your existence, and what you can offer – or about a specific new service which you are launching. Either way, you need to devise some measures to test how successful you've been. How receptive have your different user groups been? Which aspects of your message have got through and which ignored or misunderstood? Has your audience been absolutely clear what you're promoting? An ability to analyse the effect of your campaign will give you a better chance of running successful campaigns in the future.

It has long been a truism that people don't want 'information', they want solutions to problems: they want someone knowledgeable about the subject area, and experienced enough to elicit their real requirements, who will sift out irrelevant data and present them with something they can use straightaway. Your marketing activities need to hook into this idea of relevance, and sell benefits such as time saved, or more informed decision-making.

As McCarthy and others indicate, there are four basic means of promoting your services. In order of priority, these are:

- You
- The information service itself
- The way the service outputs are packaged and presented
- Promotional activities

The first three of these might be regarded as passive or 'stealth' marketing, but they are all vitally important.

To start with You. Whether you are a qualified information professional or not, it is important to present a professional (=courteous, helpful and even-handed) image to your users. This is helped if you have a set of basic procedures to work to; they don't have to be complicated, just consistent. How you deal with problems will be a yardstick your customers will use to judge your effectiveness and how useful they believe you will be to them. If a complaint is handled quickly and effectively, your complainant may be turned into a supporter; if you are seen to act positively in dealing with complaints, people are more likely to be forthcoming about their real needs and concerns, which in turn will help in building long-term relationships. Be seen to be giving consideration to user suggestions, even if the answer has to be no, and use language they can understand: 'talk in our customers' terms, not in library or research terms' (Eddison, 1990: p. 114).

What does the library itself look like? De Saez (1993: p.49) talks of the need to assess what user first impressions are, and urges a strong statement of identity and due regard for 'atmospherics'. Is the library clean, tidy, well-lit and welcoming, with somewhere comfortable to sit and read or sit and write? Are the shelves clearly labelled, the catalogue accessible and understandable? Are any guides available, e.g. a list of current journals?

The service 'outputs' or 'products' should have a consistent look, and be tailored to the needs and convenience of the user. This might include tidying up computer printout to strip out field codes or unnecessary detail, and putting a cover note on a mixed batch of results explaining what the different things are. It should be clear to the recipient that this material has come from the library, and who to contact in case of a query. This is particularly important where a priced service is concerned. In short, 'every communication which leaves the library should be an advertisement for your service' (McCarthy, 1992: p.291).

Promotional activities cover a wide range of possibilities, of which the most feasible and effective are discussed below:

(i) Brochures
Brochures have an enduring popularity. They can be picked up by personal visitors, mailed out along with the members' newsletter, made available at seminars and conferences. If you're unsure about your writing skills, get a draft vetted by your marketing department. A brochure can be devised for the information service as a whole, or to promote one particular service. Essential elements for inclusion are:

- a brief and interesting description of what the service is, and how it has come about (or been revamped);
- whether it is targeted at a particular group;
- what the benefits of using the service are;
- details of availability, who to contact and cost where applicable.

If, as a result of your user survey, you have picked up quotable quotes from some of your users, ask if you can include them in your brochure. Promotional literature should also include some indication of date, so that you can review the information and revise the text on a regular basis. With present office systems, quite professional looking results can be obtained at modest cost, and updated often enough to maintain interest.

(ii) Slogans and logos
Both may be appropriate to a one-off campaign, by drawing attention to the service, but they do date quickly, and should therefore be used with caution.

(iii) Getting out and about
Active marketing, i.e. you going out to the users, rather than expecting them always to come to you, can be a very effective way of targeting priority customers or bringing in new business. Examples might include your going to see a new member of staff to help him/her find information on the Internet, or to discuss specific ways in which you can help them to carry out their job.

(iv) Newsletter
If the organisation is a large one, or the library services remote sites, a library Newsletter may be a possibility. This could take the form of a current awareness bulletin with some added value: a selection of press comment on a relevant news story, or a summary or the conclusions of a recent report or survey within the sector.

(v) Direct mail
A targeted direct mail campaign may be appropriate, perhaps to introduce a new 'premium' service. Ensure that the text reflects the concerns of your audience, rather than yours: 'we know from speaking to several probation officers like yourself who use the library service that what you would really like to see from us is a faster response time. We are delighted to tell you we can now guarantee a 48-hour turnaround …'

(vi) House journal
An occasional write-up in your 'house' journal or professional newsletter will raise your profile with users and management. Ideally, this should be hooked into a story, rather than simply reporting the arrival of a new staff member or just to remind readers of your existence. An example might be the contribution made by the library in finding material for a recent fundraising campaign.

(vii) Use of the Internet
If your organisation has a Web site, this can provide good opportunities for information professionals to raise their own and their service profile.

Watson (1996) provides a good case study to illustrate how the Net can be incorporated into a strategic approach to the development of products and services. Gedye's article (1997), though geared to the promotion and marketing of learned societies and their publications, has useful general advice to offer on design and layout which is relevant in the present context if you are publicising your service on the Web (or indeed as an information person, find yourself drafted in to assist with the initial Web site design). For example:

- ask yourself and others what people are most likely to want from your Web site;
- use graphics sparingly: consider offering a 'graphics-lite' or plain text version so that those with slow connections can opt for a version that works on their machine;
- always include an email link which will allow visitors to contact you – and make it easy to find.

These are just a few concrete examples of promotional activities, and others are suggested elsewhere in this book. You should also be looking to promote your services in an ongoing, wider sense:

- Do information staff attend meetings of other departments? Are you included in discussions of projects, or project resourcing? You clearly need to be aware of organisational initiatives at an early stage, so that you can assess their impact on the information service. However, you should also be looking for opportunities to emphasise what information or expertise the library has to offer, and build a greater awareness of your value, e.g by negotiating library membership of influential committees;
- Cultivate contacts – ideally find yourself champions amongst senior staff, who will support you when it matters;
- If you get written appreciation for a piece of work carried out, make sure your management knows about it.

5. Evaluation

The evaluation phase brings to an end one marketing cycle and sets the stage for another. Its purpose is to assess and evaluate the different elements of your marketing plan and the assumptions that underpinned it: what changes have occurred since the start of the process in the external or internal environment that will impact upon the user population and their needs? How effective have individual elements been? Which objectives have been achieved, which not, and why? What have the costs and benefits been? The whole purpose of your marketing programme will have been to establish which services your customers need and how you can deliver them in the most effective way for the organisation. In terms of timing, the Evaluation phase of your Marketing Plan will have had to allow enough time for new or changed services or delivery modes to have bedded down, i.e. long enough for you to have gauged the costs, and your users the benefits, to note any trends, unforeseen or otherwise, and to apply corrective action where appropriate. A short informal survey of a representative sample of users (perhaps a scaled down version of your User Needs sample) will provide invaluable feedback which you can use to supplement your own financial and statistical data, and your own perceptions. Eliciting feedback can be done at quite a specific level. Eddison (1990: p.113) suggests following up work done by library staff on a specific project with a written query to the initiator along the lines of 'What was the impact of the work we did for you on the study/proposal/project?' This kind of formal written query may not be appropriate in a voluntary sector context, but the idea behind it of measuring impact rather than effort is a very powerful one.

One question (as noted in section 2.3) will be whether the benefit of a particular service outweighs the cost, but this can be difficult to judge. The cost side is easy: staff time, printed or electronic resource, an element for photocopying or faxing, etc. Benefits are often intangible, and longer term. In a commercial environment, they can be linked in to goals that relate directly to information timeliness ('To be first in the marketplace with new products') but timeliness (or responsiveness) can be equally applicable to non-profit organisations. How much of other people's time does your (timely, efficient) information service save? The mission, goals and organisational values will be different, but there will be an equal need to link the information service's goals to them, and to change with them over time. If the information service is simply seen as some undefined 'support' it may be well worthwhile trying to identify, and quantify where possible, which of your organisational goals the information service has most impact on (or could have most impact on) and make sure the value of its contribution is acknowledged by senior management. As Powers (1995: pp.490-491) so aptly puts it, 'There is no longer a valid assumption that library services are valued . . . it is vital to demonstrate that information adds value . . . The special library that monitors and evaluates services (defines and implements services) with a very specific goal of improving senior management results (decision-making, leadership, consensus building) is a special library securing a future for itself and improving overall performance of its parent organisation.'

Conclusion

The process of marketing planning, and a rolling programme of planning, implementation and review may seem like luxury in a hard pressed information unit struggling to maintain a basic level of service. However, it will reap benefits in terms of being more in tune with and responsive to the changing needs of the organisation and what it is trying to achieve, delivering a service where all effort is being used where it is most needed.

References

Coote, Helen and Batchelor, Bridget. *How to market your library service effectively*, 2nd edition. (Aslib Know-How series) London, Aslib, 1998

De Saez, Eileen Elliott. *Marketing concepts for library and information services*, London, Library Association, 1993

Eddison, Betty. 'Marketing in the special library environment.' *Special Libraries* Spring 1990, pp.111-17

Evan-Wong, Sue and de Freitas, Claudette. 'Marketing an information service: a case study of the OECS Economic Affairs Secretariat Documentation Centre,' *Information Services and Use* 15, 1995, pp.117-30

Gedye, Richard. 'Using the World-Wide Web as a marketing tool,' *Learned Publishing* 10 (1) (Jan 1997), pp.25-32

Grimwood-Jones, Diana. 'Choosing and using consultants,' *ASSIGnation* 13 (1) (Jan 1996), pp.8-10

Keiser, Barbie and Galvin, Carol K. *Marketing library services: a nuts-and-bolts approach*, 4th edition, The Hague, FID, 1995

Lindquist, Mats G. *'The marketing of information,'* News Bulletin 43 (11/12) (Nov/Dec 1993), pp.267-69

McCarthy, Grace. 'Promoting the in-house library,' *Aslib Proceedings* 44 (7/8) (July/Aug 1992), pp.289-93

One-Person Library, New York, OPL Resources Ltd.

Powers, Janet E. 'Marketing in the special library environment,' *Library Trends* 43 (3) (Winter 1995), pp.478-93

Watson, Mark 'Why should you be on the Net?' *Library Association Record* 98 (11) (Nov 1996), pp.578-81

Part C

Case Studies

Case Study 1

Archives and Records Management at Leonard Cheshire
Jill Roberts

Introduction

The voluntary organisation

The Cheshire Archive and Library serves the international voluntary organisations founded by the late war hero and charity worker Lord Cheshire of Woodhall.

The majority of archiving and records management work is done for Leonard Cheshire (formerly The Leonard Cheshire Foundation). Established in 1948, the aim of this charity remains to provide residential homes and services for people with disabilities: over the years it has expanded so that it now gives its name to more than 200 projects in 50 countries worldwide. It has a central administration based in London, but the Homes and Services – in accordance with the Founder's principles – are given a high degree of administrative autonomy and are largely run and funded as an integral part of their local communities. The Cheshire Archive takes deposits from central and regional offices: it also acts as an internal source of professional advice on archiving and records management for the Cheshire Homes and Services, but is their repository of last resort only.

Establishment of the Archive

In 1985 a Cheshire Home, which had been based for thirty years in the eighteenth century Leicestershire mansion of Staunton Harold Hall, realised the aims of a successful fundraising campaign and moved to premises purpose built to suit the needs of disabled people. Most of the vacated accommodation at the Hall was to house a Sue Ryder Home, but Leonard Cheshire had plans to use some of the ground floor space as a resource centre which would include an exhibition and archive on his work and that of his wife Sue Ryder. With the help of a volunteer, non-current records were collected from the administrative base of both charities and from Leonard Cheshire's office, and were finally collated around 1990. There was no formal system of records management at this stage, and the documents of varied media – papers, photos, videos, films, tapes, and slides – apparently did not go through any appraisal for archival value. However, as the bulk of the material was to form the Founder's collection, the significance of its provenance might be seen as argument enough for permanent preservation. With the addition of some smaller collections which continue to be donated by individuals who have been involved with Cheshire's work, and of some books and journals for loan, the Cheshire Archive and Library was born.

Overview of the Archive's role within the organisation

Leonard Cheshire took on its role as employer of its first archivist in 1993, and the post was placed in the General Secretary's Department which dealt, among other things, with general administration. This decision accurately reflected the role necessarily played by records management – and so by extension archiving – in the professional control and disposal of modern records. However, in developing the new post as part of the organisational structure, the archivist was keen to establish the archive as an alive and evolving information source for both internal and external users as well as an administrative tool. It was hopefully to be accepted as a relevant part of the organisation's internal culture, and as an asset to be used in support of fulfilment of Leonard Cheshire's mission to create opportunities with disabled people.

As a result of recent management restructuring, the archive is today placed in the Directorate of Planning and Development. The archive/library and records management functions are to sit alongside the organisation's other two information posts – those of the National Information Officer who deals with current information provision and current awareness, and the Research Officer who manages an in-house Monitoring Unit providing management information and research reports for senior staff. This rearrangement is partly the welcome result of plans for co-ordinating the three posts to produce an even more streamlined and integrated information function for the parent body.

Records management

Its relationship with the archiving function

The introduction to this chapter refers to archiving as an extension of records management. Cook [1] observes that 'in the private sector it is quite natural (though not universal) to regard archives as a specialist aspect of records management'. The National Council on Archives has recently published a statement of principles and policy objectives of a national archives policy; principle number 6 reads:

> Public bodies which create records should be required and private bodies and individuals encouraged to ensure the orderly progression of those records through their life cycle and to make adequate arrangements for the safe-guarding of and access to records which merit permanent preservation as archives.[2]

There is no doubt that, in theory, deposits of the administrative records of an organisation are ideally archived as the result of regular and controlled management of its current records. In practice at Leonard Cheshire, however, the establishment of the archive and its of first acquisitions took place before the design of a formal records management programme. This latter exercise was promoted by the archivist more easily than would otherwise have been the case precisely because the principle of an in-house archive had already been tacitly agreed. The need to ensure that non-current records of value ended up in the archive – and those with no archival value disposed of – could be argued as self-evident.

Establishing the importance of records management among other organisational priorities

Establishing the importance of records management in the wider context of overall organisational priorities was, however, not so simple. The fact that the organisation is a prominent member of the international voluntary sector added force to the completely valid and repeated arguments from some senior management about the need to minimise – and the need to be seen to minimise – administrative costs. Aware of the need to take on board these arguments and preserve good relations with the parent body, but equally aware that she could not successfully develop the archive without proper systems for ensuring that appraised material was deposited regularly, the archivist had to work to achieve a balance. Success in establishing a records management programme seemed very slow in coming and at times unattainable. With hindsight, the strategy which proved to be the most effective was two-fold: firstly to link the need for records management firmly with the successful future management of the archive function, and secondly to ensure that support for the project was won and maintained at a high enough level within the organisational structure to endow the whole exercise with the authority needed for its acceptance by staff.

Two papers on the advantages of records management were prepared by the archivist. In addition, an early visit from the Royal Commission on Historical Manuscripts, which advises on the best management of archives in private hands, resulted in an independent report which also highlighted the need for such a system within the organisation. All these documents were addressed to senior management and to Trustees and outlined the definition, aims, and advantages of records management in general and therefore its benefits to the efficient functioning of Leonard Cheshire in particular. The archivist was particularly keen to emphasise a three-fold aim: to make available a common system of control of current records as produced by the organisation as a whole, to identify material which should be preserved and so increase efficiency by identifying that which could be destroyed, and to ensure that all records – current, semi-current and archival – could be used more effectively as a pool of information both internally and externally. The general objectives of the proposed records management programme were presented as:

- reduction in volume of current records held in filing systems;
- more efficient use of storage space;
- increased accuracy and speed of retrieval of records;
- more efficient access to information;
- identification of material which could be destroyed;
- identification of material with archival potential.

As a result of the presentation of the second proposal paper to a Directors meeting, and of a visit to the archive by Directors and other staff which included a further presentation on records management in context to administrative officers, a timetable for implementation was agreed and minuted. Recommendations on records management from both the archivist (who worked alone) and the Royal Commission on Historical Manuscripts had included the need for extra resources to manage the programme. In practice, however, compromises were made and it fell to the archivist to reprioritise duties in order to accept responsibility for its management with the help of a temporary part time assistant. Nevertheless, an important leap had been made. The future of the archive as a professionally-managed information source had been accepted as linked to management of that same information earlier in its life-cycle, and the archive function itself (often seen as peripheral) was more firmly established as part of the organisation's day to day concerns and culture.

Aims and practicalities of retention scheduling

An agreed retention schedule is the key document in any records management programme. It is both a practical guide to and the authority for the disposal of the organisation's records. In the case of Leonard Cheshire, it was decided early on in the project (in accordance with stated policy) that detailed retention scheduling would be limited to its central and regional administrative offices – the provenance for previous deposits.

The Homes and Services would remain responsible for their own records management, with the archive acting as a source of advice where needed.

The aim of the retention scheduling was to agree on the potential archival value of the various types of records routinely produced by each office. After that, all material which was no longer needed day by day would be collected for the archive, and disposed of according to those agreed values. In practice staff relied heavily on the advice of the archivist in allocating retention values. She in turn was guided by professional publications such as the advisory document[3] on records management produced by the Royal Commission on Historical Manuscripts, and the special edition of the *Records Management* journal on retention scheduling[4]. She also relied on previous experience of the usefulness of certain records to users and on common sense – and erred constantly on the side of caution!

Together with the staff concerned, the archivist listed the various types of records they produced: it was important at this stage to make a distinction between the *types* of records by provenance (*classes* or *series* in archival terms) and the title which staff might give to individual files. Shifting the approach to the definition of records in this way meant that the retention schedule was appropriate to the function concerned on a long term basis rather than to its specific current projects – and also that it was a more useful tool for help with the description of archival material later. Once listed, each type of record was allocated a retention value: A for archival, D for destroy, and R for review. This last category was intended for material whose value could not be decided on immediately and so a number of years was agreed on as a waiting period – for example, R2 meant that a review should take place in two years' time. This effectively set up a small repository for semi-current records side by side with the archive. Figure 1 shows a typical layout extract from the finished schedule: record and value content details have been changed for reasons of confidentiality.

Collection and sifting of material

Two van loads of material were collected from three regional offices and the central office (a total staff of around 60) and were deposited at the archive for appraisal as a result of the retention scheduling visits. As previously indicated, the parent body agreed to increase the archive's resources to cope with the exercise by funding a temporary records assistant (whose van driving skills were an entirely unexpected bonus). This extra allocation in itself was a welcome indication of the voluntary organisation's commitment to its new records management strategy, particularly given the strength and validity of arguments against an increase in staff costs in general. The size of deposits from offices across the

REGIONAL OFFICE

Key to retention values:

A   the record has archival value. Once the record is no longer in use, it should be sent to the archive where it will be retained permanently and may be made available to researchers. If access is to be restricted, please say how.

D   the record is of no archival value. Once the record is no longer in use, it should be destroyed.

R   archival value can not be assessed immediately. Once the record is no longer in use, it should be separated out and held for the stated number of years before review.

Record	Retention value
Accounts	R6
Annual reports produced by Central Office	D
Correspondence	
– with Central Office	R1
– with Services	A
Fundraising records	R2
Minutes and Papers	
– Regional committees	A
– other committees	D
New projects reports	A
Staff records	
– annual leave records	D
– job descriptions	R2

Figure 1: Typical layout for retention schedule

organisation varied: later evaluation suggested that the main reason for this was simply the tendency of some administrative staff to produce more copies of single records than others, although there were also indications that some staff had overestimated what was being asked of them and had therefore been more reluctant to co-operate. This obviously had implications in terms of further training and of expectations of larger deposits from those staff in future.

Once at the archive, the material was dealt with by provenance and divided into three sections for disposal according to the retention schedule for each office: listing and storage in the archive, confidential destruction, or separate storage by date for review in later years. The plan allowed for the originating offices to be given details of the disposal of their records and, although retention values had been allocated by type of record, the lists to be sent back to the offices reverted to the more universally recognisable original file names.

To conclude the first part of this chapter with some statistics: the project came in just under its budget of £6000, and on time (almost exactly a year from the first retention scheduling meeting in September 1996 to the final evaluation report in October 1997). A little more than 38% of the deposited material was archived, while just over 17% was destroyed and 44.5% set aside for review. Some 43 linear feet of valuable archival material were added to the archive's resources as a result of the organisation's first formal records management exercise. So the continuation of the archive as an evolving and relevant information source for staff and other users was hopefully further ensured.

Archives

Perceptions of archiving as a function: archivist as guardian or gateway?

A recent issue of Leonard Cheshire's house magazine *The Cheshire Smile* carried a short article outlining ways in which readers could use the archive as a resource for fundraising during 1998 – Leonard Cheshire's Golden Jubilee Year. When the article was published the editor had included a photograph of the archivist and captioned it 'Guardian of the Cheshire Archives'. Correspondence addressed to this fearsome creature continued for some time.

The dual nature of archivists' duties to both preserve and make accessible the material in their care is well-documented. Some argue that the whole point of preserving records is to ensure their availability to posterity: others that without adequate preservation measures there would be no access and therefore the former should always take priority. To take two illustrations from a national level: the statement of principles for a UK national policy already quoted[5] combines both preservation and access in the same statement. By contrast, the Archives and Records Association of New Zealand's policy on access to archives has baldly stated 'ARANZ believes that the prime purpose for maintaining archives is to enable their use. In general terms therefore, access is the paramount concern of the custodian of archives'[6].

In practice at Leonard Cheshire – an environment where, as already discussed, it is productive to emphasise the practical usefulness of the archive as a resource if its retention is to be widely seen as justified – it is the importance of access which overtly takes precedence. Informing this presentation, however, is the understanding that best preservation practice is a primary tool for achieving access for the widest usership. In the context of this case study, the practical archivist is silent guardian and therefore successful gateway.

Drawing up archive policies

The drawing up of a statement of policies and associated procedures was an early and vital job for three reasons. Firstly because it established a framework of principles and practice within which the new function could operate; secondly because it afforded an opportunity for that framework to be built on accepted professional archival practice; and thirdly because the necessary agreement at Trustee level within the organisation – alongside other formal policies – offered another forum within which to demonstrate the professionalism and permanence of the function and its advantages as an organisational resource.

For an archivist working alone, this was one task above all others which called for networking with fellow professionals working in similar environments to ensure all relevant areas of operation were covered. In addition, a publication by the Australian Society of Archivists[7] was of immense help – as it had been in other more practical areas of work. Following this advice, guided by experience as to the areas of work which needed to be defined in a more formal sense, and in conjunction with the Head of Policy to ensure adherence to house style, a statement of policy was produced together with an associated procedures guideline. The policy statement covered the core archive functions of acquisition, appraisal, cataloguing, preservation, access, outreach, and general administration. The statement is shown at Appendix A to this chapter.

Storage

In common with many other archives not housed in purpose-built accommodation, the question of storage of the archival material has largely been one of making the best of what was available. Two rooms plus an office were allocated at the beginning, and subsequent discussions have confirmed that there is not likely to be any room to cater for the inevitable expansion of an ongoing archive. The recent records management exercise has used up most of the available space, so before the next major deposits are accepted, some strategy for increasing storage space must be devised.

The archive's running budget allows for the regular purchase of archival standard storage material, and the boxes are kept on free-standing bays of metal shelving. Regular checks for temperature and humidity in the store rooms show that, using the British Standard for the storage and exhibition of archival documents (BS 5454) as a guide, humidity is rather too high and – in the summer months – so too is the temperature. There is no method of controlling this apart from electric storage heaters, and as some of the storage space is shared with the office and research areas, these have to be switched on in cold weather. However, the thick walls of the old Hall go a long way towards minimising harmful sudden changes in temperature and – taking BS 5454 as an ideal to be strived for – the Cheshire Archives are not badly housed.

Preservation and conservation

On a practical level, it has been important to differentiate between these two concepts. The Cheshire Archive looks on preservation as the overall policy and practice of maximising the useful life of the records and of ensuring permanent access to their information content: practical conservation is one tool to be used towards this end.

Best preservation practice reaches into every aspect of the practical running of an archive. In summing up the results of a survey on preservation policies and strategies in the UK, Eden & Feather confirm 'Our findings, not surprisingly, highlight the fact that preservation is indeed a thread that runs through all the activities of an archive or record office'[8]. Forde agrees that 'Preservation activity is ubiquitous'[9] and argues that the reasons for the urgency of the development of preservation policies are 'both general and particular, but most have their origins in a need for accountability, for setting priorities and for justifying expenditure'[10]. This need for justification in the voluntary sector in particular has been discussed elsewhere in this chapter.

So far, the main area of detailed preservation practice to be addressed in the Cheshire Archive has been the drawing up of a disaster control plan to be put into action in the event of mishap such as fire or flood. This was seen as particularly urgent because the archivist works alone, remote from the parent body, and can not automatically call on an inhouse team for help: staff elsewhere in the Hall will have their own priorities in an emergency. As an insurance, the Cheshire Archive therefore subscribes to a commercial disaster recovery scheme which is on call 24 hours per day and whose details are held by caretaking and management staff on site. The disaster control plan then consists of two other main strands: the equipping and appropriate storage of an emergency supply for use in disaster recovery, and the laying down of procedures to be followed in the wake of an emergency.

If we define conservation as the practical workbench craft of the repair of damaged artefacts, the Cheshire Archive has fortunately not had to commission a great deal. The earliest papers date only from the late 1940s, and the worst physical damage is the result of insect infestation among papers generated at Leonard Cheshire's base in India during the 1950s. These – together with some fading and glued Minute Books – have been microfilmed to ensure preservation of their information content. In addition, conservation work has been carried out on some architectural drawings and on a Bible in the Founder's collection which were considered of significant enough artefactual value to justify the (not inconsiderable) expense of repair.

Production of finding guides

The drawing up of catalogues, lists and indexes to guide the user to the information required is obviously of immense importance. Unfortunately, it is also the most time-consuming and probably the most long-term practical task confronting archive staff. Inevitably, therefore, in a situation where the archivist works alone and has to reprioritise frequently in order to keep the function running smoothly, it is often the job which is postponed.

New deposits have to be listed, of course, and the contents recorded in such a way that the records can be retrieved if required. However, the detailed listing and cross-referencing which would ease and enhance the user's direct access to their information content has to be seen as lower priority work.

Nevertheless, since 1993 a full catalogue of the Founder's collection has been produced. This is fully listed at the series or class level of archival description, and some of the more general records are described in more detail, with a subject index as a complementary guide. Similar finding guides to the other two main collections – the administrative papers of Leonard Cheshire and the Ryder-Cheshire Foundation – are in progress. Guides to the smaller collections are very general.

In a one-person archive, it is often the case that a certain amount of the information needed to help clients is held only in the head of the archivist: this situation should be minimised if the management of the function is not be rendered vulnerable.

Publicity and user education

The archivist has been reluctant to embark on a formal programme of publicity for the archive to external users because of the limited physical space available for research, the remoteness of the site, and the fact that finding guides has been slow in production. The situation is improving with time, however: the National Register of Archives maintained by the Royal Commission on Historical Manuscripts makes reference to the contents of the archive and this is soon to be updated with a more detailed listing of the Founder's collection.

Publicity has therefore been mainly confined to the internal usership (which accounts for nearly 70% of all search requests). The archivist contributes to in-house publications and regularly visits Cheshire Homes and Services. The Golden Jubilee Year coming up in 1998 has been an ideal opportunity to offer help in organising resources for raising awareness – such as the cataloguing of photo collections, or reformatting old films onto VHS video.

A leaflet on the archive was produced in 1994, but experience has shown that its approach was not ideal. It was designed both to publicise the archive's existence as a resource to internal and external users, and also to advise on best records management internally. It was trying to speak to two separate audiences at once, and to a certain extent it fell between the two stools. A redesign is planned, which will probably take the form of two separate and more simple flyers.

In general terms, publicising the benefits of the function and educating users are seen as an ongoing part of its day to day work.

Conclusion

Archiving is a relatively new experience at Leonard Cheshire – and formal records management even more so. The absorbing of a new specialist function into a long-established organisational structure in this way is not easy. It is undoubtedly to the credit of Leonard Cheshire that it has been so supportive of a concept whose main potential contribution to its mission is long-term. The support for the establishment of the archive shown by the late Founder demonstrates that he understood its advantages, and this has further encouraged the archivist in its development over the last five years.

The Cheshire Archive and Library is now part of the structure and culture of its parent body: a living, evolving information network with links back into history and out to the organisation of today. Its resources are used to inform and contextualise current projects and to help keep them rooted in what was best about the past. Professionally managed along accepted archival principles, it will remain the objective and authentic record of the unique contribution which Leonard Cheshire and his Foundation continue to make to the work of the voluntary sector.

Appendix A: Policy Statement

Policy Statement

The Cheshire Archives and Library

Reason for Policy
This policy statement establishes the authority for the framework within which the various programmes of the Cheshire Archives and Library will function. All practices and procedures should be in accordance with provisions outlined in the accompanying procedure document, which is in line with the policy statement.

Policy Statement
The purpose of the Cheshire Archives and Library ('the Archive') is to collect, manage, preserve, and utilise the archival heritage of the Leonard Cheshire and Ryder-Cheshire Foundations, and to accept related library material for loan, with the overall aim of providing a first class permanent repository and information source for all potential users.

The Archive will acquire, and so take responsibility for the care of, archival and library material which is relevant it its purpose.

The Archive will appraise certain types of material received in order to confirm its fitness for the Archive's purpose.

The Archive will produce catalogues of material held.

The Archive will take all possible measures to prolong the life of material held.

Subject to certain conditions, material in the Archive will be made available to users, or where users can not visit the Archive the Archivist will carry out research on request.

The Archive will publicise its functions as repository, information source, and advisory body.

The Archive will manage its own administration effectively.

Procedures
The policy has accompanying procedures which must be followed.

Status
This policy statement has been agreed by the Trustees of the Leonard Cheshire Foundation in October 1996 and is mandatory on all its services.

References

1. Cook, M. *Information management and archival data*, London, Library Association Publishing, 1993, p. 17
2. National Council on Archives. *An archives policy for the United Kingdom: statement of principles and policy objectives*, London, National Council on Archives, 1996
3. Royal Commission on Historical Manuscripts. *Records management. Advice to smaller organisations wishing to introduce a records management system. Advisory memorandum no 5*, London, Royal Commission on Historical Manuscripts, 1993
4. *Records Management*, 64 (October), 1994
5. As 2 above
6. Archives and Records Association of New Zealand. 'ARANZ policy on access to archives', *Archifacts* (April 1991), p. 67
7. Ellis, J. *Keeping archives*, O'Connor, Australian Capital Territory, Australia, Thorpe & Australian Society of Archivists, 1993
8. Eden, P & Feather, J. 'Preservation policies and strategies in British archives and record offices: a survey', *Journal of the Society of Archivists*, 18(1) (April 1997), p. 69
9. Forde, H. 'Preservation policies – who needs them?' *Journal of the Society of Archivists*, 18(2) (October 1997), p. 166
10. Ibid.

Case Study 2

Christian Aid: Evaluation of Library Services

Sarah Heery

Christian Aid is an overseas development charity working in partnership with local organisations in sixty countries in Africa, Latin America and the Caribbean, Asia, the Middle East and Eastern Europe. Its staff of 280, plus volunteers, work in London and the UK regions and Ireland. London staff support partner groups in the South through local churches and organisations which work towards alleviating poverty. Funded projects include women's empowerment and credit programmes, skill-sharing, relief and rehabilitation projects and emergency work. Regional staff work towards raising awareness of world poverty issues, such as Third World debt, fair trade and the policies of international financial institutions, such as the World Bank and the International Monetary Fund (IMF), in churches, schools and among the public using education, lobbying and campaigning methods. Financial support is received from the churches, governments, the public and corporate bodies. Christian Aid Week is the charity's main source of income each year. *Christian Aid News* is its quarterly newspaper, promoting its work at home and overseas.

The library began as a press cuttings library in the 1970s, and now provides an extensive lending and proactive current awareness service which includes a daily press report, weekly publications list and Selective Dissemination of Information (SDI). The library holds an extensive collection of books and documents, a comprehensive reference collection, video library, periodicals, newspapers, CD-ROMs, and access to the World Wide Web and GreenNet conferences. A video tape library and photo library exist in the London office, independent of the document library.

A major organisation restructuring in 1995 saw the creation of thirty-two teams in the Overseas, Policy and Campaigns, External Relations, Regions and Nations, and Finance departments. At this time the library's independence and autonomy were considerably reduced. It now forms an integrated part of the Information Team, and enjoys a more hands-on management approach from the team leader. The librarian's role has changed to that of coordinator. The Information Team's aims are to promote a 'unified "one-stop shop" information service, providing a comprehensive response to the majority of information requests, a service which is valued by both Christian Aid and non-Christian Aid staff and which reflects Christian Aid's role as an authoritative source of information on development issues' to support the organisation's aims, to all staff wherever they are located.

The librarian coordinates the work of two assistant librarians who have regional and subject responsibilities, providing information, training and support to relevant staff on subjects as diverse as microcredit, gender, food security, democracy and good governance and project monitoring and evaluation.

Library services

The document collection consists of the annual reports of non-governmental organisations (NGOs) and international organisations (the World Bank, IMF and the United Nations), Economist Intelligence Unit (EIU) reports, directories, dictionaries, encyclopaedias, books on development-related issues such as economic globalisation, gender, theology, health, water and trade.

There are subscriptions to over 200 journal titles, ranging from *New Internationalist* to the *Economist*, and titles from the countries in which Christian Aid works such as *Barricada Internacional* (Nicaragua) and *Wajibu*, a journal of social and religious concern from Kenya. Partners' publications are also received. Many titles are circulated. All publications are scanned for articles and abstracts are added to the library database. Electronic copies of titles are becoming increasingly available.

A daily press report provides a selection of articles from the UK broadsheets and church press, accessible by email for all staff in the UK and overseas. Articles are maintained on a press report database. The report is available by subscription to external organisations/researchers and part of an information-sharing initiative to other charities. News clippings have been replaced and newspapers are now kept on CD-ROM. A clippings archive exists dating from 1960-1994.

The publications list is a weekly listing of new material received in the library and is a major source of borrowing. It also advertises new Web sites and the publications indexes of the World Bank and the Department for International Development (DfID). The video library holds a selection of recordings of television programmes.

SDI is a monthly targeted information service providing country and subject information including details of papers and information sources from

ELDIS (Environment and Electronic Information Development System) and the OneWorld Online partner sites and Think Tanks.

The library relies heavily on volunteers for a number of tasks including cataloguing and classification of library and non-library material, archiving, video classification, journal abstracting and responding to press report requests.

Electronic information

Electronic information is becoming increasingly available and relevant to Christian Aid's work. The library has access to the Internet and GreenNet (an NGO electronic network), use of CD-ROMs, email and a documents database of internally-produced documents. The library provides regular information updates from GreenNet conferences on countries in Latin America and the Caribbean and campaign updates on debt, trade and structural adjustment. The documents database is a networked database of internal Christian Aid documents, including policy statements and reports, Christian Aid procedures, staff handbook, overseas teams' documents, press releases and team plans.

Use of the Internet is increasing. There are two sites for public use in the library, plus several other access points in other teams. Regular sites accessed for news and information include the South Africa Press Agency (SAPA), the World Bank Public Information Centre, ELDIS, both for information and information sources, and One World Online. Christian Aid has its own Web site (http://www.christian-aid.org.uk/) managed by One World Online and updated by the Media Team with press releases, special reports and vacancies lists. One World Online has its own development-Internet and its recently-launched Think Tanks have the potential for information gathering for Christian Aid and similar organisations, in their aim of increasing dialogue between Northern and Southern partners.

Information sources and methods of access and delivery are constantly changing and Christian Aid has implemented several developments in this area. An internal email network has been in use for two years and has revolutionised information access and distribution, as well as becoming an effective promotion and communication tool. Desk-top email has enabled staff to subscribe to mailing lists of interest to them and their teams. Most library material is now sent by email which has made the library more accessible for staff outside London.

Evaluation

Evaluation has been defined as a process of critical and systematic assessment to determine, firstly, how well a system is functioning (according to previously agreed objectives, standards, or other criteria); secondly to determine if it can be improved; and thirdly to determine how best to improve it[1]. Library questionnaires have been drawn up and circulated in the past with limited results, but a major organisational restructuring and a change of personnel and management of the library with a new team leader and associate director provided an opportunity to evaluate the value of existing information services and staff responses to it.

The evaluation was conducted by a librarian with experience of information consultancies and the NGO sector in Canada and New Zealand. She also worked part-time in the library to familiarise herself with library services and users, the aims and objectives of the Information Team and the work of Christian Aid. The evaluation objectives were to improve the targeting of existing information resources; to document the extent of use of current information services and to evaluate the impact of services on the quality of people's work; to identify opportunities for improved efficiency, effectiveness or quality in these services; to identify additional services which would contribute to Christian Aid's objectives, and to suggest future approaches to the provision of information.

All members of the directorate plus 40 members of staff, selected at random, were interviewed. Staff interviewed included project officers, team leaders, policy researchers, communication officers, area staff, team administrators and library staff. One-to-one interviews were conducted with staff in London and regional staff were interviewed by telephone. The evaluation did not have time to seek out the information needs of partners overseas or members of Christian Aid's Board. Interviews concentrated on staff's work priorities and information needs and their comments on each of the library services: book lending/reference, inter-library loans, periodicals circulation, news monitoring, periodicals bulletin, publications list, videos, bulletin board and Internet access, external email access (GreenNet), access to the documents database, archives, library catalogue, CD-ROMs, library training, and networked internal email.

Members of the directorate were more general in their responses as they have people who use the library on their behalf. They expressed the need for targeted, up-to-date and more accessible campaigns and statistical information. Networking with other NGO libraries and the need to market the library externally were recommended. The directorate identified the need to prioritise tasks and services, to monitor future political and social trends as well as the organisation's changing information needs as work focuses change, and to meet the information needs of an increasing number of staff working overseas.

Area staff's work is difficult to quantify and evaluate due to their distance from the office and library staff have less contact with them to find out their needs compared to London-based staff. They work on development education to encourage their constituencies to join Christian Aid campaigns and their work is by its very nature more generalist. All staff receive the same services whatever their location, but few area staff make requests other than on an ad hoc basis. The library is more accessible to them now they are on internal email and requests are made from emailed publications. They rely largely on Christian Aid publications, staff in the overseas section and liaison with other NGOs.

In general staff were satisfied with the information services available. Their main concerns were the need for up-to-date information, particularly in new areas of work for Christian Aid; increased accessibility to Christian Aid's own material, including archives; more authoritative sources for statistics; background information on issues relevant to partners; the work of other NGOs; study space in the library; slow circulation of journals; and improved access to the library catalogue. There were certain areas of work which received less interest than might have been expected: development education; technical specialisms; training materials; foreign language materials; foreign press; development theory; video collection.

From the library's point of view, the survey helped raise our profile and reiterated the value staff place on information resources and library services. It was useful for library staff to have colleagues' work areas confirmed and therefore improve our ability to provide more targeted and packaged information. Different staff priorities were revealed in the varying levels of use by teams in the same department. Teams were found to rely to some extent on personal specialist book, journal and database collections, unknown to the library, and clearly containing some important reference collections used by Christian Aid.

Respondents considered certain areas of work as examples of information overload. The periodicals bulletin, a quarterly bulletin of journal abstracts, was considered out of date by the time it was sent out. Firstly, abstracting was rationalised and the bulletin provided only for area staff, but it was ultimately dropped. Compilation and delivery of the press report changed, with the clippings service being replaced by newspapers on CD-ROM. The majority of services have continued but have been repackaged and become more focused to staff needs.

Team liaison is now a high priority reflected in developments in information delivery. A current awareness service, SDI, was implemented in response to suggestions for more current and focused information. Staff provide their work areas and librarians send out monthly regional and subject updates. Communication links are in place to ensure librarians know about changing interests and also for the library to monitor its services and stock development to reflect changing political and social trends. The librarian also liaises with teams and experts on purchases to address information omissions mentioned in the evaluation such as new geographical regions, ethical investment, conflict resolution, economic alternatives, land rights, credit, and democratisation.

A collection policy has been drawn up to reflect Christian Aid's work and potential areas of work and a centralised purchasing policy is in place. The librarian coordinates all team spending on books and items are included on the library database on receipt, so a central record of all material coming into Christian Aid is held. Similarly, a centralised cataloguing project is underway to catalogue specialist collections kept outside the library so all staff are aware of all information in Christian Aid whatever its location. A weeding operation to remove stock more than ten years old continues with expert help from teams. The librarian and training officer manage and develop a learning centre within the library, equipped with a computer, CD-ROM and Internet access and a video recorder. It offers staff material for their professional development and other training needs, including management and self-development training, language material, IT-applications for word processing and spreadsheets.

More financial resources are being allocated to authoritative sources of information. There is now selective purchasing of EIU reports, which give up-to-date statistical information and country profiles of the campaign countries. In addition World Bank and IMF documentation is available, plus Reuters and CD-ROMs.

Increased accessibility to Christian Aid's own material has been achieved by ensuring all copies of internally-produced reports are given to the library for the document collection or for the documents database. A volunteer archivist has been appointed to oversee and advise teams on archiving in line with Christian Aid's archive policy and to limit archiving to essential material. She liaises with teams and now trains staff in archiving on disk to save space. Archives are also stored off-site at London University. Reference material can now be borrowed overnight and study space external to the library has been provided. The library catalogue will be available networked to people's desks in 1998 allowing for more user self-sufficiency.

Journal circulation is constantly monitored and extra copies of popular titles have been obtained. New titles such as *World Development* and *Microenterprise News* are now available and electronic titles such as the

Mail & Guardian, SouthScan and *Africa Confidential* are available on the Internet and distributed by email together with online news services on Southern and East African countries.

Links are maintained with other NGOs through the Overseas Aid Charities Librarians' Group (OACLG) information meetings, held quarterly with other NGO information colleagues with participants from Christian Aid, CAFOD, Save the Children Fund, ActionAid, the British Red Cross, Oxfam, Appropriate Health Resources and Technologies Action Group (AHRTAG), Plan International and Help Age International. Current information issues are raised as well as more specific policy issues such as information policy and collection policy. Such a forum provides scope for closer integration on stock development to complement each others' work. Christian Aid library also borrows extensively from DfID's Development Index of books and journal articles and receives current awareness updates from ActionAid, Oxfam, AHRTAG and Partnership House Mission Studies Library.

Library staff continue to monitor and promote electronic information sources from the Internet and GreenNet. Users of the Internet keep a record of sites visited and time spent 'surfing', which will be evaluated on an annual basis. Cybercafe Internet promotions are well-received by both experts and non-users.

External information sources are continuously monitored and close links are maintained with other agencies and their information, plus DfID, the World Bank, IMF and UN. The Internet is a new and growing source of external information. Staff ensure partners have access to the library on visits to the UK to see our information services and for advice on information sources. Librarians try to maintain a dialogue with partners on issues of aid, projects and information sharing.

Promotion

Aside from the evaluation recommendations, the library is promoted through a regular Information Team newsletter, staff guides, press report subscriptions and external meetings. New staff receive a general introduction to the library at the Christian Aid induction course. More personalised training sessions, tailored to a person's job, are offered by library staff at a later date, in order to target information more effectively and efficiently to an individual's needs and determine more adequate information provision.

The internal network is an effective tool for advertising the work of the organisation through announcing talks, courses and conferences. The library responds to particular meetings, courses and lunchtime talks with bibliographies of related materials and Internet-training on specific subject areas. Library staff could keep better informed of current developments in their areas of responsibility and exchange ideas and information through more personal staff contact at team project meetings.

The library regularly puts on exhibitions on current issues of interest such as child labour and debt, plus new book displays and book sales.

An annual report on the library's activities will be produced this year to document the role and usage of the library within the organisation, including statistical analysis and budgeted spending by teams.

Future

Since the evaluation, continuous monitoring of services and library use is in operation. It is envisaged a new library computer system will provide numerous statistics on all aspects of our work, to better evaluate the use of information and its impact on staff time. There are plans to assess information provision such as SDI and its impact on staff decision-making, possibly as a library school student project. An information audit examining use of information distributed via the internal network is also planned.

Library staff also need to assess how to best meet the needs of staff outside the London office, i.e. area staff and overseas field officers. More liaison is required with area staff. Library representation at the annual conferences of area staff and field officers will assist in assessing what their work entails and their information requirements. All field offices have access to networked information. Advice is offered on suggestions for journal subscriptions and reference material such as fundraising publications, directories, and documentation on procedures for emergency situations.

Library staff must continue to monitor use of the Internet and external mailing lists by staff accessing information, in order to contain the costs to Christian Aid.

New networked library software will enable user access at desk level and allow user independence for searching and self-reservations, which will have implications for library staff and methods of work. A development plan will be implemented for the professional development and training of all staff, notably those from the policy/research teams. The documents database will be part of the new networked library catalogue which will improve access for all staff.

Current information developments can only enhance the efficiency of Christian Aid library and free library staff time for more information developmental work, researching sources and developing ideas and training.

References

1. Freiband, S.J. 'Evaluation of reference collections in public, community college & high school libraries', *Collection Management* 3(4) (Winter 1979) pp. 353-361

Bibliography

Heery, S. 'Promotion of library services in the voluntary sector: the case of Christian Aid', *Aslib Proceedings* Vol. 46, No 4, (April 1994) pp. 101-103.

St Clair, G. *Power and influence: enhancing information services within the organisation*, London, Bowker-Saur, 1994.

Case Study 3

Library Automation at the NSPCC Library
Gerry Power

One of the principles of the NSPCC Library's service is to keep up with developments in information technology to support information provision. This case study outlines the Library's role and how it has tested and implemented different IT products during the last two years, 1995 to 1997. In early 1995 the Library had seven PCs, DOS was the main operating system, the library management system was DOS-based and character-based. Now, most of our Library applications run in Windows and many changes and developments have taken place on our local area network since 1995.

The NSPCC and its Library

The National Society for the Prevention to Cruelty to Children (NSPCC) was founded over 100 years ago to prevent children from suffering significant harm as a result of ill treatment. It aims to protect children who are at risk of abuse or neglect and to help children who have suffered significant harm to overcome the effects of such harm.

The NSPCC is active in eight regions in England, Wales and Northern Ireland, where over 120 teams and projects carry out a variety of work: investigating allegations of abuse, assessment and therapy for children who have suffered abuse, helping the families of abused children. It offers consultation and advice to other professionals and agencies who work in child welfare. The NSPCC's national training centre is based in Leicester. The Child Protection Research Group is based at the National Centre in London, as is the Library. The NSPCC also publishes a range of books, leaflets and video packs aimed at parents, practitioners, researchers and students. The Society actively campaigns on behalf of children, and provides a 24 hour telephone helpline for anyone who is concerned about the welfare of a child.

The Library, based in London, is maintained to support all NSPCC staff, to whom services are provided free of charge. Staff may visit the Library during office hours, but for most Library users this is not feasible because they are based in child protection projects in the NSPCC's eight regions. Most requests for information and for loans are made by post or by telephone, and users who have email may send their requests electronically. The NSPCC historical archive forms part of the Library service.

The services provided by the Library to staff include literature searches in the form of reading lists, loans of books, reports and audio-visual material, photocopying and a current awareness bulletin. The Library's collection contains approximately 8,000 books and 250 audio-visual items. Over 100 journal titles are regularly received. The collection also contains some CD-ROMs and a number of annual reports from the statutory and voluntary sector.

The Library's catalogue describes the collection of books and audio-visual items, and numbers over 24,000 records. The subject matter of the collection focuses on child protection, including social work, child psychology and psychotherapy, the voluntary sector and management. The Library's enquiry desk provides a proactive information service which reflects the needs of NSPCC staff. The principles and standards of the information service are elaborated in the Library services manual, a copy of which has been distributed to all NSPCC regions and projects. These standards seek to guarantee a thorough, proactive, accessible, polite, accurate, speedy and up-to-date service. One of our principles is to keep up with developments in information technology to support information provision.

The Library's IT network

The Library currently has 10 PCs, two of which are always available to users during opening hours. Windows 3.11 is now the most used operating system for workstations. Staff have access to Microsoft Office on their work-stations, and they can use networked resources via the Library's local area network. This network links the 10 PCs to a file server which stores the integrated library management system and other shared files. Novell netware version 3.12 is the network management software. Other network resources include two printers, an electronic mail network for NSPCC staff in the regions and in London, and an electronic bulletin board. High-speed modems and communication software provide access from some Library PCs to the Internet, to online hosts and to the British Library. The Systems Librarian monitors the day-to-day running of the Library network and liaises with the IT staff to solve system problems and to implement upgrades.

Library IT strategy

The Library IT strategy was drafted by the Librarian in the spring of 1995. It aims to develop the use of new technology to improve services to users.

The strategy advocates technology to help users to help themselves, and provides for a monitoring of technological developments so that Library staff continue to harness new technology to make innovations in the service.

The draft strategy was discussed by Library staff and the agreed document took effect from the Summer of 1995. The strategy seeks to plan and co-ordinate all Library IT developments. It provides a time frame (up to three years) for developments and monitoring thereof. The strategy is laid out systematically making provision for each aspect of IT development:

Information services
- purchase, install and use new CD-ROM products
- develop a user-friendly OPAC
- train staff in using CD-ROMs and OPAC

Internet
- monitor and evaluate the World Wide Web and Telnet as tools for information retrieval
- draft and agree a policy on use of the Internet in the Library

Library Housekeeping
- investigate use of barcodes to speed up circulation
- investigate new integrated systems to replace Soutron
- improve authority files in the catalogue
- develop a Thesaurus for the catalogue
- automate serials control

Documentation
- produce clear instructions for users on new products and systems

Network Development
- new version of Novell netware
- replace file server
- make best use of the network cabling and telecoms
- learn from IT innovations in other departments
- devise good front-end menus to help towards 'seamlessness'

Hardware
- review and replace printers and other peripherals
- replace personal computers, allowing for a 4 to 5 year life cycle
- purchase and install high speed modems

Office systems
- install Microsoft Office for all Library staff
- basic training in Word, Excel etc.

Each aspect of IT development in the strategy states the priority of that aspect (whether high, medium or low), the person or persons who are keyworkers, the resources and costs involved, and the time frame of implementation. The keynote of the whole strategy is the development of a user-friendly library service. The strategy is revised each year as priorities are reviewed and to take account of progress.

A key point of the strategy was the review and possible replacement of the Soutron Library system. This review was to include a look at possible serials packages to provide better control of the collection of serial publications. We also looked into barcodes as a means of identifying items of stock to help us provide a faster and more accurate loans service.

The senior management in NSPCC did not require an IT strategy from the Library, but the strategy did meet with the approval and support of the IT manager and the Head of Child Protection Research. It provides a very useful blueprint for our IT developments. It has provided for an across-the-board use of Windows 3.11 in the Library, which reflects the IT department's advocacy of Windows products throughout the Society. Providing a clear and seamless interface to a variety of new products places demands upon our IT support staff and on the Library staff. It also creates a critical agenda for continuous staff training.

The Soutron Library System

The Soutron Library System was used at NSPCC from 1989 until March 1997. It offered modules for Loans, Cataloguing, Acquisitions, Enquiry and System Management. The Enquiry module was a useful librarian's tool, but very difficult for users as it did not offer intuitive features. Effective use of Enquiry required lots of keyboarding, a familiarity with library jargon, and a knowledge of the data structure. Being a DOS-based and character-based system, Soutron was quite a robust product which performed adequately on the Library's network, did not require lots of routine maintenance, and tolerated unscheduled network interruptions quite forgivingly!

Another strong point of the Soutron system for us was that it provided a unity of catalogue database, search interface and bibliographic report, i.e. one catalogue database contained records for a variety of formats (books, journal article, audio-visual) which could be searched using one search screen. This was, and still is, very important for us at NSPCC Library because most of our users are looking for information by subject or keyword, and what format the information is in is not an initial selection criterion.

Many of the requests of the Soutron User Group to make the system more user-friendly and more staff-friendly met with the response 'system re-write required' from Soutron Limited. A sample list of enhancements considered desirable by the User Group and tabled in 1994 included the following:

- ability to display borrower's team address for loans transactions;
- better use of function keys to provide keyboard shortcuts
- improved and more flexible user reports (overdue and reserves notices)
- quicker processing of statistical reports in Circulation
- ability to record more information about inventory
- better date range searching in Enquiry
- clearer and more flexible layout of Bibliographies
- better text editing in Cataloguing

Thus we were building up a picture of the improvements we considered essential in our library system even before we decided to consider other systems as alternatives to Soutron. Soutron Limited pointed out that many of these requests required a system re-write, which meant that they would be difficult and expensive to implement in the system. Soutron Ltd also pointed out the great difficulty involved in converting the DOS-based and character-based product to a fully-functioning Windows product.

During 1995 and 1996, Soutron Ltd did some development of a Windows interface to the Soutron system. As the NSPCC Library was very keen to gain a user-friendly interface to its catalogue, to make available as an OPAC in the Library, we agreed to test Win-OPAC in its development stage. This product required a conversion of the Soutron catalogue files to Windows files, and thus it did not function in real time. We spent some time in 1996 testing this product with little success.

Investigating New Systems

During the early summer of 1996, all Library staff were asked to note down points about a new system which they considered to be essential or desirable to carrying out their work. Staff were asked to consider the catalogue from the user's point of view: what steps were necessary to doing basic and more involved searches on the catalogue. These requirements were collated into lists by function: acquisitions, cataloguing, circulation, enquiry. Some of these requirements may be summarised as follows:

Cataloguing
- one single bibliographic database to hold up to 100,000 records
- flexible record format, to allow for repeat fields
- flexible inputting and editing of data
- good Thesaurus facility

- one database to hold records for different formats of material: books, journal articles etc.

Circulation
- ability to display the user's work address for transactions
- good reservation features
- OPAC to display date due
- flexible user record format, capable of holding notes e.g. items lost and paid for
- ability to record loan history by item of stock
- ability to design clear and well arranged user reports (overdue notices, reserved notices)

Enquiry/OPAC
- good subject searching, with Thesaural display online
- ability to search by subject term and by subject keyword
- keyword searching across all text fields
- ability to sort screen and report output by different criteria: date, title, author
- ability to search by publisher
- easy search options for beginners
- expert search, with Boolean operators, for librarians
- clear and uncluttered record displays
- screen and report formats amenable to modification
- ability to provide good context specific help screens

We gathered information about different Library systems by visiting the Computers in Libraries exhibition held annually in London, and also the Libtech exhibition held in Hatfield each September. A variety of integrated library systems suitable for small libraries are usually on show. These events provide a very useful opportunity to try out different systems and to talk to suppliers. The Hatfield event in September 1996 provided a free seminar on library automation for smaller libraries which included short presentations from a number of suppliers, with question and answer sessions.

We also visited some other small libraries in the London region. One factor which emerged from visiting libraries and talking to colleagues in early 1996 was that Windows interfaces for small library systems were still either in a development stage or just emerging onto the market. Opportunities to test out a fully functioning and 'live' Windows system were therefore quite limited.

All suppliers whom we asked to demonstrate their system were most amenable to half a day, or in some cases to a full day's, visit to NSPCC. These demonstrations allowed all library staff to view and test out the system, and to ask the supplier plenty of questions. Each point on our list of requirements (some of which are listed above) was put to the supplier and we asked suppliers to demonstrate one module at a time. These visits also provided an opportunity for a member of our IT staff to check with the supplier if the system would function fully on the Library's local area network. Many questions were asked about the technical properties and requirements of the system:

- database design and file structure
- the linking of files
- the programming language
- the required disk space on the fileserver and on the workstations
- the minimum memory necessary to run the system fully
- compatibility with Novell
- future plans for developments and enhancements
- backing up files and restoring from backup
- technical help and support from a help desk
- trouble-shooting and problem-solving

All library staff were asked to note their impressions of the system as demonstrated, and to make notes on how it matched the list of functional requirements. Staff were encouraged to put themselves in the place of the user when trying out the OPAC. Staff were advised that their impressions of the system were important and would be taken into account when making a decision about which system was best for our Library.

Project Management

In addition to exploring the market-place and viewing systems, another requirement at this stage was the drawing up of an information technology standard to submit to the Information Systems manager at NSPCC. This standard provides a control framework to ensure that new systems within the NSPCC are appropriately defined, authorised and implemented.

All projects have a sponsor (a senior manager) and a project leader responsible to the sponsor. As the planned expenditure for the new library system was in excess of £10,000, the new Library system was considered a major system.

The ADLIB Library system

We chose ADLIB as our new Library system because we liked the look and functionality of the OPAC. We were satisfied that the ADLIB system would be able to accommodate our catalogue, and that a conversion from Soutron data to ADLIB data was feasible. We saw that improvements could be made to our loans system. The printed reports, such as reading lists and circulation reports, met our minimum requirements, and we were satisfied that we could develop them ourselves. We liked the flexibility and openness of the system. ADLIB also offered modules for search and interlibrary loans, which we needed. In addition, we appreciated that we could generate better management information reports from ADLIB with its toolbox and flexibility.

The ADLIB library system is an open system in that it can be installed on a variety of platforms from DOS to Windows to UNIX. Single workstation and network licenses are available. Data structures, screens, reports, menus and help screen can all be defined by the customer. ADLIB allows for the linking of databases, and this makes for interesting displays in Windows. In viewing the catalogue in OPAC, for instance, one can open extra windows for copies of information to display when a copy is due back from loan. Similarly, windows can be opened on subject terms to display thesaural links.

Other interesting Windows features of ADLIB include the ability to preview the appearance of reports on screen before sending them to the printer. Also from this preview screen it is possible to select text using the mouse or keyboard and copy it to the clipboard for inclusion in other Windows applications like Notepad or email. Many reports for different modules can be written to disk and thus be imported into word-processing or spreadsheet packages.

Testing, Conversion and Going Live

The project steering group consists of the Librarian, the Deputy Librarian and the Systems Librarian. It was clear from the outset, when we were investigating new systems, that the planning, testing and implementation of any new system would be very demanding of staff time and energy. Our IT help desk were also conscious that a new system would place demands on them.

Once we had ordered the system in December 1996, an implementation timetable was drawn up as shown opposite:

The system documentation supplied by ADLIB Information Systems has been supplemented by our own step-by-step guides to common routines. Manuals are particularly important for training and to help new staff carry out basic routines. The Deputy Librarian has prepared step-by-step guidelines on all Circulation routines, so that Library staff can deal promptly with users' telephone queries about their loans.

Date	Task, Process
Feb 1997	Test version of ADLIB installed on one PC
	Sample database of 500 records loaded
	Library staff test sample database by searching and editing
	Test versions of Acquisitions and Circulation installed and tested
March 1997	More testing of catalogue data in greater volume
	Library staff list any unresolved errors and amendments needed
	Continue to test Acquisitions and Circulation
	Barcode readers installed on two PCs
	Barcode labels applied to all stock items
	Conversion of all catalogue data to ADLIB format
April 1997	Go live at the beginning of the month
	Catalogue fully converted
	Loans and reserves converted
	Two full days training for Library staff in common ADLIB routines
Summer 1997	All barcode data scanned in to the Copies file
	Two day's system management training for librarians
	Make OPAC as user-friendly as possible
	Make OPAC available to Research and Training groups
	Written instructions for staff and for users on searching OPAC
	Input complete details of all users
September 1997	Installation of new ADLOAN circulation module in ADLIB
November 1997	Reloading the database to take advantage of better record length

A user's guide to the OPAC has also been prepared. This gives users tips on search strategies and how to search by subject. A Thesaurus project was begun in October 1997 and is due for completion in March 1998. This project will develop our in-house list of subject terms into a Thesaurus on child protection. Broader and narrower subject terms can be displayed in the OPAC by clicking on the subject terms displayed when searching the OPAC.

The modules which have been implemented since April 1997 are Acquisitions, Cataloguing, Circulation and OPAC. The Serials module will shortly be up and running. Journals, magazines and newsletters are a very important part of our collection, and records for journal articles comprise 60% of the catalogue. Using the Serials module for control of our serial publications will provide a holdings list which is easier to update and therefore more quickly disseminated to staff. We will be able to provide a link in the OPAC between the catalogue record for the part-item with the record for the whole-item, i.e. a link between the description of the journal article and the record for the journal itself.

System maintenance and trouble-shooting

Every incremental change to any database in ADLIB is recorded in a log file. This text file contains details of all material loaned and returned on a particular day, all catalogue records added or amended, and any updates to user records. For system security, it is good practice to accumulate these files for a month or so, just in case it is necessary to reload any data which gets damaged or lost. The system works best when the log file is saved for each day, and is re-started each morning.

We also keep a log of any system problems or system errors which occur. These are reported immediately to the Systems Librarian, who liaises with ADLIB Information Systems to solve problems in the running of the system. The most serious problems occur if records are being saved and there is at the same time an unscheduled interruption to the local area network. Any such 'blip' in the network can cause damage to the databases, but such damage can be repaired by 'exporting' and 'importing' the database concerned. This export and import process refreshes and rebuilds the indexes and the links between records. As the ADLIB databases are Windows files, they are by nature more complex and more sensitive than database files in a DOS system.

Installing and implementing any new library system is not without problems, and during our first few months of using ADLIB, we encountered some difficulties. During April and May of 1997, we had difficulty in editing and saving catalogue records. The error messages indicated that there was not enough 'system space' to complete the editing and saving necessary, so we had to investigate how to remedy this on our local area network. Only with trial and error, and with help from the NSPCC IT help desk, did we track down the problem and solve it. A network configuration file, which controls how each PC sends and receives data around a local area network, needed to be edited on each PC to take account of the new database system in ADLIB. For best results, the system needs to be able to open a maximum of 150 files at a time, and the network configuration file needs to take account of this factor. We have learned in the Library that databases which run in Windows are more demanding of the system and more 'resource-hungry' than databases which run in DOS.

We also encountered a problem with the converted reservations file. Because of a small bug in one of the programs, this file became damaged in April 1997, but the ADLIB help desk sent us a bug fix and promptly repaired the file for us.

Response times over the Library's local area network can be quite slow, especially if saving catalogue records or editing in barcode information. We have done several tests to try and speed up response times, and our IT department have strongly recommended replacing our existing file-server with a newer and more powerful model in early 1998. We plan to replace the file-server in April of 1998. We shall also be reviewing our network software, and will investigate both Windows 95 and Windows NT, because both of these have advantages over Windows 3.11 for running ADLIB.

Conclusion

Installing and implementing a new Library system, which runs in Windows, has not been without its challenges, but to date we are satisfied that the system we have chosen is producing the benefits for which we purchased it.

Case Study 4

Launching a Web Page: Alcohol Concern

Caroline Bradley

Introduction

Alcohol Concern is the national agency on alcohol misuse. It was formed in 1984, bringing together functions previously spread between three organisations. Our broad aims are to reduce the level of alcohol misuse and to improve the range and quality of sources of help for problem drinkers and their families.

The majority of our funding comes from the Department of Health; however, we are increasingly seeking, securing and undertaking projects funded from other sources.

In addition to lobbying and campaigning at national and local levels, Alcohol Concern acts as an umbrella body for alcohol services in England.

We aim to be an expert organisation; this can only be achieved by collecting, maintaining, managing and strategically presenting relevant information and opinion. Information is at the heart of what we do.

The Information Unit comprises four members of staff: Librarian; Information and Research Officer; Information Development Officer and Information Unit Assistant who is also responsible for the organisation's membership services. This represents 20% of Alcohol Concern's total staff.

The unit provides an enquiry service, maintains a library and database (the largest collection of material on alcohol in the UK) publishes a range of factsheets, a current awareness bulletin, a quarterly information and research update and occasional other publications. It deals with approximately 8,000 enquiries every year from students, academics, policy makers, service providers, commissioners and planners. The unit aims to use information pro-actively, to encourage a wide group of professionals to recognise the costs of alcohol misuse and to build strategies and polices to reduce these costs to individuals and local communities.

The Information Unit also contributes to the wider work of the organisation which is carried out by staff in three distinct units: Services; Press and Publications; Education and Training; in addition to the Director, two Assistant Directors and two Finance and Administration staff.

Alcohol Concern's work includes the development of national standards for people who work with problem drinkers and their families; we host conferences and events that bring experts and policy makers together; we administer a grants programme that has created 79 new alcohol services since 1990; we lobby for the adequate funding of treatment facilities and address wider practicalities such as the need for toughened glasses in pubs to reduce the annual toll of injuries from bottles and glasses being used as weapons. Recent work has included campaigning about the marketing and labelling of alcopops, holding a conference that investigated the effectiveness of alcohol services, lobbying the new government to establish a national alcohol strategy and collaborating with ChildLine to publicise the needs of children who are abused or mistreated as a result of other people's drinking.

Why we wanted to establish a Web site

Whilst use of the Internet is embryonic in the field of welfare provision generally and even more so between local alcohol agencies in the UK, Alcohol Concern felt it was important to establish a Web site as the first step in exploring how this medium could be used to forward the aims and objectives of the organisation.

We were also aware that other organisations were putting up Web sites and rather worryingly one was claiming to be the 'UK centre for information on alcohol'! With a world wide audience in mind it felt important to ensure that comprehensive and accurate information was available on this topic from the UK. As we are the national agency on alcohol misuse it seemed an obvious strategic step to establish this identity on the World Wide Web.

Visiting libraries and information centres in person is increasingly a less common means of investigation – particularly for specialist resources. We need to be proactive in exploring new ways of ensuring information is accessible to those who need it. The Internet presents a massive challenge to voluntary sector organisations whose status and ability to influence is derived from their role as an interface between practical know-how, information, opinion and policy makers.

Access to the Internet instantly creates autonomous researchers of variable experience and ability. The problem is that access to the net also confers a feeling of potential omniscience. A local government officer formulating a policy to address local alcohol misuse problems may be able to find helpful and relevant information via the Internet, but it will be nowhere near as comprehensive as that provided by Alcohol Concern's Information Unit. Individual Internet researchers are not likely to have:

- access to specialist alcohol information from sources other than the Internet;
- a guarantee as to the quality of the information that they find;
- an overview or guidance that puts the information in context;
- confidence about how up to date the information is;
- a historical perspective;
- details of similar policies developed elsewhere;
- contact details of informed individuals.

However, the problem is that they may not realise this and they may think that lack of information on the Internet on a particular topic means that there is no information on that topic, or that what they have found is all that there is.

Alcohol Concern aims to inform and influence a wide range of people. As an organisation we deal in information and opinion, it was thus important for us to establish our identity and publicise our services and activities via the Internet as it is increasingly an environment and an information resource used by the publics that we wish to reach.

Aim of the Web site

As our first step in using electronic information systems the main aim of the Web site was to make available a range of information held within the organisation to as many people using the Internet who want it. Additionally the site would provide Alcohol Concern with an identity on the World Wide Web. In this respect the aim of the site was to reflect the expertise, work and structure of Alcohol Concern as an organisation.

The Web site as a whole is not targeted at any one group but information within the pages is labelled as appropriate for specific user groups, e.g. people concerned about drinking problems or local policy makers and purchasers of alcohol services.

At present its main purpose is to reflect Alcohol Concern's activities, and act as a 'poster board' for a wide variety of information on alcohol whilst also providing direction to other sources of information on this area.

Given limited resources within Alcohol Concern the site was not intended to be used as an additional avenue for receiving enquiries about alcohol. Routine enquiries already take up a vast amount of staff time and we were wary of opening the flood gates to a world wide audience without means of assessing the level of demand. Interactive aspects of the site are therefore limited to ordering books and leaflets or booking places at our conferences and events plus of course a feedback page. Most of the information available on the site can be downloaded by users.

Technical considerations

a) Initial options

We first considered developing a Web page (as we then called it) in the summer of 1996. At that time a number of companies had set up as site developers, and a few specialists had decided to focus on the voluntary sector. We responded to a handful of offers of demonstrations. We were then better placed to compare and assess information from other site developers.

At the time we did not have a clear idea of what we wanted the site to contain or its main purpose other than the broad aims described above. There was a lack of technical expertise and familiarity with information technology within Alcohol Concern. No one was familiar with the Internet itself or the type of sites being set up. Basically the area was too new for anyone internally to have particular views about. This meant that we were very easily impressed by the products being presented, particularly as the initial outlay seemed to be an amount we could afford – in a sense as an experiment.

However, a key member of staff at Dolomite Publishing, the publisher of Alcohol Concern's directory, was familiar with the Internet and adept at using Internet publishing software. In discussions with them it quickly became clear that for someone with the technical expertise setting up a site was fairly straightforward and that we should not necessarily turn to a specialist provider. If we had not had this advice on hand from someone who was familiar with the Internet and the workings and needs of our organisation we would have probably selected one of the specialist companies – whichever one seemed to be offering the best deal at the time.

The type of package that we would have ended up with would have been:

- the design of a set number of pages (between 12 and 15);
- a set number of times in which alterations to the information could be made (12-20 per year);
- connection to an Internet server – which otherwise seemed impossible to contemplate;
- a non-specific site name.

The cost would have been between £800 and £1,500 per year. Additional services could then have been added on an ad-hoc basis if required (extra pages, pictures, interactive features etc.). The charges for this would have varied, but we would have been charged for every update or addition.

The big incentive of course was that it would not have required capital outlay and the option would not require technical expertise on our part.

However our publisher persuaded us that we should think further ahead and set up a system that over time could be operated in house thereby:

- retaining flexibility;
- creating a bigger and better Web site;
- ensuring the site address was appropriate to its contents;
- maintaining ability to instantly update at no extra cost;
- incorporate new features as and when required;
- involve staff and ensure the use of the site became ingrained in organisational practice;
- have as many links to other sites as we wished;

all achievable at a very minimal **ongoing** cost that is the rent of server space plus staff time.

What we decided to do

Having established a very happy and mutually beneficial partnership with Dolomite Publishing around the publication of Alcohol Concern's Directory (it is compiled and published at no cost to us but still brings us income) we decided to ask them whether they would be interested in working on the project. The key factors in this decision were:

- the option of a fairly large site at low ongoing costs – given the amount of information Alcohol Concern has available this seemed more appropriate option as the longer term maintenance costs are low (rental of the server site only plus some staff time);
- the site would be maintained at no extra cost for one year including any reasonable/routine updates and additions. During the year Alcohol Concern would assign responsibility to a member of staff whom Dolomite would work with to ensure they could take over the maintenance of the site in due course. We would be able to service the site without having to learn techniques or procedures that we didn't need to know;
- trust – we were confident that Dolomite would fully explain, in a language we were able to understand, resource requirements laying out clear options and making recommendations in our best interests;

- partnership – linked to the above we were confident that the project would be developed collaboratively and that Alcohol Concern staff would be involved appropriately and thoroughly.

Planning the site

It took about a month to develop the structure and content of the site. This was an almost organic process and the eventual structure of the pages reflects both Alcohol Concern's internal structure and the organisation's current focus of work.

An internal memo from September 1996 shows the initial plan of the Web site as follows. It was envisaged that the three main sections would be Alcohol Problems, Information for Trainers and Information for Professionals.

The site is structured simply with a limited number of graphics. We have not gone for an 'all singing and dancing' site as our aim is to disseminate information to a wide range of people and complex graphics could easily form a barrier to people with less powerful software or less familiarity with IT. We also feel it is important to retain some gravitas as a national agency dealing with a range of serious subjects. Also we did not want to make the site too complex for us to maintain ourselves.

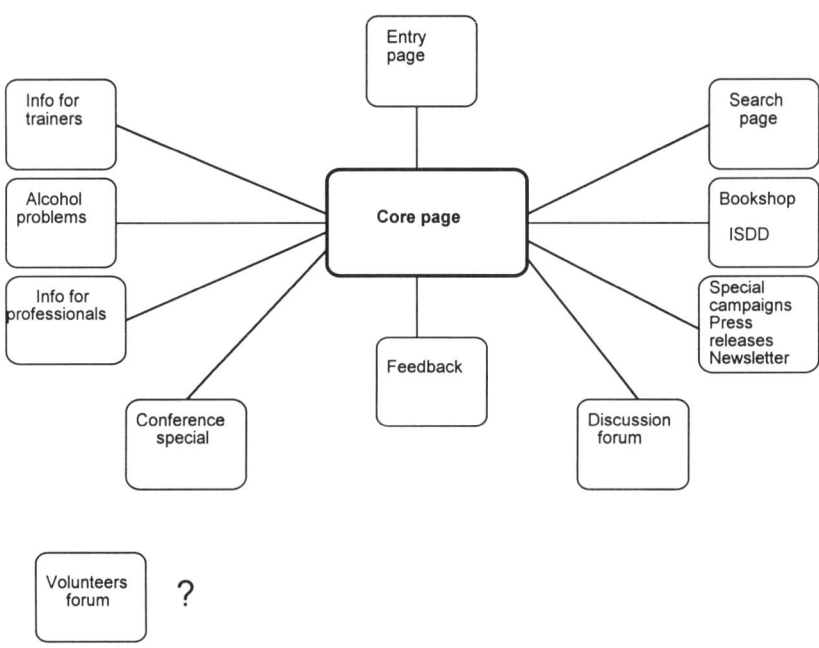

The entry page was and remains very simple. It contains our logo, our name, address and our broad aims. There is then the invitation for people to 'click-here' if they would like to find out more about alcohol – its effects and issues. A hypertext link then takes them to the core page which is essentially a menu of what is available at the site

A mock-up of the site that set out the framework and look of the basic pages was established on one of Alcohol Concern's in-house computers. Staff were invited to assess and comment on the design and wording.

The above plan was circulated to help people to visualise what the site would eventually contain. Staff were asked to make information appropriate for inclusion available on disc, it was suggested that this might include leaflets. The addresses of three voluntary sector Web sites were circulated to give people an idea of how other sites looked and worked so that they could assess the mock-up from a more informed position.

The memo stresses that any additional ideas were very welcome and looking back the overall impression is that the process of designing and establishing the Web site was very definitely owned by the organisation as a whole rather than by information staff, external consultants or management.

The site was launched in October 1996.

Initial impact and evaluation

Dolomite publishing had a demo copy of some quite sophisticated site monitoring software which they used to analyse visitors to the site. As our aim for the site had been fairly broad we didn't have specific benchmarks by which to assess the level of use and type of requests. The software showed that the site was being consulted by a wide range of Internet users and that they were downloading our information.

We now have software that enables us to produce weekly reports of activity at the site.

This is another area where our experience of launching a Web page is atypical. If we had used a site development service they would have provided us with detailed analysis and then encouraged us to fine tune the site accordingly. Our approach has meant that we have ended up with a longer period in which to see how the site is used and how we as an organisation use it. When the site is fully controlled by Alcohol Concern's Information Development Officer there will be more value in analysing traffic to the site after changes or additions have been made.

Resources

The work has cost Alcohol Concern £2,500. This includes:

- registering a domain name;
- submitting the site to all the search engines;
- design consultancy and production of the site's graphic content;
- conversion of rest of site's content from text to HTML;
- organising the rental of space with the server (we use Digiserv Corporation and rent 10 megabytes of space).

The ongoing cost is $30 per month for rental of server space (approximately £20 plus VAT).

The quality of the site is far in excess of anything we could have achieved from the specialist companies for a similar cost. However, we appreciate that we were fortunate to have a good reciprocal relationship with a publisher who was keen to branch out into the Internet. It was a new area for both parties and fortunately the partnership has worked well.

Responsibility for maintaining the site is currently shared between Dolomite Publishing and Alcohol Concern. Full responsibility will soon shift to Alcohol Concern's Information Development Officer. We originally anticipated having to purchase an Internet publishing package at this point (about £150), however Microsoft Internet publishing software (Frontpage) is now available directly from the Internet. This software will enable information to be published directly to the Web site from the Information Development Officer's networked desk top computer. We are currently waiting for the initial glitches to be removed from this software before assuming total in-house control of the site.

Current site content

Alcohol Concern home page

News & Campaigns
Copies of the most recent 14 press releases.

Factsheets index
There are 18 full text factsheets on the site.

Bookshop

A list of publications available via mail-order from Alcohol Concern. The list is split into broad categories such as Training & Resources, Workplace etc. to aid browsing.

Bookshop order form

After browsing the list visitors can leave their order and mailing details on an on-line form.

Useful Contact Addresses

Contains National Organisations, Regional Alcohol Service Offices and Organisations for Help and Advice.

Search Page

A search engine specific to the AC site. Visitors can search for documents on the Web site containing specific words or a combination of words. To assist searching the Boolean operators and, or & not are available. There is a link to the Alta Vista search engine at this point. The idea is that if visitors have not been able to discover what they were searching for at the Alcohol Concern site then Alta Vista may help them to track it down. This is a reciprocal arrangement as we gain a site specific search engine (Alta Vista provided us with the appropriate bit of code) and they gain some free promotion and potentially some new users.

Feedback Form

Visitors are invited to tell us what they think of the Web site or anything else that comes to mind. Four options are offered: complaint, problem, suggestion and praise. Visitors are then asked to categorise their comments as being about the Web site, Alcohol Concern, alcohol problems, training, purchasing services or more information, and are then invited to enter their comments.

Training Information

This section contains eight pages of information giving details of a our national forum for alcohol trainers, forthcoming events and conferences, our VACTS scheme which stands for Volunteer Alcohol Counsellors Training Scheme and is a nationally accredited set of standards for alcohol counselling agencies to aim for.

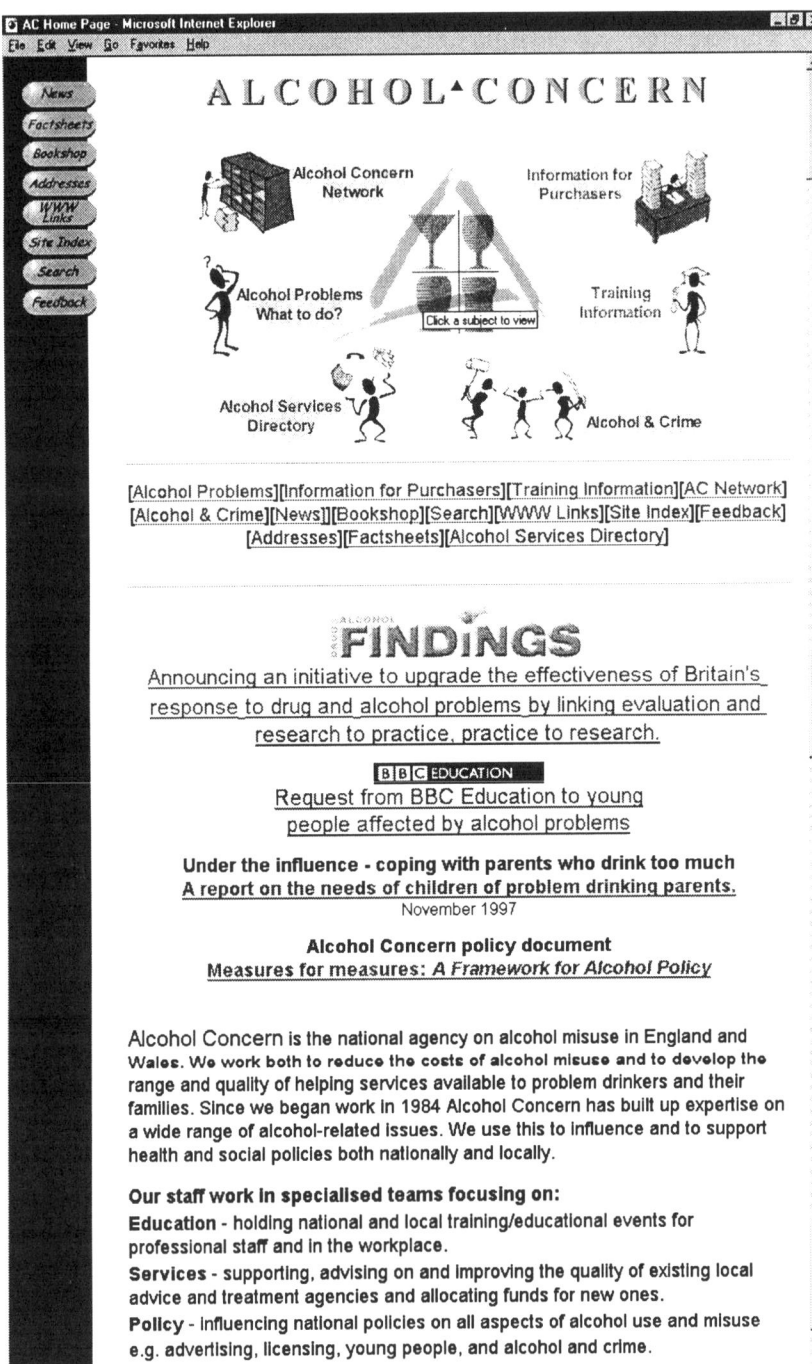

Alcohol Concern's Home Page
(Reprinted by permission of Alcohol Concern)

service on alcohol, a quarterly research bulletin, factsheets, and running a mail order book shop.

Publications - publishing a quarterly magazine, educational and training materials, and a wide range of information leaflets, booklets and posters.

Media - using radio, television and the press to raise awareness about alcohol misuse.

Services for problem drinkers - running a grants programme to extend counselling and advice services to areas where there is no existing provision.

Training - implementing a National Alcohol Training Strategy for the many different professions that come into contact with problem drinkers, and maintaining ACAC (Alcohol Concern Assessment Centre)Centre through which workers in the alcohol field can gain qualifications.

Among the issues with which Alcohol Concern has been involved recently are:

Drink driving - supporting calls for a range of measures, including random breath testing of motorists, to reduce the deaths caused by drinking drivers.

Community care - lobbying for adequate funding of treatment facilities for alcohol misusers, nationally and locally, in the wake of the NHS and Community Care Act.

Alcohol at work - running a Workplace Alcohol Advisory Service, and co-ordinating the national Federation of Workplace Alcohol Advisory Services, to tackle alcohol problems at work which result in up to 14 million lost working days each year.

Special groups - considering the particular problems faced by women, Black people and people in rural areas with drinking problems, and making help easier to find.

ALCOHOL CONCERN
32-36 Loman Street
London
SE1 0EE
United Kingdom

Telephone:(+44) 0171-928-7377
Fax:(+44) 0171-928-4644
Email: alccon@popmail.dircon.co.uk

Best experienced with

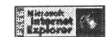

Click here to start

or other tables and frames supporting browser
Registered Charity No: 291705
A Company Limited by Guarantee - Registered in London No: 1908221

Copyright © Alcohol Concern. All rights reserved.
Revised: **30 March, 1998**

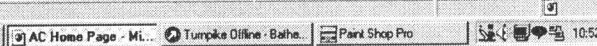

Alcohol Concern's Home Page
(Reprinted by permission of Alcohol Concern)

Alcohol & Crime

Five pages are separated into: the links between alcohol and crime; facts and figures about alcohol-related crime; Alcohol Concern's work on alcohol and crime; drink driving; and a survey of community alcohol agencies working in prisons.

The Alcohol Concern Network

This is a version of our membership recruitment leaflet; it outlines the services and benefits on offer to members of Alcohol Concern.

Information for Purchasers

This section is divided into five separate pages. As its title suggests, it is targeted at people who are responsible for commissioning/purchasing alcohol services. It includes a link to the Alcohol Services Directory Home Page. This page is maintained by Dolomite Publishing and contains information about local services taken from the directory that Alcohol Concern publishes with Dolomite. Visitors can track down their local services by county or borough.

Alcohol Problems

This section contains a range of information for people who are affected by alcohol problems. It contains health information about the immediate and long term effects of drinking; advice on sensible drinking including what is a unit; a section entitled 'Do I have an alcohol problem?'; tips for cutting down; 'Worried about someone else?'; finding help and another link to the Alcohol Services Directory Home Page so that people can find out what help is available to them locally.

Under the influence – coping with parents who drink too much

This section contains the foreword of a recent report by Alcohol Concern. The full report is available to visitors to the site in Portable Document Format. Acrobat Reader, the software for viewing and printing pdf files is available at no charge from Adobe Systems WWW site. There is a link to this site available on this page. Copies of the report obtained via Adobe software retain the formatting and layout of the original when downloaded.

Measures for Measures: a framework for alcohol policy

This is a full text version of our recent policy document. It sets out the main issues that Alcohol Concern is currently campaigning for.

Analysis of site traffic

The Web Trends™ software provides us with a detailed weekly activity report. Our site averages about 700 'user sessions' per week. 'User sessions' average at between six and eight minutes.

We now have a full year of activity reports and it is clear from these that the pace and intensity of traffic on the site mirrors the academic terms quite closely. In the third week in June the weekly total of 'user sessions' was 398, but by the third week in October it had risen to 1050.

Of the three areas that we originally anticipated would form the majority of the site (Alcohol Problems, Information for Trainers and Information for Professionals), Alcohol Problems is by far the most requested. The other popular element of the site are the factsheets, these are often the most visited and downloaded elements, which fits in with the assumption, due to increased traffic during term time, that the majority of visitors to the site are students.

It is quite exciting, but often also frustrating (see below) to know that people from all over the world are using your information. The most active country in terms of the nationality of visitors to the site is the United States, followed by the UK, then Canada and Australia. This reflects the pattern of access to the Web as well as the dominance of English as the Web's first language. However, we have also had users from Brazil, Kuwait, Finland, Malaysia and most of the European countries.

In general it appears that our site is being used by individuals to gain information about alcohol problems and the wider effects probably because they are affected by an alcohol problem or because they are studying alcohol misuse.

Effect on enquiries

There has been no significant reduction in enquiries to Alcohol Concern's Information Unit. Indeed the Web site may have added to our enquiries or at least channelled some via email.

We often receive general enquiries from school children or college students or concerned individuals in foreign countries. These can be frustrating if they clearly have come via the Web site as often the answer is within the factsheets that the enquirer would have had access to.

They are also frustrating if we are not the best source of information for the enquirer because of cultural relevance or the relative distribution of resources. For example, a schoolchild in Georgia in the US asking about sources of help for problem drinkers would be better off consulting their local library or health board or even the NIAAA (the US's national alcohol misuse agency) rather than us. And in turn we would be better off using our resources to answer UK schoolchildren's requests as that is something we are funded to do.

So a complex evaluative process evolves. For example, email enquiries from overseas generally require us to ask 'should I answer this at all?' of ourselves. The response will often be 'yes, if I can do so easily'. Because the enquiries appear as a trickle (relative to the number of phone and written enquiries that we receive) it has taken a while for their nature to register with us. When viewed from an impartial resource management viewpoint the answer should most often be 'no, I should not spend my time and Alcohol Concern's scarce resources in answering this request'. But the eagerness of the questioner, the egalitarian nature of current Internet etiquette and the natural tendencies of the Information Worker often make it hard to say no.

We need to work backwards and post clearer signposts for younger students on the Web site and develop a range of stock email answers that list more appropriate sources of information or redirect people to the Web site. But, of course, this again takes time.

Not all Web related enquiries are of this nature. Sometimes they are from individuals or organisations who clearly fall into our Information Unit's client group. A problem that then arises is which format is it appropriate to respond in? Our enquiry service is print and post based. The majority of Internet oriented enquiries provide us with an email address to respond to rather than a postal address. We can therefore either:

- indicate what kind of information is available to answer their enquiry and direct the enquirer to it (e.g. local library, our library, other organisation etc.);
- respond asking for a postal address;
- send information that we have in an appropriate form to attach to our email response (e.g. Alcohol Concern authored factsheets)

Changes and tinkering

We have experimented with a 'discussion forum'. For about six months visitors to the site were invited to post questions or queries or to report on work that they were involved in. The aim was to establish a self-contained forum where contributors questions were answered by other visitors to the site. Alcohol Concern did not intend to play any part in the forum apart from providing the space within the Web site.

People did post questions to the forum, and, encouragingly, some of these were from key groups that we hoped were using the site, such as alcohol workers, criminal justice professionals, social workers etc. Unfortunately people were very good at asking questions, but reluctant to answer them.

Additionally, a lot of questions were very general; typically they would be requests from students for explanations of whole topics like 'problem drinking' or 'alcohol and crime'. Information on these topics was included elsewhere on the site and these postings were thus quite frustrating to behold.

After a couple of weeks it became clear that visitors to the site were not going to post any responses to the forum queries (apart from 'yes, I was wondering that too') so we started supplying answers or opinions with prompts for further contributions. These responses were signed as being from 'AC Info Unit' and were intended to encourage participation. They didn't and on reflection we should have used a false identity as visitors who viewed the previous postings on the forum now got the impression that it was an enquiry service and proceeded to ask questions which we then felt mean if we didn't answer.

Site maintenance

This has been shared between Alcohol Concern staff and Dolomite Publishing.

Dolomite produce a weekly activity report from the site. Alcohol Concern's Information Development Officer checks the feedback and bookshop order forms on a weekly basis.

Currency is an important factor in the evaluation of any Web site. Our site is updated by the inclusion of organisational press releases, details of forthcoming events, details of new publications and the posting of new factsheets. The currency of the site thus depends on the wider activities of the organisation rather than any editorial policy about the site itself.

Problems

There have been no major problems associated with this project. It's been affordable, the result is better than we could have ever hoped for when we started and we will shortly be in a position to take over the site maintenance.

The only difficulties have been the speed at which Alcohol Concern could deliver a staff member to work towards taking on maintenance responsibility and concern that the Web site forum would generate unwanted extra work. The pace at which developments happen on the net has increased the reliance on Dolomite more that perhaps was anticipated by both partners. This has not been a problem for Alcohol Concern as the additional demands made on Dolomite are not considered by them overly problematic given their interest in the site. Whilst the goal of bringing this function was, and still is achievable, the pace of development of the technology suggests that if it was not for the collaborative nature of the project more investment than anticipated in respect of internal staff resources would have been required.

Possible future developments

The Internet is an environment and a tool that we can use to develop and enhance our information service. It therefore represents an exciting strategic opportunity.

Unfortunately it also represents a threat to our established position. At the moment most information services in our sector have developed to be complementary to each other. It now appears likely that voluntary sector organisations that trade in expertise will discover new competition from commercial organisations who are geared up to disseminate information electronically or from other sources such as academic institutions who are now able to exploit their information resources in new ways.

In effect our traditional markets are under threat because a new medium has arrived. The costs of the new medium are reducing all the time. The cost of using Internet is now less than fax.

We are facing a major strategic opportunity to develop our information service in new ways. Handling information electronically offers a range of benefits such as decentralised costs (if people are receiving briefings from a 'fax-back' service rather than a newsletter then they bear the cost of printing) and the opportunity to enhance or add value to existing information products and services. But because it is a fast moving and relatively new area it is easy to feel panicked into participating because everyone else is and because it is there.

Alcohol Concern's Information Unit needs to integrate the Web site and other means of electronic information management into its overall strategic development plan. The establishment of the Web site has been interesting in itself, but we now need to consider how to use it to add value to our information services, to improve our patterns of work and enable us to reach our current and potential users in more effective ways.

1. Linking up with local alcohol agencies

The site already has a direct link to Alcohol Concern's directory of local agencies where the addresses of agencies providing help, advice, detoxification and residential rehabilitation are listed. As yet few local agencies are on the Internet and are unsure about the value of establishing their own sites. Alcohol Concern proposes to make available a page for each service attached to their listed address for their own, more detailed information about the services they provide.

We could use the Web site to develop the way that we exchange information with alcohol services. As an umbrella organisation it is vital that our relationship with services is reciprocal. We rely on alcohol workers and researchers for information about current practise and concerns and in turn we hope that they value our national perspective and turn to us for definitive information, best practice advice, representation etc.

As more local services gain access to the Internet we could develop a form on the site through which they could submit information enquiries but also reports on particular projects that they have undertaken. This would assist us in building up a projects/best practice database.

2. Development of special forums for different groups within the field.

Depending on the pace of acquisition of Internet facilities, Alcohol Concern would like to consider opening special pages for communication with, and between, particular groups within the field. A page for our regional representatives for example could help ensure information is made available directly to them much more rapidly. Other Internet groups and forums may also be a good way of sharing good practice and information between agencies.

3. Linking up with other national information centres.

The Institute of Drug Dependence has been able to attract funding for the development of their site to provide access to actual text documentation on particularly subjects – drug and crime information and research for example. Alcohol Concern would like to provide this site, linked to our own, with complementary documentation on alcohol and a funding proposal has been drawn up to make available key documents in this way.

Key topics would be identified and information and research would be made available at three levels:

- basic information on the topic and statistics;
- access to overviews and reviews of literature and research;
- access to key texts and academic research literature.

Access to our bibliographic database would also be offered, probably on a subscription basis.

The difficulties in attracting funding for developments linked to alcohol issues rather than illicit drugs have so far impeded progress of this project.

4. To establish a presence on the NHS Intranet

NHS*net* is the secure national network developed for the NHS. It provides a similar range of communication and information services to that available on the Internet, but it is a closed environment (an intranet as opposed to the Internet). It is possible for health related organisations to establish a presence on the NHS*net*. As health service managers and practitioners are among the key groups that we wish to target with information this is a key area to develop. Ideally we would like to establish a targeted version of our Web site and directory information in this environment.

5. Targeting key audiences via 'push technologies'

This emerging technology enables an information provider to deliver directly onto Web users desktop computers. Visitors to the Web site will register if they wish to receive information, they then join a mailing list where information will be delivered directly to them rather than published at a static site. This technology will make the Web a more pro-active tool for information providers, enabling us to present complete documents cheaply and directly to target audiences.

Case Study 5

Information Audit at Charities Aid Foundation

Dr Susan K.E. Saxon-Harrold

Introduction

Even to the casual observer the pace of change currently being experienced by the voluntary sector is both dramatic and pervasive. The competition for funds between charities, pressures to deliver services once the prerogative of the state has resulted in an awareness of the need to operate in new ways. All the constituent parts of an organisation are required to operate through a programme of corporate objectives and to support this by the identification of information requirements. Information management and technology has thus emerged as a major issue for voluntary organisations in the 1990s.

The Internet: Opportunities

Widespread public access to the Internet combined with user friendly browsing software means that this new media has rapidly become established. For organisations with clarity and vision there is no limit to what can be achieved by using the internet. Currently, users of the Web use it for the following:

- 80% browsing
- 65% entertainment
- 60% education
- 50% work & business
- 48% academic research
- 30% business research
- 10% shopping
- 11% other

  Source: The Graphics and Visualization & Usability Center at the Georgia Institute of Technology, November 1994

A major international charity like Charities Aid Foundation (CAF) is not immune to such changes. This case study describes CAF's efforts to be at the forefront of expanding its financial and information services across borders as one element towards achieving organisational fitness through an information management review. An information audit (Hamilton, 1993) of resources, uses, flows and requirements for new information was a significant component of this review process.

Background: Charities Aid Foundation (CAF)

CAF has expanded its range of activities and has built a substantial international focus to its work which encompasses grant making, financial and consultancy services. Overseas offices in Russia and the United States are part of an international development strategy embracing India, South Africa and the Pacific Rim region. It is likely that international activity will slowly increase over the coming years as a proportion of CAF's total activity.

CAF's activities concentrate heavily upon financial services, acting as a conduit for tax efficient donations and endeavoring to stimulate levels of charitable giving. In exploring new countries and regions to operate in, CAF has realised that establishing information services may be the most appropriate entry strategy to working overseas. Strategically, CAF has established itself as an organisation that assists in the development of voluntary agencies as a supplier of finance, information and consultancy services in the countries and regions in which it operates.

CAF's Vision for its Internet Presence

CAF's vision for its Internet presence was slowly emerging amongst its Managers and Director at the time of this information audit in 1995. CAF's vision centred around the concept of a 'one-stop shop' providing information on voluntarism both in the UK and in the international arena. CAF feels it has a substantial resource base on voluntarism that any donor, charity, or individual could access to obtain up to date and comprehensive information about CAF services and the world of voluntary activity in general.

CAF has a multiplicity of audiences in Britain and from around the world that it tries to serve ranging from voluntary organisations, donors (from the public, private and voluntary sectors), researchers, voluntary sector 'professionals' and the media. CAF's vision was to become a 'one stop shop' on cutting-edge issues on the voluntary sector. To do this it would have to build up to date and more detailed information about the voluntary sector in Britain and around the world. The challenge was to try to marry information with the multiplicity of CAF audiences. CAF needed to consider not only its audiences but whether it was being philanthropic, pursuing business considerations or adding value to its clients by opening up information to others.

Internationally, the nonprofit information field was wide open and CAF was well placed as any Foundation working overseas. Whilst there was political analysis and information available about the countries CAF is currently operating in, or wishes to operate in, there was far less information available on voluntary activity. Its offices in America and Russia are endeavoring to plug this gap.

Information audit and Charities Aid Foundation

This case study describes the efforts of one major charity to recognize the importance of the information that it holds, how it can make better use of its information and what information should inform the development of its internet site. CAF recognized the importance of accurate and timely information as the core commodity to making its activities a success. Although the use of the information in other sectors e.g. the National Health Service has been a popular concept, CAF has not used information audits as a means of identifying needs or formulating an information action plan. Though comparatively late in adopting a technique that has many precedents in the corporate information world, CAF had the advantage of having information management activities positively associated with two factors:

- the direct involvement of the chief executive; and
- the adoption of a structured approach to the analysis, concentrating all the time on corporate objectives.

The impetus for an information review came from an informal discussion between the Project Leader, Susan Saxon-Harrold and CAF's Chief Executive, Michael Brophy in the summer of 1995. The recent appointment of new Publications, Research and Internet managers was seen as an opportunity to co-ordinate dissipated energies in information management.

It can be seen from the case study that the audit was based on existing documentary evidence in addition to new data gathered by a needs analysis. This approach applied to the objectives: only when the data that has been gathered is juxtaposed with what the organisation is trying to achieve does it become a true information audit. The information audit project included objectives both through specific questions and by reference to key planning documents such as CAF's Corporate Plan.

The information audit process

Charities Aid Foundation's Chief Executive undertook to facilitate the information review and to provide an internal Project Manager, David Moncrieff and an external Project Leader/auditor, Dr Susan Saxon-Harrold. The terms of reference were as follows:

> 1. to advise on the CAF's review of information management in relation to its proposed internet site by liaising with CAF departments and managers, mutually agreed with the Project Director;
>
> 2. to design and facilitate an information audit to ascertain what information departments hold that could be readily used for the CAF internet site;
>
> 3. to report on the results of the information audit.

The original brief for the project was revised on two occasions to meet the requirements of a dynamic project. It was agreed as part of the project that:

> a) historical research and statistical data would be identified for possible future Internet presentation;
>
> b) external organisations holding relevant data on charities and donors were to be identified and initial discussion undertaken to explore organisation alliances with the data holders.

Throughout the audit period the Project Leader would work with the Project Manager and managers at CAF. The Project Leader was also able to draw on the expertise of staff at the European Foundation Centre (EFC) in Brussels and Independent Sector in the United States of America for technical skills elsewhere in the field for the production of the report.

Carrying out the information audit

The information audit was carried out in the following stages which are described in turn:

Formation of an internal steering group

Immediately, following a consultation exercise with CAF's Chief Executive, the internal Project Manager convened an internal steering group of ten middle management representatives from each directorate. This group was to comment on the interim and final report and offer a corporate view of how CAF's internet site should be constructed and what it should contain. These individuals would also be subjects of the pilot phase of the face-to-face interviews.

Designing the questionnaire

A selection of potential questions on CAF's development of its internet site, its current information provision and needs were refined with the assistance of the internal Project Manager and staff at the European Foundation Centre. The resulting draft of open-ended questions was presented to members of the internal steering group for comment. A set of questions was developed which resulted in an interview lasting approximately an hour covering the following:

- external and internal sources of information
- use of printed sources/bibliographic databases
- information flows
- information requests
- personal and departmental collections in CAF's offices in the UK and overseas
- distribution of information
- information needs
- general statements, random thoughts about information at CAF
- organisational objectives
- training

The interview schedule was designed to yield a mixture of lists of information held and 'soft' subjective reflections of staff experiences, perceptions and need.

Conducting interviews

In order to select the right people to talk to, the project manager provided details together with identifying managers from the staff list. Appointments were set up by phone with the nineteen managers and four CAF Directors. It was a time-consuming process, but paid off as it gave the project leader/auditor the opportunity to give brief details of what it is that the project was trying to achieve. Explaining the focus of the study, which only took a short time, was a means of ensuring an adequate amount of time at the interview stage.

The external project leader, Susan Saxon-Harrold, conducted interviews with 20 CAF managers, the first four of whom were guardians of CAF information on the voluntary sector, nationally and internationally. On average an hour was spent with managers with the exception of CAF Russia and CAF America, where correspondence supplemented an interview in one case and was the only contact in another.

All managers within CAF's headquarters in Kent were to be interviewed by the project leader as opposed to a member of the steering group. There were a number of reasons for this: firstly, managers were more likely to be more open with people from outside their own work area; secondly, it would be beneficial to the auditor to visit different parts of the organisation, and finally, the audit would encourage cross-organisational working.

Support given to interviewees included a sample interview script upon which to base their comments. This included definitions of terms such as 'information' and 'the Internet'. This was extremely important within the voluntary sector at a time when few organisations really understood the power of the Internet as an information tool or what lay behind the Chief Executive's interest in this subject. The interviewees were given a preamble which explained the purpose and scope of the survey. Nevertheless, at the time it came as no surprise that there was distrust of the underlying motives for the study.

All managers received verbal notification explaining the information audit and outlining general topics to be covered. Before each interview the project leader contacted managers to flag up topics for discussion beforehand and then supply the exact layout and wording of each question at the time of interview. Over a ten week period between June-August 1995, 19 CAF managers and four CAF Directors were interviewed and 11 other relevant national and international agencies that CAF had a working relationship with. Despite a tight time-frame to complete the project there was on average an hour and a half allocated for all interviews, which took place either face-to-face or by telephone to overseas agencies. This good response rate was attributable to the support of upper management and to the auditor's persistence and knowledge of the organisation.

The interviews ascertained what information managers and directors held which may have been suitable for loading onto the Internet in the medium term. A semi-structured questionnaire enabled the manager and auditor to have a structured conversation finding out how individuals use information while carrying out their jobs. The advantage of visiting people at the office site where they were working was that they told the auditor about information resources which she did not know it existed, but also suggested other people that the auditor should speak to. A pattern emerged early on in this project, and indicated similar usage of information across several departments. Confirmation of a pattern enabled the auditor to cut down on the number of additional staff interviewed, leaving time to see those not included before, but who turned out to be important in completion of the project. Interviewees were asked to tell the auditor:

a) what material they held, and how it was organised;
b) what interviewees thought the Internet could be used for in relation to their current or planned activities;

c) what external agencies they contact regularly for information as part of their activities.

Communicating with the auditor

Running in parallel to the interview process, this step warrants special mention because of maintaining consistency and communication between the auditor and CAF's steering group. During the interview period, the auditor received a considerable amount of written information about CAF services, plans, and information held that could be put to better use. Written material supplemented informal communication with managers and directors. In addition, in a large organisation with offices on a number of sites and countries, feedback from the auditor was seen as an important source of subjective data from the actual interview interactions. A series of debriefings was held between the Chief Executive, the auditor and the project manager as an opportunity for individual consultation. These revealed general feelings within CAF about the audit together with any persistently problematic questions or other issues.

Processing interview data

All 53 interviews were tape-recorded and transcribed for analysis. Given the qualitative nature of the project it was not felt to be either practicable or necessary to seek a fully representative sample. All the data was inputted onto an Access database. Downloading of responses to selected questions from the database enabled specific sections of the report to be written.

Presenting results

It is difficult to do justice to the complexity of a large organisation when using a 'snapshot' approach. This is particularly the case when organisations are facing environmental change. However, all the interviews and written material was analysed and a final report was completed. The project leader/auditor considered that the consultative nature of the process, together with the importance of 'soft' data to the intelligence gathering, made techniques from Soft Systems Methodology (Davies & Leddington, 1991) appropriate to the presentation of the report. This method has already been used in other contexts, principally in the National Health Service (Hepworth, 1992) and is designed to achieve desirable changes by taking a holistic approach.

Information was categorized as either giving expertise, publicity, contacts, enabling new markets to be entered or existing markets expanded. The findings of the report were presented at two meetings of CAF staff – in October and November 1995. The first meeting was to members of the steering group and the second was a formal presentation to the Chief Executive.

Benefits to Charities Aid Foundation

Charities Aid Foundation benefited in a number of ways from the information audit in relation to the development of its internet site. These can be divided into 'process' (those accruing from the techniques themselves) and 'outcome' (those resulting from the implementation of the report).

Process:
- information has been placed higher on the agenda with awareness being increased amongst staff at managerial level;
- CAF has a large body of information to support the planning process;
- the auditor developed a new approach and a greater understanding of CAF's role and their contribution to the process;
- the need for staff to have access to a number of external databases was recognized;
- procedures and protocols for keeping bibliographical and statistical information were reviewed.

Outcome:
- CAF has been able to identify individual areas of duplication and information gaps;
- CAF has been able to identify responsibilities for the individual information functions – e.g. database and records management, technology and current internet awareness;
- CAF has been able to identify individual areas of expertise, and common training needs;
- CAF considered offering company and charity clients a free home page service and/or technical support on how to go about getting a presence on the Internet;
- CAF developed its presence on the Internet as part of its overall mission;
- CAF investigated using the Internet as one way to improve data collection in relation to its various services;
- As a leading charity with its own presence on the Internet, CAF was able to consider educating other charities about the benefits of the Internet by convening an Internet charities/foundation group;

- As CAF's site was developed, collaboration with external agencies was also encouraged and the Internet project regularly re-assessed. CAF continued to identify other agencies in the UK and abroad to add further information about its services;
- CAF deposited a copy of some of its major research surveys with the ESRC data archive to encourage wider access and usage by researchers.

References

Davies, L. and Leddington, P. *Information in action: soft systems methodology*, Basingstoke/London, Macmillan, 1991

Hamilton, Feona. 'The information audit'. In Lawes, A (ed.) *Management skills for the information manager*, Aldershot, Ashgate, 1993

Hepworth, J.B. et al. 'The enhancement of information systems through user involvement in system design'. *International Journal of Information Management* 12 (1992) pp.120-129

Orna, E. *Practical information policies: how to manage information flow in organisations*, Aldershot, Gower, 1990

The Graphics and Visualization & Usability Center, Georgia Institute of Technology, November, 1994

The Charities Aid Foundation can be found on the World Wide Web at: *http://www.charitynet.org*

Case Study 6

Information Collection and Dissemination in an International Context: the Case of CRIN

Becky Purbrick

Introduction

The Child Rights Information Network (CRIN) was formally launched at an international meeting in July 1995, five years after the United Nations (UN) Convention on the Rights of the Child (the Convention) entered into force as international law. Sixty representatives from non-governmental organisations (NGOs), UN Agencies and academic institutions involved in children's rights activities participated and decided the network's aims, activities and structure. Three broad aims were adopted:

- Support and promote the implementation of the UN Convention on the Rights of the Child;
- Help to meet the information needs of organisations and individuals working with and for children's rights; and
- Support organisations to gather, handle, produce and disseminate child rights information through training, capacity building and the development of electronic and non-electronic networking tools.

This case study of CRIN will outline the rationale for the network, its activities, participation of its members and its achievements so far to highlight issues concerning information collection and dissemination in the international context.

Children's Rights, the Convention and the growth of networking

CRIN has developed within the framework of the Convention and growth of the children's rights community. The Convention entered into force on 2 September 1990. Seven years later 191 countries had signed and ratified the Convention, making it the most universally accepted international human rights instrument. Its articles outline the protection and promotion of children's development and participation in society in the broadest sense by combining the human rights of the child, the child's civil and political rights and the child's right to participate in decisions which affect them. The adoption of the Convention and its almost universal ratification has contributed to the growth of children's rights NGOs and networks. For example, there are now over 60 national coalitions of children's rights organisations working in countries throughout the world. The Children's Rights Office based in the United Kingdom set up in March 1992 is one example. It specifically promotes and monitors the implementation of the Convention in the United Kingdom. The Convention has also contributed to the adoption of a children rights perspective by the more established child welfare organisations. Recently, the United Nations Children's Fund (UNICEF) changed from a needs-based to children's rights-based approach.

The implementation of the Convention in 191 countries, with the first States reporting in 1992 and the attendant growth of the children's rights community has led to new information needs and demands. The Convention sets out the monitoring and reporting obligations of states party to the Convention, i.e. national governments. Two years after each State has ratified the Convention, it is obliged to present a written report to an expert committee of ten detailing the progress of national implementation. (States are then obliged to present periodic reports every five years.) Unlike any other international treaty, the Convention sets out a unique monitoring and reporting role for UNICEF and NGOs. Article 45 states that UNICEF and other competent bodies (meaning NGOs) can be invited by the Committee to give 'expert advice'[1] and information. The production of NGO reports presented to the Committee on the Rights of the Child has brought new demands to gather, analyse and disseminate information about the situation of children and their rights as well as the need to exchange experiences at the national and international level.

Networking as one of the modus operandi of NGOs has also increased over the past decade. Not least because of the so called 'new age of information' where access to and use of information is recognised as essential for NGOs to meet their organisational objectives. This is particularly true of organisations who work in partnership and do not undertake the work themselves, as argued by Mike Edwards[2].

The idea for CRIN

Against this background UNICEF, the international secretariat of Defence for Children International (DCI) based in Geneva and Rädda Barnen (Swedish Save the Children) convened a workshop in 1992 to examine the potential for effective information exchange to strengthen the implementation and monitoring of the Convention. The workshop brought together a number of NGOs and UN Agencies with existing but varying experience in managing information. The need for common and internationally recognised concepts concerning children's rights arose as a key issue and the development of a children's rights thesaurus to support communication and information handling was proposed by Rädda Barnen and DCI.

The workshop inspired the idea for an information network. A group of international NGOs with UNICEF (later known as the Facilitating Group[3]) continued to meet informally to develop this proposal. The need for a network was based on several assumptions. First, there is a wealth of information about children and the issues that affect them held by governments, academic institutions and non-governmental organisations but access to this information is neither easy or systematic. Second, there is no comprehensive picture of who holds what information, what type of information is available and how it can be obtained. Third, once it is known where information is held, a network would be the most appropriate mechanism for connecting these 'information centres'. Fourth, the child rights community is very diverse, operates on many different levels and handles information in different ways. This context requires a networking approach to information exchange rather than the adoption of one system for information collection and dissemination. Finally, creating co-operation between children's rights organisations on information handling could avoid duplication and would support mutual learning.

Initially, the Facilitating Group concentrated on mapping out the existing information handling capacities of children's rights organisations. In 1993, Human Rights Internet (HRI) was commissioned to undertake this survey. The organisations who responded were divided into three categories[4]: organisations with computerised information collections (As), organisations with information collections but not computerised (Bs) and organisations without collections (Cs). A majority fitted category B and of those in category A, just under 50 percent collected information on children but described children as a secondary focus of their work. C organisations were the smallest group, although it may be assumed that many organisations did not respond as the did not systematically collect information[5]. The survey provided the first data on the status of information collection within the children's rights community.

Drawing from the survey results, the information handling capacities of children's rights organisations did not appear to be either sophisticated or widespread. However, information management and the use of information technology was and still is relatively new among NGOs, particularly, although not exclusively, among smaller and southern-based organisations[6]. The HRI survey showed 11 percent of organisations were using email systems. At that time, a children's rights approach to collecting, analysing and disseminating information was also underdeveloped. There is still a long way to go before specific tools for managing children's rights information are developed and widely used. In 1993, UNICEF's International Child Development Centre commissioned the production of a children's rights thesaurus. The English, French and Spanish versions will be available in 1998, the publisher is to be identified.

By 1994, it became clear to the Facilitating Group that a network which would simply connect existing information centres was not yet possible. A different approach to information networking was needed.

Setting up CRIN

In January 1995, the Facilitating Group, appointed a coordinator (the author) for 6 months to develop a network proposal to be discussed at an international meeting. A questionnaire[7] was sent to 172 southern-based and 50 northern-based organisations to identify their information needs and the services they could use. A 59 percent response indicated the timeliness and interest in a network to meet their needs.

Eight preliminary project proposals were drafted based on the results of the questionnaire and previous consultations within the Facilitating Group. A traditional structure for the network with a general assembly, an executive committee and secretariat was also prepared for discussion.

The international meeting was held in July 1995 and attended by 60 participants who represented decision and policy makers as well as, although not predominately, information workers. This was a deliberate decision to engage primary information users who could assess the potential use of a network and who could harness organisational commitment. It became apparent that needs were broad and far-reaching. Priorities included access to qualitative and quantitative data on the situation of children; guidance on accessing and retrieving information; and capacity building, particularly in the use of electronic information systems. Not surprisingly, obstacles included the lack of resources, technical expertise, managing too much information and often the wrong kind and the absence of an information and knowledge-based culture.

While the proposed network could not address all of these needs, the proposed projects were intended as a beginning. The participants agreed to support the development of an informal, open and free network, with an expanded Facilitating Group[8] to steer the work, and a small coordinating unit hosted by an international organisation (currently Save the Children UK).

CRIN's projects

CRIN's newsletter was launched in January 1996, as the first project. The newsletter is a primary communication and promotion tool. Each issue includes news from the Facilitating Group and the coordinating unit, profiles of members, news of initiatives such as a new clearing house of media violence on children, references of new children's rights publications, Web sites of interest and forthcoming conferences on children's rights issues. Each issue includes a membership form, is available in English, French and Spanish and mailed to 1, 300 organisations and individuals working in some 130 countries. By September 1997 and before distributing the fifth issue, over 400 organisations in 101 countries had joined CRIN, a strong indication that the network and the newsletter is satisfying a need.

By March 1996, work began on a database of children's rights organisations. Lotus Notes software was chosen because of its decentralised access, its replication facility via telecommunications networks and interface with the Web. The database is designed to hold information about the aims and activities of each organisation; their programmes and work; their information collections organised according to the articles in the Convention; and details of their research and publications. It is intended as a tool for identifying who is doing what in the field of children's rights and retrieving information produced by network members. The database is published on CRIN's Web site and a printed directory is being prepared.

A questionnaire[9] for gathering information is distributed with each issue of the newsletter. Initially, the number of responses to the questionnaire were not encouraging. The coordinating unit actually needed a fully functioning and responsive network of members to gather information systematically. The quality of responses were also variable as organisations were asked to describe their own information collections according to the Convention. As noted earlier, specific tools for cataloguing children's rights information are not fully developed and so many collections are not organised according to the articles of the Convention. Furthermore, members were not necessarily clear why this information was needed or would be of use to them. More recently, gathering information from member organisations has improved because other CRIN services are now available. Members are beginning to see the direct benefits of using and contributing to the network.

Developing a participatory network to collect and disseminate information has been a guiding principle throughout CRIN's evolution. Thus decentralised access and updating of the database is an important goal. So far, local copies of the database are being piloted with CRIN members in Sweden, Switzerland, Uruguay and India. Each member is requested to add information, send and receive updates to the Lotus Notes server at UNICEF in Geneva. Already, this pilot is highlighting some of the wider difficulties of international information collection and dissemination. For example, replicating the database between Uruguay and Geneva incurs high communication costs, local training and technical support to use the software is difficult to find, providing technical support at a distance has cultural and language implications, integrating internal databases with CRIN's is not always appropriate or simple, and member organisations have limited resources to gather information on behalf of the network.

CRIN MAIL, the network's third project is a private mailing list, introduced in January 1997. (Over 60 percent of CRIN's members now use email, a significant increase since the initial HRI survey.) The CRIN MAIL is used to post news and announcements and to pose questions to other network members. Although a majority of CRIN members are using email, for many it is still a new tool. The first months of the CRIN MAIL were beset with teething problems. Members unfamiliar with mailing lists often sent individual messages. The number of messages beginning 'Dear Becky ...' were frustrating for many and annoying to some. Now the mailing list is very active with only occasional mis-postings.

The CRIN MAIL has dramatically changed the nature of communication within the network. For the first year, top-down links between the coordinator and individual members dominated communication. The CRIN MAIL has opened up horizontal links between network members. Members are able to see inputs from others, often encouraging their own contributions. The CRIN MAIL has also provided a means of tapping into information and knowledge which is so often in people's heads rather than stored in a database or library. Responses to questions posted on the CRIN MAIL often arrive within a few days and are based on members personal knowledge and experience.

In August 1997, members were asked for their views of the CRIN MAIL, characterised by one:

> NFTC is constantly receiving mail from CRIN members, they provide us with very interesting information about the activities of other organisations working in the field of child welfare all over the world. CRIN MAIL gave us the opportunity of contacting, opening communication channels and exchanging information with these organisations
>
> Hayat Malhas Yaghi, National Taskforce for Children, Jordan[10].

In March 1997, development of CRIN's Web site began in earnest, even though full Internet access lags behind the network members' use of email. (Even within resource-rich organisations such as Save the Children UK access to the Internet is limited.) However, 16 percent of the membership are creating their own Web sites such as Casa Alianza from Costa Rica and Child Workers in Asia based in Thailand. Implicit in the development of CRIN's Web site is that full access to the Internet will increase among network members. Although access and use of the Internet is likely to remain unequal between the North and South. CRIN's training and capacity building initiatives (see below) will need to take this into account and devise strategies to address these issues.

CRIN's Web site is designed to provide a first port of call for anyone seeking children's rights information on the Internet. The site is complemented by CRIN's directory of Web sites on children and children's rights information. The site is divided into five sections:

1. Issues relating children's rights which includes full text documentation, information relating to the Convention, who is doing what and conference information;
2. Publications – a growing bibliographic reference of children's rights publications;
3. Databases – direct access to CRIN's organisations database and links to other useful databases;
4. The Convention on the Rights of the Child including full text documentation, guidelines, monitoring information and ratifications; and
5. Information about CRIN including project details, membership details and links to members' Web sites.

Increasingly, CRIN's newsletter and the CRIN MAIL is used to update members on new information published on the site, so that members without Internet access can request hard copy documentation.

CRIN's members are actively encouraged to contribute information to the site through the establishment of thematic desks (see below). Most of CRIN members do not have the resources, technical expertise or capacity to publish their own documentation on the Internet. The coordinating unit provides this service thus giving members an additional channel to disseminate their own documentation at a low cost.

CRIN's training and capacity building project for information handling remains to be developed. Despite being a priority at the international meeting in July 1995 and highlighted by the African participants' joint statement: 'The group from Africa wishes to emphasize the critical importance of providing it with support and resources for capacity building so that Africa can participate fully and equally in an international network.'[11]

Understanding and addressing the training needs of a wide range of organisations is extremely complex and will require different approaches. Although its priority has not been ignored, the network needs to reach a level of maturity before it can realistically assess the training and capacity building needs of its members. With a membership of over 400, the network is now much better placed to tackle this project.

Building a network to gather and exchange information

CRIN is still a very young network just beginning to learn how to collect and disseminate information on an international scale. CRIN was originally established because a networking approach to the global collection and dissemination of children's rights information was perceived as more practical, sustainable and desirable than creating one organisation which would assume this role, even though the opportunity to go to one place to retrieve information may be an attractive proposition to many working in the field of children's rights.

The initial concept of CRIN as only facilitating the exchange of information assumed that information was already systematically collected, processed, stored and retrievable within organisations. CRIN would simply provide the mechanisms for exchange and help to identify existing resources. Despite internal and external pressures on NGOs for improved accountability, more effective collaboration in lobbying and advocacy and improved practice based on knowledge and institutional learning, for most managing information effectively is still a battle to be won.

Out of necessity CRIN has developed as a network which seeks to facilitate information exchange and through its projects it collects and disseminates information about children and their rights. If CRIN had developed only to facilitate information exchange it may have become an exclusive network of information providers. CRIN's informal structure and its broad aims to support information exchange and handling within the children's rights community has created a different kind of network. CRIN works almost despite its diverse membership ranging from UN Agencies such as UNICEF with considerable resources at its disposal to grassroots organisations with limited resources such as Concern for Children and Environment, Nepal. Members continue to demonstrate the will and necessity to find a common ground. This has been and remains one of the biggest challenges of all.

The last two years have been about building a communication network and developing tools for gathering and sharing information. Furnishing these tools with substance and quality has been the major challenge of the last six months. This has required the active participation of CRIN's members and a range of incentives to ensure contributions. Throughout 1996, membership of CRIN did not amount to much as the only tangible project output was CRIN's newsletter. Other projects and services were introduced in 1997 such as the CRIN MAIL, the membership directory, CRIN's Web site and Web site directory. Members began to see the potential benefits of CRIN. Quid pro quo relations for exchanging information between members and between the coordinating unit have become possible.

Thematic desks creating a participatory network

The concept of virtual thematic desks was introduced in June 1997 to further encourage the participation and contributions of CRIN's members and to provide a mechanism for systematic and focused information collection and dissemination. Members with expertise in a particular theme are invited to contribute information to one or more desks. A common structure for each desk has been defined to include different types of information which are then stored and thus disseminated through CRIN's Web site. The types of information include full text and bibliographical material on each issue; conference information including agendas, participants, papers and reports; information about activities and research; and information relating to the Convention and other international treaties.

Over twenty CRIN members are currently contributing to CRIN's first theme, child labour, by providing electronic and printed materials. The coordinating unit is responsible for the technical aspects of managing the Web site. Members are enthusiastic and see the benefits of disseminating their own information to a wider audience at a low cost to themselves. However, not all members are providing information proactively and the coordinating unit plays a crucial role in reminding and prodding members to contribute. Some members are clearly better equipped to do so, often because they have given organisational priority to advocacy, campaigning and information dissemination. Feedback from members is encouraging and two new desks are being created, one on sexual exploitation of children and the other on monitoring the Convention through national coalitions of children's rights organisations. The Taskforce on National Coalitions[12] approached CRIN to establish this desk, a positive development.

A regionalised approach

CRIN's projects, particularly the CRIN MAIL and Web site have highlighted issues raised at the international meeting which launched CRIN, namely the challenge of language and technology. English dominates communication within the network, except CRIN's newsletter. A number of members cannot fully participate and share their knowledge and expertise because of the language barriers. Members from Latin America are keen to adopt a regionalised model for CRIN to diversify the culture and language within the network, an inevitability and necessity.

The challenge of technology is equally important. CRIN is committed to developing tools that are appropriate and accessible to its diverse membership but in contradiction has concentrated on projects which are dependent on information technology. This dependency is borne out of necessity within the coordinating unit. Furthermore the rapid growth and use of information technology cannot be ignored. CRIN's efforts to create an information-rich Web site reflects the assumption that use of the Internet will continue to grow, however unevenly. The coordinating unit's use of information technology and particularly communication technology is both cost effective and more efficient as it communicates with a growing and disparate membership. However, CRIN seeks to promote a wide range of tools for gathering and disseminating information. Increasingly, the newsletter is used to inform the membership of the content of CRIN's Web site and offers hard copy documentation to those members without Internet access. The production of paper directories represents a continued commitment to share information across a range of formats.

Once again a regionalised approach may provide opportunities for members to find solutions to collaborative access and use of the Internet. As well as the challenge to develop appropriate and innovative means of collecting and disseminating information within the network. (Although regionalisation is not perceived as a panacea for all those issues which are difficult to tackle.) A CRIN member, the Arab Resource Collective is committed to investigating the information and training needs within its region. This investigation will consider questions of language, culture and what information is specific to the region and what could be shared globally.

In many ways CRIN is only at the beginning, but it is becoming a vibrant network. It is now in a position to explore the information needs and capacities within the children's rights community in a meaningful way and develop a variety of tools for handling and managing information within an international context.

References

The Convention on the Rights of the Child adopted by the United Nations General Assembly on 20 November 1989 and entered into force on 2 September 1990

Edwards, Mike. 'NGOs in the Age of Information' in 'Knowledge is power? The use and abuse of information in development' *IDS Bulletin* Vol. 25, No. 2 April 1994

Human Rights Internet *Children's Rights Information Sources: A listing of organisations with information on the rights of the child*, Ottawa, Canada, Human Rights Internet, 1995

Purbrick, Becky. *Establishing a Child Rights Information Network: Report of the proceedings of an international meeting, July 3rd - 5th, 1995*, London, Child Rights Information Network, 1996

Notes

1. See Article 45 *The Convention on the Rights of the Child* adopted by the United Nations General Assembly on 20 November 1989 and entered into force on 2 September 1990.
2. See Mike Edwards 'NGOs in the Age of Information' in 'Knowledge is power? The use and abuse of information in development' *IDS Bulletin* Vol. 25, No. 2 April , p. 117.
3. The Facilitating Group initially included Defence for Children International, International Secretariat, International Centre for Childhood and the Family, International Save the Children Alliance, NGO Group for the Convention on the Rights of the Child, Rädda Barnen, Save the Children UK, UNICEF's International Child Development Centre, UNICEF and the High Commissioner for Human Rights. Membership later expanded to include southern representatives (see footnote 6).
4. See Human Rights Internet *Children's Rights Information Sources: A listing of organisations with information on the rights of the child*, 1995.
5. Computerisation of the organisation's information collection was used as a measure of the sophistication of information handling.
6. Southern-based is defined as all countries which are not located in Western Europe and North America. Eastern and Central Europe are included in southern-based.
7. For the results of the survey see Appendix One.

8   The Facilitating Group was expanded to include southern organisations: African Network for the Prevention and Protection Against Child Abuse and Neglect, Arab Resource Collective, Butterflies, Concerned for Working Children and Instituto Interamericano del Niños.
9   See Appendix Two
10 Personal communication to the author
11 See Becky Purbrick, *Establishing a Child Rights Information Network: Report of the proceedings of an international meeting, July 3rd - 5th, 1995*, p 18
12 The Taskforce on National Coalitions is a subgroup of the NGO Group for the Convention on the Rights of the Child, a member of CRIN and part of the Facilitating Group.

Appendix One

Results of the Information Needs Questionnaire prepared for the Child Rights Information Network

In preparation for the meeting in Paris on 'Establishing a Child Rights Information Network', 3-5 July 1995, a questionnaire was designed to identify the information needs of child-rights and child-focused organisations. It was sent to 222 organisations, 172 based in the south and 50 in the north. Organisations were asked to identify which type of information on children's rights is most useful in their work; what type of information from other organisations is useful; on which areas of the Convention on the Rights of the Child (CRC) they require information, particularly in terms of its implementation; what sources of information and services do they find most useful and what method of communication is used most effectively.

There was a very good response – 59% of the organisations returned their questionnaires. This percentage indicates the level of interest and support for the establishment of an information network. It also reflects the effectiveness of using an existing network to gather information, Save the Children and Defence for Children International offices throughout the world helped to target organisations and solicit responses to the questionnaire. The highest response came from Africa and South East Asia and the lowest from Latin America. It is assumed that the lower response from Latin America was mainly due to language barriers as the questionnaire was not translated into Spanish.

Responses from the Northern and Southern based non-governmental organisations (NGOs) were analysed separately and in combination, to identify any possible difference in terms of information needs. Organisations were asked what type of child-rights and child-focused information they found the most useful. 35% ranked information about the CRC, its implementation and interpretation as the most useful, 32% ranked the national situation of children as top priority and 25% identified practical information on 'working' with children as the most useful.

When gathering information from other organisations, 44% of the responding organisations identified exchanging practical experience in specific areas of work as a priority, and 36% ranked background information about other organisations as a top priority. Additionally, knowing about current programme activities and contacts of other organisations was identified as a key resource.

Organisations were asked to identify their most important information needs in relation to the CRC, 42% ranked 'special protection measures' as the greatest need, followed by information on civil rights and freedoms. The remaining areas of the CRC were given fairly equal weighting. The results give a very high demand (44%) for case studies of the implementation of the CRC. Southern organisations indicated a greater demand for training materials on the CRC in comparison with Northern organisations (38% and 22% respectively). Also there is a greater demand from the South for information on the NGO group for the Convention on the Rights of the Child and information about national coalitions.

Project related information deriving from direct experience was identified as the most useful type of information for organisations working in the field of child rights, again Southern organisations ranked training materials as very important. Findings from research, reviews and evaluations were also valued by Southern and Northern organisations.

The results demonstrated that organisations mainly use their own internal sources of information and information from personal contacts and informal networks. Information gathered from meetings and from other NGOs were identified as the second most important sources. Information from external resource centres was not ranked highly by Southern and Northern organisations. Respondents were also asked to comment on information services which they found useful. Databases or directories of organisations was overall the most useful source. Southern organisations rely on newsletters and media services as key sources whereas Northern organisations identified bibliographic information as a valuable source.

Organisations were also asked to comment on the most effective methods of exchanging information. 61% ranked face-to-face meetings, conferences and workshops as the most effective method of exchanging information, followed by mail, telephone and fax. Southern organisations rely more heavily on mail in comparison with Northern organisations which rely heavily on faxing. Only 7% identified email as the most effective means of communication and there was no difference between Northern and Southern organisations. However, a significant number of organisations are currently investigating or introducing email and linkages with the Internet.

Organisations were asked to comment on their own experience of networking and some of the problems that they encounter. Many of the organisations noted that they are not currently involved in any formal and effective information networks. Despite this, the benefits of networking were highlighted, such as the opportunity to exchange expertise and reflect on various issues, greater access to information sources, saving of time and resources and building up internal capacity. Some of the problems that the respondents identified were as follows:

- it is difficult to maintain regular contact with other organisations, particularly ones based in other countries
- some organisations are not willing to share information
- a lot of unsolicited information does not have any relevance to the needs of the organisation
- networks are not coordinated properly
- networks can collapse if key people are not involved
- sustaining the interest of members is difficult
- poor communications infrastructure prevent effective exchange of information

Additionally, organisations were asked to identify some of the problems they face when obtaining information. The most common problems are not knowing where information is held, who to contact on a particular issue and who is doing what and where in the field of child rights. The timeliness of receiving information is also a major constraint, as is the capacity to meet an organisation's information needs. Respondents highlighted the need for training in the collection, documentation and dissemination of information relating to child rights.

The results of this questionnaire provide a 'picture' of the information needs of organisations working to make a reality of children's rights and should help to shape the nature and scope of the Child Rights Information Network (CRIN). In this way CRIN can be sensitive to the needs of its members and users. Drawing from the results, the network should consider the following as priorities:

1. Gathering and exchanging information on the interpretation and implementation of the Convention on the Rights of the Child, particularly case studies.

2. Gathering and exchanging information on 'special protection methods and civil rights and freedoms', whilst not excluding the other articles in the Convention.
3. Gathering, exchanging and developing training materials on the Convention and its implementation.
4. Collecting and disseminating information on 'who is doing what' in the field of child rights, the current activities of organisations, contacts and background information.
5. Building up a knowledge of information sources and how to access them and raising awareness of the existence of these sources.
6. Developing a range of services for information exchange but giving priority to developing a network newsletter and an organisational database.
6. Maintaining a range of methods for communication, but developing the capacity for electronic communication.
7. Providing training or capacity-support in managing, processing and disseminating information relating to children's rights.

August 1995

Becky Purbrick
Coordinator of the Child Rights Information Network
C/O Save the Children (UK)
17 Grove Lane
London SE5 8RD
Tel: +44 171 703 5400
Fax: +44 171 793 7630
Email: *crin@pro-net.co.uk*

Appendix Two

Child Rights Information Network: Organisations Questionnaire

(Please write in black and as clearly as possible)

About your organisation

1. Name of organisation (In English):

2. Alternative organisation name, including local language names:

3. Acronym:

4. Year of establishment:

5. Postal address:

Country:

6. Telephone (with country and area codes):

7. Fax (with country and areas codes):

8. Email address:

9. Web site Address:

10. Name of director:

11. Name of the contact person (s) for CRIN:

12. Number of staff:

13. Average annual income:

Your aims and programmes

14. Aims and programmes (please provide a short description of the aims of your organisation, your programmes and their intended impact.)

15. Please list your main areas of work with children eg. primary education, adoption, juvenile justice.

16. Type of organisation (please tick as appropriate)
- National
- Regional
- International
- Non-governmental
- UN/Multilateral
- Grassroots/Community Based Organisation
- Academic

17. Please indicate your main target audiences or intended beneficiaries of your programmes (please tick as appropriate)
- Children (0-4)
- Children (5-15)
- Children (16-18)
- Women
- Families
- General public
- Communities
- Governments
- Media
- Commerce
- UN Agencies
- NGOs
- Other:

18. Countries in which your organisation works (attach a country list, if necessary)

19. Regional focus of your work (please tick as appropriate) NB. Regional means group of countries
- North Africa
- North America
- Western Europe
- South Asia
- West Africa
- South America
- Central and Eastern Europe
- South E Asia
- East and Central Africa
- Central America
- Former Soviet Union
- Central Asia
- Southern Africa
- Caribbean
- Arabic Countries
- Pacific

20. *Please indicate your main approaches or methods of working (please tick as appropriate)*
- Funding
- Operational
- Partnership
- Service provision
- Hands on technical support
- Training and advice services
- Advocacy
- Research and information
- Other

Your organisation's research programmes

21. *Please provide information on your organisations research programmes.* Please attach a list of programme titles, researchers names, dates covered by the research and brief details of the programmes (ie. an abstract, executive summary or contents pages)

Your organisation's publications

22. *Please provide details of publications produced by your organisation*
We would be grateful if you could provide sample copies of newsletters, bulletins and brochures produced by your organisation and details of any publications you produce that specifically relate to child rights (ie. publications lists, publishers summaries, contents pages or abstracts).

About your information resources or documentation centre

The questions below relate to your information resources. If you do not have an organised information collection you do not need to complete these questions. Please go to question 29.

23. *Please provide a brief description of your documentation centre, resource centre, library or information collection. (Please include purpose of your centre, main users, subject and specialist collections, size and services)*

24. *Please indicate the main subject areas of your information collection, according to the articles in the Convention on the Rights of the Child. Please only tick as appropriate.*
- General principles
  Definition of the child
  Non discrimination

- Best interests of the child
  Implementation of the Convention
  Right to life
  Existing standards
- Civil rights and freedoms
  Name & nationality
  Preservation of identity
  Freedom of expression
  Freedom of association
  Protection from cruelty
  Protection of privacy
  Protection from libel & slander
  Access to appropriate information
  Protection from injurious information
  Standard of living (rights)
  Children of minority & indigenous peoples
- Family environment and alternative care
  Parental guidance
  Extended families & child development
  Children separated from their parents
  Family reunification
  Illicit transfer & non return
  Parental responsibilities
  Child care services
  Child abuse & neglect
  Alternative care
  Institutional care
  Adoption & intercountry adoption
  Placement evaluations
  Children & social security
  Standards of living (provision)
  Street children
- Basic health and welfare
  Disabled children
  Disease control
  Family planning

      Harmful traditional practices
      Health services
      Health & hygiene education
      Infant & child mortality
      Mother & child health
      Nutrition & malnutrition
      Pollution & the environment
      Preventative health care
      Primary health care
      Water & sanitation
      Rehabilitative treatment & care

- Education, leisure and cultural activities
      Compulsory education
      Free education
      Higher education
      Illiteracy & literacy
      Primary education
      School discipline
      School attendance & dropout rates
      Secondary education
      Vocational guidance
      Aims of education
      Play & leisure
      Cultural life

- Special protection measures
      Refugee children
      Refugee protection
      Refugee law
      Family tracing & unaccompanied children
      Humanitarian aid
      Children in armed conflict
      Child soldiers
      Humanitarian law
      Civilian protection in war
      Landmines

- Legal

- Capital punishment
- Detention & imprisonment
- Torture cruel treatment & punishment
- Alternatives to judicial proceedings & imprisonment
- Charging children
- Convicted children
- Children & judicial bodies
- Juvenile offenders
- Legal assistance for children
- Trials & hearings involving children
- Minimum age & legal rights

- **Exploitation**
  - Child labour
  - Slavery & bonded labour
  - Drug abuse & drug protection
  - Sexual exploitation & abuse
  - Child pornography
  - Child prostitution
  - Sale trafficking & abduction
  - Other forms of exploitation

- **Implementation of the CRC**
  - Monitoring
  - Ombudswork
  - National Coalition
  - Legislative reform
  - Advocacy
  - Other:

25. *What types of documents do you hold in your documentation centre? (Please tick as appropriate)*
- UN/Multilateral
- Legal
- Country-specific
- Policy-related
- Governmental
- Statistical
- Global

- Press-related
- Academic
- Case study
- Project-related
- Public education
- Other

26. What language(s) does your collection include?:

27. Please provide a brief description of the databases that you have developed eg. bibliographical on child labour, full text on education, projects, etc.

28. Are any of your databases available on CD-ROM, on-line or on the Internet, if so please provide brief details of how to access them. (eg CRIN's web site http://www.crin.ch)

29. Do you give permission for this information to be published in a directory and on CRIN's web site? (Yes /No)

30. Is your organisation willing and able to respond to information requests from other organisations? (Yes / No)

31. What information services can you provide eg literature searches, accession lists etc?

32. Completed by _____ Date: _____

Please return as soon as possible to the address below. Please include any relevant supporting materials and documentation eg annual report, research reports etc.

>Child Rights Information Network,
>Becky Purbrick, Coordinator,
>c/o Save the Children (UK), 17 Grove Lane, London, UK,
>SE5 8RD
>Tel +44 171 703 5400, Fax +44 171 793 7630
>Email crin@mail.pro-net.co.uk

Appendix

Appendix

Electronic Information Resources for the Voluntary and Community Sector

Compiled by Communities Online Forum (http://www.communities.org.uk) and Partnerships Online (http://www.partnerships.org.uk)

Main gateway sites for voluntary organisations, with mailing lists and newsgroups

Black information link
http://www.blink.org.uk
Providing information to bring about improvements in race relations and to act as a forum where ideas can be freely shared.

Community Development Foundation
http://www.cdf.org.uk
Focusing on social inclusion, regeneration, capacity building and the community sector.

Community Work Training
http://www.community-work-training.org.uk
Training materials, articles and links from West Yorkshire Community Work Training Group.

CVSNet
http://www.neilirving.demon.co.uk/cvsnet
Useful mailing lists offering discussion of all aspects of the work of Councils for Voluntary Service.

DisabilityNet
http://www.disabilitynet.co.uk
An information, discussion and news service for disabled people and those with an interest in disability issues.

Fundraising UK
http://www.fundraising.co.uk/
Information about grants and partnerships, examples of fund-raising on the Internet, events and resources.

Funderfinder
http://www.funderfinder.org.uk/
Funderfinder is a charity that develops and distributes software to help individuals and not-for-profit organisations in the UK find charitable trusts that might give them money. Their Web site includes an online advice pack, links to other sites and a discussion forum.

InfoRurale
http://www.nrec.org.uk/inforurale
Information gateway for rural development, part of the national rural enterprise council.

Local Government
http://www.open.gov.uk/index/filclgov.htm
An official list of local authorities on the UK Government's open.gov server.

Mailbase
http://www.mailbase.org.uk
Electronic discussion lists for the UK higher education community, many of which are open to all.

National Council for Voluntary Organisations
http://www.vois.org.uk/ncvo
Includes news, a calendar of events and links to other sites of possible interest.

National Organisation for Adult Learning in England and Wales (NIACE)
http://www.niace.org.uk
Including discussion list on 'The Learning Age' – at *http://www.lifelonglearning.co.uk/consult/*

Nua
http://www.nua.ie
An Internet consultancy and developer which offers a regularly updated survey on use of the Internet.

OneWorld
http://www.oneworld.org

An alternative news 'supersite'. Edited routes into many groups working for social justice and sustainable development, including Oxfam, Save the Children and Amnesty International.

The Site
http://www.thesite.org
An enormous umbrella site for resources for young people on the Web.

UK Public Libraries on the Web
http://dspace.dial.pipex.com/town/square/ac940/weblibs.html
This site by Sheila and Robert Harden has a comprehensive list of resources.

Organisations offering advice to voluntary organisations

CharityNet
http://www.charitynet.org/index.html
The Web site of the Charities Aid Foundation, with a search engine listing over 70,000 community groups, links to corporate community involvement pages on company Web sites, and the CharityCard Directory.

ChurchNet
http://www.churchnet.org.uk/churchnet/
For all Christian churches, groups and organisations in the UK with a resource base, technical training and help.

GreenNet
http://www.gn.apc.org/gn/links
Menus of members, environment, progressive, spiritual and government links and support for these groups.

Poptel
http://www.poptel.net/sales/
A co-op set up to provide Internet access and publishing services for non-profits including major trades unions, the UK Labour Party and voluntary sector organisations.

Voluntary Organisations Internet Server
http://www.vois.org.uk
Voluntary Organisations Internet Server (VOIS) offers a resource centre, a volunteers notice board and a searchable database.

Online publications offering practical help

Benton Communication Best Practices Toolkit
http://www.benton.org/Practice/Toolkit/
A site which aims to help non-profit organisations make effective use of communications and information technologies.

Community Network Movement
http://www.scn.org/ip/commnet/home.html
A Web site providing information for the community network movement. Contains resources and links to other organisations.

Coyote Communications Tip Sheets
http://www.coyotecom.com/tips.html
Coyote Communications post a variety of tip sheets aimed at the non-profit and public sector. Topics include Web development and maintenance, the Internet, and databases and software.

Legal, Political and Social Issues of the Internet
http://www.venables.co.uk/legal/issues.htm
This paper gives a general overview of the legal concerns of an organisation going online, and includes links to legal resources and further information on specific issues.

London Advice Services Alliance
http://www.lasa.org.uk
LASA is development and resource agency for providers of advice and information. Through their 'Computanews' factsheets they provide free advice on computers for voluntary organisations.

Netskills
http://www.netskills.ac.uk/TONIC
A free, online, full tutorial on Internet tools, complete with exercises, from the University of Newcastle Upon Tyne. Lets you work through in sections, picking up where you left off last time.

New Community Networks: Wired for Change
http://www.scn.org/ip/commnet/wired.html
A Web site relating to Douglas Schuler's book of the same name, which discusses how grassroots activists are using IT to build community networks designed to reinvigorate communities by providing a forum for dialogue. The site contains chapter abstracts, an extensive bibliography and appendices on community networks, listing sites, bulletin board systems, software etc.

Partnerships Online
http://www.partnerships.org.uk/pubs/
Includes advice on how to use IT in the community, 'Getting Connected' on Internet basics, and articles from community practitioners on the community uses of information technology.

Total Net Value
http://www.totalnetval.com/
An Internet and online consultancy service from the authors of *Making the NetWork*, the best guide to getting your organisation online, including a 'Freebies' area offering advice and help in the promotion of your Web site.

Key policy reports in the field

BT's vision of community networks
http://www.labs.bt.com/ourwork/cnet/index.htm
Research from the BT Labs team highlighting connectivity as a key issue in local community networks.

Down-to-earth vision
http://www.uk.ibm.com/community/uk171.html
An evaluation of community based IT initiatives and social inclusion.

Government Direct
http://www.open.gov.uk/citu/gdirect/greenpaper/index.htm
The green paper suggesting that in future some government information provision will be solely electronic and attempting to highlight the issues this raises, including responses.

Inventing the Future
http://www.partnerships.org.uk/itf/itfsum.html
Text of a booklet about what the Information Society may mean for communities, produced by Partnerships for Tomorrow in 1996.

Living in the Information Society
http://www.uk.ibm.com/comm/community/uk007.html
Further IBM sponsored reports into the social consequences of new technologies.

The Net Result – Social Inclusion in the Information Society
http://www.uk.ibm.com/comm/community/uk117.html
A major work warning against social exclusion and covering far-reaching recommendations and debate around that theme.

Universal access to email
http://www.rand.org:80/publications/MR/MR650/
As the government and Microsoft move towards universal email, the RAND group looks at feasibility and societal implications

Other useful sites

Community Networks and Teleworking
http://members.aol.com/telework/netpage.htm
Offers some pointers to links between teleworking and the community at large.

Communities Online
http://www.communities.org.uk
A network for community networkers – activists around the country exploring ways in which new communications technologies can be used for the benefit of local communities.

EARL: Electronic Access to Resources in Libraries
http://www.earl.org.uk
EARL is a consortium of UK Public Library Authorities and other organisations which aim to make available the advantages of the Internet to all library users and other members of the public. Includes a list of partners with links to their sites, as well as listings by subject with links to their sites.

ETO European Telework Organisation
http://www.eto.org.uk
An information and discussion site on the use of teleworking, teletrade and telecooperation.

Information Society Initiative
http://www.isi.gov.uk/
The government project aimed primarily at businesses, but of relevance to the independent sector.

IT for All
http://www.itforall.org.uk/
The government initiative promoting awareness and use of information technology.

Panos: information and communication for sustainable development
http://www.oneworld.org/panos/.

A Web site which gives news, opinions and perspectives from developing countries, with the intention of stimulating debate on global environmental and development issues. Topics include the impact of the Internet, telecommunications issues, the repercussions of climate change, women's health issues, and the social impact of HIV/AIDS.

Partnerships Online
http://www.partnerships.org.uk
How to use the Internet for community benefit, partnership building and organisational change.

UK Citizens Online Democracy
http://www.democracy.org.uk
Discussion and pilot studies on the use of new technology in the democratic process.

Notes on Contributors

Graham Bennett

Graham has an MA in Information Management from Sheffield University, and has worked as a librarian, information officer and library manager in both the academic and voluntary sectors. Most recently, he has worked for both VSO and, currently, for Amnesty International as Director of Information Resources. He has broad experience of management and organisational development in the voluntary sector, both in the UK and overseas, notably in the Philippines where he worked for two years in the non-governmental sector. As part of his work with Amnesty, he has been responsible for developing an information management strategy for the organisation, as well as acting as project manager for large-scale organisational restructuring.

Caroline Bradley

Following a year as a library assistant for a trades union, Caroline Bradley completed an MA in Information & Library studies at Loughborough University in 1992. She then worked in local radio for two and a half years, producing programmes with community groups. From there she moved to a local Age Concern group where she managed a scheme tackling social isolation amongst older people, before moving to Alcohol Concern as Information Development Officer in January 1997.

Rodney Breen

Rodney Breen graduated from University College Dublin with a BA in History in 1980 and a Diploma in Archive Studies in 1981. From 1987 to 1991 he worked for the BBC as part of its Records Management team. Since 1991 he has been the Records Manager and Archivist of Save the Children, where his brief covers everything from setting up filing systems to producing promotional materials for the archives. He is an active member of both the Charity Archivists and Records Managers group (CHARM) and the Voluntary Action History Society.

Lynette Cawthra

Lynette Cawthra is Library and Information Service Manager at the King's Fund, an independent charitable foundation working on health policy research, service development and educational programmes, as well as giving grants to other organisations. Its library is open to the public, and contains a unique collection of material on UK healthcare policy and management (with a particularly strong emphasis on both official and 'grey' literature). The service also acts as a conduit for information about developments and good practice in health and social care services. Lynette also manages the Fund's Web site. From 1991 to 1996 she was Information Manager at Age Concern England, with responsibility for the information phoneline, Web site and the editing & production of factsheets and the monthly bulletin, as well as for the library. Since training as a professional librarian, she has also been bibliographic researcher for a charitable art foundation, and librarian for a civil service trades union. As a Mancunian, she is a lifelong Manchester United fan.

Jacqueline Cropley

Jacqueline Cropley consults in IT, knowledge management and marketing. She has installed information retrieval and other computer systems (including mainframes, PCs, networked services, client/server, Internet and intranets) for a variety of companies, local authorities, and health and social services. Her past employment includes information management, marketing and IT roles in law, financial services and education. She is a Council member of the Institute of Information Scientists, the Library Association, and the British Library Advisory Council. Recent publications include a chapter on business and economic databases in the *Manual of Online Search Strategies* and an article on knowledge management for *Business Information Review*.

Nicholas Deakin

Nicholas Deakin has been Professor of Social Policy and Administration at Birmingham University since 1980. Previously, he worked in central and local government and at an independent research institute. His recent major publications include *The Enterprise Culture and the Inner Cities* (with John Edwards), a new edition of his text *The Politics of Welfare* and a study with Birmingham colleagues entitled *Contracting for Change*. In 1996 he chaired the Independent Commission on the Future of the Voluntary sector in England set up by the NCVO. He is currently working with Richard Parry of Edinburgh University on a study of Treasury approaches to social policy.

Pesh Framjee

Pesh Framjee, Head of the Charity Unit at Binder Hamlyn and Arthur Andersen, has been involved in the not for profit sector, both professionally and as a volunteer, for over 20 years and writes and lectures extensively on matters affecting the sector. He has undertaken special work for the Charity Commission both in UK and overseas and was seconded to a major international charity as finance director. He is the Special Advisor to the Charity Finance Directors Group and a committee member of the Charities Strategic Management Forum.

Pesh was also a member of the Charity Commission/NCVO Working Party which prepared the report *?On Trust?* and is a member of the Charity Commission monitoring group and the committee that prepared the Statement of Recommended Practice (SORP) on Accounting by Charities. He is also a member of the Institute of Chartered Accountants Charity Accounts Advisory Group and briefed members of the House of Lords Committee that debated the Charities Bill.

Christine Forrester

Christine Forrester is Senior International Consultant for CAF Consultants. She has worked as a freelance consultant for over four years, and specialises in organisational and management development. She has recently worked extensively on NGO and Civil Society development in Central and Eastern Europe, and has worked with organisations in Poland, Hungary, Slovakia, Bulgaria, Romania, Latvia, Lithuania, Estonia, Bosnia, Ukraine and Russia and in Palestine. She currently manages the UK Know How Fund Health Sector Small Partnership Schemes for Russia and the Ukraine. She has also worked with a wide range of organisations in the UK, particularly those working in the information and advice, HIV/AIDS and community development fields.

Prior to moving into consultancy, Christine was Assistant Director at the London Lighthouse, and the first Director of the Globe Centre (and HIV/AIDS centre for East London). From 1983 to 1990, she was Director of Voluntary Action Resource Centre (Falkirk and District), and a Board member of Scottish Council for Voluntary Organisations and of Volunteer Development Scotland and Chair of the Urban Programme Action Committee in Scotland. She has also been an elected member of a London local authority, the Chair of a Parish Council, a lay member of a District Health Authority, a Trustee of the Housing Associations Charitable Trust and a Board member of Kington Development Trust, and is immediate past Chair of Open Door Housing Trust, a special needs housing association operating in London.

Previous publications include reports on housing in London and on women in local government. She is a co-author of the recent Scottish Homes HomePoint *National Standards and Good Practice Manual* and the author of a series of distance learning materials for HomePoint on Strategic Planning and Working with Staff and Volunteers that have been developed for information and advice providers in Scotland.

Diana Grimwood-Jones

Diana Grimwood-Jones is an independent consultant with a particular interest in organisational effectiveness, user needs analyses and new product development. Her career includes 12 years in academic libraries as a Middle Eastern specialist, and nine years at The British Library in a variety of managerial roles. She was Senior Consultant at Aslib from 1992 to 1997, which included working with some household names in the voluntary sector. Most recently, she has been managing a long term project to design and build the London Reference Database of business support services for Business Link London.

Emma Hallam

Emma Hallam has a degree in Law and an MA in Information and Library Studies. Her background is in academic libraries, but her interest in the development of access to information has led to her working for a short time as a freelance researcher. She is currently working as Project Researcher at Southmead Hospital Library and Information Service, Bristol, on the regionally-funded and managed Database Access Project.

Kevin Harris

Kevin Harris is Information Manager at Community Development Foundation, where he has worked since 1986. In addition to running CDF's Information Unit he carries out research, consultancy and development work in two fields: (i) public libraries and communities; and (ii) information technology and communities. He was Secretary to the INSINC Working Party on Social Inclusion in the Information Society and has been Database Manager of the Volnet UK online and CD ROM information service since 1987. He is a member of the national committee of the Community Services Group of The Library Association, and of the Board of UK Communities Online.

Sarah Heery

Sarah Heery is currently Acting Librarian at Christian Aid. She has previously worked as assistant librarian for the Overseas Development Administration and the Ministry of Agriculture, and as librarian at the College of the Transfiguration, Grahamstown, South Africa.

Nicola Hilliard

Nicola Hillard graduated in Sociology and Social Anthropology from the University of Hull and then took a postgraduate diploma in librarianship. Before joining the National Children's Bureau in 1987 as Head of the Library and Information Service, she worked at the Centre for Policy on Ageing and at the Tavistock Library.

Nicola is the editor of Highlights, a series of research summaries on key child care issues and is joint book review editor of the Bureau's journal *Children & Society*. She has developed a number of other library services including the *ChildData* CD-ROM, containing five of the library's information databases, and *Children in the News*, a weekly media abstracting service, and also manages the Solvent Misuse Project which collects and disseminates information on solvent misuse.

Until recently chair of governors of a London primary school, Nicola is a committee member of the Aslib Social Sciences Group and of the National Play Information Centre. She has provided advice and consultancy to a number of library and information services in the UK and Europe and represents the Bureau in the European Forum on HIV, Children and Families.

Carys Hodges

As a student Carys Hodges volunteered in the information unit of Oxfam. After graduating, she worked in the information unit of the UK office of an international organisation in the corporate sector. This was followed by a period as a fund-raiser and user of information in Book Aid International. Carys then moved to ACTIONAID where she set up a Resource Centre of 10,000 items and an extensive range of services for UK and overseas staff. Carys has also worked for PLAN International, where the main focus of her work was the provision of information services for staff overseas. She has visited and liaised with information managers in a range of other international organisations based in the UK and overseas, as well in some national organisations.

Jeremy Phillips

Jeremy Phillips, an intellectual property consultant with London-based solicitors Slaughter and May, is Managing Editor of the loose-leaf reference work, *The Aslib Guide to Copyright,* and a co-author of *Whale on Copyright* (Sweet & Maxwell, 5th edition 1997). He has recently been appointed Visiting Professor in the Faculty of Laws, University College London; and Professor, Magister Lucentinus programme, University of Alicante, Spain.

Gerry Power

Since 1993, Gerry Power has worked at the Library of the National Society for the Prevention of Cruelty to Children in London. As Systems Librarian, he is responsible both for maintaining the Library's catalogue database and for the day-to-day running of the Library's IT network. From 1990 to 1993, he worked as a documentalist in human rights in the Gambia, West Africa, and prior to that, from 1987 to 1990, he was Cataloguer at the Library of the University of Limerick, Ireland.

Becky Purbrick

Becky Purbrick read Political Theory and Institutions at Liverpool University (1985-1988) and from 1989 to 1991 completed a Masters of Philosophy on the Impact of Labour Migration in Rural Zambia at the Liverpool Institute of Public Administration and Labour Management. Becky has been the Coordinator of the Child Rights Network since January 1995 when the network was initially established. From 1991 to 1994 she was employed by Save the Children to manage the overseas programme's information service. This covered all of Save the Children's field offices in over 50 countries. Between 1992 and 1994 Becky ran regional workshops in East Africa, Latin America and South East Asia, training local Save the Children staff in information management.

Jill Roberts

Jill Roberts BA (Hons), ALA, has been archivist and librarian to the Leonard Cheshire and Ryder-Cheshire Foundations since the beginning of 1993. After a first career in the civil service, she graduated from Loughborough University in Information and Library Studies in 1992. Whilst there, she specialised in archive administration and preservation studies and produced a dissertation on archive provision in a sample of UK charities. After graduation she worked on a research project for the University before joining the Foundation. She is currently working towards a PhD comparing approaches between archivists and librarians to the accessing of information.

Colin Rochester

Colin Rochester has worked in the voluntary sector for thirty years, including posts with the Workers' Educational Association and Cambridge House and Talbot Settlement. Since 1987 he has undertaken research and dissemination work for the Centre for Voluntary Organisation at the London School of Economics. His publications include *An Introduction to the Voluntary Sector* (edited with Justin Davis and Rodney Hedley) (Routledge, 1995) and *Social Benefits: Measuring the Value of Community Sector Organisations* (Charities Aid Foundation, 1997).

Susan K.E. Saxon-Harrold

Susan holds a Doctorate in Strategic Management and has taught Organisational Analysis at Bradford University Management Centre, and joined Charities Aid Foundation (CAF) as Head of Research in 1986. CAF became internationally known for its research and information on charity resources and the development of comparative charity statistics. In 1992, Susan was elected as a Research Fellow at the University of Kent. Her many publications include *Dimensions of the Voluntary Sector* (1995) and *Researching the Voluntary Sector* (1994). Susan was European Grant Making Director for NEP International Trust for four years prior to forming her own company. Saxon-Harrold & Co. Ltd provides research, organisation development consultancy and training in the UK and internationally. Recently, Susan has worked in the Baltic States training and assisting organisations in their development, and at present is working with the Institute for Volunteering Research/University of London as a Research Fellow. Additionally, she is a Consultant with CAF Consultants where over the next two years she will be re-establishing the Templeton Institute organisation development courses for small charities across the country.

Sylvia Simmons

Sylvia Simmons is an information consultant and social researcher with an interest in the application of information management to social and public policy. Her consultancy InfoResponse Associates specialises in the not-for-profit and public sectors. Between 1992 and 1997 she was a Senior Consultant with Aslib, The Association for Information Management. She was previously Information Officer, and subsequently Development Officer, at SKILL (National Bureau for Students with Disabilities), and has also worked with the British Library Research & Innovation Centre, British Library Consultancy Services and the World ORT Union.

Frances Tait

Frances Tait ALA, MIInfSc is a Consultant, Trainer and Facilitator with SolutionSearch, specialising in library and information service provision and management. She is also Information Resources Manager at the International Planned Parenthood Federation responsible for the development and delivery of all aspects of the small Library, Information and Records Management service. She was previously the Information Research Manager for BBC TV, managing a large, multi-site operation providing information to programme makers and managers on all subjects. Formerly she was the Manager of the Information Centre at Aslib.

Mark Walker

Based in Brighton, UK, Mark Walker is a freelance writer and marketing consultant working chiefly for clients in the voluntary sector. He also works for Sussex Community Internet Project, which provides training and other support for community and voluntary organisations.

Mark Watson

Mark Watson (BA, ALA) is Head of Library and Information Services at the National Institute for Social Work, where he is responsible for a range of library and information services, including a local government subscription-based scheme, the Caredata CD-ROM database, and Internet services. A Web-accessible version of Caredata is scheduled for mid-1998. He has recently led two projects: a Bridge House Estates funded project 'Getting Voluntary Organisations Online' and a British Library Research and Innovation Centre project 'Digital Libraries, Special Libraries and Practitioners'. Further details of these projects, information services, and publications are available from *www.nisw.org.uk*.

Index

access, to information 67-70
accessibility, of information 114
accountability 17
accounting standards 25
accounts, purpose of 25-6
acquisitions
    archives 277
    automation 210-11
    informing staff of new 118
    library material 190-2
    software 220-1
active marketing 319
ADLIB Library system 356-9
advice, on automation 226-7
Age Concern Leicester 290
AIDS crisis 83
Alcohol Concern, Information Unit 361-2
    web site
        aims of 363-4
        analysis of site traffic 373-4
        changes to 374-5
        contents 368-73
        decision-making 365-6
        future developments 376-8
        impact and evaluation 367
        maintenance 375
        planning 366-7
        problems 375-6
        reasons for 362-3
        resources 368
        technical considerations 364-5
Amnesty International 126, 129, 133

archives 113, 263-4
    acquisitions policy 277
    external deposit or internal storage 278-9
    as fundraising resource 275-6
    information strategy 265
    organisational resource 276
    raising awareness of 280-1
    resources 278
    searchroom services and finding aids 279-80
    specialist problems 264-5
    storage and preservation 277-8
    value of 275
    see also Leonard Cheshire Archive and Library

articles, periodical 199-200

audio tapes 202-3

audits, records management 267-8
    see also information audits

authors' works, copyright 254-5

automation *see* library automation

benchmarking 56

bibliographic databases 116

books, on management 146-7

boundaries, voluntary agencies 12-13

brochures 318-19

budget reviews 310-11

bulletin boards 241-2, 293

Cadbury Code 39-44

campaigning 92-6

capital costs, automation 217

capital funds 28

capital gains, gifts 38

card catalogues 175, 176

Cardbox 175

career development 298-9

catalogues 118, 175-6, 200

cataloguing
    automation 209-10
    library management systems 221
    material 194-5

Index | 431

CD-ROMs
    acquisitions 203
    publishing options 178-82
    in voluntary sector 177-8

central information units *see* library and information services

change, managing 45-58
    library and information services 144-5
    staff resistance 300

changes
    organisational structures 129
    in social policy 83-4

charges 160-1

charismatic leaders 17

charitable status 15

Charitable Uses Acts 10, 15

Charities Act 1993 23, 25, 30

Charities Aid Foundation (CAF) 11
    background 380
    information audit 381
        benefits of 386-7
        carrying out 382-5
        process 382
    Internet vision 380-1

Charities On-Line Express for Libraries 165

Charity Commission 2-3, 15, 24, 30, 40

charity governance 39-44

CHARM 278

chat facilities, Internet 244

Child Rights Information Network (CRIN) 389
    development of 396-7
    growth of networking 389-90
    idea behind 390-2
    projects 393-6
    regionalised approach 398
    setting up 392
    thematic desks 397

ChildData Abstracts 157-8, 159, 179

Children in the News 158

Children and Parliament 158, 183

Children's Residential Care Unit 151

Children's Society 153, 290

ChildStats 157

Christian Aid library 339-40
    electronic information 341
    evaluation 342-5
    future of 346
    promotion 345-6
    services 340-1

circulation
    automation 211
    lists 116, 117, 118

Citizen's Advice Bureaux 11, 86, 87, 241

citizenship, voluntary action 80

classification
    of expenditure 29-30
    of organisations 77
    schemes 111, 196-7

Codes of Governance 4

collaboration, Internet 244-5

collective self help 83

commercial storage 271

Commission on the Future of the Voluntary Sector 20-1, 78, 79

COMMIT report 70

communication
    community sector 59-71
    with information auditors 385
    managing change 53-4
    technology *see* information technology
    voluntary sector 234-7

community sector, information and communication 59-71

Community Sector Coalition 13

competencies, librarians 169-70

computerised catalogues 200

confidential information 252-3

conservation 333-4

constitutional forms, voluntary agencies 15, 31

consultants 289

consultation 130

consumer influence 65-6

continuing professional development (CPD) 298-9

contract culture 52-3

contract law, copyright 253-4

contracts, staff 289

control environment, financial 40-1

conversion, to ADLIB Library system 356-8

copyright 251-61
    authors' works 254-5
    Database Directive 256-7
    Internet and Intranets 257-9
    legal status of information 252-4
    liability 259-60

Copyright, Designs and Patents Act 1988 253, 256

corporation tax 31

costs, automation 217-18

Council for Charitable Support 4

council tax 35-6

CRIN *see* Child Rights Information Network

CRIN MAIL 394, 395

CRIN newsletter 393, 395

cultural diversity 133-4

cultural shifts 83-4

current awareness bulletins 116, 118, 174

data
    analysis 89
    inputting 112, 216

Database Directive 254, 256-7

databases 110-11
    CD-ROMs 177-82, 203
    communicating information 234
    copyright protection 254, 256-7
    international organisations 119
    on the Internet 184-5
    library 175-6
    library automation 223-4
    online 176-7
    see also bibliographic databases

Deakin Review 20-1, 78, 79

decision-making 130-1

deeds of covenant 36-7

Department of Social Security's Benefits Integrity Project (BIP) 98

Dialog 184
direct mail 319
directories
    library systems 226-7
    voluntary sector information 234
    web-based 241
Disability Advice and Information and Advice Lines (DIAL) 57
disability movement 85
Disabled Young Adult Centre, email service 243-4
disaster planning, records management 273-4
discretionary relief, council tax 35-6
document management systems 223
documentation, internal 110, 116
domestic property, council tax 35

Early Childhood Unit 151
effectiveness
    campaigning 94-6
    financial control 40-4
    of training 297-8
ELDIS 121, 341
electronic information 341
Electronic Libraries Programme 169
electronic networking 246-8
electronic publishing 175-8
electronic records 273
email
    capabilities 238
    in information services 118
    organisational communication 236
    private 242-4, 394
    social inclusion 69-70
    staff networking 293
empowerment 86, 87
enquiries
    impact of Alcohol Concern web site 373-4
    logging 172, 173t
    services 119, 159-60
    subject specific 118-19
environmental analysis 307-8

equal opportunities 133-4
equity law 254
evaluation
   Alcohol concern web site 367
   campaigning 93-4
   Christian Aid Library 342-5
   library services 161-2
   marketing 320-1
exempt supplies, VAT 33
exhibitions, library systems 227
expenditure
   classification of 29-30
   library and information services 139
experience, staff 134, 283-5
external deposit 278-9
external service reviews 82
external strategic reviews 80

Facilitating Group, CRIN 391, 392
feedback, library and information services 174
Filer Commission 11
files, current information 195-6
filing systems, records management 268-9
financial planning 138-9
financial reporting 23-9
Financial Reporting Standards (FRSs) 25
financial transactions 43
finding aids 279-80, 334-5
fire risks 274
fiscal issues 30-8
fixed-term contracts 289
flooding 274
flyers, dissemination of 118
focus groups 172-4, 313-14
formalisation, of voluntary agencies 16, 20
formally organised, defined 12
forums, Internet 377
Framework for Continuing Professional Development (CPD) 298-9

FRS *see* Financial Reporting Standards
functional classification 29-30
fund accounting 27-8
funding 15, 17
fundraising, archive material 275-6
funds, use of designated 28-9

game theory 95-6
Gift Aid 37
governance 39-44
government
    relationship with voluntary agencies 15-16, 86
    role of 1, 10-11
GreenNet 241, 294
group dynamics 286

Hansard 157, 158
hard data 87
health and safety 286
health sector, librarians 169
Highlights 157
Home Office Regulations 23-4, 30
house journals 319
human resources 17
Human Rights Internet (HRI) 391

ICT *see* information technology
income generation 165-6
income tax 31
Independent Commission on the Future of the Voluntary Sector in England 4
induction, of staff 285-6
infomapping 135-6
information
    accessibility 114
    charging for 160-1
    communication 234-7

    in the community sector 59-71
    dissemination of 156-7
    encouraging use of 120
    importance of 103-4
    needs assessments 106-8, 167-8, 311-14
    overload 166-7
    policy and strategy 73-99
    relevant 108-9
    value of 88-92
    voluntary sector 232-3
information audits 171-2, 308-11
    see also Charities Aid Foundation
Information for Development Co-ordinating Committee (IDCC) 122

information management 86-8, 231-49

information professionals *see* staff

information retrieval, automation 212, 222-3

information services *see* library and information services

information systems 56-7, 87, 109-13

information technology 3
    changing context of 69-70
    introducing new 45
    library and information services 140-1, 164
    NSPCC network 350-9
    and power 67-8
    training 248

Inmagic database 175

innovation
    voluntary action 80
    volunteers as source of 290-1

INSINC Working party 70

Institute of Development Studies (IDS) 121, 184-5

institutions, information provision 64-6

intermediary bodies 14

internal documentation 110, 116

internal service reviews 82

internal storage 278-9

internal strategic reviews 80, 82

International Development Research Centre (IDRC) 121

international perspectives 103-22

International Planned Parenthood Federation (IPPF) 188, 291, 292

Internet
- accessing 239
- acquisitions 192
- capabilities 237-8
- Charities Aid Foundation 380-1
- collaboration 244-5
- copyright 257-9
- databases on 184-5
- forums 377
- knowledge management 240-4
- library automation 140, 225-6
- opportunities 379-80
- promotion 319-20
- as social learning space 69
- voluntary sector profile 165
- *see also* web sites

interviews
- CAF information audit 383-5
- library and information services 172-4
- marketing 312

Intranets
- copyright 257-9
- NHS 378

Investors in People 297

ISO 9000 56, 297

isomorphism 20

job descriptions 286

job-sharing 288-9

Joint Monitoring Steering Committee 62

Joseph Rowntree Foundation 4

just in case/time, material collection 188

key conduits, community information 60

key performance indicators (KPIs) 42

keywords, subject 197

King's Fund Library, staff involvement 287

knowledge culture 67-8

knowledge management *see* information management

leaders, charismatic 17

Legal Aid Board 56

legal forms, voluntary agencies 15

Leonard Cheshire Archive and Library 325
- archive
  - establishment 325-6
  - finding guides 334-5
  - perceptions of function 331-2
  - policy statements 332, 336
  - preservation and conservation 333-4
  - publicity and user education 335
  - role within organisation 326
  - storage 332-3
- records management
  - establishing importance of 327-8
  - material, collection and sifting 329, 331
  - relationship with archive 326-7
  - retention scheduling 328-9, 330f

liability, copyright 259-60

librarians
- organisational recognition 301
- profile 168-70
- working alone 291-3, 302
- working for non-qualified 300-1

Library Association
- Framework for Continuing Professional Development (CPD) 298-9
- registration of associates 297

library automation
- advice 226-7
- allocation of time 214-15
- applications and systems 219-26
- approaching suppliers 227-9
- exhibitions 227
- finance and justification 217-18
- identifying priorities 209-14
- planning 207-8
- time consuming tasks 216
- *see also* NSPCC library

Library and Information Commission 299

library and information services
- change, managing 144-5
- designing 135-6
- feedback, gaining 174
- financial planning 138-9
- improvement of 174
- income generation 165-6
- information overload, managing 166-7

library and information services (continued)
    international 114-20
    management 138-9
    marketing 142-3
    new products and services 163, 170-5
    in organisational structures 128-9
    space, managing 142
    technology in 140-1, 164
    see also Christian Aid library; librarians; material; National Children's Bureau

library management systems 176, 220-2
    ADLIB Library system 356-9
    directories and publications 226-7
    investigating new 353-5
    Soutron Library system 352-3

life cycles
    organisational 75, 81f
    records management 265-6

links, via Internet 376-7, 377-8

loans
    automation 211-12
    to overseas staff 116-17

logos 319

mailing lists 235, 241-2, 294

management
    attitudes of staff towards 132-3
    information reports 212
    library and information services 138-9
    reading about 146-7
    style 131-2
    see also information management; project management; records management; team management

Management Committees 55, 128, 143

managers
    decision-making 130-1
    networks for 120, 121-2
    non-librarian 300-1
    profile of 145-6
    records management 265-9
    role of 87

Manchester Community Information Network 241, 245

market influence 2

marketing 93, 305-7
    environmental analysis 307-8
    evaluation 320-1
    library and information services 142-3
    needs assessments 106-8, 167-8, 311-14
    plans 314-20
    see also information audits
material
    acquiring 190-2
    classifying 111, 196-7
    finding what's available 189-90
    integrated records 200-1
    managing 141-2
    recording 111, 193-5
    shelving 197-8, 271-2
    storage 277-8, 278-9, 332-3
    subject coverage 187-9
    see also CD-ROMS; microfilm; non-text material; periodicals; photographs; publications
media
    coverage 91-2
    information from 68
meetings 235, 237
memos 237
Mental Health Handbook 244
mentoring 293
microfilm 270
mobile shelving 271
monitoring
    demand and need 89-91
    financial control 43-4
motivation, staff 286-7
motivation-hygiene theory 139
multiculturalism 133-4
mutual aid 10

National Association of Citizens Advice Bureaux (NACAB) 90, 233
National Child Development Study 150
    library and information services
        charging for information 160-1
        evaluating services 161-2

National Children's Bureau
   aims and objectives 150-2
   library and information service 152-4
      services 156-60
      users 155-6
   membership 154-5
   web site 183

National Council for Voluntary Organisations 11

National Lottery 1, 307

National Standards for Housing and Advice Information providers 56

National Vocational Qualifications (NVQs) 296

NCH Action for Children 153

needs assessments 106-8, 167-8, 311-14

Net Result, The 70

networking
   electronic 246-8
   process of 71
   staff 293-4

networks
   for information managers 120, 121-2
   see also Child Rights Information Network; NSPCC library

newsgroups 293

newsletters 235, 237, 319, 393, 395

NHS Intranet 378

Nolan Committee 5

non-business supplies, VAT 33

non-domestic rating 35-6

non-text material 201-4

not profit-distributing, defined 12

notice boards 235

NSPCC library 349-50
   IT network
      ADLIB Library system 356-9
      investigating new systems 353-5
      project management 355
      Soutron Library system 352-3
     strategy 350-2

office automation systems 225

One-Man Bands Group 293

online databases 176-7, 184-5
Online Public Access Catalogue (OPAC) 176
Open Door Housing Trust 52-3
operational information resources, Internet 245
operational planning 136-8
optical character recognition 225
ordering 115, 190-2
orders, recording 193
organisations
    and change 46, 47-51
    classifying 77
    communication 235-7
    conflicts, informational needs 77
    international 104-5
    life cycle 75, 81f
    records management 281-2
    structures 125-8, 128-9
    visibility, benefits of 245-8
outcomes, measuring 54

Parliamentary Liaison Officer 98
part-time workers 287-8
partnerships 3
Patents Act 1977 253
payroll giving 37-8
performance appraisals 298
performance evaluation, campaigning 93-4
performance measurement
    financial control 42
    managing change 54-6
periodicals 198-200
    automation 211
    house journals 319
    ordering 116
person specifications, managers 146
personal interviews 312
PESTs 307
photographs 203-4
place, marketing mix 316-17

planning
    automation 207-8
    disaster management 273-4
    web site, Alcohol Concern 366-7
    see also financial planning; strategic planning

plans
    disaster 274
    marketing 314-20

postal service 235

posters 201-2

power, and information 67

preservation, archive material 277-8, 333-4

price, marketing mix 315-16

print-based knowledge culture 67, 69

private email 242-4, 394

proactive campaigning 93

procedures manuals 204

product, marketing mix 315

professionalism 2, 20

profiles, Internet 165

profits, taxes on 31

project management, NSPCC IT network 355

promotion
    Christian Aid library 345-6
    of library and information services 142-3
    marketing mix 317-20

public libraries 62

publications
    on library systems 226-7
    ordering 115

publicity, archive 335

qualifications, training 296

quality standards 56, 297

questionnaires
    CAF information audit 383
    library and information services 172-4
    marketing 312-13

RADAR 98
rates 35-6
rationality, campaign strategies 96
reactive campaigning 93
reconciliation, of information 43
recording
    material 111-12, 193-5
    orders 193
records
    electronic 273
    integrated 200-1
records management 263-4
    disaster planning 273-4
    disposal of records 272-3
    filing systems 268-9
    information strategy 265
    managers, function of 265-9
    retention scheduling 269-70, 328-9, 330f
    security 272
    specialist problems 264-5
    storage options, semi-current material 270-2
    see also Leonard Cheshire Archive and Library
recruitment 285
recurring costs, automation 218
registration
    Charity Commission 30
    Library Association 297
    VAT 33
relational databases 224
representation, voluntary action 80
resource centres, community 70
resources
    Alcohol Concern web site 368
    archives 278
    marketing reviews 310-11
restricted income funds 28
retention scheduling 269-70, 328-9, 330f
review dates, records management 273
risks, financial control 41
Royal Commission on Historical Manuscripts 278

salaries 139-40

Samaritans, email service 243

sanctions, underperformers 140

Scottish Homes HomePoint 55-6

SDI *see* selective dissemination of information

searchroom services 279-80

secondment, of staff 38, 291

security
    of information 112-13
    records management 272

selection, staff 285

selective dissemination of information 117-18, 340-1

self-governing, defined 12

self-help 10, 78, 83

serials *see* periodicals

service contracts 83

service reviews 82

services
    voluntary sector 20
    see also library and information services

shelving 197-8, 271-2

Shetland Times v. Wills 258

SilverPlatter 184

skills
    information handling 68, 283-5
    information management 71

slogans 319

social exclusion 3

social inclusion 66-9

social movements 85-6

social origin, of information 68

social policy
    access to information 65
    changes in 83
    value of information 88-92

SOFA *see* Statement of Financial Activities

soft information 87, 97

software
    acquisitions 220-1
    library management 176
    text retrieval 222-3
    workflow 224-5
    workgroup 223

SORP *see* Statement of Recommended Practice

Soutron Library system 352-3

space, managing 142

Special Library Association, competencies 169

SSAP *see* Statements of Standard Accounting Practice

staff
    attitudes to management 132-3
    and change
        impact of 84-5
        resistance to 300
    continuing professional development 298-9
    induction 285-6
    managing 139-40, 286-7
    networking 293-4
    secondment of 38, 291
    selection and recruitment 285
    skills and experience 283-5
    survey on 77-8
    training 294-8
    see also librarians; managers; volunteers

standards
    accounting 25
    performance measurement 55-6
    quality 56, 297

Standards and Good Practice Manual 57

start-up costs, automation 217

Statement of Financial Activities (SOFA) 24, 26-7

Statement of Recommended Practice (SORP) 23-4, 25, 27, 29, 30

Statements of Standard Accounting Practice (SSAPs) 25

statistical information 88-91

STATS system 88, 89

statute law, confidential information 253

steering group, CAF information audit 382

storage, of material 277-8, 278-9, 332-3

strategic planning 47, 136-8

strategic reviews 46, 80, 82

strategies
    campaign 95-6
    and change process 46
    information 265

structural-operational definition 12-13

subject coverage 187-9

subject keywords 197

sui generis right 256

suppliers
    archive storage and conservation material 282
    library automation 227-9

surveys
    Human Rights Internet 391
    records management 267-8

Sussex Community Internet Project (SCIP) 241-2

SWOT analysis 308-9

systems
    maintenance 358-9
    trials 228-9
    see also document management systems; filing systems; information systems; library management systems; office automation systems

tax
    effective methods of giving 36-8
    on income and profits 31
    overview 30-1
    see also council tax; VAT

Teaching Aids at Low Cost (TALC) 121

team management 286-7

teleworking 289

terminology, voluntary sector 11-12

testing, of ADLIB Library system 356-8

text retrieval software 222-3

thematic desks 397

thesauri 197

Three Worlds Model 19f

Traditional Model 18f

training
    IT 248
    staff 290, 294-8

transfers on death 38
troubleshooting, ADLIB Library system 358-9

UN Convention on the Rights of the Child 389-90
UnCover 184
university librarians, USA 169
unrestricted funds 28
usage analysis 309-10
usage statistics 172
user education, archive 335
user empowerment 85

values 16
VAT 31-5
verbal information 109
video tapes 202-3
virtual libraries 188-9, 225-6
virus protection 113
visibility
    electronic networking 246-8
    voluntary agencies 245-6
VolNet 177, 179, 184, 236
voluntarism 16
voluntary action 78-80
Voluntary and Community Unit at the Home Office 11
voluntary governing bodies 17
voluntary sector
    challenges and implications 19-21
    common features 16-17
    defining 11-14
    distinctive nature of 17-19
    formalisation 16
    functions 14
    funding 15
    historical background 9-11
    legal and constitutional forms 15
    relationship with government 15-16, 86
    scale and area of operation 14
    voluntarism 16
Voluntary Sector Information Workers Forum (VOLSIF) 78

volunteering 17
volunteers 134, 289-91, 341

web sites
   archive 282
   CRIN 394-5
   as information providers 182-4
   international 122
   see also Alcohol Concern, Information Unit

Wolfenden Committee 11, 14

workflow software 224-5

workgroup software 223

working, alternative ways of 287-9

World Intellectual Property Organization (WIPO) 257

World Wide Web *see* Internet

zero rated supplies, VAT 33